Enduring Words

Enduring Words

Literary Narrative in a Changing Media Ecology

Michael Wutz

The University of Alabama Press
Tuscaloosa

Copyright © 2009
The University of Alabama Press
Tuscaloosa, Alabama 35487-0380
All rights reserved
Manufactured in the United States of America

Typeface: Adobe Caslon Pro

∞

The paper on which this book is printed meets the minimum requirements of American National Standard for Information Sciences-Permanence of Paper for Printed Library Materials, ANSI Z39.48-1984.

Library of Congress Cataloging-in-Publication Data

Wutz, Michael.
   Enduring words : literary narrative in a changing media ecology / Michael Wutz.
      p. cm.
   Includes bibliographical references and index.
   ISBN 978-0-8173-1670-9 (cloth : alk. paper) 1. Literature, Modern—20th century—History and criticism. 2. Postmodernism (Literature) 3. Literature and technology. 4. Narration (Rhetoric) 5. Lowry, Malcolm, 1909–1957—Criticism and interpretation. I. Title.
   PN771.W88 2009
   809'.93356—dc22

                                                2009010164

Contents

Acknowledgments   vii

1. Introduction   1
   Mediating Narrative   1
   Unusual Suspects, Unusual Subjects   6
   Narrative Niches in a Postprint World   20

2. Frank Norris and the Modern Media Ecology   28
   Zoning the District: Photography, "Chromoliterature," and Literary Naturalism   29
   Relegitimizing Print: Cinema, the Body, and the Big Stink   37
   Agency and Angst: Mangled Hands and Machined Writing   46

3. *The Pit:* Locating Modernism's Other   55
   Blending the Wheat with the Chaff   56
   Art and Dandies in the Cornbelt   62
   Of Cablegrams and First Editions, or Short Circuits of the Wired Mind   74

4. Archaic Mechanics, Anarchic Meaning: Malcolm Lowry and the Technology of Narrative   85
   The Engineer, the Hand, and the Machine   87
   Narrative Technology: The Myth and the Machine   98
   The Narrative Engine as Difference Engine   103

5. License to Shoot (and Live): Malcolm Lowry
and the Captivity of Cinema   107
   Inside "the Cabinet of Dr. Caliglowry"   109
   Trains, Planes, and Automobiles: The Cinematic Real in *Tender Is the Night*   115
   Incarceration and Imaginary Liberation in *October Ferry to Gabriola*   123

6. Literary Narrative and Information Culture: Garbage, Waste,
and Residue in the Work of E. L. Doctorow   133
   The Stuff Novels Are Made On, or the Artist in Stitches   134
   Literary Recycling, Postmodernism, and the Novel Nomad   141
   Half-Life, Shelf-Life, and Literary Fallout, or Waste Making Noise   151

7. *The Waterworks:* Knowledge and Cognition
in the Early Age of Data Storage   156
   Stars at War, or Data in Gotham   157
   Brains, Waves, and Recording Machines   164
   Modularity, Information, Narrative Knowledge   173

8. By Way of Conclusion: *City of God, Galatea 2.2,*
and the Case of No Body in Vain   181
   Cognition in Circuit City, or City of Circuits   181
   Language and (Narrative) Cognition in *Galatea 2.2*   189
   Posthuman Embodiment, Writing, and Print   196

Notes   205

Bibliography   247

Index   271

Acknowledgments

A book that takes distributed cognition as one of its themes would be doubly remiss if it did not acknowledge the truism that books are collective efforts in which authors—often reduced to an "effect" or "function" of late—avail themselves of what they have learned from others. In that spirit, I want to acknowledge the community of individuals and institutions that have helped me in what turned out (with periods of fruitful intermission) to become an almost twenty-year project, fully acknowledging that all the mistakes in this book are my own and that, human nature being what it is (which is to say, fallible and forgetful), I will not be able to thank everyone who has had a hand in this book.

The manuscript began under the generous guidance of Walter L. Reed, William B. Dillingham, and John Johnston. From there it morphed into a different project and, during its genesis, benefited from the insights of numerous friends and colleagues. Joseph Tabbi, University of Illinois–Chicago, read early chapters of the manuscript and generously shared his extensive observations. Geoffrey Winthrop-Young, University of British Columbia, knows media theory and critical theory, Continental or otherwise, better than anybody in North America and, despite numerous commitments of his own, was always willing to offer insightful comments. At Weber State University, I benefited from illuminating conversations with John Schwiebert and Bob Hogge. Clara Mucci at the Università degli Studi Gabriele D'Annunzio in Chieti, Italy, offered friendship and encouragement at critical moments, and Maria DiBattista at Princeton University believed in my work when I didn't and is a guiding presence in this book. Kerstin Schmidt and Klaus Benesch of the Julius-Maximilians-Universität München, Germany, gave of their friendship and generously shared their time and knowledge. I would also like to thank Patrick A. McCarthy (University of Miami) and Fredrick Asals (University of Toronto) for their expert knowledge in fine-tuning my understanding of Malcolm Lowry and for helping me navigate the maelstrom of the Malcolm Lowry archive. I would like to acknowledge the reviewers at The University of Alabama Press for their constructive feedback in refining this book. Finally, I would like to thank the superb staff at The University of Alabama Press for their help in preparing the final manuscript, and to Jenn Backer for her sure-handed copyediting. My debt to all of them is tremendous.

I have had the privilege of working in a series of extraordinary libraries and have had the benefit of consulting with their dedicated archivists and interlibrary loan desks. I wish to thank the excellent staff of Stewart Library at Weber State University in Ogden, Utah; the Special Collections at the University of British Columbia, Canada; the Bancroft Library at the University of California, Berkeley; and the Universitätsbibliothek at the Universität of Bayreuth, Germany.

My research has been supported by repeated grants from various agencies and institutions: the Weber State University Research and Professional Growth Committee, which generously funded writing time and research trips to various libraries; the College of Arts and Humanities and the Department of English at Weber State University, in particular, June K. Phillips, Madonne Miner, and Candadai Seshachari, for in-kind support and moral encouragement; the International Council of Canadian Studies for travel and research support; and the National Endowment of Humanities, which enabled me to study modernism in Paris in what turned out to become an extraordinarily stimulating summer seminar under the leadership of Maria DiBattista and Suzanne Nash. I also received a one-year fellowship from Emory University Graduate School. I acknowledge these individuals and sources with gratitude.

As always, my greatest debt and warmest gratitude are to Marilee Rohan, my best reader, closest friend, and much more, who has read every single page and contributed to my work in ways too numerous to mention. My debt and gratitude also go to our children, Christian and Anja, who, though they may not know it, have been with me all the way and nourished my work in invaluable ways. I would not have been able to finish this book without their presence and support. I dedicate this book to them.

Parts of this book, in earlier versions, have appeared in the following journals and collections: chapter 4 on Malcolm Lowry and the technology of narrative in *Reading Matters: Narrative in the New Media Ecology*, ed. Joseph

Tabbi and Michael Wutz (Copyright © 1997 by Cornell University Press); chapter 6 on E. L. Doctorow and information culture in *Contemporary Literature* 44, no. 3 (Fall 2003): 501–35 (Copyright © 2003 by the Board of Regents of the University of Wisconsin System). I am grateful for the permission to reuse this material.

Enduring Words

1
Introduction

Mediating Narrative

On the eve of World War I Fillipo Tommaso Marinetti, the noisy maestro of the Italian futurists, declared with characteristic bravado, "Those people who today make use of the telegraph, the telephone, the phonograph, the train, the bicycle, the motorcycle, the automobile, the ocean liner, the dirigible, the aeroplane, the cinema, the great newspaper (synthesis of a day in the world's life) do not realize that these various means of communication, transportation and information have a decisive influence on their psyches" (*Manifestos* 96). By 1913 such statements had entered the high-flying rhetoric of the avant-garde and appeared in the barrage of manifestos that defined the turn-of-the-century futurist moment.[1] As a catalogue of the transportation and communication technologies emerging between the 1840s and the first decade(s) of the twentieth century, the pronouncement maps the range of modernist media that have fundamentally altered human modes of being, seeing, and speaking—in short, the human subject—and, as a properly "futurist" dictum, Marinetti's declaration easily invites extension into the contemporary mediascape and their effects on the human psychic apparatus. In fact, in what amounts to a panegyric to corporal hardware that anticipates current notions of cyborgism, Marinetti demands to "destroy the *I* in literature: that is, all psychology," and to replace the soft flesh of self with the hard bodies of machined humans: to "put matter in his place" and "to make literature out of the life of a motor" (*Writings* 87). What is more, the convergence of "this nonhuman and mechanical being" shows first evolutionary signs of "a bodily development in the form of a prow from the outward swell of a breastbone, which will be the more marked the better an aviator the man of the future becomes" (*Writings* 91).[2] This decidedly futurist version of *Homo Icarus Mechanicus* anticipates the hybrid discourse of Donna Haraway's evolutionary cyborg in the same manner as it does Paul Virilio's "dromological" project on the collusion of flight, vision, and (what is a central concern of the Italian futurists as well) warfare.[3]

Marinetti similarly informed the world about what has by now become a familiar refrain in the history and theory of narrative: the death of literature, and of the novel more specifically, in a world dominated by the assemblage of (post)modern communications technologies. While "the necessities of propaganda will force us to publish a book once in a while," he conceded, the book per se is "a wholly passéist means of preserving and communicating thought" and "has for a long time been fated to disappear like cathedrals, towers, crenelated walls, museums." A "static companion of the sedentary, the nostalgic" (with occasional use for political mobilization), print is doomed to go the way of other archaic holdovers, soon to be superseded by the visual media, "the cinema . . . and mobile illuminated signs" (*Writings* 130). Fredric Jameson, for one (perhaps with a silent nod to the Italian grand master), noted that "for seventy years the cleverest prophets have warned us regularly that the dominant art form of the twentieth century was not literature at all . . . but rather the one new and historically unique art invented in the contemporary period, namely film" (*Postmodernism* 68); Vilém Flusser similarly observed that "letters have served their purpose more or less well, but they are no longer very useful," further noting that the shift to image-based surface thinking coincides with the spatial mapping of photography and the subsequent concentration of visual codes ("Taking Leave" 6). And Friedrich Kittler, in a more strictly hardware fashion, has argued that print, and with it the novel as one preeminent form of alphabetic knowledge transmission, had to surrender its long-held storage monopoly when writing's form of symbolic mediation had to compete with new technologies capable of recording the physical effects of the real, that is, sound and light. Once the gramophone and film had emerged as the new bullies on the media block, there to absorb the acoustic and visual data streams hitherto confined to print, writing lost its erstwhile centrality and was forced into the margins of discourse, a demotion that the advent of the binary code has accelerated further (*Gramophone* 1–19).[4]

The position of literary narrative in a postprint world and, secondarily, the media-technological re-formation of the human subject (its senses, its body, and its mind) as it is represented in the senescent medium of literature—these are the large, twin focal points of *Enduring Words*. Its title is meant to acknowledge the obvious: namely, that the words that make up literary narrative have endured for centuries; they have passed the test of time and, as material artifacts, have underscored their lasting cultural relevance. At the same time, words have demonstrated their endurance at a media-historical juncture when their durability has been under siege by the successive pressure of the electric and electronic media following the long dominance of print culture. Embedded within the complex media ecology of modernity, the world of print has variously been able to withstand the challenges of oblivion by repositioning itself in the field of always-already-mediated representation. *Enduring Words* charts this temporal and functional endurance of literary print.

The subtitle of *Enduring Words*—*Literary Narrative in a Changing Media Ecology*—ought then to be seen as an extension of this double durability in the sense that literary narrative, as part of the subset of print culture, is a medium in its own right negotiating between its textual self-presence and the world. Suitably conditioned readers, that is, alphabetized minds that have internalized the codes of reading, are able to translate the black marks against a differential background, a.k.a. letters, into imagined sensory phenomena and hallucinate the world laid out symbolically for them. Reading a novel becomes, hence, an act of mediation that closes the feedback loop between author and reader, the one coding her scenarios in the software of the alphabet, the other recoding these scenarios into her own cognitive constructs, subject to the interpretive bandwidth of language.

As such, print narrative also has a specific materiality that expresses itself, among others, in layout and page design, the feel of paper, and the lettering of fonts, all of which are constitutive of its signifying range. While print in the Gutenberg Galaxy has primarily served as a vehicle for linguistic meaning, it is precisely the novel's location within a postprint mediaverse that foregrounds textuality per se and "resists any processing that would simply treat it as a set of referential signs pointing beyond themselves to a semantic content" (McGann 74). Indeed, *Enduring Words* understands itself in part as a study that takes a fresh look at the physicality of print culture. If literary studies has, until recently, "generally been content to treat fictional and narrative worlds as if they were entirely products of the imagination," this book wants to turn an open, not blind, eye to the matter of printed matter and break down the traditional "sharp line between representation and the technologies producing them" (Hayles, *Machines* 19).

Similarly, what critical theory following Freud has been fond of calling "the scene of writing," that is, the writer's material circumstances of producing text, not only acknowledges the irreducible materiality of the textual artifact but also allows insight into the media-technological circumstances of its evolution.⁵ Put differently, specific practices and the choice of particular writing instruments, including the peculiarities of handwriting, typewriting, and keyboarding, physically register the conditions of mediality under which particular texts have been written, just as they can register authorial anxieties. Writing in the mid- or late nineteenth century certainly presumes a different understanding of authorship and selfhood than does working at the beginning of the twenty-first century.

More important, *Enduring Words* also circumscribes the novel's awareness of its location within (and endurance in) a modern media ecology beginning, as Flusser and Kittler suggest, with photography in the 1840s, soon to be followed by additional breakthrough developments in visual storage, such as color photography, silent film, and eventually sound and color film early in the twentieth century, including its influential precursors, the kinetoscope and the vitascope. At the same time, Edison's phonograph and Emile Berliner's gramophone, each with its peculiarities of inscription, enabled the recording and playing back of sound, respectively, and thus made voice and noise, in various stages of technological authenticity, into retrievable commodities. Add to this such media as the (oft forgotten) player piano in the early twentieth century, which allowed for the playing of pre-recorded music by attaching a pre-inscribed roll onto a piano, and you have an increasing distribution of technologies giving an increasing spectrum of data streams their peculiar storage channels.⁶ Eventually this modernist differentiation was further refined through more contemporary media such as the video and of course the computer, whose binary coding currently promises, or threatens, to subsume other media into its totalizing reach. The Gutenberg Galaxy and the Edisonian Universe are on the threshold of being absorbed, in Hegelian fashion, into the Turing World, a kind of *binary (d)esperanto* that could easily swallow older and analog forms of storage into a gigantic Digital Soup and mix previously distinguished data streams into a bland Broth of Bits (Kittler, *Gramophone,* esp. 242–63).

If we take a large enough view, this response can be described in terms of a cascading feedback loop that charts the novel's shifting position within these shifting media constellations. For if the novel's traditional mission was to conjure up an effect of realism in print, of producing an authentic experience of mimesis, it also paradoxically engendered within its readers an increasingly pressing desire for the real only later, nonverbal media could meet, thus preparing the cognitive and intellectual conditions of possibility for the media-technological inventions to follow. In the canonical words of Walter Benjamin, "It has always been one of the primary tasks of art to create a demand whose hour of full satisfaction has not yet come. The history of every art form has critical periods in which the particular form strains after effects which can be easily achieved only with a changed technical standard—that is to say, in a new art form" (*Selected Writings* 3:118). Print, to put it differently, demoted itself in the same measure as it promoted new, more ostensibly authentic forms of virtual reality, which in turn laid the groundwork for the development of contemporary forms of computer-based virtual reality.[7] Thus, the novel—especially during its heyday in the nineteenth century, when literacy and mass printing led to high distribution volumes—and the computer can, equally paradoxically, be seen to have traded places, the one a universal discrete machine of print disseminating the interests of Europe's post-Enlightenment powers, the other a digital universal discrete machine marshaling the interests of corporate power (read: Microsoft, Silicon Valley, and Google) in the global village of the future. The virtual storage monopoly once possessed by print has, indeed, largely been taken over (in more senses than one) by the storage monopoly of digitalization, creating a cultural effect that is not altogether unlike narrative's homogenizing function of yore.

Thus, *Enduring Words,* the title, in combination with *Literary Narrative in a Changing Media Ecology,* the subtitle, above all suggests the novel's resilient response to what might appear as its almost complete loss of representational territory and the corresponding migration of visual, acoustic, and digital information strains into more appropriate channels of communication. Turning the former storage responsibility of print into a liberating virtue, in the manner of a media-technological reaction formation (or Oedipal conflict), the serious modern and postmodern novel often makes a virtue of necessity by integrating, co-opting, or rejecting the techniques and effects of later technologies of representation, in the process not only expanding its own repertoire of the real but, in a contrary gesture, also reconsidering and insisting on its own irreducible mediality. Its marginal status within an expanded media ecology, as Carlos Fuentes put it, "in itself brings the novel back to the elementary position in which it has to become everything to become itself" (in Doezma 493). Instead of a narrative retreat into a verbal hideout, there to linger as an endangered species, the novel capitalizes on its technological belatedness or anachronism to claim and reclaim new vistas of representation, similar to the way its postprint environment enabled narrative's textuality to take on material significance. If the novel thus participates in what J. David Bolter and Richard Grusin have described as practices of remediation—"the representation of one medium in another"—it does so in a way fundamentally different from that of contemporary digital environments. While the computer and the World Wide Web are governed by a "logic of immediacy," suggesting that "the medium itself should disappear and leave us in the presence of the thing represented" (5), the novel tends to foreground, not erase, its act of mediation and draw attention to its artifactuality, even as it sometimes wants to uphold the illusion of the real.[8] That, as I hope to show, is one of the hallmarks of literary narrative's status in the modern media ecology, and one that bodes well for its enduring genetic resilience and viability.

Unusual Suspects, Unusual Subjects

Gilles Deleuze once famously said that "machines are social before being technical. Or rather, there is a human technology which exists before a material technology" (*Foucault* 39). This observation might well serve as a tutelary prompting for the range of approaches employed in this book. Eschewing any form of technological determinism that might assign agency to the media under discussion here, while reducing humans to supplementary actants, *Enduring Words* proceeds on the assumption that technological and cultural changes are part of a vast, chaotic, and level playing field in which energies and interests intersect and mutually determine and reshape one another. Instead of the traditional diffusion model, in which technologies are seen to structure the practices of everyday life in the fashion of a top-down hierarchy, such a more horizontal approach is closer to what Bruno Latour has described as a "translation" model, that is, a model more cognizant of the reciprocities between technology, media, science, and their embeddedness within a viscous cultural context (132). In such a network of interaction, not only is power dispersed among the numerous nodes and clusters of social, institutional, and economic relations; media technologies themselves are never prior and autonomous but rather the expression of these confluent and divergent power relations that have contributed to their coming into being as well as their changing use. As Jonathan Sterne puts it, "Technologies are repeatable social, cultural and material processes crystallized into mechanisms" (8).[9] Edison, for one, originally envisioned his phonograph as an office machine facilitating the high-speed processing of text, but public opinion, massive commercial interests, and emergent mass culture quickly redefined his machine into the primary entertainment device of turn-of-the-century America (see Gitelman 62–96); the bildungsroman would never have assumed the forms it did had it not been for a host of social, institutional, and economic forces vested in the formation of a bourgeois subject ready to behave and consume. Inquiring similarly into the interactions between print narrative and its succeeding technological environment not only presumes a functional equivalence between the media of different historical orders but also necessitates understanding cultural work as a complex *assemblage* and overlay of competing discourses and practices engaged in perpetual realignment. Thus, folded into the close, media-oriented readings I offer in what follows, I delve briefly, when appropriate, into the history of technology and the history of the subject, the history of the body and the history of science, and popular science and cognitive science to acknowledge their imbrication in a larger cultural field that has contributed to the relocation and redefinition of the novel in the mediaverse of modernity.

Subscribing to a similar cross-disciplinary methodology, Sara Danius in *The Senses of Modernism* analyzes how the transport, media, and medical technologies at the turn of the century did their work on the canonical giants of modernism and led to a redistribution of perceptual labor. Arguing that "the emergence of modernist aesthetics signifies the increasing internalization of technological matrices of perception," and that "categories of perceiving and knowing are reconfigured in a historical situation in which technological devices are capable of storing, transmitting, and reproducing sense data," she demonstrates how the work of Marcel Proust, Thomas Mann, and James Joyce acutely registers the impact of train and car travel, the cinema, the X-ray, and the whole array of modernist machines of vision and speed (2–3). Her book is an installment in the afterhistory of modernism, because it understands high modernism "not as it wanted to understand itself, that is, as autonomous aesthetic performance at a safe remove from the encroachments of technology, massification, and commodification, but rather as historically mediated, semiautonomous cultural practices responding to, expressing, or managing conceptual, ideological, social, and cultural crises" (26). By historicizing the senses and their registration in fictional form, she demonstrates *in nuce* what Karl Marx had urged in the mid-nineteenth century: namely, that "[t]he forming of the five senses is a labor of the entire history of the world down to the present." When the senses are "cultivated or brought into being" through social and material practices, body history, subject history, and media history indeed become one (140).

Tom LeClair's *The Art of Excess*, working in the tradition of systems theory and its attention to scaled levels of relationships, similarly centers on the reciprocities of media and narrative form by taking a close look at eminent American novelists. Emerging within a cultural field marked by an "implosion of meaning," Thomas Pynchon, William Gaddis, Robert Coover, Ursula LeGuin, and others build themselves back into the proliferating data streams of today's global village by analyzing and criticizing the "master ideologies of American and multinational cultures" that are largely responsible for their very generation, and they do so by utilizing the specific resources of the novel (16). LeClair notes that such "masterworks take full advantage of the possibilities of their technology (the book) and medium (language) to represent large cultural and often global wholes" by advancing "against the mass media's thin layer of superficial information their massive novels of thick and profound information" (2, 16). Combining the encyclopedic impulse with the specific materiality of their medium—a double awareness already fully present in the achievement of the high modernists—such writers, rather than retreating from the capabilities of the book, use "the scale of information storage that textuality provides" by "collecting and testing stores of information, often from nontextual culture" (23).

John Johnston's *Information Multiplicity* shares a similar attention to the novel's location within a postmodern order of information. Diagnosing a condition of "information multiplicity" that tends to meld older cultural forms and identities into switch points of unceasing cycles of information exchange, Johnston develops two complementary models of serious fiction emerging in postwar America. Represented by the early work of Pynchon, Joseph McElroy, and Gaddis, "the novel of information multiplicity" emerges "between the modernist era defined by the separation of media (film, phonograph, the typewriter) and a new era defined by a global communications assemblage in which the television and computer assume essential functions" (57); in the manner of its high-modernist precursors, it attempts to register the informational surcharge of the world "by articulating new multiplicities through novel orderings and narrativizations of heterogeneous kinds of information" (3).[10] Following a "shift in the conditions of mediality" in the 1980s and 1990s—from a system of separate media to one "of partially connected media systems"—the "novel of media assemblage," by contrast, evolves "when information becomes fully quantified and digitalized ... and no longer carries its former viral and semantic potential" (4). Exemplified through Don DeLillo, William Gibson, Pat Cadigan, and the later Pynchon, such novels "take for granted a new level of informational control" and, by participating subversively in the mass media assemblage surrounding them, extend "the forms of subjectivity produced by new regimes of information production, storage and communication" (5).

Such a shift in the conditions of mediality, and in the conditions of consciousness, is observed by Joseph Tabbi in *Cognitive Fictions*. In his earlier *Postmodern Sublime*, Tabbi had noted that the novels of Don DeLillo, in particular, share an acute media-ecological awareness visible in the resistance to global networks and, more formally, in the "arrangement and release of cultural data into a narrative flow [that] intricates the postmodern literary imagination in nonliterary material" (183). The coedited collection of essays *Reading Matters* focuses more distinctly on the role of literary narrative in the mediaverse of the twentieth century, including the material import of print in a culture of flickering dots and bits. *Cognitive Fictions* extends these concerns into the domain of thinking by arguing that from its position "to the side of the dominant media of our time, print narrative . . . might recognize itself, at the moment it is forced to consider its own technological obsolescence, as a figuration of mind within the new media ecology" (xi). Thought, in the work of Richard Powers, Paul Auster, Stefanie Strickland, and others, takes form not, as in Bergson, "as a 'stream' or 'monologue' so much as an aggregate of conscious and unconscious, interacting and self-correcting, processes," a cognitive field in which "thought in its interiority and immateriality is present, but cannot be positively identified or isolated" (xxii). Narrative literature, to put it differently, locates itself at the blind spot of other media by "registering and reproducing their effects *as conscious experience*" (xii).

More generally, in *How We Became Posthuman* (which also includes the more recent *Writing Machines* and *My Mother Was a Computer*, which are part of a conceptual trilogy) N. Katherine Hayles draws on biological autopoiesis to argue for the continued importance of embodiment, for an understanding of consciousness-as-embodiment, and for a recognition of cognition as distributed cognition, if you will, rather than as the autonomous act of a monadic (and often male) subject. Concerned that information technologies have led to fantasies of immortality in computer science and cyberpunk, where consciousness becomes a downloadable database severed from the flesh, Hayles celebrates "finitude as a condition of human being" and that human life is life in a body embedded in a complex world "too unruly to fit into disembodied ones and zeros" (5, 13). Analyzing how information theory has repressed embodied knowledge, she looks toward literary narratives (by Neal Stephenson, Philip K. Dick, and others) as passageways affording the transfusion of science into culture (in the sense of Michel Serres's "Northwest passages") and as an embodied discourse resistant to abstraction: "Embedding ideas and artifacts in the situated specificities of narrative, literary texts give these ideas and artifacts a local habitation and a name through discursive formulations whose effects are specific to that textual body," and a textual body often as "prolix and noisy as the body itself" (22). Such texts contain her definition of the posthuman as, among other things, an understanding of consciousness as "an evolutionary upstart" and a view of the "human being so that it can be seamlessly articulated with intelligent machines" (3).

I want to continue in the tradition of these interdisciplinary *literary* scholars by offering not media-*theoretical* but more properly media-*oriented* readings of novelists whose work has escaped attention of being read in those terms. Danius studies the relays between technological media and narrative in the fiction of canonical modernists; LeClair, Johnston, and Tabbi extend these relays into a range of emergent and established postmodern writers (leaving aside the fact that even such eminent writers as Gaddis and McElroy have received little attention outside the academy); and Hayles investigates (dis)embodiment in the fields of informatics, cognitive science, and contemporary literature. I want to draw on the joint insights of these critics—and have for that reason provided capsule summaries of their work—to focus on writers whose oeuvre is, at least in some instances, not only lesser known and little studied (even when commercially successful) but rests on the fault lines of the media-technological shifts I have been delineating, rather than being wholly positioned inside of them: Frank Norris, Malcolm Lowry, and E. L. Doctorow (as well as, in the concluding section, Richard Powers, a writer studied by Hayles and Tabbi as well). Such fault lines, to be sure, are not meant as radical Foucauldian ruptures ushering in, at a historical moment's notice, a new technological order paradigmatically different from previous ones.[11] Rather, such shifts are fluid and serial to allow room for numerous interstitial and interlocking steps within which writing, in equally fluid and serial forms, takes place. (Typewriting and word processing, after all, have succeeded handwriting without eliminating the latter.) I devote one substantive chapter each to locating these writers within the media-technological configurations that inform their work, including the way such configurations frame notions of writing, perception, narrative form, and cognition. In a series of second, more concentrated chapters, I offer readings of a representative text of each to demonstrate the interactions between literary narrative and postprint media in more focused form. Here, I want to preview the larger trajectory of my argument and articulate the connections between the writers under discussion.

Working essentially in the last decade of the nineteenth century, when train and urban transit travel have become thoroughly habitual, while the premodern media network—with the exception of photography—still has the bedazzling charm of novelty, Frank Norris registers with particular acuteness the perceptual shifts taking place within human subjects, as well as the impact of the typewriter and visual and sound storage technologies on the culture of writing and print. As a threshold modernist knocking at the gates of the modern, Norris often propels his fictions by *narrative engines* that are commonly found in literary naturalism, such as the locomotive in *The Octopus* or the cable cars in *McTeague*. Such steam-driven, electric, and fundamentally mechanical engines carry a highly allegorical surcharge as they emblematize the narrative momentum of the text, the dynamic and speed with which the novel propels itself toward its often inevitable conclusion. At the same time, as we shall see, such machines also enable the mobilized vision of early film, for "cinema finds an apt metaphor in the train, in its framed, moving image, its construction of a journey as an optical experience, the radical juxtaposition of different places" (Kirby 2). Furthermore, trains and cable-powered urban transit also embody the late nineteenth-century techno-scientific worldview that grounds subjectivity in thermodynamic models of pressure and release and in velocity vectors predetermining character behavior, and hence signify the instinctual world of naturalism. If track-bounded vehicles, as Michel de Certeau has noted, suggest "something at once incarcerational and navigational," they also circumscribe the narrow radius of naturalist subjects, often behaving as though they are running in grooves or being pulled by subterranean strings, much like the cable cars driving *McTeague* and its eponymous hero (113).[12]

This underground remote control, in turn, suggests limited human agency and is intimately related to the media technologies of Norris's day. For Norris, in both his fiction and in his theory of fiction, phonography and photography—the *one* medium fully familiarized by the 1890s—are superficial inscription technologies capable only of recording bodies and their noises, but not the motivating forces of human agency. His characters utter "words with as little consciousness as a phonograph," whose unconscious tremors (a form of the Lacanian real) meanwhile inscribe themselves in the deep structures of naturalist fiction (*Woman* 169). Surpassing "the meticulous science of the phonograph" or "the incontestable precision of the photograph," the naturalist novel cuts "straight through the clothes and tissues and wrappings of flesh" to lay bare "the red, living heart of things," much like a scriptive X-ray stylus (*Criticism* 73, 75).[13] Similarly, amid paradoxical gestures that devalue writing and anticipate Marinetti's attack on the book, especially in *McTeague*, Norris insists on the fullness of literary experience compared to the flattening rendition of film, whose manifold techniques Norris co-opts into his fiction, perhaps through familiarity with the time-motion studies of Eadweard Muybridge and Étienne-Jules Marey. Arguably the first to include a "kinetoscope" in American fiction (while killing off a photographer as the immediate media rival in the same novel), Norris installs lower-order characters as flat, unself-conscious, and (dis)embodied processing subjects ideally equipped to record, like a camera, the world around them, in effect instantiating an early filmic point of view in narrative form and deploying cognitive shields capable of filtering out, as Georg Simmel has noted, the sensory overflow of urban data threatening to dissolve the self.[14] As well, montage and jump cuts give his (better) fictions strongly cinematographic qualities and were, for that reason, among the first to be considered for film, a full decade before Erich von Stroheim made *McTeague* into his well-known *Greed* (1924). However, as with early photography, with which naturalist fiction does after all share the logging of criminal stereotypes, Norris ascribes to print a representational density, particularly of that of the body in its materiality and sensory reach, that exceeds superficial inscription technologies.[15] This is one reason why naturalist fictions smell so much and why, as I argue in my reading of *The Pit*, Norris articulates a protomodernist sensibility that variously juxtaposes the aesthetic and durable materialities of the book to the high-speed processing technologies of ephemeral business data.

These conflicting impulses, vacillating between the adoption of postprint techniques that seem to give new life to a moribund medium and the simultaneous insistence on the representational superiority of print, are also evident in the stress within Norris's idea of *authorial* agency, registering as it does the discursive shift from a culture of handwriting to that of typewriting. As Kittler has demonstrated, the typewriter is a fundamentally prosthetic device that enables writing when the physiological linkage between eye, hand, and pen—as in the case of blindness—is suspended. Unlike writing by hand, the typewriter "creates in the proper position on a paper a complete letter, which not only is untouched by the writer's hand but is also located in a place entirely apart from where the hands work" (Beyerlen, qtd. in Kittler, *Networks* 195). Thus, while Norris recommends the virtues of a typewritten draft, as a novel is submitted to a publisher, his obsession with the scene of writing in his work suggests a premechanized investment in the hand and the consequent triangulation between mind, hand, and paper, that is, the compositional fluidity between conception, articulation, and self-expression. His fixation on manual disfigure-, or, rather, dis*finger*-ments, is so strong that it lays bare the repressed return to a kind of primal scene involving the loss of agency and authority, the loss of limb leading to a loss of self and power (at one point correlating the loss of McTeague's dental licensure with amputation: it's "just like cutting off your husband's hands," as a character puts it to McTeague's wife, Trina). Writing by hand is for Norris an act of authorial mastery and aesthetic self-expression, of physical and stylistic control over the materials of writing, and a virile exercise of self-generation, and hence part of what Amy Kaplan has called the naturalist "spectacle of masculinity," often under the admiring gaze of female eyes ("Romancing" 675). Typewriting, by contrast, has for Norris the associations of machined production, aesthetic devaluation, and, most important, of an assertive female labor force entering the world of work in increasing numbers. For that reason, compounding his investment in the hand, he tended to see the typewriter as an engine of effeminacy and re-production, not production, as a machine of industrialized domesticity allowing busy women to meddle with the original scripts of real men.

Writing roughly two generations later, in the years before, during, and after World War II and with the intellectual heritage of modernism largely behind him, Malcolm Lowry worked at what one could call a post-high-modern media moment, when radio and film, and car and train (and, eventually, plane) travel at high speed, had become internalized processing modes and working on a typewriter a widely accepted professional norm. Nevertheless, Lowry cultivates a premodern ethos about writing by hand that is similar to Norris's investment in manual embodiment, and he uncannily replicates Norrisian fears of manual incapacitation indicative of the truncated sphere of authorial agency working under conditions of mediality. Lowry's scene of writing, however, is more properly modern as his nostalgic glance back at pre-industrial notions of craft intersects with his simultaneous commitment to engineering as a form of textual control and design, evident in the engineering genealogy of his work as well as in his technology of narrative: the conceptual use of component-part machine designs to structure his novel forms into, again, narrative engines, often with a deliberately archaic and mythological patina to mute their contemporary edge. Thus, evident in his novels and manuscripts, handwriting for Lowry carries strongly romantic overtones of unmediated naturalness, self-generation, and embodied self-expression, of being purposefully out of the loop in a culture demanding the regular and regularized production of machined script. With Heidegger he would agree that "[m]echanical writing . . . conceals the handwriting and thereby the character. The typewriter makes everyone look the same" (81). Typewriting, by contrast, while in theory congenial to the formal austerity and clean efficiency of textual engineering, suggests the standardization of text through identical, prescribed letters and the conversion of writerly craft into a form of text processing. Like Norris, Lowry composed longhand

and had his (often illegible, hence "authentic") texts typewritten by female hands, including those of his second wife, and like Norris, Lowry may have come to see typing as a form of female intrusion, in his case, a pruning of his overly luxuriant prose by Margerie's restraining hands (from which Norris's prose would also have benefited). However, Lowry, unlike Norris, also saw the typewriter evolve into an instrument of "companionate authorship and parallel writing," as Margerie added her own suggestions to evolving drafts during the typing process while shaping Lowry's verbal lava (Bowker 292).

This postmodern media divide and distributed authorship is also visible in Lowry's dual allegiance to written narrative and film as the newly naturalized medium of artistic representation (as it is in his double life as a shack dweller living in romantic isolation and an urbanite in search of cosmopolitan stimulation). As a lifelong film buff with an encyclopedic knowledge of everything cinematic, importing techniques of film into his fiction became for him standard procedure, as with every modernist worth his or her salt, and like many a fellow novelist he had visions of joining the Hollywood dream factory, where he lived for a while. Few novelists working in the modern media ecology could heed Erich Auerbach's advice not to employ "the structural possibilities of film in the interest of the novel," for "a [cinematic] concentration of space and time . . . can never be within the reach of the spoken or written word" (546).[16] As well, in keeping with Lowry's visual sensibilities, bus, train, and plane rides become occasions for filmic panoramas on wheels and wings far more sophisticated than Norris's simple presentations, as they splice together outward-directed vision with the slow, internal ruminations of the perceiving subject. However, what distinguishes Lowry from most other late modernist writers is an increasing boundary conflict between film and fiction that expresses itself in numerous ways. Lowry did not only integrate, much more so than his fellow writers, sustained allusions to numerous films into his fiction to serve as cinematic leitmotifs counterpointing literary plots. For a good part of 1949 and 1950, following the publication of *Under the Volcano*, he also shelved his own literary endeavors to work, with Margerie, on a script of F. Scott Fitzgerald's thoroughly cinematic novel about cinema, *Tender Is the Night* (which yet awaits production because of its significant literary qualities that are difficult, if not impossible, to translate into film). During that time, Lowry formulated a virtual aesthetic of film, including provisions for a subliminal apparatus of cinema that is close to Walter Benjamin's "optical unconscious" (*Selected Writings* 3:117), and, most important, he came to believe that film might be a contemporary and more truly mimetic art form superior to print in capturing the perceptual and cognitive labors and the internal fluidities of the modern subject. This profound reorientation, away from the book, may help explain why Lowry suffered from a prolonged writer's block and why all of his longer post-*Volcano* texts, particularly *Dark as a Grave Wherein My Friend Is Laid, October Ferry to Gabriola,* and *La Mordida,* have remained unfinished: he was unable to reconcile the conflicting impulses of what is, in effect, a media schizophrenia with one another.[17] *October Ferry,* I want to suggest, registers Lowry's compromised fealty to writing particularly well, just as it registers a change in Lowry's philosophical outlook that, for him, was intimately connected to film: the shift from a deterministic mode of thinking in his (pre-)*Volcano* work to the distinctly fluid and provisional closures in *Tender, Dark as the Grave, La Mordida,* and *October Ferry,* in which the protagonists recuperate their agency after prolonged periods of paralysis. While Lowry may originally have seen both fiction and film as complementary manifestations of his mythopoetic mastertrope, *la maquina infernal,* unspinning a prescribed fate with inexorable logic, he came to understand cinema as a more fluid medium true to its animating premise—a *maquina viva.* Animating him, it may paradoxically also have stopped him from continuing to write. In that sense, as well as in his desire for Hollywood fame, Lowry thus once more followed in the footsteps of the author who saw in film the writing on the wall: "I saw that the novel, which at my maturity was the strongest and supplest medium for conveying thought and emotion . . . was becoming subordinated to a communal art . . . capable of reflecting only the tritest thought, the most obvious emotion. It was an art in which words were subordinate to images, where personality was worn down to the inevitable low gear of collaboration. As long past as 1930, I had a hunch that the talkies would make even the best-selling novelist as archaic as silent pictures" (Fitzgerald, *The Crack-Up* 78).

Nevertheless, as long as Lowry did write, he met the challenge of swelling data streams not just with cinematic and radiophonic imports but also by extending the resources of narrative fiction to the limits of readable print. While *Under the Volcano* is not *Finnegans Wake* (in which Joyce claimed to "roll away the reel world" [64]), it is a novel stuffed with every conceivable noise and voice, perspective and elective, to produce a narrative density bordering on semiotic overload. Stretching the tradition of high-modern encyclopedias, such as Proust's *Remembrance of Things Past,* Joyce's *Ulysses,* or Musil's *The Man without Qualities,* Lowry squeezed what Italo Calvino called "the multiplicity of the writable" into one single text(ure) bulging at its seams (112). Correspondingly, sentences tend to trail off into inconclusiveness or enmesh themselves into arabesque loops that defer closure, not only entrapping the reader in a seemingly endless process of signification but also acknowledging that the object of representation forever eludes verbal containment. In its orchestrated thickness forever on the verge of overreaching itself, *Under the Volcano* is a "novel of information multiplicity" that takes account of the processing capabilities of postprint media while insisting on the alphabetic resources of the book, now stretched to capacity and anticipating hypertext.[18]

If Lowry registers the crisis of narrative in the media ecology of the mid-twentieth century as few writers do, including the prospect of envisioning processing and thinking in visual terms, E. L. Doctorow celebrates the capaciousness of narrative to accommodate and reflect on all other discourses, including that of the (mass) media, on the threshold of the postmodern, when film and television have begun to dominate the public space of communication.[19] While Lowry saw artistic promise in film, possibly surpassing print, Doctorow experiences film and television (and radio to a certain extent) largely as conventionalized and commercialized mass media under the sway of corporate interests, hence compromising their artistic-critical edge and obliterating literary culture. Doctorow of course is no stranger to the art of the film and has frequently acknowledged the general impact of cinema on the evolution of twentieth-century narrative forms, including his own; similarly, mindful that screenwriting "is a kind of self-negation as a writer" (*Screenplays* 8), Doctorow has authored scripts from his novels *The Book of Daniel*, *Ragtime*, and *Loon Lake* that have been produced to small but critical success (or, as in the case of the latter two, have remained unproduced because of their irreducible literariness, that is, their unfilmability, similar to that of Lowry's work). *Ragtime* has since been adapted (by Michael Weller) into a lucrative blockbuster, as has *Billy Bathgate* (by Tom Stoppard), and even Doctorow's very start as a novelist grew out of his dissatisfaction with reading hackneyed film scripts for a publisher, resulting, in turn, in his first novel, *Welcome to Hard Times*, a parody of the Western. Nevertheless, for Doctorow (and very much in contrast to theoretical image-champions like Flusser), visual media remain vastly inferior to print because they subordinate language to image (and time to space) and, consequently, reduce the complexities of thought to an uncontoured void. Literary discourse, by contrast, lays bare the processes of cognition, conception, and the self through verbal elaboration and development.

Digital technologies carry the promise of such cognitive and substantive flattening as well, given that such technologies are often controlled by global software players managing the information streams of the World Wide Web. In *Loon Lake*, it is "data linkage" that "disestablishes human character," as the swapping of digital files composes and recomposes binary bipeds in a cascade of changing subjects (14). In *City of God*, the divine is seen to reside "in the blinking cursor," a cybergod or digital deus ex machina immanent in a binary network (8); the "simplest digital invasive techniques" lay bare a person's entire record to make it available for surveillance and manipulation, just as characters in the novel morph from their "real" alphabetic existence into fictions within fictions, film scenarios, and surgically reconstructed doppelgängers whose presumed identity is less than skin deep. Movies themselves, in fact, "today no longer require film. They are recorded and held in digital suspension as ones and zeroes," their changed material base facilitating infinite manipulations, similar to digitized identity theft or the silicon makeovers advertised in the award-winning television series *Nip and Tuck* (257). If representation as one of the quintessential modes of artistic work switches from the alphabet to digits, Doctorow urges, humans are in danger of surrendering the complexities of their self and thought to corporate software engineers controlling the (surface) codes within which the work of the imagination and the writing of history will take place.[20]

Being resistant to the digital regime, however, does not mean outright refusal of its corresponding means of composition. Doctorow's writing practices merge a distrust in the writing hand with mechanized and electronic forms of text processing that are in keeping with the fluidity of emergent thought (whose speed, in turn, could be seen to express postprint forms of mediation). Paralleling the postmanual and predigital moment from which he emerges, Doctorow learned how to type in middle school and started composing on a mechanical typewriter, perhaps because he "could not take seriously (and sometimes could not decipher) what I had written by hand." Realizing "early how the typing more closely kept up with the speed of thought," he soon graduated to an electric typewriter and, in the mid-1980s, switched to a computer keyboard, whose even more increased facility of composition is markedly noticeable in *Billy Bathgate*, the first novel written on the new medium whose verbal fluidity and luxuriance express the medium's decreased material resistance and the concomitant release of ideational flow. Authorial agency, for Doctorow, is not disrupted in the dislocations between body and machine but rather channeled into the keyboard-cum-conduit that facilitates writing in a digital age in the first place.[21]

Availing himself of contemporary writing technologies, Doctorow is yet concerned about the "vast and trembling shift from the magic of writing to the magic of electronics," a concern he meets by invigorating writing with renewed magic that aims at the blind spots of contemporary media and that engages the formal possibilities of the new communicative order (Postman 13).[22] He inserts the novel itself into the alphanumeric gap left by the binary code, extending from film and television to other discourses such as journalism, history, and science, literally by spelling out what has been left out of these knowledge domains. Understood as what information theory calls a "noisy channel" and what Michel Serres called a *parasite,* a viral agent causing static within a communicative system, Doctorow's narratives not only acknowledge, as these other discourses often do not, their rhetorical assembly by a human agent from the material building blocks of letters but also rewrite and rethink the information and mythmaking of other disciplines and media. Doctorow, I suggest, sees the novelist as a collector of discarded materials, as an archivist of unacknowledged knowledge or, in more senses than one, a refuser, and the novel as a collection of "non-disciplinary" debris or media edits translated into forms of telling knowledge about a culture's historical moment. Often integrating what would go by cultural residue in the media and in established fields of formalized knowledge, his novels propose themselves as assemblies of what has remained unassembled or remained invisible to assembly by other discourses.

At the same time, Doctorow's more recent writings also register the effects of networked environments on narrative form and on cognition and the subject. Negotiating within fields of data, several of his novels stage crises in information processing, as new technologies of storage and mediation lead to new informational spikes—and human brains struggling to deal with such plenitude of data. *The Waterworks* maps the challenges of a postbellum data surplus through the novel's rhetoric of skulls and brains, a doctor's pioneering work on brains and medical technologies, his work on premodern subjects suffering informational overload, as well as a detective whose knack for new but arcane data makes him into a veritable Lord of Information. Set in New York City after the Civil War and understood as a "negative imprint" of later, twentieth-century data booms, *The Waterworks* reads like a retrospective precursor to the novel of information multiplicity and suggests that rising levels of data are not the sudden result of modernism's eruptive forces but part of a techno-historical continuity that goes back to the energies of urbanization and to what the historian of information James R. Beniger has called the "crisis of control" of commodity and distribution flows in mid-nineteenth-century America. For that very reason, the novel not only models the memory function of print and the cognitive distance necessary to translate history into knowledge but also suggests numerous thematic and formal parallels between current notions of modularity and its narrative structure, such as distributed cognition, the emergence of memory gaps (Daniel Dennett), spatial re-cognition, and the narrator's highly responsive role as a decentered and perpetually self-correcting node processing parallel narrative fractals.

City of God is written with an even more acute awareness of the premises of cognitive science and the rising waves of information washing through cerebral folds. Albert Einstein and Ludwig Wittgenstein, the two thinkers who gave science and language philosophy their modern inflections, are given ample space to describe their theories of mind and selfhood—embodied, in the final analysis, even in the linguistic constructs of the analytical philosopher. The putative narrator Everett develops characters suspended between their wish for the old-fashioned autonomy of the self and an awareness that cognition is the effect of chemical reactions traveling along neuropathways, but they are fundamentally unable to see the mind in posthuman terms as what J. Francisco Varela, Evan Thompson, and Eleanor Rosch have called "a disunified, heterogenous, collection of networks of processes" (107). Everett, by contrast, aware of the fiction of autonomous agency, variously entertains cognitive modularity as an explanatory model of synergy and communication. Just as the individual ants of a colony can be seen to operate "like parallel processors, or in fact our own cortical structure of neurons," so individual humans, he reasons (in an analogy that replicates the cognitive parallelism he is describing), at times participate as independent agents in the "pulsing communicating cells of an urban over-brain," there to coalesce into a systemic unison that recalls the autopoetic processes of a gigantic cell (242–43). Even the encyclopedic form of *City*, assembling as it does numerous discourses and sign and signal systems, including those of radio, film, television, and the computer, derives from a conception of mind as clustered nodes of Web sites generating knowledge discontinuously and in discrete bits and pieces. Knowledge from within the chaotic structures of narrative, Doctorow suggests, emerges in steps of self-organizing processes that provide temporary closure but no permanent equilibrium.

These reciprocities between narrative and cognition and between narrative and network connect the later Doctorow with Richard Powers. While Doctorow's interest in cognitive science and in the effects of a totalized media field are more punctual and recent, and hence indicate his transition to a more broadly conceived moment of knowledge production (however filtered that moment may be through texts taking place at a century's remove), Powers, as a younger writer, works in an environment of full electronification and scientific theorizing that, for him, is thoroughly natural. Powers has repeatedly emphasized "the bidirectional relation between narrative and cognition" and the work of narrative consciousness to "make a continuity out of the interruptive fragments of perception" (qtd. in Neilson 14–15). Evident in all of Powers's fiction, it is particularly so in *Galatea 2.2*, the novel organized around cognition in both human and machined form, and the novel, as I argue in my conclusion, that correlates literary language, the canon, and cognition as analogous processes of evolutionary condensation (however vastly different in scale, given that language is an only recent addition to humanity's cognitive toolbox). Furthermore, just as the novel's dual-digital title indicates the rewriting of the Pygmalion story in the language of a software upgrade, thus adding an iterative and refractive doubling to a myth already multiply rewritten, it also indicates the synergy of brain and body as one indivisible unit of being, which is precisely what the digitized Galatea 2.2 in the alphabetic *Galatea 2.2* falls short of. In that sense, the novel retraces the general issues that preoccupy the writers of this study, and the issues that begin to chart the continued resilience of the book in the digital age: the links between language and cognition, and between agency, embodiment, and the materialities of writing.

Narrative Niches in a Postprint World

Powers, Doctorow, Lowry, and Norris each at their specific media-ecological moment and each in their idiosyncratic way reassert the continued vitality of narrative in a postprint world by drawing on the temporal extension of language as a syntactic extension of thought. Literary narrative, in particular, with its self-reflective texture of artifice, can achieve a level of reflective thought, lexical density, and cognitive thickness unmatched, in their view, by most other print and certainly postprint media. If the complexities of language are captured especially well in literature, it does so to express within its own medial constraints what the processes of the brain do in nonsymbolic form. The linearity of print, as McLuhan and his colleagues have taught us, has brought forth typographic man and the sequential logic of rational thought, and with it historical, evolutionary thinking—qualities that are in themselves worthy of preservation, particularly at a moment when electronic mediation, its popular claims toward multiplicity notwithstanding, threatens to erase historical nuance and critical distance in favor of one-dimensional or streamlined thinking: of sound bites and flat screens, if you will. Narrative can, however, also engender and engage the spatial, multivectored nature of cognition that is the hallmark of high modernist literature and its contemporary instantiations. While television and the computer can be seen as the current embodiments of "our collective imagination projected outside of our bodies"—thus taking the place formerly occupied by the book—and while these technologies "have moved information processing from within our brains to screens in front of, rather than behind, our eyes," it is still the processing within the brain that is the primary cognitive act, and an act that (at least in the current historical moment of human being) has the greatest affinities with alphabetic thought (De Kerckhove 5).[23] Narrative, to put it differently, with its affinity for conceit and metaphor and its sensitivity for rhetorical grace, beauty, and wit, while not presuming to represent the powers of the mind, comes closer than do other media to capturing at least a faint platonic shadow of the brain's cognitive brilliance. Its semantic density and temporal elasticity make it an ideal vehicle for the infinitude of thought that resists reduction into flattening ones and zeroes. Troping, indeed, as Richard Poirier has put it, gives "evidence of the human involvement in the shaping of language, and it prevents language from imposing itself upon us with the force and indifference of Technology. It frees us from predetermined meanings. Troping is the turning of the word into directions it seemed destined to avoid" (131).

Similarly, all four writers variously acknowledge an embodied and distributed notion of selfhood at odds with Enlightenment notions of autonomy. While Norris is a century removed from the cognitive models of the self, his naturalist subjects live in a Freudian world of instinctual knowledge that undercuts the unity of reasoned being. (As well, Norris figures the internal machinations of his characters in the discourses of thermodynamics, hydraulics, and electrics that also underlie Freud's models of the psychic apparatus.) Dissolving in multiple streams of time, Lowry's subjects are bundles of the voices of others and nodes of conflict as blurry as the moirés of their filmic mode of knowing. Doctorow explicitly invokes cognition to describe intentionality in terms of neuronal firings, mindful that such models may still not be far-reaching enough to map behavior. And Powers, as the schizoid doubling of 2 in *Galatea 2.2* suggests, unravels agency as a complete illusion, opting instead for a radically fluid and decentered notion of selfhood based on media-enabled physiological changes in brain structure. Print narrative, in that sense, can serve as an archive of historically specific models of selfhood embedded in located actions and personified agents (even if some of those agents, as in *Galatea*, are computational or machinic in nature).

In addition, all four writers variously use the materialities of writing and print to ground their *authorial* agency in the face of writing technologies severing the writing body from its work. Norris and Lowry both meet the anxieties of typewriting with a premechanized investment in the hand to ensure the compositional continuity (however illusory) between body, word, and self. Writing when the typewriter has become conventionalized and (not unlike Lowry) distrustful of the squiggles produced by the writing hand, Doctorow (very much unlike Lowry) sees no disconnect between keyboards, body, and authorial will, but rather a writing form that affords seamless compositional fluidity and speed. Like some of Doctorow's characters, but not Doctorow himself, Powers is anxious about dissolving into a network, and he counteracts, as I argue, such authorial dispersion with the classic materialities of print. Aware that books and humans are endowed with a "resistant materiality that has traditionally marked the durable inscription of books no less than it has marked our experiences as embodied creatures," Powers multiply links the heft and bulk of books with a weighted sense of authorship to secure his own embodied being (Hayles, *Posthuman* 29). At the same time, as a writer participating more fully in the digital age, Powers's writing practices—ranging from a wireless keyboard to beam his prose on a computer screen to voice-activated dictation software—also point to a more properly posthuman notion of authorship in which embodiment becomes a human-machine interface that is increasingly light and lithe. Even more than in the case of Doctorow, such practices are in sync with the speed of thought (that is, speech) as it emerges and is recorded, in almost-real time, as a data file, in the process short-circuiting the manual labor of typing in favor of digital registration. While seeking to embody himself in the traditional materialities of print, Powers (and his narrative incarnations) also strives for more immediate, and less closely embodied, forms of composition that incarnate presence through the virtual simultaneity of cognition, articulation, and digital inscription. And such cognition, for all its registration as only flickering signifiers, as Powers acknowledges, is nevertheless always cognition-in-the-body.[24]

From a media-technological perspective, these larger reciprocities are predicated on narrative's ontological function to commute experience into meaning and point to its genetic resilience in the contemporary order of mediation. Niklas Luhmann's notion of "preadaptive advances" (his own adaptation of Darwin) may, indeed, be useful to illustrate the changing, that is, multifunctional, position of the novel within the equally changing media system of data storage and circulation. Luhmann saw in the interlocking succession of speech, writing, and print "evolutionary achievements" that brought about wide-ranging structural changes within the system of communication, arguing that each such technology goes through stages of "preadaptive" functionality. Just as the wings of an insect, for example, served as a thermoregulatory and/or balancing device, before adapting for purposes of flight, so the printing press "was first designed and used as a technology for calligraphic standardization, before its exposure to market forces foregrounded its ability to produce immaculate repetitions and standardized knowledge" (Winthrop-Young, "Sociology" 402). Analogously, one might say, print narrative assumes different but often overlapping and complementary functions within changing media-technological orders.

One such changing function—similar to the narrative affirmation of language, cognition, embodiment, and agency—is the novel's task as a one-time carrier of factual truth, its eventual association with "fiction," and the eventual dissolution of these ontological distinctions under the influence of media technologies in contemporary literature. In his genealogy of print narrative in England, J. Lennard Davis has argued that the modern understanding of the novel emerges from a "news/novel discourse" in the sixteenth century, an amorphous complex of all printed prose narratives that is initially undifferentiated but eventually bifurcates, owing to ideological maneuverings distinguishing truth from falsehood in English courts. Thus, while early news ballads reported on matters of public interest and gave narrative "the ability to embody recentness, hence to record that which was novel—that is, to be a 'novel'" (48), the juridical sorting of fact from fiction also separated out into "journalism and history" and "novels," so that "factual narratives [were] clearly differentiated from fictional ones" (67). This relegation of the novel to the nonfactual continued throughout the eighteenth and nineteenth centuries under the influence of romanticism, and, importantly, the initial impact of media technologies. When Charles Baudelaire famously declared in 1859 that photography should not be allowed to "encroach upon the domain of the impalpable and the imaginary" but instead serve as "secretary and clerk of whoever needs an absolute factual exactitude in his profession," he bracketed literature from the empirical ethos of pictorial representation, even as the emergent culture of positivism pressured narrative precisely into assuming the burden of mimetic verification ("Salon" 153). Similarly, when Guillaume Apollinaire observed fifty years later that "it is possible to foresee the day when the phonograph and the cinema will be the only current forms of reproduction, and when as a result poets will enjoy a freedom hitherto unknown," he previewed with uncanny precision the development of electronic mediation and the consequent liberation of literary modernism from the weight of realism ("The New Spirit" 334). Yet, it is under the influence of the mass media of the twentieth century that the ontological separation of fact and fiction and illusion and reality begins to de-differentiate, leading, under the general rubric of postmodernism, to a self-conscious acknowledgment, among historians no less than the spinners of other tales, that venerable categories of truth and falsehood are constructs after all—false documents or factual fictions that the novel's capacious reach has been easily able to accommodate. Far from being constrained by specious distinctions (such as "fiction"), the novel has refunctionalized itself in the current mediaverse by assuming new cultural assignments in the form of "historiographic metafiction" (Hutcheon 88) or, as we saw earlier, novels of information multiplicity, media assemblage, or narratives of cognition. It is the medium's true return to a polymorphous "news/novel discourse," which at the same time holds open renewed adaptations within future discursive fields.

Similarly, literary narrative may see itself as the repository of a specific notion of information and knowledge in the digital moment of the present, when these very terms are subject to negotiation. The viral proliferation of data *is* no doubt the information condition under which writing today takes place, and more than one contemporary observer—Luhmann perhaps being the most well-known—has noted that just as film has penetrated the collective sensorium to the point of being virtually coterminous with consciousness over a wide array of experiences, so the computer, in the not too distant future, could redefine consciousness and communication, and hence identify as information and knowledge only that which fits into the operational parameters of digitalization.[25] Kittler, for one, collapses communication into information and at the same time discards "so-called Man" (*der sogenannte Mensch*) as a romantic holdover nourishing bygone dreams of autonomy, and he reduces all media, including literature, to the processing and storage functions of the computer. Literature, he observes, "is first of all a form of data processing; it receives and stores, processes and transmits information in a manner in no wise structurally different from computers" ("Benn's Poetry" 11). Digital sorting and storage, however, are vastly different from alphabetic processing and registration, just as *information* coded in binary terms (leaving aside the cybernetic understanding as information divorced from meaning) differs significantly from the condensing and compacting function of human memory, both individual and collective. Put differently, not only does Kittler transfer the model of computerized storage (*speichern*) onto other media without probing their specific resources or constraints, he also assumes a homogenous and transferable "notion of information" that "has not been sufficiently defined to warrant such generalization" (Winkler, *Docuverse* 83). While the novel generalizes as little as the term is elusive, it can yet insist on a notion of information, and on the processes of commuting such information into such (often construed as humanist, and hence old-fashioned) terms as *knowledge, insight,* and *wisdom,* that are qualitatively different from the binary bits of computer processing. As the contemporary novelists under investigation demonstrate, print narrative can offer a system of information and knowledge self-consciously different from the computable databases of mainframes and networks.[26]

Analogously, print narrative can offer a time horizon and thinking mode radically different from that of postliterary forms of information flow and consumer culture. If acceleration, as Paul Virilio and Derrick de Kerckhove have variously shown, is *the* defining criterion of the present (and thus threatens to press each moment into the historical past with dizzying speed), stories in print can provide both temporal and temporary retreat from such unrestrained velocity.[27] Powers, for one, has noted that "when we read, we stand in the flow of thought and outside the flow of ephemeral events," but "new media often reverse this relation. In place of the time of thought—the time of Chartres, of Angkor, of the Taj—they serve us *real* time, *transparent* time" ("Being and Seeming"). Opposed to this real and transparent time, narrative can provide a space of freedom that invites a more measured and reflective mode of historical thinking that is commensurate with the decoding processes of alphabetic reading and very much at odds with the high-volume, high-speed processing of television and digital media that is frequently instrumental in nature. "Reading is the last act of secular prayer," a way of "making a womb unto yourself" and "blocking the end result of information and communication long enough to be in a kind of stationary, meditative aspect" (Powers in Berger 113). As a medium from a different technological order, literary fiction can create a constructive vacuum of time in which the pressures of informational gain and loss are, for the time being, suspended while fostering resistance to the teleological imperatives that define late capitalist market culture. Reading literature is productive, not in a consumerist sense but in the sense of pondering and mulling over—free from the constraints of goal-directed time—the conditions that have brought about the culture of speed and splurging (and, incidentally, have nudged narrative into its meditative niche).

What lies behind this emphasis on narrative time are the critical constraints of literary fiction as opposed to the often nondirectional sprawl of hypertext structures. Not only does hypertext surrender the authorial control and direction of print to the free play of the reader's navigational drive, but virtual hopscotching, while guided by strategic hyperlinks, does not require having to work *through* language in the same resistant manner, as does the reading of print narrative, and to generate a sense of time within the reader that emerges from the materialities of print to be negotiated. One does not have to believe, with Gore Vidal, that "the word-processor is erasing literature" and marshal the energies of literary fiction to do media combat with a new and exciting technology, whose stock-driven dynamism reaches into the most remote corners of the globe (qtd. in Heim 1); not to be connected, after all, signals belatedness, anachronism—being out of touch. Further, given the feverish growth of Internet connectivity, the integration of word and image into a new electronic *Gesamtkunstwerk* suggests the probing infancy of an as yet new medium exploring its possibilities (and limits) within the twenty-first-century media ecology. Far from trying to swallow alphabetic text into its digital maw, hypermedia, if anything, "is the revenge of text upon television," for "in television, text is absorbed into the video image, but in hypermedia the televised image becomes part of the text" (Bolter 26). Redefining text and integrating what cultural conservatives like Neil Postman and Alvin Kernan considered the greatest challenge to print into a new medium is part of the intermedial system of checks and balances, after all, and furthermore a canonical insight of media theory.[28] Still, Myron Tuman's concern (echoing Winkler's) that hypertexts are essentially "systems for storing and retrieving information" but "not documents prepared by authors to convey a distinct world view to readers" opens up an interventionist space for narrative fiction that it has been occupying all along (75, 78). Instead of infinite electronic expansiveness, it offers a vision of the world that is bound (in more senses than one) and that engages the integrative function of literary prose to literally constructive effect. While reading ambitious literature is as participatory as the navigation of hyperlinks, such engagement with material text not only affords closure (that is fundamental to life and human embodiment) but, contrasting hypertextual drifting, also insists on an authorial vision of nonauthoritative control. As the novelist Mary Caponegro put it, "I want to invite my reader in, and while I want anything but a passive guest inside my page, I want also to be mistress of my own hospitality" (25).

Thus, to sing elegies bemoaning the demise of the Gutenberg Galaxy is to be unmindful of literary fiction's role in the mediaverse of the twenty-first century. While many, if not most, of print's traditional functions, particularly in the domains of data management and storage, have migrated to the computer, and will continue to do so, literary fiction seems far from becoming obsolete. The survival of print narrative, to be sure, is determined by more than "pure" media-ecological considerations. Time-honored (and hence naturalized) cultural attitudes often lag behind changes in technology and delivery, such as the oft-cited resistance to online reading as the singular preserve, in a humorous formulation, of "Twinkie-charged insomniac dweebs" (Weinberger 42). Similarly, no less than the corporate drive behind Internet expansion, the continued existence of print will depend on "industry perceptions of the most lucrative product structure," such as, for example, the current shrink-wrap packaging of literary anthologies with paperback (and non-copyrighted) classics for university classrooms in an effort to increase sales. Looking at technological possibilities that might portend the demise of print "is not the same as identifying corporate priorities, school board politics, teenagers' habits, or advertisers' whims" (Murphy 90).[29] Still, as reflections even by advanced practitioners of hypertext fiction show, the media-specific qualities of literary print are worthy of imitation and thus suggest their continued resilience in electronic environments. "The Web is a pretty difficult space in which to create an expressive surface for text," Michael Joyce observes, further noting that "to achieve a feeling of depth and successive interaction unlike most Web fictions," he enriches his hypertexts with print-based constraints. *Twelve Blue*, for example, contains the word *blue* on every screen to create a self-conscious leitmotif and verbal resistance that makes readers pause, and each screen contains only one hyperlink that sinks the moment it has been clicked to allow for narrative direction guided by the reader's sensibilities ("Forms" 233). As the remediation of fundamentally print-based forms, such strategies demonstrate the present limits of hyperfiction, just as they emphasize once more the constructive constraints of its medial predecessor and its place in the current media ecology.[30] Indeed, Amazon's recent strategy to offer downloadable books online through its Kindle device—while understood as a complement to print for a new generation of digital readers—may well have the effect of rekindling a desire for hard copies and the felt materiality of the bound page, and the current record number of books in print worldwide seems to suggest a Renaissance of the Book (that is aided, in another media-related twist, by the release of scores of film adaptation of literary classics and contemporary fiction).

Language, as Joyce (Michael, not James, though he would have agreed) reminds us, is characterized by "its intrinsically multiple forms," "its age-old engagement of eye and ear and mind," "its ancient summoning of gesture, movement, rhythm and repetition," and "the consolation and refreshment it offers memory." If, as such, it offers the best possible model for what will emerge as a "truly electronic narrative art form" in the future ("Forms" 231), it has already done so, and will continue to do so, for the print-based narrative art form of the present and the future.[31] Its belatedness/anachronism and verbal and cognitive thickness as well as its specific materiality and temporal unfolding suggest that literary fiction—understood as a self-re(de)fining medium—will continue to be a player in the media ecology of the future perpetually engaged in the process of process, leading to new (and synergistic) forms of representation, cognition, and (both authorial and readerly) embodiment.

2
Frank Norris and the Modern Media Ecology

What a denouement we should have if we could suppose the secrets of the darkened chamber to be revealed by the testimony of the imprinted paper.

—Fox Talbot, *The Pencil of Nature* (qtd. in Green-Lewis 145)

Reading Frank Norris is in many ways like taking a walking tour through the fashionable Mechanics Fairs of the late nineteenth century, local spinoffs of the spectacles of technological achievement such as the Centennial or the Columbia Exhibition. While his machines are part of the narrative equipment of verisimilitude, they also and in no small part bespeak what he called the novelist's "*sense of fiction,*" his attempt to invest technology with a figurative surcharge (*Criticism* 67). Most prominent among these is the trope of the universe as a gigantic engine that circulates, like an epic set piece, through his oeuvre and that derives largely from his exposure to Herbert Spencer. Norris saw in the idea of a universal machine a fitting mastertrope or ideological superstructure to validate his predetermined world with contemporary scientific authority.[1]

This chapter seeks to contribute to the discussion of technological models in Norris's fiction, particularly in *McTeague*, the novel in which the relays between technology and late nineteenth-century American culture become most visible. It examines how Norris negotiates "the uncertain and shifting line between the natural and the technological" in turn-of-the-century America and how his machines offer suggestive models to reflect on the increasing industrialization of writing and the consequent anxieties of writerly self-investment (Seltzer 3).[2] Most important, it situates Norris's work within the emergent media culture of the late nineteenth century—in particular, photography, film, and the typewriter—which pressured print narrative into redefining its modes and domains of representation. As such, this chapter is concerned with permeable zones and boundaries: boundaries between media, boundaries between handwriting and machine writing, boundaries between hardware and software, and boundaries between women and men.

Zoning the District: Photography, "Chromoliterature," and Literary Naturalism

Norris's work hovers between the discursive span of news and novel. Prior to his career as a novelist, Norris honed his craft as a reporter and editor at *McLure's* and at San Francisco's society weekly, *The Wave*, and his best fiction derives from newspaper stories to suggest a congenial reciprocity between reportorial and literary narrative.[3] But unlike his contemporary Henry James, who understood journalism as "the great new science of beating the sense out of words," Norris saw in newspapers and magazines no assault on the institution of literature (James, *Novels* 22:45).[4] Instead, these forms of writing too had their place within the ecology of print, side by side with more "ambitious" forms of textuality. Nevertheless, despite this ostensible leveling of hierarchies, Norris's work points to distinctions between newspaper work and his idea of the literary that provide a suggestive template to investigate the boundary oscillations between naturalist narrative and the new kid on the media block: photography.

The advent of instantaneous photography in the 1870s and 1880s is largely the result of increased shutter speeds and more reactive plates, and it allowed for the first Kodak moments, the fast freezing of the fluid real into a stable image. As such, instantaneous photography posed anew, as it had done during its infancy, questions about the nature of truth: "If, at the center of the problem was the degree to which the camera—a mechanical instrument—could deliver a picture of reality that was truthful, the real question was of course buried in the question itself: what was a 'truthful' picture of reality?" (Orvell 85). Norris, too, was centrally concerned with this question and frequently argued that empirical accuracy puts undue limits on the literary imagination. While writers frequently insist on realistic descriptions, such descriptions are "not always true to life, from the point of view of the artist" (*Criticism* 56). Since the very perception of reality is radically heterogeneous, lodged as it is in individualized apprehension, scientific observation or technologically mediated forms of recording are necessarily inadequate and prescriptive: "Not even science is going to help you; no two photographs, even, will convey just the same impression of the same actuality" (*Criticism* 57).[5]

Romantic at their core, Norris's sensibilities raise profound questions about the phenomenology of perception and being, which philosophers such as Edmund Husserl, Charles Sanders Pierce, and William James were posing in their own domain.[6] As well, Norris insists on the power of imaginative freedom to define the otherness of the literary vis-à-vis the new medium. In his pre-Formalist quest for an understanding of literariness, Norris brackets off the imaginary and the non-real as exclusive to literature—its quality of estrangement that allows the world to be seen anew rather than with the jaded eyes of photographic vision. What is at issue is Norris's emphasis on the stress between positivist accuracy as a techno-scientific category and the expansive imagination of art (even allowing, anticipating Andy Warhol, "pea-green horses"). Artistic license compromised by technological modes of representation is no license at all but a surrender to the protocols of industrialized knowledge. Opposed to "truth," "accuracy" is a "mere machine-made thing," a technological replica emphasizing factual verisimilitude, not literary verity (*Criticism* 58). Photography is such a "machine-made thing," a medium bound by the mimetic codes of verisimilitude, and as such an ideal medium supplementing discourse that is not literary: journalism.

Throughout his career, Norris associated photography with journalistic writing. In a review on recent nature books, he compliments the "marvelous life-photographs of birds" (*Criticism* 41), and when he responds to an inquiry about the makings of a correspondent, he urges "an observation almost photographic" (*Letters* 175). Similarly, even after establishing himself as litterateur, the evidence suggests that Norris went on assignment with camera in hand. Based on the photographs illustrating many of his journalistic writings (and the unlikelihood that periodicals sent a separate photographer), Norris may have been among "the early photojournalists in the United States" (Katz, "Publications" 156).[7] Thus, whenever it was a matter of complementing the documentary claims of a newspaper or magazine report, Norris affirmed the powers of the new medium.[8] In semiotic terms, one might say that Norris the journalist subscribed to the iconic quality of the photographic sign, its putative ability to record something as real through a relation of literal resemblance, which in effect allows for a kind of transparency of the object world; and this transparency, in turn, is premised on the indexical relation of the photographic sign with the object world, the photochemical process linking the image and referent as an analogical, factually truthful transcription of the world.

To emphasize the documentary quality even of literary narrative, Norris routinely implanted photographs as well as daguerreotypes and (chromo) lithographs into his novels. They provided a visual mapping of the contemporary real and allowed for socioeconomic distinctions. A seaman's cabin in

Blix is given a rustic flush by an "old daguerreotype" and an "array of photographs thrust into the mirror between frame and glass" (25); the Big Dipper Mine in *McTeague* sports an unframed "chromo" on the wall of "a couple of peasants in a ploughed field (Millet's 'Angelus')" to capture the popular aesthetic (210); and *The Pit* is cluttered with photographs of persons and objects. When Laura Jadwin's provincial aunt counts "the number of photographs" in her hostess's family album as art expert Corthell discusses "the spring exhibit of water-colors," Norris juxtaposes photography as a form of low-class consumption with the high-class presumptions of art (97). While low- and middle-brow Americans flip through photo albums in the parlor, upper-crust upstarts give themselves a patina of culture by pillaging through European galleries. The Jadwins spare no money to invest in paintings by Bouguereau and Detaille, among others, to buy themselves some old world sophistication (175–76).

Underlying this division is the emergent dialectic between authenticity and imitation that characterizes much of the nineteenth century. As technologies of reproduction, photography, the daguerreotype, and chromolithography were frequently seen as agents "for democratizing luxury and diffusing high culture through imitations of elite forms" (Orvell xvi), and as such they began exerting cultural pressure on the distinction between the real thing and its simulacrum. While training at the Académie Julian in Paris in the 1880s, Norris witnessed the forays cameras were making into the visual arts. Photography captured in a flash what it took a painter weeks of labor and skill to do. Conversely, painting responded to photographic representation by approximating or superseding it, as in the minutely detailed and colorful paintings of the pre-Raphaelites, or, as with the French Impressionists, by duplicating and refining the blurred images of early photographs, and later, when the advent of color photography seemed imminent, by enriching their land- and cityscapes with an unprecedented plethora of pigments and tonal shades.[9]

The evolution of Norris's idea of fiction, developing after his sojourn in Paris, can similarly be linked to the encroachment of photography on naturalist representation. His narrative theory and practice both suggest that while photography may be useful for empirical data storage, it is not an artistic means commensurate with the sensibilities of literary narrative. In 1859 Baudelaire had noted that photography should be "the secretary and clerk of whoever needs an absolute factual exactitude in his profession" but should not be "allowed to encroach upon the domain of the impalpable and the imaginary" ("Salon" 153–54). Congruent with Baudelaire, Norris implanted photos and chromos into his work as instances of documentary precision and in line with the material accumulations of late nineteenth-century culture. Novels, however, that imitate other novels or current tastes (such as those written within pseudo-literary coteries) subscribe to the ethos of the photograph and are, hence, a form of "chromoliterature": Norris's version of pulp fiction.[10] The ambitious novel, by contrast, allows for a representational reach exceeding that of visual data storage. Juxtaposed to the qualifications of the camera, Norris claims for narrative a more wide-ranging register of codes and, quite literally, reauthorizes print in the postprint age.

Most prominent among Norris's strategies is a kind of chromatic overcompensation. He infuses his novels with a surcharge of color that was beyond the scope of contemporary photography. In San Francisco's Chinatown, "color was everywhere. A thousand little notes of green and yellow, of vermilion and sky blue, assaulted the eye. Here it was the doorway, here a vivid glint of cloth or hanging, here a huge scarlet sign lettered with gold, and here a kaleidoscopic effect in the garments of a passer-by." On the other side of the street, "gigantic pot-bellied lanterns of red and gold" swung from a balcony, "while along its railing stood a row of pots—brass, ruddy bronze, and blue porcelain—from which were growing red, saffron, purple, pink, and golden tulips without number" (*Blix* 29). Similarly radiant passages can be found in most of Norris's novels and suggest not only his own painterly eye but, in their narrative particularization of pigments and tonal shades, also the Impressionist and Divisionist canvases with which he was familiar. They evoke a visual surplus or, in the lexicon of media studies, a proliferation of pixels beyond the processing of the camera.

Extending this expansive reflex, Norris elevates naturalist narrative also by juxtaposing photographic surface to textual depth. In his fiction and theory of fiction, Norris notes that photographic (and phonographic) storage is capable of recording only the visible (or audible) traces of human being, but not the motivating forces of human agency. Naturalism, by contrast, pries open this gloss of inscription and lays bare humanity in all its (degenerate) rawness. The realist novel, much like journalism, only notes "the surface of things. For it Beauty is not even skin-deep, but only a geometrical plane, without dimensions of depth, a mere outside." The naturalist novel, by contrast, exceeds "the incontestable precision of the photograph" (or "the meticulous science of the phonograph") because it probes "the unplumbed depth of the human heart" (*Criticism* 73, 78). Similarly, Zola's writings reach beyond "the truthfulness of a camera" and go "straight through the clothes and tissues and wrappings of flesh down deep into the red, living heart of things" (*Criticism* 71, 75). Naturalism, for Norris, is a kind of scriptive X-ray, the new subsurface imaging technology of the body's shadow world that eclipsed other surface inscriptions such as film, particularly in Norris's San Francisco. It allowed medical and literary examiners to reach beyond hair and skin into the body's deep structures and to suggest correspondences (phrenological and otherwise) between what the new rays had, in effect, obliterated: "the distinction between the outer and inner spaces of the body" (Reiser 62).[11]

Significantly, the surface-subsurface dichotomy is inscribed in the gold motif of *McTeague*, the mastertrope of a novel written during the gold standard of America's currency. Its pages are stuffed with gold and its simulations—ranging from plates and coins to picture frames—which make distinctions between the real and the fake difficult. In this novel about mouths and teeth, Maria Macapa and Zerkow resort to the old practice of testing the metal's mettle by biting into it, and McTeague is told the difference between expensive "French gilt" (manufactured from gold leaf) and less costly "German gilt" (made simply from thick gold paint), as he inquires about coatings for his dental sign, but neither knows how to distinguish between them (77). In the Gilded Age, little, if anything, is what it seems, covered as it is by a patina of preciousness. Structurally analogous, the characters in *McTeague* are glazed with a thin veneer of civilization that is recordable by the technology complementing that veneer: a shiny and superficial surface (consisting, not coincidentally, of metallic compounds) capable of inscribing outer appearances. Such photographic surface records cannot, however, shed light on the complex metallurgy of character in *McTeague*, many of whom find, again not coincidentally, their greatest fulfillment when fondling metals. To uncover the base metal, "the foul stream of hereditary evil," requires the diagnostic practices of literary naturalism (22). Analogous to the simulation of gold, photography for Norris is a technology of both duplication and duplicity; literary narrative, by contrast, is a technology of truth.

In what can only be described as an anxiety of technological influence, Norris writes out of existence narrative's competitor, the "bankrupt" photographer whose vacated suite is inhabited by Trina and McTeague (77). He is present only as an absence, the residue of his soft hardware leaving a lingering reminder of his craft: "Try as she would, Trina could never quite eradicate from their rooms a certain faint and indefinable odor.... The smell of the photographer's chemicals persisted in spite of all Trina could do to combat it" (125).[12] By expunging the picture taker, Norris relegates him to the invisible shadow world of the narrative, even as his subdued olfactory traces hint at a return of the repressed that refuses to go away completely. As an Oedipal struggle in the new mediascape, Norris felt the need to kill narrative's emerging rival that had begun to make inroads into its monopoly of representation.[13]

And yet, despite this ostensible reaction formation, Norris's work shows genetic affinities with the cultural norms of photography. In terms of their logistics, both shared a fundamentally typological notion of representation. In photographs of the time, "the pictured subject, with all its concrete particularity, *stands* for a more general class of like subjects" (Orvell 88)[14]; naturalist narrative similarly underwrites a typology, whereby specific character qualities do double duty as individualized and generalized traits. Each tick, idiosyncrasy, or inclination contributes to an essentialized ethnicity, such as Trina's hoarding impulse, which is the presumed effect of "a good deal of peasant blood still [running] undiluted in her veins" (78).

In large part, this photo-literary typology derived from the nineteenth-century interest in criminality and the invention of essentialized ethnicities to regulate social hierarchies and immigration flows. Picture archives, as Allan Sekula has noted, were devoted to "new techniques of social diagnosis and control" and "to the systematic naming, categorization, and isolation of an otherness thought to be determined by biology and manifested through the language of the body itself" ("Traffic" 16). The naturalist novel can similarly be understood as a "set of representational techniques" that "systematically participate[s] in a general economy of policing power" (Miller 2). Forms of data collection both, photographic and naturalist archives often catalogued undesirable subjects (which were hence desirable for print and camera for precisely that reason) in the service of marking deviance. Conversely, looking at or reading about pathological souls and bodies allowed readers to gauge and recalibrate their own physical and mental normalcy. (And such bodies and souls do not have to be photographed—or written about.)

Norris fully subscribed to the racist hierarchies of his time. As is well-known, many of his disturbing profiles derive from Cesare Lombroso, the Italian criminologist whose genealogy of misfits was popularized by Max Nordau's 1895 eugenic blockbuster *Degeneration* (Dillingham 67).[15] Equally likely, Norris absorbed criminal typology through a lively market of popular books on character richly illustrated with photographs and phrenological charts. T. Appleberg's *Know Thy Future* (1892), La Vergne Belden Stevens's *Faciology* (1893), and William Seymour's *Key to Character, or Everybody Their Own Detective* (1894) were just a few of numerous publications that offered sustained face readings in tandem with evidentiary photographs, frequently gesturing toward the Other (Green-Lewis 183–84). In one of the ironies of nineteenth-century cultural history, both occult science, which the culture of empiricism had long believed to have discredited, and photography, which had received empiricism's highest imprimatur, conspired to produce a kind of indisputable facial hermeneutics.[16] When Norris observes that "detectives would rather have for identification purposes a good description of the criminal, than a photograph of him," because "a man carries about with him a certain distinct impression—a sort of symbol of his personality," he links the scopic truth of the photograph with physiognomic evidence but at the same time upholds the surface-depth split that underlies his separation of photographic from literary truth (*Apprenticeship* 1:54). Diseased minds carry their imprint in the face. Ineradicably inscribed in their physiognomy is a pathology evident in the square heads, squinting eyes, and bulging bumps of Norris's culprits. While some detectives (and writers) may, indeed, identify criminality in a photograph, "the ideal detective" would be a blinded face or body reader running "his hands over the bodies of the hundreds of sleeping inmates, almost in the dark, until he reaches a certain one" (*Apprenticeship* 1:54). As flat renditions of faces, mug shots can lie; the bumps of bodies do not. Even literary typologies of such bodies, derived though they may be from dissimulating photographs, are more knowing than their "original" source.

To obtain a more truthful picture of racial purities, and hence to surpass the two-dimensional, and possibly fraudulent, flatness of the conventional portrait photograph, criminal or otherwise, the English scientist Sir Francis Galton invented the practice of composite photography. One of the chief architects of the eugenics movement, and cousin of his ideological bedfellow Darwin, Galton suggested that no single photograph is able to record a sitter's ethnic self. Instead, he photographed his subjects as much as twenty times and then, as a form of typological synthesis, sandwiched the resultant pictures into "a single homogenized facial image" meant to capture the sitter's ethnic core, further suggesting that a series of such composites would reveal an archetypal typology of racial origins (Orvell 92). As an optical abstract or visual mean, the composite photograph was understood to bypass the informational blind spot of the single shot and allowed the camera to make unprecedented claims toward truth.

Norris's narratives offer similar equivalents of composite photographs. While many of his character types originate in Lombroso's picture books, they might also be seen as multiple exposures condensed into essentialized portraits. This may help account for Norris's repetition of stock phrases to portray character. Epistemologically, certainly, Norris's literary narratives share with Galton's photographic narratives anxieties about degeneracy and faith in the ultimate improvement of (naturally, only select) types. Witness Laura Jadwin in *The Pit*, as she arrives at her version of evolutionary meliorism by considering her typology of Womanhood: "The individual—I, Laura Jadwin—counts for nothing. It is the type to which I belong that's important, the mould, the form, the sort of composite photograph of hundreds of thousands of Laura Jadwins.... [W]hat I am, the little things that distinguish me from everybody else, those pass away very quickly, are very ephemeral. But the type Laura Jadwin, that always remains, doesn't it? One must help building up only the permanent things. Then, let's see, the individual may deteriorate, but the type always grows better" (217).

With its peculiar presumption of depth, the composite picture as visual narrative could make revelatory truth claims similar to those of Norris's literary narratives and, hence, be seen as their technological equivalent; Laura's condensed photographic typology certainly suggests as much. Unlike the flat quality of the single shot, which Norris deemed commensurate with the journalistic real, the composite picture accrues a cumulative truth that is close to the depth claims of his fiction: it can do photographically what literary narrative does verbally. By laminating serial shots into a visual narrative, composite photography thus bridges the oscillating boundary between Norris's naturalism and the camera in the late nineteenth century (just as it relays the policing function of both as archives of aberrancy). While photographs may be useful to supplement a magazine report or to indicate imitative tastes in fiction, Norris never fully legitimized their "machine-made" accuracy (verisimilitude), which was at odds with the handiwork of the writer: the truth (verity) of the novel.

Of course, young Norris had already seen it all in Paris. While fooling around at the Julian, he realized that many prominent French painters, most notably Edgar Degas, had begun using the qualities specific to the photograph—in particular, its ability to freeze-frame urban life—as scenic models for their paintings, thus, similar to Norris, validating the new medium without relinquishing the touch of the artist (Scharf 181–95).[17] Around the corner from Degas's studio in the rue Laval, two brothers of light were soon to tinker with strings of photographs and to throw them up against a wall. True to the canonical insight that old media look forward to the new, Norris gives us a preview of coming attractions. Stephen Crane's *Maggie*, he observes, reads like "scores and scores of tiny flashlight photographs, instantaneous, caught on the run, as it were. Of a necessity . . . the movement of his tale must be rapid, brief, very hurried, hardly more than a glimpse" (*Criticism* 164). The moving pictures have arrived.[18]

Relegitimizing Print: Cinema, the Body, and the Big Stink

Erich von Stroheim claimed not to have left out a single scene from *McTeague*. "It has always been my determination to produce the story exactly as it was written," he observed (Koszarski 117), further acknowledging that he first wanted to become a filmmaker while reading Norris's novel (Weinberg 114). No doubt von Stroheim sensed the affinities between Norris's vision and his own. With 446,103 feet of negative, somewhere between forty-two and forty-five reels, and about nine hours of projection time, *Greed* in its original 1923 version was as monstrous and grotesque as the literary characters it features. (Eventually the film was, repeatedly, severely edited to make a viewing in one screening possible.) Like many contemporaries, von Stroheim wanted to make, not what in today's parlance would go by "adaptation" but a complete and faithful transcription of a literary text: a translation from one medium to another.

Von Stroheim's techniques of cinema, in fact, are more fully based on literary modes of presentation than on those of Norris himself. The barn doors and irises in *Greed*, for example, which serve as editorial devices to establish continuity between scenes, are very much at odds with the novel's many "abrupt transitions," which are more characteristic of film itself (Lawlor 8). While Norris was at the cutting edge of technical experimentation (anticipating the new medium), von Stroheim fell back onto the narrative strategies of literature (which gave rise to film in the first place).

Such reciprocities, and there are more, illustrate the claim that media of different conceptual orders are imbricated in a web of interactions that exerts pressure upon their mutual evolution. Judging by von Stroheim's narrative traditionalism, film, for all its fundamental newness, had not yet fully understood itself as a medium with radically different possibilities of presentation. Conversely, though Norris is often reactionary and nostalgic, his range of techniques suggests a filmic imagination then still in its infancy.[19] Extending my discussion of photography, I want to suggest that Norris reaches beyond the limits of print to approximate filmic vision but that he at the same time meets the cultural devaluation of print by recuperating the fullness of literary experience. Specifically, Norris ascribes to literary narrative a representational density of the body that exceeds superficial inscription technologies: its material being, its sensual reach, and its instinctual complexity. While film records only flimsy footage of the body in motion, the body as such, so Norris's logic goes, constitutes an irreducible essence that can be captured only by the verbal elaborations of naturalist narrative.

By his own account, Norris's "first ambition was to be [an] animal painter" (*Letters* 108). He enrolled at the San Francisco Art Foundation in 1886 but spent his days at the stables of the Presidio where he "studied the horses of the cavalry barracks, making sketches of legs, rumps, hoofs, and heads" (Walker, *Norris* 25; see also McElrath and Crisler 142–43). Acutely perceptive to the muscular labor of speeding steeds, as in "The Coverfield Sweepstakes," he rendered their movement with precision and claimed that Frederic Remington's horses (which later publishers would use to illustrate his fiction) "should be accorded a place in the world's art.... Perhaps no artist who ever lived understands horse action so well as this American illustrator of ours" (*Apprenticeship* 2:209). Remington made extensive use of the equestrian time-motion studies done by Eadweard Muybridge, as did a famous contemporary in Europe.[20] Anton Meissonier, widely known for his historical tableaux, took great pride in painting "horse action" better than any other painter dead or alive, but following Muybridge's first public appearance in Paris in the fall of 1881, he "based all of the scenes in which the horse appears on chronophotographic documents" (Marey, qtd. in Rabinbach 102).[21]

At issue was the age-old question whether galloping horses always have at least one hoof on the ground or whether they are momentarily airborne. In 1878, at the invitation of Governor Leland S. Stanford, Muybridge began photographing speeding horses with a trip-wire installation that triggered sequenced camera shutters, intending, as Kittler put it, "to instruct ignorant painters what motion looks like in real-time analysis" (*Gramophone* 116). A year later he published a series of six new photographs titled *The Horse in Motion*, taken with shutter speeds of 1/500 of a second. Working on similar studies, the French engineer Étienne-Jules Marey suggested to Muybridge that he mount his photosilhouettes on a revolving wheel to create the illusion of motion—an idea Marey had derived from the principle of the zoetrope, a popular children's toy at the time. When Muybridge eventually came to Paris to parade his flickering animal motions to an excited crowd (appropriately enough, first in Marey's house), his "zoetropic device signaled the first dramatic example of the photographic synthesis of movement" (Rabinbach 102).

No sketches of Norris's horses survive, nor do we know whether he knew of Marey and Muybridge, but the coincidence of their work is suggestive. Muybridge was a celebrity in California, who began part of his studies at the Presidio, Norris's equestrian hangout (Haas 14). Both had repeatedly published their photographs in the Parisian journal *La Nature* and were the buzz in the ateliers where Norris was to dabble before long. What is known is that Muybridge, following another demonstration of his (by now renamed) "zoopraxiscope" in New Jersey in 1888, went to the Wizard of Menlo Park to suggest a business venture. Thomas Edison, initially impressed with Muybridge's idea to link a zoopraxiscope with a phonograph to make "live" recordings of actors, declined, but during that meeting "Edison's motion picture may well have received its first spark" (Musser, *Edison* 5).

This confluence may help explain a suggestive mix-up in *McTeague*, when Norris includes Edison's early form of the motion picture, the kinetoscope. Invented by Edison and his chief assistant William Dickson in 1892, it makes its (arguably) first appearance in American fiction when McTeague wants to show his bride a good time at the local Orpheum. A poster announces it as "the crowning scientific achievement of the nineteenth century" (58), and when they finally see its choppy images, indeed, "the kinetoscope took their breaths away" (62).[22] In reality, however, the kinetoscope was a one-person peephole that allowed for brief single-reel viewings, not the projection we see in *McTeague*. Like McTeague, who confuses the new technology with a "magic lantern" (64), Norris might have thought of the vitascope, a successor to the kinetoscope and forerunner of the film projector, which Edison demonstrated in New York in the spring of 1896 and began marketing in San Francisco's Orpheum in June of that year (Mottram 586).[23] The point is that the vitascope, in both its technology and subject matter of usually large animals or objects in motion, has strong affinities to Muybridge's zoopraxiscopical projections, which horse lover Norris may have had in mind.

It is certainly no coincidence that Norris's projector first features a moving horse and that he included a new, competing narrative technology into his own in the first place. In the mechanical regularity of the "kinetoscope," he may have recognized an allegory or narrative engine from a different conceptual order than Spencer's cosmic machine to represent the operational dynamic of *McTeague*, the precision with which the novel unwinds itself. In a world in which character-puppets are pulled by subterranean strings as much as the cable cars, inscribing the story on quasi-filmic sheets of paper may have suggested the inexorability with which the narrative unrolls toward its "prerecorded" end. The grooved parade of naturalist figur(in)es, their frequent association with the linear velocity of pressurized locomotives, and their predetermined inscription in a novelistic screenplay are at the center of Norris's "mechanics of fiction" and show strong affinities with the cinematic apparatus.[24] Uncannily, in a sequence of local shots fashionable at the time, when Norris's film shows a horse followed by a cable car, he projects retrospectively the change in San Francisco's mass transit systems, as cable cars replaced horse-drawn carriages following a viral epidemic in the 1870s. Analogously, through this filmic recording, Norris might project the shifts in the media system, as narrative anticipates filmic vision and recalibrates its narrative strategies.[25]

Most prominently among these strategies is what Sergei Eisenstein has called the "extra-ordinary plasticity" or "optical quality" of character delineation. Like Dickens's figures, Norris's "are rounded with means as plastic and slightly exaggerated as are the screen heroes of today" (208). Certainly, Norris's premise "to take cognizance of variations from the type of normal life" is a natural for the unnatural freaks of film (*Criticism* 76). They can be easily visualized because they are wife beaters, sex maniacs, and metal fondlers with prominent bumps on their heads. Brutal, living intensely in the flesh and relishing magnified ticks, naturalism's gallery of physical and psychological deformities lends itself to film. Erich von Stroheim realized that early on.[26]

In addition, *McTeague* is distinguished by what the literary sensibility of von Stroheim tended to elide: montage. Norris's texts are firmly grounded in filmic design or the calculated sequencing of narrative scenarios. His "Mechanics of Fiction" describes a conception of narrative as "a series of pictures" spliced together from chapter-shots, each of which serves as "a unit, distinct, separate" (*Criticism* 61). In particular, Norris is fond of the elliptic montage of sequential scenes to regulate narrative tension and speed, as when, following the mutilation of Trina's right hand at the end of scene XVIII, he opens scene XIX with a brilliant sentence that contracts time as it leaps over the amputation to Trina's new job: "One can hold a scrubbing-brush with two good fingers and the stumps of two others even if both joints of the thumb are gone, but it takes considerable practice to get used to it" (193). Similarly, Norris employs parallel montage to achieve filmic concentration and concurrence, as in the cut between sections XX and XXI, when children discover Trina's body while McTeague, more than a hundred miles away, meanders through Placer County.[27]

Most important, Norris's work illustrates the feedback loops between consumer culture, point of view, and filmic mediation. Already photography "greatly extend[ed] the sphere of commodity exchange . . . by flooding the market with countless images of figures, landscapes, and events" beyond the imagination of the private customer (Benjamin, *Selected Writings* 3:36). By the end of the nineteenth century, film's spec(tac)ular breadth had begun to reify commodity culture and, along with it, the visual regime desiring those commodities. As one such commodity (rendering commodities in lettered form), print narrative developed a "point of view" that was centered around a perceiving subject (or desiring machine) positioned outside the reader. Anticipating filmic vision, such centers are frequently "accompanied by the verbal or narrative equivalents of techniques characteristic of film ... the medium which will shortly become the hegemonic expression of late capitalist society" (Jameson, *Unconscious* 160), and Norris's work indeed features modern subjects whose modes of cognition correlate to the "scanning" procedures of film.

In "Metropolitan Noises," an essay as ingenious as it is racist, Norris notes that in "highly organized subjects," urban noise produces "hysteria, mild insanity.... The lower the type, however, the less irritating is the effect produced. With the savage, noise is music and music noise, but delicate and highly specialized organisms can be influenced by sound as mercury is influenced by temperature" (*Apprenticeship* 1:276). Georg Simmel similarly observed that the modern "*intensification of nervous stimulation*" is manageable by absorbing "sensory mental imagery" in "the transparent, conscious, higher layers of the psyche" precisely because such processing is "remote from the depth of the personality," and hence assures the integrity of selfhood (175–76). Building on Simmel, Benjamin has theorized that the shock experience constitutive of modernity has an anesthetic effect on consciousness so as to manage trauma and secure an intact self: "The greater the shock factor in particular impressions, the more vigilant consciousness has to be in screening stimuli" (*Selected Writings* 4:319).[28] In all these instances, the intellect operates as a cognitive shield that registers traumatic experience on the surface only. Proustian moments all, they describe the realignment of the perceptual field and the psychic apparatus to buffer sensory surplus.

In Norris's fiction, such surface processing is evident in *Blix* when reporter Condy hurries unreflectively through his day, but at night, as his "tired eyes closed at last, occurred that strange trick of picture-making that the overtaxed brain plays over the retina. A swift series of pictures of the day's doings began to whirl *through* rather than *before* the pupils of his shut eyes," eventually trailing in a catalogue of fleeting sensations, registered but not processed (41). Condy's internal film allows him to revisit his experiences and expresses his mental fatigue as a psychological reflex demarcating the self awash in a sea of stimuli. Similarly, while Lloyd Searight in *A Man's Woman* is not embattled by sensory overload but private complications, she escapes into the writing on the wall of her dark room, "staring at the shifting shadow pictures that the electric lights, shining through the trees down in the square, threw upon the walls and ceiling of her room" (53; see also 112). This film takes the projections of city lights as its raw material, and if the images don't enable Searight to see right, at least they distract from her emotional upset.

What is more, Norris registers the panorama as a fundamentally cinematic form of perception. Wolfgang Schivelbusch has shown that the sights rushing past a train window "transformed the world of lands and seas into a panorama that could be experienced. . . . [I]t turned the travelers' eyes outward and offered them the opulent nourishment of ever changing images that were the only possible thing that could be experienced during the journey" (Sternberger, qtd. on p. 62). By gliding without effort on rails, the passenger became a stationary register whose former depth perception, owing to the speeding train, melded fore- and background into a monoperspectival flatness. Often, travelers lost their sense of time and started counting mile or telegraph poles to retain a sense of speed, which the smoothness of railroad travel did no longer permit immediately. Accordingly, in *A Man's Woman*, Lloyd "took an interest in every unusual feature of the country through which the train was speeding, and noted each stop or increase of speed. She found a certain diversion, as she had often done before, in watching for the mileposts and in keeping count of the miles" (158). More important, while the train window served as a framing device for serial panorama shots, the poles functioned as a, as it were, frame within the frame. Schivelbusch notes that the "outer world beyond the compartment window was mediated to the traveler by the telegraph poles and wires which flashed by. . . . The landscape appeared *behind* the telegraph poles and wires; it was seen *through* them" (31). Analogously, "while the train carried her swiftly back to the City," Lloyd "sat quietly in her place, watching the landscape rushing past her and cut into regular divisions by the telegraph poles like the whirling pictures of a kinetoscope" (158). Norris's acknowledgment of railroad travel as a protocinematic mode of perception could not be more clear.[29]

McTeague is not, as is Condy (and Lloyd), a modern subject seeking protection from sensory overload. On the contrary, he is one of Norris's "lower types," a flat processing surface ideally equipped to record camera-like, that is, unself-consciously, the world around him.[30] Instead of a moving point of view, the novel features McTeague's own panning but stationary vision: "Day after day," the narrator observes in cinematic parlance, "McTeague saw the same panorama unroll itself. The bay window of his 'Dental Parlors' was for him a point of vantage from which he watched the world go past" (9). This world includes "corner drug stores with huge jars of red, yellow, and green liquids in their windows"; "stationers' stores, where illustrated weeklies were tacked upon bulletin boards"; "barber shops with cigar stands in their vestibules"; and, in a catalogue extending over half a page, "subservient provisionmen . . . scribbling hastily in [their] order books" (7–8).

What is important here, from a media-oriented perspective, is not solely Norris's triangulation of cinema and consumption that (pace Jameson) is central to the evolution of filmic vision, nor that the passage illustrates Paul

Virilio's claim in "Cinema Isn't I See, It's I Fly" (*War* 11). Rather, what is of interest is McTeague's increasing disembodiment during his overview, almost as if Norris wanted to suggest the dematerializing effect of cinematic recording. Introduced as a giant whose "mind was as his body, heavy," McTeague "heave[s] himself laboriously" out of his chair and assumes a viewing position at the window (6). Once his vision takes over, however, McTeague's body largely disappears; his materiality reduces from that of a hefty processing subject to an invisible, disembodied consciousness. Both writer and reader lose sight of what is actually a fully embodied camera eye.[31]

It is tempting to read this separation of vision from the body along the lines of a technological unconscious, a prefigurative capitulation of literary narrative to cinema. Does Norris suggest, however unconsciously, that the traditionally embodied point of view in fiction will give way to the disembodied vision of the apparatus of cinema? Other, more clearly conscious gestures support such a view. Characters involved in writing and drawing illustrate in their decline the decline of print and reading in a world increasingly shaped by other medial inscriptions. Mrs. Heise is a "decayed writing teacher" who can, it appears, no longer make a living from her craft (112). Trina's friend Selina with "'elegant' handwriting" "overworked herself giving lessons in hand painting" and ends up living in a boardinghouse, unable to compete against the images of the camera (144, 40). The "stationery and 'notion' bazaar" on Polk Street is going out of business (114). And for Old Grannis, the gluing of old pamphlets and newspapers on his "little binding apparatus"—"uncut" and "never read"—becomes an occupational therapy, a way of sealing into oblivion printed words whose status in the new media ecology has become precarious indeed (140, 13). As Maria Macapa observes, with the romanticized clairvoyance of the demented, "He takes his amusement in sewin' up books" (68).

Even the public reaction to the kinetoscope points toward a medial change of guards. Interspersed as the second-to-last feature of the evening, its projections mesmerize the Orpheum's clientele until "fully half the audience left immediately afterward," suggesting not only cinema's future as a mass anesthetic but also its nonverbal, more easily accessible form of mediation (63). A visual inscription without the detour through letters requires less effort and no command over the alphabet. It can be "read" even in cases of illiteracy, as with the "awe-struck" McTeague, and reach into unalphabetized imaginations (62).

Norris, however, counters such devaluations of narrative by complicating the disembodiment of filmic mediation. He revalidates print by emphasizing what, in his view, eludes superficial inscriptions of the body: its materiality, its instinctuality, and its sensual and sensory register. McTeague's perception of Trina's hair as "heaps of blue-black coils and braids, a royal crown of swarthy bands, a veritable sable tiara, heavy, abundant, odorous," is memorable precisely because it orchestrates the senses in ways no close-up can approximate (17). The novel famously figures Trina's hoarding impulse as an ecstatic intercourse of warm body with cold metal, pulsing flesh with static matter (198).[32] And in the novel's most concentrated embodiment, McTeague's mass distills into hypersensory perception when his "sixth sense" warns of his pursuers, and he metamorphoses into a pure chunk of instinct that "hastened on furtively, his head and shoulders bent. At times one could almost say he crouched as he pushed forward with long strides; now and then he even looked over his shoulder" (229). Such moments deploy verbal friezes that, in Norris's view, induce in readers a mise-en-scène more precise and suggestive than any visual recording and endow the narrative with a textured temporality that tunnels into the characters' evolutionary complexity.[33]

Paralleling this narrative fullness of instinct, Norris develops a sensory spectrum that absorbs the blind spots of contemporary media. While the physiological effects of eye and ear have their technological extensions in photography, film, and gramophone, the effects of the proximate senses of hand and nose are without corresponding inscriptions. Analogously, complementing this separation of data streams, Norris enlivens his work with clouds of smell and bouts of touch that slip between the media-technological cracks (even as his characters hear and see all the time and have elective affinities to filmic vision). His characters, as in *McTeague,* are repeatedly identified by what they grab and sniff. McTeague possesses a "manual dexterity that one sometimes sees in stupid persons" (14); Trina is a woodcarver who "turned the little figures in her fingers with a wonderful lightness and deftness" (160); Zerkow's "claw-like, prehensile fingers" are those of a man "who accumulates, but never disburses" (28); and Zerkow and Trina, when they can't fondle metals themselves, indulge in a kind of manual ersatz erotics, their fingers touching and rubbing their mouths and chin (29, 199). Similarly, McTeague's parlors "exhaled a mingling odor of bedding, creosote, and ether," frequently mixed with "an acrid odor of ink" rising from the post office below (7); Zerkow's shop was "foul with all manner of choking odors," and the "certain faint and indefinable odor" of the photographer's studio has lodged itself irrevocably into the McTeagues' apartment (28, 125). This big stink comes to a symbolic head when McTeague, while digging through Trina's clothes, catches a whiff of her smell and, in a case study of fetishistic displacement, "plung[es] his face deep amongst them, savoring their delicious odor with long breaths of luxury and supreme content" (47).[34]

These representations of embodiment and sensory plenitude must certainly be seen in the context of late nineteenth-century America's love affair with Darwinism and thermodynamics that had a distinct interest in the body and collective and individual (d)evolution.[35] As well, from the neuroscientific perspective that is never far from this study, Norris's emphasis on smell, in particular, echoes current findings that "odor receptors take up more than 3 percent of the human genome" (Lehrer 65) and demonstrates in narrative terms that the proverbially strongest of the senses is deeply grounded in the body. Indeed, for a lumbering giant working in mouths and on teeth, as for everybody, "the taste of most flavors is smell," be it ether steam beer or French kisses (Lehrer 64). Inscribing such neuroscientific evidence into the novel *avant la lettre* thus gives literary naturalism a contemporary scientific resonance and once more—now on the level of genetic coding—literalizes its canonical classification by drawing attention to the biological, that is, natural and naturalist, range of its themes. At the same time, I would urge that this focus on the body be seen in relation to new inscription technologies and a changing logistics of perception. Hans Rindisbacher has demonstrated that much of nineteenth-century fiction is characterized by "olfactory repression," but is re-odorized under the influence of a modernist subjectivity (viii). Beginning with the French Symbolists and continuing into naturalism, literature evolved a new understanding of sensory perception and olfactory significance: "smells are no longer perceived as a reality 'out there' that leaves a sensory imprint on a subject. Rather, their meaning is constituted in and by the perceiving subject itself" (167). I would add that this revaluation is intimately linked to the redistribution of sense ratios brought about by new media. In the manner as sight and sound were channeled into phonograph and camera—thereby releasing and recalibrating these very senses—touch and smell remained without corresponding media inscriptions and were hence absorbed, in multiply nuanced forms, by the old medium of print.[36]

Thus, Norris's work registers literature's imbrication with the new media technologies of his time. While insisting on the continued viability of the novel and demarcating its conceptual order from photography and film, he also intimates its possible senescence and anticipates elements of filmic narrative. Interestingly, these formal reciprocities also look forward to the commercial links between camera and print in the near future. Norris died too young to witness these links firsthand, but a decade after his death, and a decade before von Stroheim's *Greed* (1924), Norris's publisher filed a "Memorandum of agreement between Doubleday, Page & Company and William Brady," the director of *The Pit*'s successful stage adaptation, "for motion picture rights to *The Pit, The Octopus, McTeague, Blix, Moran of the Lady Letty,* and *Man's Woman* [*sic*]" (FNC 6:35). One year later, Norris's brother and executor, Charles G. Norris, observed that in the face of a royalty dispute and "moving picture rights," Doubleday and Page should not sign up "with Edison Co. or any other moving picture concern" (FNC 1, May 1915). Did Edison, America's entrepreneur extraordinaire, smell a quick buck and attempt to secure film options for Norris's novels? Certainly, the strong interest in Norris by several studios testifies to their filmability that, as I have argued, originates in the boundary oscillations between fiction and film. With the release of the first films based on Norris's work—D. W. Griffith's *A Corner in Wheat* (1909) based on *The Pit*, two versions of *McTeague* titled *Desert Gold* (1914) and *McTeague* (1916), and a version of *Moran of the Lady Letty* (1922)—as well as a subsequent reissue of *McTeague* as a "photoplay edition" to coincide with *Greed* that featured shots on the dust cover (1925), Norris's Edisonian "kinetoscope" in *McTeague*—the splicing of fiction and film—has come full circle.[37]

Agency and Angst: Mangled Hands and Machined Writing

In 1928, when Doubleday, Doran began publishing a ten-volume edition of Norris's works, they lured prospective buyers by inserting a page of *McTeague*'s original manuscript into each volume of the book. Roughly twenty-five years after his death, Norris's holographs were not deemed valuable enough to warrant preservation in climate-controlled archives, yet they were enough of a prize to attract subscriptions to a new edition of his works. What today are seen as irreplaceable artifacts of authenticity were three generations earlier there for the giving away and taking.

This curious footnote in the annals of literary marketing nicely adumbrates a third issue that further delineates Norris's work within the new media ecology: the practice of writing in the brave new world order of information. Paralleling the complex dialogues between fiction, photography, and film, Norris's novels and essays point to the problem of agency in the machined world of the turn of the century. His work registers the anxieties authors felt as they transitioned from a culture of handwriting to that of typewriting, a shift that severs the writer's body (attuned to a handheld pen) from the act of writing itself. Norris responds to the resultant feeling of estrangement by defining writing as an exertion of authorial power and mastery over the materials of writing. This fear of technological disempowerment is deeply implicated in his anxieties about gender and authorship in a technologized world.

The loss of agency in turn-of-the-century fiction is nowhere more visible than when naturalist characters are at the mercy of instinctual pressures overpowering their cultural veneer or, alternately, in locomotives hurtling confined bodies through pre-tracked space. By contrast, the loss of *authorial* agency is more closely tied to the hands as the organ that traditionally defines the novelist. Extending Norris's hand-based notion of character, as I suggest above, he is preoccupied with injured hands and manual incapacity. In his essays on writing, a feisty Norris notes that of the current U.S. population, "100,000 ... have lost the use of both arms" and are hence unable to plagiarize, for which "grammar and a right hand unparalyzed are all that is necessary" (*Criticism* 141, 186). In *A Man's Woman*, a novel opening with a polar expedition, ship doctor Dennison, "having slipped his mitten, had his hand frostbitten before he could recover it" (288), and the right hand of expedition engineer Ferriss became so frostbitten that the doctor "was obliged to amputate it above the wrist," followed by the amputation of the left shortly thereafter (291). In *McTeague*, "Old Grannis's fingers trembled so that he pricked them with his needle" (25); when the men wrestle in the park, Mr. Heise "believed himself to be particularly strong in the wrists, but the dentist, using but one hand ... all but strained the harness-maker's arm" (129). McTeague breaks his rival Marcus's right arm shortly thereafter, and Marcus eventually involves himself in a gunfight in which "two fingers of his left hand were shot away" (237). An enraged McTeague gnaws "at his hands in an excess of silent fury" (26), and Trina's fingertips become mutilated by McTeague's "crunching and grinding them with his immense teeth" and by her contact with poisonous paint, eventually resulting in a partial amputation (171).

These mutilations—and the list goes on—suggest Norris's abiding concern with incapacitation and reveal a compulsive fear of mangling or losing the organ elemental to his craft. Indeed, the fixation on disfigurements, or, rather, dis*finger*-ments, becoming visible here lays bare the return to a primal scene involving the loss of agency and authority, the loss of limb leading to a loss of professional life. Not coincidentally, as a sixteen-year-old preppie, precisely when he began working more seriously with pen and ink, Norris double fractured his left arm and soon afterward wrote his first fantasy of manual disfigurement. The juvenile poem *Enerves de Jumièges* featured "the half-mythical sons of Clovis, whose father had punished them for revolt by cutting the tendons of their legs and arms and setting them adrift in a barge on the Seine" (Walker, *Norris* 51; see also McElrath and Crisler 67).

Consider the relays between manual incapacitation, professional livelihood, and survival in *McTeague*. Trina receives a letter from her mother as "an answer to one she herself had written just before the amputation of her right-hand fingers—the last letter she would ever be able to write" (194). Toward the end of the novel, the heat of Death Valley controls McTeague "like a muffling Titanic palm," pulled forward as he is by "an unseen hand" (227). When a dying Marcus handcuffs his hand to McTeague's, the latter notes that "he felt a pull at his right wrist; something held it fast"—suggesting that the arrest of McTeague's hand clinches the text's closure (243). As a symbolic gesture to intimate the coincidence of manual with textual standstill, Norris's fatigued hand brings to a halt the hands of the person who made a living with his "manual dexterity." And in what may be the most suggestive link between disfigurement and professionalism (paralleling the final immobility of McTeague's hand), a neighbor observes to Trina that revoking the dentist's license by the city is "just like cutting off your husband's hands" (155). The dentist, no less than the novelist, depends on his hand to make a living. It is the embodiment to achieve professional status, the elemental marker of their ability to do the work they are "licensed" to do: pull teeth or write texts.

Significantly, Trina's poisoned hand may well signify the effects of industrial modes of production on manual processes: for while Trina has fine carving skills, "she could not whittle [figures] fast enough and cheap enough to compete with the turning lathe that could throw off whole tribes and peoples of manikins" (78). Manual skill may be an anachronism in the age of machines, at best reducing the hand to a supplement, at worst making it fit for poisoning and amputation. Significantly as well, the "printed notice" revoking McTeague's licensure is stamped with the "seal of the State of California" and codifies the text processing of Kafkaesque bureaucracies. Juxtaposed to the letter next to it, written in Selina's "'elegant' handwriting," "the oblong letter" (containing "a legal extract" in "small type") dramatizes the conflicting modes of textual production in turn-of-the-century America (144–45). If the document suggests Norris's thoughts, however cryptic, on the legitimacy of handwriting in the world of text processing, and perhaps the administrative reaches of state power that complicate professional autonomy in all domains, it also opens the discursive bifurcation I have been delineating: the rupture between handwriting and typewriting.[38]

Thus I argue that just as Norris's hand-injured subjects are unable to exercise their full agency, so Norris was anxious about losing the organ central to his craft (or having it rendered immobile). His fixation on mutilation is intimately linked to his investment in his *hand*writing and a corresponding resistance to typewriting. While the hand, in the logic of logocentrics, allows for the continuous articulation of the self—it affords a seamless transition from mind to pen to paper—the dislocations encountered during typing make such uninterrupted articulation impossible; they suspend the compositional fluidity between conception, articulation, and self-expression. Put differently, what is fundamentally at stake for Norris is the agency of his authorship: the exercise of authorial power.

Norris's holographs, for example, are written exclusively by hand and suggest an investment in aesthetic penmanship, inscribed as they are "on great foolscap paper, in fine handwriting, 600–800 words on a page," as one of his coworkers put it (FWC 1, 30 April 1931). Written with a fountain pen, whose built-in ink supply allowed for sustained compositional flow, they are a visual pleasure to behold, an inked decoration on thick, white, lined sheets.[39] Likewise, Norris appears to have handwritten all of his personal correspondence. If his letters are retyped, as many housed in the Bancroft Library are, they are usually corrected in Norris's hand, suggesting a professional type service. This is also true of business letters written on his publishers' stationery. In every instance, Norris's holographs are retyped on thin yellow paper, including numerous mistakes (such as the consistent misspelling of *Morau* for *Moran*) that suggest reproduction by someone other than himself.[40] Norris would typically correct these drafts and, presumably, have a secretary type a final copy. Indeed, reflecting the division between public and private self and Norris's investment in his cursive gracefulness, his friend Gelett Burgess observed that "Frank had two handwritings ... one for letters of almost microscopic characters, the smallest handwriting I have ever seen except Kipling's. At other times he would write large. He was at the age when one has affectations and indulges one's self" (FWC 1, 18 October 1930). Or, as Norris's early critic Isaac F. Marcosson noted in his obituary, in which he reproduced the handwritten outline of *The Pit:* "The signature is characteristic. Norris was proud of its many curves" (FNC 7).

Norris's scriptive flourish was so floral, in fact, that it was frequently mistaken for *Morris,* inviting his contemporaries to associate his name with William Morris, whose lavish book designs Norris imitated in his first book, *Yvernelle* (appropriately, a medieval romance), and whose sagas served him as models for his early fiction. As well, throughout much of his career dating back to Les Jeunes, a San Francisco–based group of aesthetes, Norris embellished his signature with the fleur-de-lis of Bourbon kings that was irreproducible in typewritten form. That Norris did not "adhere to the usages dictated by the grammar-based punctuation style" commonplace in typesetting establishments by the 1890s, but typically employed an "older 'rhetorical' style of punctuation," suggests in itself his pre-typographical sensibilities (McElrath and Burgess 268).

Being personally resistant to the typewriter did not, however, mean refusal to recommend it altogether. For a syndicated author who got paid by

1. The first manuscript page of Frank Norris's *The Pit*. Frank Norris Collection, Bancroft Library, University of California, Berkeley.

the word (keeping lists of word counts, as did F. Scott Fitzgerald), a typewritten script had its advantages. While "it is not always necessary to typewrite the manuscript" (*Criticism* 148), submitting a typed draft of a novel had the virtues of legibility, cleanliness, and editorial processing speed that ensured a first reading upon submission, as Norris suggested to fledgling writers: "First have your manuscript typewritten. The number of manuscripts is too great and the time too short to expect the reader to decipher script, and, besides, ideas presented or scenes described in type are infinitely more persuasive, more plausible than those set down in script" (*Criticism* 141). As such, a typescript also allowed a male self to become visible. When one of Condy's stories in *Blix* "came back from the typewriter's," he could "not repress a sense of jubilation" because of "the additional *strength* that print lends to fiction," suggesting not only the first step in the outward manifestation of authorship but also, in this novel of education, a young male ego in the process of self-formation (75, my emphasis). Similarly, the Norris of international fame insists on having his name printed in "'larger type,'" afraid that "to tuck away the scribe's patronimic so inconspicuously is a little undignified," further urging his publisher, "please do let me strut a little in the eye of the public" (*Letters* 195).[41] Notwithstanding these printed forms of public authorship, however, typewriting itself was not a matter of self-investment or agency but rather of a *material product* independent of the *process of writing*.

What looms behind this hand-machine rift is Norris's problematic gender typology and the division of labor in the late nineteenth-century writing market generally. Paralleling the submissive females of his oeuvre, women in unprecedented numbers entered typewriting schools, there to stage what Gregory Anderson has called the "white-blouse revolution" (1–26).[42] What used to be a male privilege—writing as the exclusive domain of men with pens—could easily be understood as a site of contention for authorship, especially by those who perceived that their sovereignty was under siege. Norris was one of many (pre)modernists who developed a pronounced unease about women in the work(place) of writing and projected his own inflections onto the emergent culture of typewriting. Compounding his investment in handwriting as both aesthetic labor and self-expression, Norris tended to see the typewriter as an engine of effeminacy and reproduction, not production—a gender dimension that is intimately related to the ethos of male power underwriting his styl(iz)ed scripts.

Norris's comments about style are well-known and encapsulated in his statement, "We don't want literature, we want life" (*Letters* 67). In lieu of mots justes and polished circumlocutions, the reader encounters a raw demonstration of lexical power that sometimes borders on parody. Many of Norris's set pieces bespeak a disorienting reach for verbal registers intended to communicate the sublime of Nature or City. While such stylistic eruptions are ostensibly uncontrolled, Norris's rhetoric seems, in part, crafted to achieve precisely such an effect. They reveal the writer "as a coercive presence" who manifests his authority "in powerful molestations, in mangling the characters, in lording one's control over them" (Cain 205). To this I would add Norris's control over his readers, inscribing his violating presence onto their imagination. As Derrida reminds us indeed, "style is always the question of a pointed object. Sometimes only a pen, but just as well a stylet, or even a dagger" ("Question" 177).[43]

This stylistic agency applies quite literally to the material act of putting pen to paper. In *Blix*, the military trope for writing suggests the links between power and style. When Condy is about to finish a novella, "words came to him without effort, ranging themselves into line with the promptitude of well-drilled soldiery." With increasing facility, "sentences and paragraphs marched down the clean-swept spaces of his paper, like companies and platoons defiling upon review; his chapters were brigades that he marshaled at will." As "commander-in-chief," Condy deploys his lettered foot soldiers on the battlefield of the page and leads them "straight to the goal" (117). What is more, such stylistic muscle flexing is even more suggestive in moments that bring the repressed moment of inscription to the surface. Michael Fried has observed that Stephen Crane "unwittingly, obsessively, and to all intents and purposes automatically metaphorized writing and the production of writing . . . in images [and] passages . . . that hitherto have wholly escaped being read in those terms" (120). A similar case could be made for Frank Norris.

Consider McTeague's recognition of the similarities between dentistry and mining. In the Burly drill in the mine, "he saw a queer counterpart of his old-time dental engine; and what were the drill and chucks but enormous hoe excavators, hard bits, and burrs? It was the same work he had so often performed . . . only magnified, made monstrous, distorted, and grotesqued" (213).[44] This association, in McTeague's only moment of abstraction, suggests that Norris himself recognized—in however repressed a way—the resemblance between inscriptive instruments and his own writing tools (here overlaid with the telling motif of disfigurement and distortion). Through their shape, function, and usage, the drills are analogous to writing with a pen, just as they suggest continued agency by extending the operator's body. Just as dentist and miner operate their drills on metal and enamel, so the writer works his pen on paper, inscribing himself in the process. The "hand" of their profession is in each case impressed on the surface of their raw material. Tooth, rock, and paper carry the signatures of their agency and power.

What is more, these inscription surfaces carry the gender inflections mapping the naturalist project. While nature "east of the Mississippi" may be "cosey, intimate . . . like a good-natured housewife," the novel's mining region is a "vast, unconquered brute" crying out for subjection. Accordingly, McTeague and his cohorts dig into "the very entrails of the earth" and "bor[e] into the vitals" of the mountains (208–9).[45] Prefiguring these penetrations, McTeague kisses Trina's mouth, "perfect, with one exception—a spot of white caries," and restores the blemish through male know-how and agency (20). Similarly, the "clean-swept spaces" of writing paper call for a filling of a different sort, a blanketing with signs or the inseminating imprint of the author's hand. When the arctic explorer in *A Man's Woman* records his forays into the white continent, he writes "with ragged, vigorous strokes of the pen, not unfrequently driving the point through the paper itself," thus inscribing himself onto the virginal sheet and rehearsing *in nuce* the naturalist project of male authorship and spatial conquest (436).[46] As Kittler has observed, "the deeply embedded metaphysics of handwriting" unearthed by psychoanalysis centers around an "omnipresent metaphor [that] equated women with the white sheet of nature or virginity, onto which a very male stylus could then inscribe the glory of its authorship" (*Gramophone* 186).

Writing by hand is thus a theatrical display of masculinity that, in both its visible and repressed forms, traverses the naturalist topography, "a labor of words" physical and adventurous "to the point of athleticism" (Wilson 2, 14).[47] This embodied sense of authorship is partly a response to the perceived fear of an effeminating softness and a distinctly female tradition of (largely sentimental) fiction dominating late nineteenth-century America, but also to an emergent culture of (almost exclusively female) typewriting to which writing with the presumed-to-be natural extension of the body, the pen, is juxtaposed.[48]

Like his contemporary Theodore Dreiser, Norris had most of his later manuscripts typed at the bureau of Anna Mallon, who employed "a battery of typists" on 309 Broadway (Swanberg 84), and he felt the financial obligations rendered for the reproductive services of women: "I have not forgotten that I owe [Ms. Mallon] money and shall send her a check in a few days" (*Letters* 144). Women not only softened the contours of the once largely male province of writing by making it a parlor entertainment; they also exacted their price as they inserted themselves in the (re)creative process. To Hamlin Garland, Norris apologizes for the brevity of his missive because "the Lampson Type setter must be fed and men must work to buy shoes

& socks for the children" (*Letters* 194). Real work is the work of men fending for their families, while the typewriter is a devouring machine gobbling up and reproducing the male labor of the hand. Paralleling Selina's "fingering [of] the keys" on the melodeon, or Trina's fingering at the sewing machine, the typewriter, for Norris, was fundamentally a machine of (paradoxically) industrialized domesticity, allowing busy women to meddle with the original scripts of real men (94, 91).[49] Opposed to the labor of handwriting, it signified the labor of rewriting. At best, as does Lloyd in *A Man's Woman*, woman may function as an ersatz for the male hand, an "amanuensis" domesticating the illegible script of the writing brute by taking dictation. Aghast at Bennett's "hieroglyphics"—at handwriting that is "nothing else but a sin"—Lloyd "took her place at the desk, pen in hand, the sleeve of her right arm rolled back to the elbow ... her pen traveling steadily from line to line" (436). For Lloyd, the ideal of Anglo-Saxon womanhood, as for Norris and his males, writing is work, but even in such a division of labor, Bennett does not yield to his manly woman, instead remote-controlling his substitute through voice recognition. (Lloyd also urges her husband to seek immortality not through biological reproduction but through a renewed arctic expedition in the name of America, to be written about upon his return.)

Thus, just as the late nineteenth-century emphasis on male physical culture is a reflex toward "the machine" and its "fierce artificiality [that] threatened to consume and exhaust man," so Norris's insistence on writing as manual labor and aesthetic art expresses a reinvigorating masculinity uncompromised by female bodies operating machines of reproduction—at least in the originary act of creation (Haraway, "Teddy Bear" 279).[50] The writer with an effete face and body who suffered from "sexual nervousness" and masculinized his heroines no less than his daughter ("Billy") saw in the productions flowing from his hand a sign of his manhood that brooked no adulteration by female hands (Lutz 146).[51] This ethos of duplicitous duplication also underlies Norris's relationship to photography and film. While the camera is not immediately tied to naturalist questions of gender, the division of labor between print and pictures—both still and moving—in Norris still presumes that the verbal resources of literary narrative are better equipped to render bodies in all their complexity than these newer media, and that print (notwithstanding its status as copy) has a greater claim toward authenticity and originality than do image-based duplications. In my media-centered reading of *The Pit* to follow, I would like to illustrate how the relays between gender and the body and between art and consumption operate in the emerging information culture of the fin de siècle.

3

The Pit

Locating Modernism's Other

Radiators and fans running on liquid air
Twelve telephones and five radios
Wonderful electric files contain endless and scientific dossiers
    of every kind of business
The only place the multimillionaire feels at home is in this office
The big plate-glass windows overlook the park and the city
In the evening the mercury vapor lights shed their soft bluish
    glimmer
This is the origin of the orders to buy and sell which sometimes
    cause
the Stock Markets of the entire world to crash
    —Blaise Cendrars, "IV. Office"

At the end of *The Pit*, Frank Norris's second installment in his planned Trilogy of the Wheat, the narrative is exacting in its meting out of desserts and punishments. Curtis Jadwin, the fallen wizard of Chicago's wheat exchange, and Laura Dearborn, his wife of histrionic talent, are both chastened and chastised. Financially bankrupt but ethically replenished, they (like Huck and Norris before them), light out into the territory, the West, where they are given a second chance. Sheldon Corthell, the artist and object of Laura's affections, does not get the girl of his dreams and instead retreats into the world of Parisian art (the site of Norris's formative years). And Page Dearborn and Landry Court, whose youthful naiveté grants them immunity from the ethical complications besetting their older role models, find themselves in a promising position in New York City (the site of Norris's professional arrival). All the pivotal figures have variously been overtaken by the reality principle of naturalist narrative and have been assigned their rank on the Tally Sheet of Merit.

Such adjudications are not untypical of naturalist narrative, and *The Pit*, like most of Norris's fiction, indeed has the normative function of reproducing turn-of-the-century values of justice and rightfulness.[1] What, however, are we to make of the naturalist myth of brute forces from which moral agencies of any sort have been evacuated? How can the post-Nietzschean universe of naturalism, with its random acts of violence and violation, be brought in sync with the idea of human or divine ethics? I will not, in this chapter, attempt to reconcile these positions (around which an entire critical industry has gathered), beyond noting that such dichotomies render the status of *The Pit*, as that of many similar novels, as a properly *naturalist* narrative of amoral agencies problematic.[2] Instead, I argue that *The Pit* not only transcends the frequently confining period modalities of *naturalism* but also suggests a recuperation of Norris's jejune aestheticism gathered in Paris. The unhewn harshness permeating his early work, such as *McTeague* and *Vandover and the Brute*, cedes to a set of nuanced sensibilities that, cumulatively and more than a decade before the Armory Show, points to the germination of a modernist aesthetic in fin-de-siècle America.

In particular, I will take a close look at the relays in *The Pit* between literary narrative, modern communications media, and contemporary art, as well as their attendant configurations of gender and embodiment. Tracing these relays will allow us to see, if not epistemological fault lines, then certainly the conceptual fissures that lay bare Norris's shift to a broadly conceived modernist sensibility. My hope is to suggest that the various notions of naturalism, realism, and modernism are enmeshed in discursive webs that make separation into distinct literary "schools" difficult to justify. Conversely, I would urge a more resilient notion of literary periodization whereby overlapping narrative tendencies ought to be seen as sharing a discursive space that serves as a reservoir for narrative strategies and concepts, indeed, for the very production of narrative itself.

Blending the Wheat with the Chaff

It has long been a critical commonplace that naturalist writing can be seen as a literary reaction formation to the perceived effeminating tendencies evident in turn-of-the-century America (Norris, *Criticism* 19–20).[3] The Wilde trial in England had drawn considerable attention in both Europe and the United States and unmasked what was widely understood to be the prevailing image of the artist: an effete and effeminate figure of dubious sexual orientation, cloistered away in the rarified atmosphere of wallpapered studios. Renditions of such artists in the work of the Goncourt brothers, Huysmans, and Walter Pater came eventually to be embodied in Wilde at the same moment that they were popularized in the Gilbert and Sullivan shows and reappeared time and again in the pages of *Punch*. Literature, it appeared, long the well-nigh exclusive occupation of (what Hawthorne called) "scribbling women" and just recently reclaimed as the province of a hardened masculinity, was again in danger of degenerating into roseate indoor diversions.

Countering this model of a decadent aestheticism, Norris and his naturalist brotherhood (in the wake of their British idol, Kipling) advanced a type of fiction that sought to reinvigorate a beleaguered Anglo-Saxon manhood and reaffirm the gender boundaries in danger of dissolution. Against "the studios and the aesthetes, the velvet jackets and the uncut hair, . . . the sexless creatures who cultivate their little art of writing as the fancier cultivates his orchid" (*Criticism* 14), Norris not so much cultivated but culled a literary rhetoric that reinstalled a fragile masculinity beset by the twin evils of effeminacy and homosexuality. The strongly xenophobic tendencies in Norris's journalistic output for *The Wave* and in *McTeague* and *Moran of the Lady Letty*, particularly in their portrayals of deviant immigrants, not only reproduce prevailing racist sentiments (just as they come on the heels of the America's first major discriminatory legislation, the Chinese Exclusion Act of 1882) but also celebrate an undiluted Anglo-Saxon maleness singularly equipped to go where no man had gone before. Similarly, in *Blix, Moran,* and *A Man's Woman* (and, to a certain degree, in *The Octopus*), the select She-Hulks held up as role models, usually for partially effeminate males, are not primarily the products of drawing rooms but of some of the quintessential sites of the male world: a ship, a ranch, and the West more generally.[4] Many of the dichotomies organizing Norris's theoretical writings, indeed, such as the tension between an overly refined American East and the more energetic, rejuvenating West, between the conflicting conceptions of literature as an aesthetic exercise and a labor of blood, sweat, and tears, among others, carry highly charged gender inflections and underwrite an antidecadent ethos of muscular virility.

In their valuation of hard bodies and pure blood, Norris's writings thus anticipate the gender system of many representative canonical high modernists. His males share the stalwart determination of Hemingway's bullfighters and big-game hunters, just as they possess the grace under pressure embodied in Mailer's combat soldiers (and the Weimar storm troopers in Klaus Theweleit's *Male Fantasies*). Jadwin's attempt in *The Pit* to corner the worldwide wheat market, for example, is the naturalist-capitalist version of territorial expansion that Norris renders in the discourse of military conquest, "the Napoleon of La Salle Street" preparing for "the grand *coup*, the last huge strategical move, the concentration of every piece of heavy artillery" (325). Conversely, the patronizing misogynism permeating his fiction suggests the anti-feminist rhetoric of Ezra Pound and Wyndham Lewis, among others, who, like Norris, associated fin-de-siècle aestheticism with "the feminization of culture" and sought to resurrect an essentially WASPish, if not Aryan, malehood as a bulwark against soft-bellied mass culture (Lewis, *The Art of Being Ruled*).[5] As Jackson Lears has observed, many male writers at the turn of the century and beyond sought "alternatives to modern softness" engendered by what they saw as the overly refined tastes of the genteel tradition (113).[6]

Looking closely at *The Pit*, however, I want to suggest that this particularly Anglo-American form of modernism is folded into the French antecedents leading up to the mainstream modernist configuration—the Symbolist and decadent tradition against which another part of Norris purported to write against. Norris's description of the female body as a site of commodified display has strong affinities with Baudelaire's pronouncements in "The Painter of Modern Life," the summa of his aesthetic (and a founding text of modernist misogyny). For Baudelaire, bourgeois Woman is characterized by "the muslins, the gauzes, the vast iridescent clouds of stuff in which she envelops herself,... the metal and mineral which twist and turn around her arms and her neck" (*Painter* 30); Norris's women in *The Pit* are similarly decked out "almost without exception, in light-coloured gowns, white, pale blue, Nile green, and pink, while over these costumes were thrown opera cloaks and capes of astonishing complexity and elaborateness.... Everywhere the eye was arrested by the luxury of stuffs, the brilliance and delicacy of fabrics" (9). Both writers in effect reinscribe the age-old dichotomy of female Matter and male Mind, female Chaos and male Spirit, in terms of an implied polarization and in the decadent lexicon of stuff and fluff.

More important, Norris also follows Baudelaire in the political import of such gendered dichotomies. For Baudelaire, especially the late Baudelaire disillusioned by the Second Republic, art was the prerogative of male brilliance, the last remaining bastion of intellectual work in a culture under assault from commerce and consumption typified by Woman (*Painter*). Norris similarly construed the Female as the site of mass culture and pulp fiction. The best way to decline into literary mediocrity—that is, to write for "safe" magazines catering to a female audience—is to associate with aesthetic coteries and, "worst of all," with "a number of women who neither wrote nor reviewed, but who 'took an interest in young writers'" (*Criticism* 32). By virtue of their leisure and inborn compassion, women should write the best novels, but they do not because they exhibit "speedier mental fatigue" and because it is "inconceivably hard for the sensitive woman to force herself into the midst of that great, grim complication of men's doings that we call life" (*Criticism* 36). The "muse of American fiction" is "no chaste, delicate, super-refined mademoiselle of delicate roses and 'elegant' attitudinizings," but such mademoiselles, for Norris, encapsulate the reading tastes of the American public and the current bulk of literary schlock (*Criticism* 13). Consumer rather than producer of fiction, Woman—as does *The Pit*'s token mademoiselle, Page Dearborn—keeps to scribbling "lucubrations quite meaningless and futile" into her journal, with "a cone of foolscap over her forearm to guard against inkspots" (147).[7] And instead of reading recent (proto)naturalist fiction, such as Stevenson's *The Wrecker*—one of Norris's favorites that anticipates his brand of naturalism—they consume such staples of Victorian evangelism as Ruskin or Browning, with a rare glimpse into Howells or the "trashy novels" that instill chivalric notions of romance (143, 149).

Complicating this gendered rhetoric of literary production and taste formation, Norris also develops the idea of Woman as a machine of desire and imitation that, in terms of a literary typology, also originates in the premodernist moment in mid-nineteenth-century France (and runs parallel to Thorstein Veblen's notion of ornamental wifehood in his *Theory of the Leisure Class*). In Emma Bovary, Baudelaire's confrere Flaubert created a canonical modern heroine whose entire fantasy structure is nourished by romantic fictions; she is the very embodiment of secondhand desire, a collection of roles and models mediated by her readings that add up to a print-based form of virtual reality *avant la lettre*. And Laura Dearborn, the protagonist of *The Pit*, imitating the imitations of Emma, as it were, can easily be seen as an American version of *bovarisme*.[8] Analogous to that of Emma, Laura's life is largely one of fantasies, projections, and role-plays whose scripts derive from her readings. To her, "all things not positively unworthy became heroic," such as the triad of her suitors: "Landry Court was a young chevalier, pure as Galahad. Corthell was a beautiful artist-priest of the early Renaissance. Even Jadwin was the merchant prince, a great financial captain" (21). Spurred by her desire to play "the rôles of Shakespeare's heroines" (41), she evolves a life of impersonation in which authentic self and enacted other meld into a schizophrenic consciousness: "She had begun by dramatizing, but by now she was acting—acting with all her histrionic powers at fullest stretch.... She was sincere and she was not sincere. Part of her—one of those two Laura Jadwins who at different times, but with equal right called themselves 'I'—knew just what effect her words, her pose, would have upon a man who sympathised with her.... But the other Laura would have resented as petty, as even wrong, the insinuation that she was not wholly, thoroughly sincere" (258). Eventually, like those of Emma, Laura's dramatizations culminate in a complete erasure of the self, and she flirts with marital transgression. Announcing to Jadwin that "I am anything I choose" (272), she acknowledges a form of (Bakhtinian) being inhabited by the voices of others, the self becoming an echo chamber of prior impersonations.[9]

Thus, concurrent with proleptic tremors of canonical Anglo-American modernism, *The Pit* strongly resonates with the field of ideas derived from the French precursors to that tradition. Baudelaire and Flaubert, the dandies incarnate of high modernism, as well as their (proto)Symbolist circles, ushered in what one could describe as the split rhetoric of modernism whereby, as Andreas Huyssen has observed, "the political, psychological, and aesthetic discourse around the turn of the century consistently and obsessively genders mass culture and the masses as feminine, while high culture, whether traditional or modern, clearly remains the privileged realm of male activities" ("Mass Culture" 47). *The Pit* clearly participates in that rhetoric, even as Norris condemned aestheticism, French or otherwise, as too literary, unmanly, and highbrow in his essays. To be sure, once the individual talents of tradition had recognized their affinities across the Channel (as well as the Atlantic), the French were quickly installed as the fountainheads of what can, in retrospect, been seen as one of the most ominous developments in the political trajectory of canonical modernism. As Richard Burton has observed, if the literary practice of the late Baudelaire indicates a modernist esthetic, his politics points to "something resembling fascism, the whole of his post-1851 development posing the question, fifty or more years in advance of Pound, Eliot, T. E. Hulme, Yeats, and Wyndham Lewis, of the relationship—still fully to be charted and explained—between modernism, prejudice (both racial and sexual), and political authoritarianism" (364). Indeed, Norris's political authoritarianism, his strongly hegemonic and patriarchal tendencies, mark his work as a prelude to what Geoffrey Herf has called "reactionary modernism," an early literary manifestation of an incipient fascism, arguably beginning with Baudelaire (and Flaubert), composed of the fundamentally conservative and orthodox impulses that, collectively, make up an important element of the canonical modernist project.[10]

Integrating Norris into these literary-political developments is an attempt to help chart a more finely nuanced history of modernism or, rather, to propose a field of convergences and turbulences in which Norris functions as an unacknowledged missing link, an American point of connection between proto-reactionary literary developments in France and their eventual manifestation in turn-of-the-century Anglo-American literary culture. And how could it not be so? When Norris, chaperoned by his mother, left for France at age seventeen for two years (1887–89), he was one of hundreds of juvenile American dandies strutting with gold-plated cane, powdered hair, and silken top hat on Haussmann's elegant boulevards; Baudelaire look-alikes all, Norris, like many of his wealthy expatriate friends (the trip was sponsored by his father, a wholesale jeweler), was on his own personal *grand tour* trying to give himself some old-European polish, a cachet of culture well liked by the Ivy League, where he was to seek admission before long (Walker, *Norris* 27–42). Intellectually curious, languishing idly frequently, and working his way through the coffeehouses and salons, he could not but be au courant about contemporary literary developments such as the aesthetic and Symbolist circles, evident, among others, in his (albeit short-lived) membership in Les Jeunes, San Francisco's literary-aesthetic fraternity.[11] His politics were very much in keeping with his chosen posture as an artiste (not yet manqué), a flaneur meandering in, yet aloof from, the laboring rabble. As one of his friends recalled upon Norris's return to the United States, Frank "cared little for the crowd . . . and thought and expressed himself frequently . . . in terms of an aristocrat of the period of the French Revolution—it was not a pose—despising the 'canaille.' . . . [H]e 'wanted to see em all drowned on one raft.'"[12]

No doubt, as Norris witnessed dramatic economic disparities at home and fell increasingly under the spell of his "other" French model, Emile Zola, he became, at least punctually, sympathetic to issues of capital distribution, labor reform, and anti-trust legislation, eventually resulting in the "muckraking" *Octopus* (and, earlier, at the behest of his mother, leading to the rejection of his father's alimony checks); and, no doubt, writing in an age of corporate industry, Norris's vision of art is fully in tune with the increasingly shorter cycles of production and consumption of the American economy. As Norris said time and again, fiction writing is "a [matter of] business," a way of making a living by turning out quickly salable material (*Criticism* 146). But I would urge that these Progressivist tendencies coexist side by side with a more conservative and aestheticist quality in his work. Such a schizoid politics is evident not only in the revisionist reassessments of *The Octopus* as a model of what Walter Benn Michaels has called "corporate fiction" (189)—a novel overtly and covertly supporting the various economic discourses circulating in its pages—but also in the conflicted double allegiance of Norris's politics more generally. Christophe den Tandt has noted that Norris's works "do not display sufficient ideological closure to be read exclusively as pro-business tracts." Rather, their "unresolved tensions" bespeak "the persistent instability of Norris's politics" (*Urban Sublime* 71) and hence register a mind torn between contemporary forms of imperialist discourse and a belief system located in genteel values of honor, hand-based craftsmanship, and essentialized class distinctions. What Lears has described as Norris's "antimodern nostalgia" took the form of a sustained interest in things medieval and a vocation "susceptible to such 'feminine' maladies as intellectualism or aestheticism" (128, 130). Beginning his artistic career by copying medieval armors in the Musée D'Artillerie of the Hôtel des Invalides and by writing French medieval romances in the spirit of William Morris, Norris revisited his old-fashioned sensibilities in his last novel, where he interrogates another central modernist concern (that grew, not coincidentally, out of the Medieval Revival): the cultural location of art in an age of mass communication and commodification. Unlike Presley in *The Octopus*, the wannabe poet who never writes his "Epic of the Wheat," Sheldon Corthell, the aesthete, glass artist, and connoisseur of wines and words in *The Pit*, makes significant pronouncements about literature and the work of art in the age of its mechanical reproducibility.

Art and Dandies in the Cornbelt

The logic of a novel driven by economics positions Corthell as one of its losers. While *The Pit* foregrounds the local and global repercussions of Jadwin's speculations, Norris's conflicted allegiance to corporate and aesthetic appreciation(s) does not allow him to privilege Corthell's function in the novel without question. On the contrary, to balance his critique of commercial practices, subdued as it is, Norris takes great pains to equivocate on Corthell's views. In contrast to Jadwin's business bravado, for example, Corthell is a "*woman's* man" (66) endowed with accoutrements that—in Norris's typology of masculinity—compromise his position as sage and savant (66). He is described as "critical to extremes" and an eclectic elitist disdainful of popular culture: "Just let anything get popular once and Sheldon Corthell can't speak of it without shuddering," as Landry puts it (22, 52). And he does of course not get the girl in the end, when a momentarily audacious Laura, nourishing plans for an elopement, is pulled back onto the carpet of respectability, while the artiste, realizing the futility of his efforts, is banished into the congenial atmosphere of distant Paris (which the novel posits as an absent utopian space uncontaminated by the American business world).[13] Such narrative gestures complicate Corthell's pronouncements, just as they reinforce the novel's trajectory. For when *The Pit* opens with a Grand Opera performance in Chicago, "the jar of commerce" already counterpoints the harmony of song, eventually reaching its sober climax when Laura (returning home through the "commission district") muses that business "invaded the very sanctuary of art, and cut athwart the music of Italy and the cadence of polite conversation" (22, 38). Norris's sympathies for the practices of corporate America prefigure from the outset the victory of economics and stalwart manhood (and domestic femininity) over literary estheticism.

And yet, precisely because Corthell is not networked into the business culture he has the power to reflect on art in a global economy. As an agent of independent wealth, as the young hobnobbing Norris was at one time, he is not at home in the world of profit. Living off his parents' inheritance (19), he is nonproductive in an economic sense but instead can afford to circulate on the margins of the world of trade without being a part of it. Looking from the outside in, tethered to the world of goods without being severed from it, he is ideally positioned to meditate on the mechanics of artistic creation in an age of worldwide commerce. In that sense, Corthell functions as a point of ideological critique in the novel; his observations map out an almost utopian space of reflection, an idealized, slightly archaic point of view that offers perspectives at odds with the novel's mastertropes of consumption and production.

In the lexicon of dynamical systems theory, Corthell operates as a strange attractor, as an intellectual (and, in the case of Laura, emotional) site of turbulence causing local disturbances and adjustments in the narrative system.[14] In the language closer to Norris, Corthell performs the work of a (Baudelairean) dandy, an intellectual aristocrat with authority in the cultural realm. Endowed with "divine gifts which work and money are unable to bestow," dandies are, above all, driven by the "doctrine of elegance and originality" and "the compelling need, alas only too rare today, of combating and destroying triviality" (*Painter* 28). Precisely because of their half-outsiderhood can they insist on a niche for beauty and splendor within the world market. What is more, for Baudelaire the emergence of dandies is a symptom of bourgeois empowerment and mass democratization in the mid- and late nineteenth century that parallels the expansion of capitalist markets and mass consumerism: "Dandyism appears above all in periods of transition, when democracy is not yet all powerful, and aristocracy is only just beginning to totter and fall" (28). To stem the disintegration of taste, he contends, dandies are important bastions of conservative thought that allow due space for the cultivation of leisure and art. They serve as intellectual elitists, often with a flashy panache, in lieu of aristocratic lineage and as the counterweight to the emergent and unrefined moneyed aristocracy. Unfortunately, however, "the rising tide of democracy, which invades and levels everything, is daily overwhelming these last representatives of human pride and pouring floods of oblivion upon the footprints of these stupendous warriors" (29). Last of the Mohicans all, dandies are pushed to the brink of extinction in an international economy. While insisting on the preserve of art, their protests are washed away by a global avalanche of schlock, their shrinking numbers expressing the flattening of mass refinement and the dangers of political empowerment.

In fact, as Baudelaire argues, it is precisely in countries with a history of democracy that dandies are becoming an increasingly unusual breed. In France, the land of *liberté, égalité, fraternité*, dandies "are becoming rarer and rarer, whereas amongst our neighbours in England"—a country with a constitutional democracy and a long conservative history—"the social system and the constitution ... will for a long time yet allow a place for the descendants of Sheridan, Brummel, and Byron" (29). Corthell is such a descendant, and he serves as Norris's lingering bulwark against the corruption of taste in the country that was helped onto its democratic feet by the French and that, by the late nineteenth century, had taken great strides in terms of a political and economic democracy. If Jadwin is the "Napoleon of La Salle Street" who, with proverbial swiftness and a strong American sense of the pragmatic, climbs the ladder of success, Corthell is the Beau Brummel of Chicago's Lake Front who provides an aesthete's perspective to the unimpeded enrichment of the Jadwins. If Jadwin serves as *The Pit*'s economic parvenu, ruled only by the doctrine that money can buy everything, Corthell serves as its artistic parvenu, the elitist conscience of the race of Jadwins seeking to critique the leveling practices of American bourgeois culture.

Symptomatic of Corthell's position in the novel, Norris describes him as a scholar-dandy whose chosen modus vivendi is not affected role-play as much as a lived and genuine identity. In one of the novel's mirror constellations, Calvin Crookes, Jadwin's major antagonist, adopts the dandy image as a vapid pose. Equally ruthless in his business practices, and without any inkling of aesthetic refinement, he sports "the very newest fashion," a "white waistcoat, drab gaiters, a gold watch and chain, a jewelled scarf pin, and a seal ring. From the top pocket of his coat protruded the finger tips of a pair of unworn red gloves" (238). Draped in the trappings of cultivation (and "unfolding a brand-new pocket handkerchief," as he speaks), he tries to give himself a cachet of polish that masks the cutthroat machinations of his business. In that, perhaps unwittingly, he adopts the dandy's rehearsed insouciance and nonchalance that is historically linked to the advent of consumer capitalism but is completely anathema to Baudelaire's dandy resistant to the hegemony of the commodity. As Walter Benjamin observed:

> It must be recognized that the features which are combined in the dandy bear a very definitive historical stamp. The dandy is a creation of the English who were leaders in world trade. The trade network

that spans the globe was in the hands of the London stock exchange people; its meshes felt the most varied, most frequent, most unforeseeable tremors. A merchant had to react to these, but he could not publicly display his reactions. The dandies took charge of the conflicts thus created. They developed the ingenious training that was necessary to overcome these conflicts. They combined an extremely quick reaction with a relaxed, even slack demeanor and facial expression. (*Baudelaire* 96)

Corthell, by contrast, communicates his aesthetic poise not so much by his social appearance, even though his attire is immaculate as well and, as a mark of distinction, he wears "a small pointed beard, and a mustache that he brushed away from his lips like a Frenchman" (19). Instead his refinement comes through in his quietly authoritative discourses on art and in the solemn eclecticism of his studio, in which every object had been "chosen with care and utmost discrimination. The walls had been treated with copper leaf till they produced a sombre, iridescent effect of green and faint gold," and everywhere "the eye rested upon some small masterpiece of art or workmanship," ranging from "an antique portrait bust of the days of decadent Rome" to an "ivory statuette of the 'Venus of the Heel,' done in the days of the magnificent Lorenzo" (251).

Juxtaposing the noisy theatrics of Crookes (that prefigures the flashy histrionics of the Futurists a decade later), Norris is careful to develop Corthell's authentic bohemianism through the subdued privacy of his lifestyle, in full awareness that self-conscious artifice, narcissistic introspection, and a performative self are part of Corthell's makeup. Unlike Crookes's veneer of culture, which remains mere surface adornment—the hallmark of a poseur—Corthell's polish is more than skin deep; it permeates the fabric of his being. And even though the clichéd nod to "the days of decadent old Rome" might suggest the specious bohemianism of a Walter Pater or an Oscar Wilde (though Corthell's heterosexuality, reserved as it is, is not in doubt), Norris describes the studio as a gilded shrine, a calm oasis unperturbed by the world of commerce. As the only major room in *The Pit* without electric lights (or telephone), illuminated only by smoldering logs and a gas lamp of "corroded bronze" (250), Norris gives it an antiquated flush, a patina of belatedness soothing in its dimness. Corthell's quiet joie de vivre, indeed, is legible as a pièce de résistance against what Rhonda Garelick has called "an economy of ever-increasing 'exchangeability' and the accumulation of mass-produced products. The dandy attempts to block this development by stepping outside of the system" (5).

As well, Norris underwrites Corthell's intellectual authority through involvement in the public appreciation of art and through art education, as well as his own artistic labors. An artist, collector, and designer of "stained windows," who had "studied, occasionally written, and in matters pertaining to the coloring and fusing of glass was cited as an authority," he puts his knowledge into public service as "one of the directors of the new Art Gallery" (eventually to become the Chicago Art Institute [19]). His distinguished position is also seen in the respect the men of business reserve for Corthell, as it is in his weekly studio sessions, where he read to his circle "'Saint Agnes Eve,' 'Sordello,' *The Light of Asia*," and subsequently discussed their "inversions, obscurities, and astonishing arabesques of rhetoric" (100). Norris no doubt invested his artist figure with the cultural authority necessary to articulate credibly his own sometime elitist sensibilities and his reflections about the precarious status of art in times of commodification.[15] At the same time, Corthell's tastes provide a glimpse into current artistic developments abroad and shed light on the formation of Norris's own aesthetic. I want to draw attention to two symbolic key scenes in *The Pit* in which the convergence of (pre)modern art, politics, and mass consumption is most suggestive.

Upon his arrival in Paris in 1887, Norris, like hundreds of American and European student artists, studied at the Académie Julian under the renowned tutelage of Guillaume-Adolphe Bouguereau and his disciples.[16] A master painter (with a Premier Grand Prix de Rome to his credit) whose large canvases in oil of Greek and Roman antiquity were favored by the official Salon, he became known early on as a defender of the academic tradition and was appointed a professor at the École des Beaux-Arts in 1888. His idealized subjects of times long past, pastoral scenes with fleshly nymphs and playful children, gave much of his work a staid sentimentality removed from the concerns of daily life, just as they developed his, particularly American, reputation as a decadent painter preoccupied with forms of illicit sexuality.[17] Indeed, the teachings Norris received at the Julian were very much at odds with what was abuzz in the cafés and the Salon des Refusés. The critical demand for a new art centering on urban industrialism and the quotidian life of the middle and working classes was heeded by several artistic developments emerging concurrently: a new order of illustrators, among them Honoré Daumier and Constantin Guys, who rendered the daily life of urban Paris in quickly executed sketches; the Impressionists, who in 1886 had just closed their eighth and last exhibition and were (at the moment they agreed to let go of the "Impressionist" label) well on their way to establishing a counteracademic tradition (Herbert 303–6); and a new visual naturalism (which conventional histories of art often ignore in favor of an almost exclusive Impressionist focus) that quickly gained international momentum (Weisberg 7–23). Within such a context, Bouguereau's academic teachings, while congenial to the medieval Norris, were not in line with a developing West Coast upstart interested in American urbanism and the repressed drives and desires of the human heart. As Richard Lack has observed, although Bouguereau's work was "widely collected by the English and more especially by the Americans in his lifetime, [his] reputation in France was more equivocal—indeed quite low in later years." Popular with the public and mainstream critics, "his work ignored the increasing demand for paintings of modern life which had been made by Charles Baudelaire." A staunch supporter of the academic training system "when it was criticized for stifling originality and nurturing mediocrity," he was scorned as one of the most visible representatives of everything an emergent modernism opposed: "high technical finish, narrative content, sentimentality and a reliance on tradition."

In *The Pit*, Norris presents Bouguereau's work precisely in such traditional terms, and it is through Corthell's bohemian sensibilities that he articulates this critique and advances a (pre)modern counteraesthetic. When Jadwin and his business associate enter the art gallery in the Jadwins' new mansion, they enter a seemingly random array of bric-a-brac: "Here and there about the room were glass cabinets full of bibelots, ivory statuettes, old snuff boxes, fans of the sixteenth and seventeenth centuries. The walls themselves were covered with a multitude of pictures, oil, water-colours, with one or two pastels" (175). In what one could call a rhetoric of accumulation, Norris suggests that the Jadwins amass art without discrimination. Unlike Corthell's carefully arranged studio, their collection is mere status symbol, an expression of being nouveau riche, of having arrived and of having money to spend. Amid this medley hangs a "large 'Bouguereau' that represented a group of nymphs bathing in a woodland pool" (176).[18] When Laura proudly praises her prize possession to Corthell, he draws attention to the painting's sentimental flatness that precludes any intellectual engagement. Bouguereau's work is popular, he observes, because "it demands less of you than some others.... It pleases you because it satisfies you so easily. You can grasp it without effort," eventually concluding that "a beautiful vase would have exactly the same value upon your wall" (218).[19]

Corthell's proposed exchangeability of a Bouguereau for a vessel in itself suggests that what is at stake for the Jadwins is not the form of art or its content but solely its material value. Paintings, porcelains, and bibelots all have an equal function in an upscale economy of appearances and acquisitions. What counts is that the objet d'art, whatever it may be, signals the buying power of bourgeois cash—a sign of the conspicuous consumption of Veblen's leisure class—and along with it a spectrum of taste unchallenging in its presumptions.[20] What is more, Corthell draws attention to an unnoticed small "twilight landscape" done by a "Western artist" that embodies precisely the sensibility absent in the Bouguereau next to it. In his reading of the painting, Corthell observes that the artist saw "something more than trees and a pool and afterglow"; he had "that feeling of night coming on," which he projected into his work: "he put something of himself [into it], the gloom and the sadness that he felt at the moment. And that little pool, still and black and sombre—why, the whole thing is the tragedy of a life full of dark, hidden secrets. . . . That little pool says one word as plain as if it were whispered in the ear—despair. Oh yes, I prefer it to the nymphs" (218–19).

Rescued from obliteration next to the domineering canvas of bourgeois propriety, the twilight landscape, for Corthell, is not an expression of moneyed taste but rather, on one level, of the viability of the art of the American West. Like the Norris who never tired of advertising the West, and, more properly, the city of San Francisco, as a site of artistic (and economic) invigoration, Corthell praises the expressive virtues of the unknown artist. And like Norris, it is, paradoxically, only the sharpened sensibilities of the artist trained in the (post)Impressionist milieu of Paris that allow him to appreciate the darkly expressive art of the Western frontier, which frequently took its impetus from the Old World, over dated Old World dust collectors; artistic sensibilities formed in Europe enable him to bridge the continents.[21] What is more, on a second, more aesthetic level, Corthell's devaluation of Bouguereau suggests a reorientation in the canons of artistic taste that was already in full swing on the Continent. By moving beyond the literal to a more figurative landscape of psychological inwardness, Corthell shifts to a more allegorical register of meaning. Instead of the mimetic rendition of an idealized terrain (which the Impressionists had dubbed "*bouguereauté*"),[22] the "twilight landscape" appears to map figuratively (and autobiographically) the terrain of the Symbolist or Expressionist real: the anguish, desire, and despair of the psyche. Roughly coincident with, say, Edvard Munch's "The Scream" (1893)—the modernist icon of existential angst (painted by a young man after, like Norris, spending formative weeks in Paris)—the Western artist captures the somber mood of the fin de siècle. In that sense, the painting can be understood as a kind of visual naturalism in which literal and Symbolist representation, as well as the private symbol system of a traumatized self, coexist. Through Corthell, Norris suggests that the dark recesses of the mind, which have long been the other of academic art, are the true subject of naturalism (and of much of [pre]modernist art). In contrast to Bouguereau's romantic classicism, desire and despair are best investigated without the gloss of Victorian decorum. Through Corthell's hermeneutics, and his implied call for a more challenging art, Norris in effect pleads for a naturalist art that unmasks, rather than mutes, the post-Darwinian complexities of human being.

Equally important, Norris's allegory of representation also involves an element of perception that evolves out of the (post)Impressionist context. When Jadwin's business partner inspects a French cuirassier by Édouard Detaille hanging in the gallery, he reacts with a layperson's confusion: "Look at it close up and it's just a lot of little daubs, but you get off a distance . . . and you see it now. Hey—see how the thing bunches up" (176). Norris himself, distinguishing between surface accuracy and a more authentic form of artistic truth, provides a more expert reading of the same or a similar painting: "Consider the study of a French cuirassier by Détaille, where the sunlight strikes the brown coat of the horse, you will see, if you look close, a mere smear of blue, light blue. This is inaccurate. The horse is not blue, nor has he any blue spots. Stand at a proper distance and the blue smear resolves itself into the glossy reflection of the sun, and the effect is true" (*Criticism* 57). What underlies this distinction is of course the brushwork common since the Impressionists, in particular their thick and dotty application of colors in rapid and "comma-like" strokes (Rewald 281), and the rough texture of their pigments, which demands of the eye to recompose the multiplicity of dots into a composite image. Widely practiced since the Impressionist craze, that method was further refined in the Divisionist canvases of Georges Seurat, who broke down pictorial perception into still more minute fractals of coloration. Seurat had studied Michel-Eugène Chevreul's *De la Loi du contraste simultané des couleurs* (Chevreul was a supervisor in the dyeworks of the Gobelins tapestry factory), and he infused his work with the newest scientific insights derived from *Modern Chromatics*, a book on color psychology written by Ogden Root, a professor of physics at New York University. Fundamentally, he realized that "although you could not paint the natural world with pigments whose colors were the same as the colors you saw, it was still possible to evoke those colors in the eye by manipulating the effects of juxtaposed patches of paint" (Everdell 71).

Seurat showed what would become one of the most celebrated paintings of the turn of the century, *Sunday Afternoon on the Island of la Grande Jatte*, in the eighth and last exhibit of the Impressionists in 1886 and was the talk of Paris when Norris arrived. Its sheer size and revolutionary execution dwarfed the work of Gauguin and Degas concurrently on the walls, and critics (of all colors, if you will) pronounced it a scientific breakthrough whose effects traveled immediately into the galleries and studios of Paris (notwithstanding the academic tradition that clung to its entrenched foothold). Not only did

Camille Pissarro, among others, become an immediate convert to Divisionism, but Seurat himself, for the rest of his brief career, drew one large masterpiece per year, such as *Les Poseuses* (1887), *Parade du Cirque* (1888), and *La Poudreuse* (1889), that dominated the columns of *La Vogue* and the *Revue indépendante* (under the editorship of Félix Fénéon) as well as the buzz in artistic circles. Norris was no doubt cognizant of Seurat's innovative technique (as was a twenty-three-year-old visiting art student from Norway), as is evident in his review of an exhibition featuring paintings based on "the vibration theory of color." Seen close up, Norris observes, these pictures "show hundreds of little color dabs of green and vermillion and yellow—sometimes the crude, unmixed color. At a distance these dabs run together and produce a brilliant atmospheric effect that is at times very effective" (*Apprenticeship* 1:188)—what Seurat himself called a "chromo-luminarist" effect (qtd. in Broude 1).[23]

What is important here is not solely Norris's knowledge of Seurat's Divisionist method, which (as we saw in the previous chapter) enriched his own literary palette, but also that his literary empiricism and his demand for the erasure of the human imagination (also a subject of the previous chapter) are fundamentally based on similar epistemological premises as is Seurat's vision. Just as *La Grande Jatte*, "by dividing optical perceptions into their discrete elements," suggested that the phenomenal world "was itself irreducibly divided into parts, that continuity was an illusion and atoms the only reality," so Norris's world is composed only of particulate matter registered by the human mind (Everdell 64). In his own words, "what we elect to call imagination is mere combination of things not heretofore combined," a "matter of selection of details," the combination of elementary building blocks into a total design. At the same time, as Everdell continues, despite this materialist footing, the reality Seurat wished to seize "was ultimately more phenomenological than material" (70). For Seurat (and his Impressionist precursors), as for Norris, artistic truth was not a matter of realist precision, in the sense of a positivist cataloguing or precise chronicling. "Accuracy," he observed, is "the achievement of the commonplace, a mere machine-made thing that comes with niggardly research and ciphering and mensuration and the multiplication table" (*Criticism* 58).[24] Truth, by contrast, was a way of seeing beyond observable data to a perception understood as mental (or retinal) construction or, in the language of painting, of inviting the eye to recompose the multiplicity of dots into an image closer to an authentic perception of the real than a single, consistent color (or brushstroke) would be. The pixels of (post)Impressionist pigments, just as Corthell's stained glass mosaics that he developed "piece by piece" (59), yield reality as Gestalt and thus throw into relief the debate between scientific objectivity and a phenomenological truth that defined the late nineteenth-century discourse on knowledge, just as they point to the heart of Norris's romantic naturalism: a literary-phenomenological life world that is constructed from the data of everyday life.

Paralleling this modernist hermeneutics of painting, Norris suggests the convergence of class and art also through differing musical appreciation. From the opening of *The Pit*, the novel's business culture understands the Opera as a site of ongoing transactions, where discussions continue sotto voce while Italian arias provide edifying background noise; and Jadwin, the arch-representative of the nouveau riche, matches the grandiosity of his business coups with the grandeur of a massive organ—in the vast gallery of an equally grandiose mansion—to signify his Napoleonic aspirations. Jadwin cannot play the instrument himself but, equipped with a "perforated roll" attachment (177), sits down, works the pedals, and pulls the stops to give his business partner a sample of prefabricated music. Gretry, indeed, is treated to the overture of *Carmen*, which the "sliding strip of paper" teases out of the organ in a "full-bodied, satisfying amplitude of volume," each note emerging "with a precision that, if mechanical, was yet effective" (178).

While the play on/of the organ serves no doubt as an expression of excess capital (and other assorted inadequacies), not of musical talent and understanding, it also signals the listeners' astonishment at the capabilities of seemingly authentic technological reproduction (just as it anticipates the player pianos that would, within a decade, hammer out ragtime in the joints of Chicago's South Side). Both Jadwin and Gretry, who compliments the performance with excited exclamations, are mesmerized by the machine-made reproduction of classical music. The two men who make their living on the stock exchange by manipulating the newest technologies of communication (and a grain that is harvested mechanically) behave in a manner typical of their profession: "with the solemn interest . . . all American businessmen have in mechanical inventions" (177). And Norris, in harmony with the Progressivist part of his sympathies (and notwithstanding the irony leveled at the businessmen), praises the virtues of engineered virtuosity and the "resistless charm" of the music (178). The indistinguishability of hand- and machine-made music, rendering mute questions of human agency or expression, is at hand, or so it appears.

Enter Sheldon. As with his reframing of the canons of pictorial value, he provides a suggestive foil to complicate the indiscriminate consumption of canned music by the petty bourgeois. Contrasting the light-heartedness of *Carmen*, Sheldon "without comment" removes the "self-playing" attachment and plays a series of concert pieces with increasing technical and expressive complexity on the organ for Laura (219). The simple call-and-response structure of Mendelssohn's *Consolation* is "possibly not [yet] a very high order of art . . . a little 'easy,' perhaps like the Bouguereau," but the piece, not unlike Bizet's preinscribed overture, "should appeal very simply and directly, after all" (220). The second movement of Beethoven's *Appassionata* has a much greater range of emotional nuances and is followed by Liszt's *Mephisto Walzer*, one of the technically and tonally most demanding orchestral pieces of the mid-nineteenth century, which Sheldon counterpoints with a sensual commentary on the emotional turbulences of the music.

The succession of pieces Sheldon chooses function as a crescendo to his dalliance with Laura. In lieu of a physical seduction, and very much parallel to Mephistophelian whisperings, he attempts to reach her through her ear: "And now this movement; isn't it reckless and capricious, like a woman who hesitates and then takes the leap?" (220). What is more important here, however, is the suggested refinement of Laura's musical tastes. As she comes to appreciate the "prolonged chords of Liszt's, heavy . . . with passion," she realizes that "here was something better than Gounod and Verdi," eventually resolving to let her musical reeducation be guided by the musical connoisseur, not public sentiment (221). As with Bouguereau, the Norris in tune with his artistic sensibilities—the Norris whose first apartment in Paris was behind the new Opera and who forsook a fauteuil in favor of the claque—enables Laura to graduate beyond aesthetic mediocrity through the agency of Sheldon, and he thus, in keeping with his gendered topography, allows Woman once more to be lifted from the realm of mass culture to the world of male refinement. If only for the moment, Laura forsakes the mass appeal of lavish yet undemanding opera productions in favor of the more sophisticated canons of classical and romantic music—canons that are endangered by the middle-class demand for operatic spectacles, as the novel's opening suggests, and are available for instant replay in the cushy domesticity of bourgeois parlors. In Sheldon's elitist typology of art and class, which he elaborates following his performance, music with a large audience appeal, that is, music requiring little trained discernment, is equivalent to architecture, "which is an expression of and an appeal to the common multitude, a whole people, the mass" (222).[25]

Viewed from the perspective of this chapter, the attempt to locate the fault lines between modern media, artistic production, and the human body, Norris is equally unequivocal about the difference between art made by humans as opposed to machines. For when Jadwin performs on the organ, Norris is careful to emphasize the contrast between mechanical sound reproduction, where each note—in keeping with the regularity of a perforated roll—emerges "clear cut" and "sharply treated with . . . precision" (178), and Sheldon's much more fluid modulation of tonal shades that allows for a much wider range of emotional expression. As well, Norris quite literally sheds light on the human hand as the expressive organ of the body, the embodied organ to play on the mechanical organ in a wide spectrum of nuances. In a moment revealing as it is rare in premodern writing, Norris suggests that behind the machinic production of art is still an embodied human agent: "The moment was propitious. The artist's profile silhouetted itself against the shade of a light that burned at the side of the organ, and that gave light to the keyboard. And on this keyboard . . . lay his long, slim hands. They were the only things that moved in the room, and the chords and bars of Mendelssohn's 'Consolation' seemed, as he played, to flow not from the instrument, but, like some invisible ether, from his finger-tips themselves" (219).[26] As in *McTeague*, Norris here identifies the hand as the crucial organ of artistic expression, the part of the body without which the music on the organ would not be. Notwithstanding complex mechanical contraptions that can elicit a preprogrammed sequence of tones, physical being is still necessary for what goes by the name of art—a contrast that is, as noted above, accentuated by the jovial lightheartedness of an operatic overture versus the emotional gravity of Sheldon's selections. The body is still crucial in imparting feeling onto the inorganic organ.

And yet, if understood as an allegory of the increasing suture between body and machine (analogous to Trina's work at the turning lathe in *McTeague*), the scene could also invite a reading that complicates the presumed priority of the body in the production of art. First, while Norris draws attention to the agency of human hands, Sheldon's body itself is effaced, put into shadowy relief by the light installed on the organ. Second, the sense of physical immobility, partly owing to a pair of vibrant hands that seem, as if disembodied, attached to a static torso, is also attributable to the "electric motor" powering the organ and rendering pumping action unnecessary (178);[27] and third, the "dulled incandescence of the electrics" illuminate the "mighty pipes" of the organ, while dwarfing human proportion and reducing Sheldon's body to an ethereal silhouette (175). Given the schism of Norris's mental topography—his allegiance to both corporate-industrial and manual-aesthetic practices—this scene might well advance a conflicted yet fundamentally symbiotic interaction between bodies and machines in the making of art. While still putting a premium on embodiment, Norris might in effect suggest, perhaps unconsciously, that the domains of human being and machinic making have entered, or are about to enter, a new order of relations.

Given Norris's obsession with the scene of writing, caught as he was in the transitional phase between professional handwriting and typewriting, as we saw in the previous chapter, I would further suggest that the structural analogies between the organ and typewriter keyboard, and their joint operation by artistic hands, may well point to a repressed meditation on the production of manuscript in the age of its mechanical reproducibility. The turn-of-the-century writer, no less than the fin-de-siècle artist, subscribed to the premise of logocentric continuity whereby only the presumed-to-be-seamless linking of brain and hand and manual instrument can bring about an exfoliation of the self from subjective interiority to performative exteriority—an expressive, that is, interpretive exfoliation no less. The transition from nature to culture, to put it differently, can be achieved with full effect only through the conduit of the hand as the embodied switch point between being and making. But whether legible as pleas for hand-based artistic expression or a more symbiotic collaboration between bodies and machines, Norris's sustained meditations on the making of art register a fundamentally modernist crisis around 1900: To what degree is art tied to embodied being? What is the cultural location of art, especially art partly wrought with old-fashioned sensibilities, in the new industrial order? In the concluding segment, I want to examine another, intimately related modernist crisis: the problematic status of literary print in a culture dominated by information and the new technologies of mass communication.

Of Cablegrams and First Editions, or Short Circuits of the Wired Mind

Benjamin has observed that the political emergence of the middle class in the nineteenth century, and with it the rise of a critical mass of alphabetized readers, coincides with a new form of communication: information. Information realigns the discursive relations among readers, writers, publishers, and events by deemphasizing experiential wisdom and the giving of counsel, as in oral or preliterate cultures, in favor of easily consumable news, informative pieces of local interest available to a wide readership. In the words of Villemessant, the founder of *Le Figaro*, "To my readers, an attic fire in the Latin Quarter is more important than a revolution in Madrid" (qtd. in Benjamin, *Selected Writings* 3:147). The shift in interest from significant events and cumulative knowledge to bite-sized morsels of yesterday's neighborhood happenings—nicely encapsulated in *Tit-Bits*, the premier easy-reading magazine for London commuters[28]—delineates one of literary modernism's central struggles: how to locate print and the values contained in the traditional print format in a culture of the perpetually new, an ephemeral world of immediate oblivion encapsulated in the newspaper. As with the problem of aestheticism and the visual arts, *The Pit* nicely illustrates this double allegiance to both the cult of information and literary print culture, thus further complicating Norris's transitional status in the modernist field.

Norris, like many of his fellow "naturalist" writers—Zola, London, and Dreiser, among them—wrote himself into literary existence as a journalist. After working for years as a contributing editor for San Francisco's society weekly, *The Wave*, publishing mogul McLure lured Norris to New York in a dual capacity as fiction reader and fiction writer, maintaining his work as a journalist on the side. It is no surprise, then, that Norris's most enduring novels, *McTeague, The Octopus*, and *The Pit*, owe their literary existence to newspaper reports of dentist murders, railroad chicanery, and, in the latter case, wheat speculator Joseph Leiter.[29] Norris, in fact, cannibalizes Leiter's stock market career in the same way, in *The Pit*, "the newspapers, not only of Chicago, but of every city in the Union, exploited [Jadwin] for 'stories'" once his dealings traveled beyond the trade floor (291). Just as newspaper "anecdotes" and "interviews" establish Leiter's mythological status as the "Napoleon of La Salle Street" (to prepare the way for the tycoons of F. Scott Fitzgerald), so Norris repossesses the newspaper story and makes it into his own, until Jadwin's "name was familiar in the homes and at the fireside of uncounted thousands" (292). *The Pit* as literary text is occasioned by the pretext of news, the medium par excellence of information; the literary condition of being has been engendered by a fleeting, historical, and reported datum: ostensible fact has morphed into more permanent and consumable fiction.

Analogous informational impulses are visible elsewhere in Norris's work. He enriches his fiction with descriptions and technical terms that are frequently lifted from current encyclopedias. The technicalities of Lloyd Searight's nursing expertise in *A Man's Woman*, just as the elaborations on dental technology in *McTeague*, are borrowed from contemporary medical textbooks. In *Blix*, journalist and would-be writer Rivers authors an article titled "Industrial Renaissance of Japan" from information "compiled after an hour's reading in the Lafcadio Hearn and the Encyclopedia" (42). During the writing of a story about a deceased diver, "in order to get the 'technical details,'" Condy "consulted the Encyclopedias again, and 'worked in' a number of unfamiliar and odd-sounding names" (42). And when he reads Blix one of the colonial stories of Morrowbie Jukes, he "prided himself upon having discovered" the technical accuracy of the story which, "so far as he knew, all critics had overlooked.... Jukes was a civil engineer, and Condy held that it was a capital bit of realism on the part of the author to have him speak ... in such technical terms" (33).

Thus, as we have already seen in the pictorial context of *The Pit,* Norris's fiction and theory of fiction fully partake in the late nineteenth-century ethos of information and information processing and suggest an increasing textual reciprocity between journalistic and literary narrative. At the same time, Norris in *The Pit* (unlike in his other major fiction) resists the pressures of literary commodification that come about in a global economy. Juxtaposed to the language of economics and journalism, literary discourse in this novel is not described as an archaic holdover in a world of business and sensational news—interfering background noise tolerated on the margins of corporate practices. On the contrary, he characterizes literature as a desirable space worthy of preservation that should not be subject to the vagaries of commercial transactions. Norris emphasizes this recuperative value of narrative by juxtaposing the transitoriness of business news and its channels—that is, information and its processing technologies—with the durability of print. Commodity fetishes if seen as investments in an economy of high-speed communication, books can yet function as resistant sites questioning the consumer effects of information flow.

Already in his essays, Norris is acutely sensitive to the turn-of-the-century World Wide Web: "To-day the globe is wrapped in telegraph wire as a boy's baseball is wrapped with string, and continent and city gossip together as so many old maids on the hotel veranda, often about matters no less trivial" (*Apprenticeship* 2:233). Correspondingly, *The Pit* pays attention to the communications networks that regulate emergent global economies. Detailing a routine day on the trade floor, Norris goes to great pains to elaborate on the gradual increase in telecommunications. Long before the opening of the market, "hundreds of telegraph instruments" of Western Union perforate the air with an "intermittent clicking of a key ... like a diligent cricket busking himself in advance of its mates" (82–84). Once the day's rumor about falling grain prices in the Far East spreads, "the clicking of the throng of instruments rose into the air in an incessant staccato stridulation" (85), punctuated by the shouts of messenger boys and the interminable "whirring of telephone signals" (88). Eventually, this electric cacophony reaches its crescendo as the market opens, and "on the instant hundreds of telegraph keys scattered throughout the building began clicking off the news to the whole country" (88). Similarly, when the price of wheat breaks the magic barrier of one dollar, "the news flashed out to the world on a hundred telegraph wires; it was called to a hundred offices across the telephone lines" (239). And when Jadwin's empire collapses, his downfall becomes a McLuhanesque moment, an instantaneous media event spreading from New York and Boston to "London, Liverpool, Paris, and Odessa"—the global village connecting through the "clicking of telegraph keys" and "the trilling of telephone bells" (332–33). This is the symphony of a wired society *avant la lettre.*

More important, Norris presents communications networks not only for reasons of historical verisimilitude but also to emphasize the speed with which their commodity—processed information—degenerates in value. After a market day, the trade floor was (in the military tropes characteristic of naturalism) "littered from end to end . . . with a countless multitude of yellow telegraph forms, thousands and thousands. . . . It was the débris of the battle-field, the abandoned impedimenta and broken weapons of contending armies, the detritus of conflict" (94). Once telegrams have fulfilled their function as carriers of momentary price quotes, they remain useful only to idling traders, who found "an apparently inexhaustible diversion in folding their telegrams into pointed javelins and sending them across the room" (91). *The Pit,* in fact, develops a veritable hierarchy of informational topicality. While a bankrupt speculator nourishes fantasies by reading "a newspaper two days old" as he sits in Gretry's offices, this already consumed and dated information is juxtaposed to the fresh news about prices. Paralleling the ticking of a telegraph that was "screwed to the blackboard," a young employee "chalked up cabalistic, and almost illegible figures under columns headed by initials of certain stocks and bonds. . . . One quotation replaced another, and the key and the chalk clicked and tapped incessantly" (75). But while the present volume of exchange is dictated by the tap dancing of telegraph keys, it is only advanced global insider information supplied by Jadwin's Parisian connections—the "'exclusive news'" from the Bourse "a day or so in advance of everybody else"—that will determine overnight gains in the market (77). Only the news not yet in circulation and not yet relegated to the data heap of business history is of (greatest) value to insiders, precisely because its secret transmission will have had crucial effects on the Chicago market by the time, as Gretry puts it, such news will have become "public property in twenty-four hours" (79).

Significantly, Jadwin and Gretry are concerned about an economic Watergate, the possibility of wiretapping that might leak news, as yet unconsumed, into the hands of the opposition, hence instantly deflating its exclusive value (245).[30] Significantly as well, the "cabalistic" blackboard entries at Gretry's brokerage point to the invaluable dimension of modern data processing: the encryption of sensitive, that is, volatile, information. While the trade publications in *The Pit* are controlled by the two contending conglomerates with the express intention of doctoring, in solid black and white, news to bring about market swings—Crookes's group could "make Bear sentiment with the public" because he "owns most of the commercial columns of the dailies" (241–42); Jadwin's circle has "fixed the warehouse crowd," as they "about 'own' the editorial and news sheets of these papers" (295)—encrypted information coming through telegraphic channels, while similarly capitalizing on market swings, remains precisely the opposite: private, and short-lived in its privacy, before being disseminated by the mass media twenty-four hours later. Jadwin has no use for a "novel," and in response to Laura's inquiries about his reading can only say, "Isn't it about time for lunch?" before admitting that fiction (after acknowledging that he has "looked ahead in it") seems "terribly dry" (226). Yet, when transmissions "in cipher" arrive from Europe, he eagerly consults his "key book," "one finger following the successive code words of the despatch," translating the news with an informational half-life of less than a day into a decisive market advantage (206–7). Against key books decoding transatlantic business events in almost-real time, the invented reality of fiction is no match.

Eventually, Norris symbolizes literature's marginal status in a world of data by integrating books into upscale patterns of consumption (and he does so by upholding the gender demarcations of naturalist discourse, which assigns information to the male world of business, books and bookishness to Woman). As part of her consumer inebriation—a hoarding fever not unlike Trina's in *McTeague*—not only does Laura begin to amass objets d'art that make up a virtual iconography of the leisure class (175), she also evolves an impulsive "mania for old books and first editions." Previously oblivious to books beyond their use as behavioral scripts, Laura suddenly "haunted the stationers and second-hand bookstores, studied the authorities, followed the auctions, and bought right and left, with reckless extravagance" (309). Like most everything, books for her become items of purchase, abstract investments associated with ostentation and cash flow value, not intrinsic value contained in the object, that is, print, itself; and, not surprisingly, her book fetish ebbs as quickly as it flows, largely because her surplus of capital diminished "the spice of the hunt in the affair. She had but to express a desire for a certain treasure, and forthwith it was put into her hand." Not perceiving the relations between material product, content, and historical moment, books for her quickly degenerate in value, turning into bulks of boredom without acquisitive thrill: "Her desires were gratified with an abruptness that killed the zest of them. She felt none of the joy of possession; the little personal relation between her and her belongings vanished away" (309).

Corthell, by contrast, does perceive the little personal relation between himself and his belongings, just as he perceives the little personal relation between books, their content, and their history of production. As a craftsman sensitive to the materialities of art, he is not only an authority on "the coloring and fusing of glass" (19) but also knowledgeable about pictorial brushwork, "color scheme," and the "management of light and shadow" (103). Mindful of the specifics of each medium, he observes that "the water-color that pretends to be anything more than a sketch oversteps its intended limits" (97). An avid reader and connoisseur of print, his studio was lined with "shelves bearing eighteenth-century books in seal brown tree calf—Addison, The Spectator, Junius, and Racine, Rochefoucauld and Pascal hung against it here and there," and one wall features "a framed page of a fourteenth-century version of *Les Quatre Fils Aymon*, with an illuminated letter of miraculous workmanship" (250). Unlike for Laura, for him each book has been carefully chosen over time and for the time, each artifact representing an embodiment of its history. Old leather- and felt-bound books are not abstract investments but works of art deriving their value from their content and the manual processes of book crafting. As Benjamin has noted indeed, "a collector of older books is closer to the wellsprings of collecting than the acquirer of luxury editions" because he is animated by the desire "to renew the old world" (*Selected Writings* 2:487). Out of sync with the turnover of consumer culture, collectors own books, as does Sheldon, for their embodied history: "The most profound enchantment for the collector is the locking of individual items within a magic circle in which they are fixed as the final thrill, the thrill of acquisition, passes over them. Everything remembered and thought, everything conscious, becomes the pedestal, the frame, the base, the lock of his property. The period, the region, the craftsmanship, the former ownership—for a true collector the whole background of an item adds up to a magic encyclopedia whose quintessence is the fate of his object" (2:486).

Norris thus presents Laura and Corthell as inhabiting two fundamentally different responses to turn-of-the-century American book culture. The triangulation between manual art, content, and historical moment, which is so central to the marginal artist, is of no import to the moneyed consumer. Without any felt appreciation for the crafted volumes, and without any personal cost to her, Laura finds that her acquisitions degenerate into an unsatisfying purchase in the never-ending chain of consumer desire and data surplus, and the effortless instantaneity of her purchases is fully in sync with the real-time communication of telegraphy and telephone invented precisely to ease the speedy capital and commodity flow she participates in. Corthell, by contrast, appreciates handcrafted books for the sake of their artisanship (their embodied skill) and content, and cherishes each artifact in his studio because of its historicity, its unique and manual origin. The artist who, unlike everybody else in *The Pit,* is not networked into the circuits of consumption via phone or electricity (250) may well understand the felt tangibility of old volumes as a counterweight to the flimsy messages of ticker tape; opposed to its unlettered code on thin paper strips, books are palpably heavy and contain knowledge—often distilled over generations—of a more durable sort. Certainly Norris, like his fictional alter ego, appreciated the solidity of crafted books, as he went "to unending trouble to bind his paper-backed French novels" to give them greater durability (Walker, *Norris* 284). Like Pound, Lewis, and a host of modernist writers for whom the materialities of books would become crucial elements of meaning constitution and alternatives to commercial text processing, the Norris interested in things medieval insisted on careful and lavish book design. His first book, *Yvernelle,* a medieval romance in ballad form, was privately printed and bound in handsome cloth with numerous decorative engravings produced in monotint and an embossed gilt top. Deriving in both design and theme from William Morris, the founder of the English Arts and Crafts movement (with whom Norris's floral signature was frequently confused), it outdid the ornate productions of the Kelmscott Press. For the premodernist Norris and the arch-modernists both, the materialities of print became the defining element to embody a more serious and durable textuality—a literary textuality worthy of preservation in the face of informational, high-speed signals.

The wizard of wheat, of course, who is largely responsible for the telegraphic blitz in *The Pit,* has no use for outdated forms of communication. He converts the traditional site of bibliophilia—his library—into his domestic business headquarters (250). As a man in possession of a good fortune in want of a wife, he subjects himself to Laura's readings, but soon after the wedding, as Page puts it, he "don't care for literature now as he did once, or was beginning to when Laura used to read to him" (230). And yet, continuing this gesture to recuperate print in a postprint world, Norris maneuvers his protagonist to where he rediscovers the values of (literary) reading. In what one might call an etiology of networking, Norris describes Jadwin's involvement in the channels of communication as a progressive entrapment in a self-destructive feedback loop. Instead of sorting information to free his mind, Jadwin finds himself overwhelmed by a data overflow unmanageable in its global sweep. The result is a mental surcharge, a short-circuiting of his processing capacities that is intimately linked to the realigned relays between bodies, minds, and machines at the turn of the century. Jadwin, one might say, becomes one of the twentieth century's first victims of the information explosion.

True to McLuhan's canonical insight that media are human extensions, Norris notes that the office of the Postal Telegraph Company "is a ganglia, a nerve center of the body of the earth not only for the transmission, but also for the reception of news and messages" (*Apprenticeship* 2:233). Similarly, the wires stretching out of the offices of the San Francisco *Chronicle* "are hardly more than a network of nerves that transmit sensation without appreciable lapse of time" (*Apprenticeship* 1:155). In one specific instance, which prefigures aporias of technological autonomy erasing human agency, Norris describes, admiringly, the mental capacities of a man sandwiched between two text-processing systems, a completely integrated link between humans and machines: "In one corner of the room sat a telegraph operator, who was also a typewriter—a miracle of a man—flanked on one side by a telegraph instrument and on the other by a chuckling, clucking Remington. A special loop from the Western Union had been run in, and the *Chronicle* tapped the circuit here by four or five operators. A dispatch arrived. The wonderful man in the corner took it off the telegraph instrument and type-wrote it as he listened, then passed it over to the Managing Editor at a near-by desk" (*Apprenticeship* 1:154). As he decodes and transmits information virtually simultaneously, the teletypewriter's processing capacities earn him a rightful slot in the assembly of machinery. Working in the vicinity of what would, a century later, be known as Silicon Valley, he performs as a perfect chip in the circuitry of information. In exemplary form, his cognitive skills have been calibrated to fit into the niche assigned to him by the apparatuses of communication and to operate in sync with industrialized data flows. As information historian James R. Beniger has put it, the "use of human beings, not for their strength and agility, nor for their knowledge or intelligence, but for the more objective capacity of their brains to store and process information," became "a dominant feature of employment in the Information Society" of the late nineteenth and twentieth centuries (225).

Jadwin too is integrated into networks of communications, and he too—albeit only sign by sign—can decode encrypted information coming through the wires. But unlike the teletypewriter, Jadwin is the cognitive inheritor of a fundamentally print-based order of knowledge whose brain is not fully attuned to the parallel and multiply staggered levels of information processing required of modern forms of communication. Thus, while he is ingenious at orchestrating global markets for a time, his empire of speculation collapses coincident with a prolonged processing crisis (or, to speak, with Beniger, "a control crisis"). For weeks he had been "struggling with a fog in the interior of his brain," and he would lie awake, "concentrating his thoughts upon the vast operation in which he found himself engaged, following out again all its complexities, its inconceivable ramifications" (282), acknowledging that "judgment, clear reasoning, at times, he felt, forsook him" (307). Then, at the moment when Jadwin—already dependent on secret transatlantic cables—demands around-the-clock access to telegraph and telephone, he experiences a mental overload articulated in terms of a processing breakdown:

> A new turn had been given to the screw . . . a slow, tense crisping of every tiniest nerve in his body. . . . A dry, pringling aura as of billions of minute electric shocks crept upward over his flesh, till it reached his head, where it seemed to culminate in a white flash. . . . And then, under the stress and violence of the hour, something snapped in his brain. The murk behind his eyes had been suddenly pierced by a white flash. The strange qualms and tiny nervous paroxysms of the last few months all at once culminated in some indefinite, indefinable crisis, and the wheels and cogs of all activities save one lapsed away and ceased. (305, 343)[31]

Tom Lutz has rightly noted that Jadwin's collapse is one of "the most detailed literary representations of a neurasthenic crisis" in American fiction (156), the disease de rigueur of turn-of-the-century middle-class America suffering, alternately, from ennui and excitement. I would add that Jadwin's breakdown is rendered specifically in the discourse of telegraphic lags and relays, of synaptic jumps and failed connections that signal a profound processing impasse related to the communication networks enmeshing him. As George M. Beard, the first diagnostician of this disease, averred in 1881, "the moderns differ from the ancient civilizations mainly in these five elements—steam power, the periodical press, the telegraph, the sciences, and the mental activity of women. . . . When civilization, plus these five factors, invades any nation, it must carry nervousness and nervous disaster along with it" (96). Leaving aside Beard's painful gendering here, his description reads like an inventory of the disciplines and technologies that enable modern cultures to regulate their massive information and material flows—a culture in which Jadwin is at home, and yet not at home. As market fluctuations amplify, and amplify nervous fibrillations, the Lord of Information is dangerously close to a total short circuit. And such an overflow, Norris suggests, may benefit from a medium that is cognitively more enriching and more resistant to yielding its meaning in one cycle of decryption or consumption: literature.

For Jadwin's erstwhile business model, Hargus, such enrichment comes too late. The man who preceded Jadwin in his machinations is a shell of his former self, a homeostatic cipher with an "atrophied brain"—the result of a cerebral short circuit following a major market crash years earlier (296). He replicates precisely the systemic disconnects and misfirings of a global network Norris noted in his essays: "it would be well to try to imagine what we would do if every wire on earth were cut to-morrow, or if even half of them were cut. It would have much the same effect upon the world at large as a stunning blow on the back of the head has upon an individual. It would not be far from paralysis" (*Apprenticeship* 2:235). Jadwin, by contrast, heals his cognitive breakdown through reengagement with the world of print. Even during his crisis, he claims "to read" his competitors "like a book," figuratively acknowledging his print-based processing horizon (284). And while he appears to have sold all of their books to finance their relocation, the therapeutic benefits of reading have not escaped him: when Laura wants to cut short a long letter from her sister, the man who used to take shortcuts in reading insists, "Read it, read it. . . . Don't skip a line. I want to hear every word" (363–64).

Similarly, Court, Jadwin's filial reincarnation in corporate America, heeds the advice of his betrothed. Page, whose very name suggests the elemental property of books, recommends to counteract the business world "starving his soul" by indicating "a course of reading for him" (192). Later, upon the couple's arrival in New York at the novel's end, Landry shows himself "intensely interested" in "a really fine course of lectures . . . on 'Literary Tendencies'" (364). This, of course, is Norris's own concluding pitch at current literary trends, and Court indeed champions not the icons of tradition but "the modern novel" and "the newest book"—Stevenson's *The Wrecker* and novels such as *The Pit* and *The Octopus* (192). These novels are, indeed, hot off the press, yet for all that no less worthy of preservation than Shakespeare, Meredith, and Browning, and very much in contrast to the informational half-life of newspapers. Through Court (a syllable short of Corthell), Norris suggests the rapprochement of economics and art—a concluding reaffirmation of the Literary as a category of cultural value, what Barbara Hochman calls the "life-giving power of narrative" (38).

The person embodying the values of literary print culture is of course Corthell himself, ranging from his collection of books and popular reading circle to his own theory of narrative: "the novel of the future is going to be the novel without a love story" (52). While Norris variously qualifies Corthell's narrative status, he invests him with the cultural authority to discriminate and judge. Indeed, Larzer Ziff has noted that in *The Pit*'s modeling of competing masculinity, Corthell becomes an increasingly "attractive male" to Laura and Norris himself. In the same way as Jadwin invests his erotic energies in the market, both Laura and Norris discover Corthell's increasing desirability. Afraid of the sexual logic of such a convergence, however, Norris did not follow "the implications of the Jadwin-Corthell tension to the very end" and instead drives a rueful wife back to her (emasculated) husband (272). Such authorial maneuvering notwithstanding, the libidinal economy of the novel—the erotic and economic "reappraisal" of both Jadwin and Corthell—certainly elevates the artist's sensibilities, just as it underwrites Norris's literary aspirations in the face of mainstream cultural expectations.[32]

No doubt, this ideological oscillation about the location of literature, and art generally, in a commodified world is one of several tensions traversing Norris's oeuvre, such as his conflicted allegiance to corporate politics and muckraking tactics, Progressive and medieval sensibilities, manly women and womanly men. But it certainly invites a reading that makes Corthell a perhaps utopian site of resistance in a world of data flows, instant communication, and the devaluation of print. Through Corthell, Norris suggests that the deluge of information processed by telephone, telegraph, and the press is at odds with the cultural value of the literary book. The information sphere inhabited by Jadwin is certainly far from the data flows in today's integrated circuits, but when he loses control of the market, he experiences not only a cognitive short circuit but also intimations of a more postmodern network of ultracommunicativity—an expanding dissipative structure divorced from human agency (see Lyotard 69–71). To resist such technological entrapment, Lyotard advocates practices of resistance that accord, at a century's remove, with Norris's utopian space for literature. As William Paulson has put it, "certain qualities of printed texts" may be "worthy of cultivation as practices of resistance to the hegemony of electronic [in Norris's case, electric] information," and create "spaces of turbulence and even fixity within it" ("Literary Canon" 245). For Lyotard, Paulson, and Norris, the category of the literary embodies a durability and stability that can interrogate the ephemeral commodities of a (post)modern culture of information and consumption: sound bites, statistics, and stock quotes. Even reformed speculators come to find that out.

4

Archaic Mechanics, Anarchic Meaning

Malcolm Lowry and the Technology of Narrative

"The typewriter," observes Martin Heidegger, "tears writing from the essential realm of the hand, i.e., the realm of the word. The word itself turns into something 'typed'" (81). As if sharing Heidegger's humanist resistance to the technologization of the word, Malcolm Lowry (much like Frank Norris) avoided using a typewriter to compose his fiction drafts. At the same time (again, much like Norris) he conceived of himself as an engineer of fiction and of his writerly practice as a narrative technology. This form of textual engineering is evident in the component part assembly of his texts and in his use of machine models, and has its origin in a modernist aesthetic of design. It is particularly visible in his masterpiece *Under the Volcano*—a novel whose machine design Lowry envisioned as an assembly of one of the oldest human technologies, and a model he appropriated from numerous cultural traditions: an aggregate of interlocking wheels. The assemblage of this *narrative engine* in the manner of a collage also puts Lowry in the proximity of postmodernism's play with intertextuality and signification, as does the resultant textual apparatus that affords virtually anarchic semiosis. If, however, *Under the Volcano* operates as what Gilles Deleuze has called a "literary machine," as a text drawing attention to the process of meaning making and to its condition as a commodity available for readerly consumption, the novel's postmodern ethos is counterbalanced by its archaic mechanical design that codifies, on the level of form, Lowry's ambivalence toward technology.

The schism between romantic artificer and narrative engineer, between the hand-based production of script and aesthetic formal design, is already suggested by the topographical coordinates of Lowry's life and work, which generally unfolds along the fault line of Nature and Culture. As is well-known,

Lowry progressively removed himself from the cultural centers of Europe and America to a wooden shack on the Pacific waterfront in British Columbia, in part because of what he called "the sthenic confusion of technological advance" (*Hear Us O Lord* 180). Eridanus, the prelapsarian sanctuary his post-*Volcano* alter egos inhabit, is indeed endangered by the onrush of civilization, as when, in a propitious moment in *October Ferry to Gabriola*, Ethan Llewelyn envisions progress as technological apocalypse, when the forces of progress will have "totally ruined most of the beauty of the country with industry, and thoroughly loused up the watersheds and the rainfall, and the last old sourdough [will have] traded in his gold sifting pan for a Geiger counter and staked out the last uranium claim" (202).

But while this passage, in the fashion of his romantic predecessors, ostensibly rewrites Genesis as a dialectic between the natural and the technological—the presence and absence of prelapsarian perfection—suggesting the Fall of the global pastoral community into an industrial wasteland and, indeed, associating machines with diabolic machinations, Lowry's oeuvre also complicates this binary. While technology can doubtlessly be destructive to the natural, Lowry describes it as an appropriate and aesthetic fixture of the modern world. In his project statement to *Hear Us O Lord from Heaven Thy Dwelling Place*, Lowry suggested that even though the protagonists should, through their life at Eridanus, experience intimations of a lost Paradise, the story "has no 'back to nature' or Rousseau-like message: there is no 'back' *permanently* to anywhere, the aim is harmony, so that the view is not to be sentimentalised."[1] Appropriately, while concerned with environmental pollution, the narrator of "The Forest Path to the Spring" finds the oil floating on the water—remnants of a refinery across the bay—"oddly pretty" (236). The brilliance of the sunrise, they come to realize, "isn't pure nature. It's the smoke from those wretched factories" across the bay (235). And in what may be the most poignant moment of industrial pastoralism in all of Lowry's work, he transvaluates the nature-culture dichotomy in favor of the latter, as he contemplates the beauty of the night sky from his wooden shack.

> It was not the moonlight or even the inlet that gave the scene its new, unique beauty, but precisely the oil refinery itself, or more precisely still, the industrial counterpoint, the flickering red pyre of the burning oil waste. Now over the water . . . came the slow warning bell of a freight train chiming on the rail over Port Boden as for a continual vespers, now closer, now receding, . . . but always as if some country sound heard long ago that might have inspired a Wordsworth or Coleridge to describe church bells borne over the fields to some wandering lovers at

evening. But whereas the moonlight washed the colour out of everything, replacing it by luminousness, providing illumination without color, the flaming burning vermilion oil waste below the moon . . . made the most extraordinary lurid color, enormously real. (*Hear Us O Lord* 193–94)

By inverting the romantic aesthetic of natural beauty, Lowry in effect suggests the fluid renegotiation, if not the deconstruction, of the opposition of the natural and the technological. In the age of massive resource management and energetic consumption—that is, in a world of consumer culture—"nature" and "technology" have become unstable categories that interpenetrate and mutually implicate one another, even if they are not necessarily interchangeable. More important, the destabilization of this romantic binary also locates Lowry's politics of technology. Rather than succumb to an unreflected nostalgia for a pretechnological utopia, a Garden without Machine, Lowry in this passage harbors "a nostalgia conscious of itself, a lucid and remorseless dissatisfaction with the present on the grounds of some remembered [imaginary] plenitude" (Jameson, *Marxism and Form* 82). He advocates a kind of technological realpolitik that mediates between nature and machine without (as in Don DeLillo's sunsets in *White Noise*) fully naturalizing the machine and mechanizing nature. Certainly, throughout *Under the Volcano* especially, Lowry reminds the reader continuously of the ultimately colonial history of the industrialized world, such as Geoffrey's mysterious involvement as a submarine commander during World War I, the Spanish Civil War, and the technological specter of World War II—Geoffrey's vision of "the inconceivable pandemonium of a million tanks" and "the blazing of ten million burning bodies" (375). Such references become a kind of ground music announcing the apocalyptic potential of the machine while reiterating the political dimension of Lowry's work. The harmonizing tendencies between Nature and Culture in Lowry's fiction, however, the breakdown of the romantic binary in favor of a fluid interimplication, are more representative of his position toward technology. As he comments in *October Ferry* on their life on the edge of the wilderness, "Back to nature, yet not all the way. Rousseau with a battery radio, Thoreau with a baby Austin" (154).

The Engineer, the Hand, and the Machine

As is generally acknowledged, Lowry was a self-styled possessed artist with an ailing soul who subscribed to the romantic mystifications surrounding the creative process. Writing, in that sense, was fundamentally a matter of inspiration, of a divine afflatus engendering creative activity—a kind of transcendental agency exercised, in Lowry's case, by an infernal demon. Feverish creative outbursts mixed with long creative dry spells suggesting the agon and absence of inspiration; unfinished fragments evoking a hieratic celebration of the fragment; an obsessive fear of plagiarism betraying the concern with genius and original creation; and the heavy use of mescal to facilitate artistic activity (Lowry's version of laudanum)—these are the elements of Lowry's romantic self-definition.

Less often acknowledged, however, is Lowry's second artistic self-conception as an engineer of fiction. While Sherrill Grace has demonstrated that Lowry's notion of engineering partly derives from Ortega's theory of self-fabrication in *Toward a Philosophy of History*,[2] Lowry's interest in the nexus of engineering and form is complemented by his recognition of the engineer as an icon of modern ingenuity and the maker of aesthetic design. Witness the following genealogy of engineering: The protagonist of "June the 30th, 1934" was "training to be an engineer at Bradford Tech" before the war (*Psalms and Songs* 42); Sir Thomas in the story draft "Noblesse Oblige" had been "in the Engineers" during the war, "so that he was an extremely handy man" (UBC SC, 16–6: 3); Ethan Llewelyn in *October Ferry* was conceived as "an electrical engineer, a child of machinery and the modern age" (UBC SC 12–13: 23); the great-great-grandfather of the writer in "Elephant and Colosseum" was "not only a poet but a successful inventor and engineer," and the first to propose a scheme for the Panama Canal (*Hear Us O Lord* 151); and Sigbjørn in "Through the Panama," continuing the lineage, is "hereditarily disposed in favor of canals" because an "ancestor of [his] also had a plan for the Panama Canal that was favorably received."[3] Sigbjørn, in fact, suggests that building a canal is "the first piece of engineering a child does figure out," only to correlate, shortly afterward, the engineering of water with the engineering of words: "the Panama Canal ... is a work of genius—I would say, like a work of child's genius—something like a novel—in fact just such a novel as I ... might have written myself" (*Hear Us O Lord* 58–61). This novel is titled *The Valley of the Shadow of Death*, Lowry's one-time alternative title for *Under the Volcano*.[4]

Lowry, indeed, developed an aesthetic of engineering, a sensibility for the gear-and-girder design of modern technology. In *October Ferry*, Lowry's doppelgänger Ethan (who is "no enemy per se of the machine: quite the contrary," as Lowry suggested in an early draft [UBC SC 12–13: 24]) begins to study a series of books on "modern architecture" and discovers himself "to be an admirer of Le Corbusier, Frank Lloyd Wright, and in general agreement with the socio-architectural tenets of Lewis Mumford" (166).

These designers and cultural critics, of course, largely formulated the early twentieth-century aesthetic of the machine that encouraged the formal and functional interdependence of structure and machine designs. "The clean surfaces, the hard lines, the calibrated perfection"—this is how Lewis Mumford described the essential components of this sensibility "that the machine has made possible" (*Sticks and Stones* 178). Ethan remembers Mies van der Rohe's famous dictum, "Less is more" ("Which meant having the greatest effect with the least means," Lowry adds in an early draft [UBC SC 16–14: 207]), and he comes to revision the oil refinery across their bay in precisely such minimalist and functionalist terms. Early in the novel, Ethan deciphers the structure as a portent of infernal doom, when the burned-out S of the SHELL sign looms as HELL, before his emergent engineering sensibilities allow him (and Jacqueline) to appreciate it "as an entity aesthetically pleasing," whose "cylindrical aluminum retorts and slim chimneys like organ pipes" (158) suggest the engineered blend and proportioned balance of a "well-behaved Meccano structure" (166).

Thus, combined with Ortega's theory of self-construction, modern engineering provided Lowry with a complementary model for his narrative practice—for seeing himself as a technologist of narrative and for using machines as structuring devices in his fiction. The efficient engineering of functionalist machine design, in particular, valorized his belief in the necessity of structure and elegance, and in the structural reciprocity of form and function: the modernist reformulation of the Aristotelian balance between form and content. As well, the clarity of form and minimal structure of engineering provided Lowry with a restraining counterpractice to his own impulse toward excess, an infinite proliferation of signs and an uncontrollable encyclopedism that threatens to turn his texts into loose baggy monsters, or what Lowry himself called "the Battle of Bulge or overstuffed glowering illegible and anyhow incomprehensible page" (*Letters* 2:604). Engineering, in that sense, afforded him a model of discipline and formal restraint that held in check his drive toward "churrigueresque" overloading, toward narrative surplus and superfluity (*Letters* 1:502), while the idea of the romantic craftsman—the erratic manuscript worker laboring in suffering seclusion—upheld and legitimized the impulsive element of art in his mind. The presence of this dual definition of authorship, the interimplication between "old-fashioned" writing and "contemporary" engineering, is another symptom of the ideological rift traversing Lowry's mental topography.

This schism, the difficulty of writing in a consumer culture, is also visible in the disparity between Lowry's writing practices and the pressures of the market, asking (as his publishers did after the publication of the *Volcano*) for the measured production of publishable script. Lowry's prodigious output—the multiple drafts of each of his novels and novel fragments, his prolix correspondence, and his impulse toward incessant note taking—suggests a textual production akin to the industriousness of a machine and is easily legible as a response to a publication environment in search of commodifiable text. Yet Lowry's very definitions of authorship deny such regularized production. Just as the writer-qua-craftsman suggests a casual pacing without an eye toward market demands, the engineer, as Lowry understood that profession, suggests formal elegance and unique design, not the machine processing of text. (In that sense, the trope of engineering may be a kind of metaphorical compromise, since Lowry, for the moment, appears to ignore the engineer's "other" associations of natural exploitation and despoliation that were dear to his environmental heart.) As models of writing, both (romantic) craftsmanship and (modern) engineering elevate the creative process and distance writing from the commodifications of the machine age. Similarly, and more importantly, Lowry did not as a general rule avail himself of the typewriter, the technology that could have enabled the speedy generation of script and the machine that, in theory, "fuses composition and publication, causing an entirely new attitude toward the written and printed word" (McLuhan, *Media* 260). Instead, Lowry composed (both his fictions and most of his letters) in longhand and then, customarily, hired a female typist or, following his second marriage, had Margerie generate a typescript from his holographs (Day 250, 270). Why did Lowry resist using a machine for the generation of text?

Lowry's resistance to the typewriter is intimately connected to his double conception as romantic craftsman and romanticized engineer, a conception based on the assumption that both are original creators and that, the craftsman no less than the engineer, are "extremely handy" men. In terms of Lowry's writerly romanticism, the hand—without any mediation beyond quill, pen, or pencil—functions as the central organ of artistic execution, the corporeal transfer point between divine inspiration and human expression. "True art," therefore, is the result of ingenious and unmediated creative activity, whereas "false art" is the result of mechanical intervention that cheapens both the writing process per se and the result of that process: the degeneration of art into artifact—into commodity.[5]

In the context of Lowry's infernal productivity, Patrick A. McCarthy has argued that "Lowry seems precariously poised between romantic and modern concepts of art and reality, a situation that undoubtedly contributed to his anxiety over the nature of his work and made it even more difficult to complete his projects" (210). When Wilderness, suffering from writer's block, begins to admire writers who "turned out their work as easily as if it came out of some celestial sausage machine," and when he yearns to read an undisguised account of a writer's struggle, for "to learn something of the mechanics of his kind of creation, was not that to learn something of the mechanism of destiny?" (*Grave* 12), he crystallizes these conflicting impulses in Lowry's thinking. The repeated (semi)ironic association of writing with mechanical, assembly-line production suggests its status as a commercial trade, as a full-time profession in the age of text-qua-commodity. A writer's success is primarily determined by the steady flow of his productions, his "mechanism of destiny." On the other hand, conceiving of writerly art in such a regularized and unmanual fashion demystifies the essential mystery of creative activity and depreciates the craft of writing.

Equally important, the protocols of standardization and regularization built into the typewriter, as well as the manual dislocations of typing itself, would have militated against Lowry's hand-based definition of art as well. As Kittler has demonstrated, the typewriter evolved as a fundamentally prosthetic device that enables writing when the physiological linkage between eye, hand, and pen is suspended, in the process creating (unlike handwriting) "a complete letter, which not only is untouched by the writer's hand but is also located in a place entirely apart from where the hands work" (Beyerlen in Kittler, *Discourse Networks* 195). For Lowry, this ruptured act of typing, the unlinking of hand and key and the imprint of the letter—and the separation of the body from writing, generally—disrupted the creative continuity between conception and articulation, and along with it authentic *self*-expression, since it compromised Lowry's philosophical belief in the hand as fundamentally human.[6]

Deep-seated as these associations are for Lowry, they could not always have been evident even to him. For once, Lowry could have understood the typewriter as an enabling technology that facilitated writing during periods when his proverbial clumsiness was compromised further by his signature condition: a state of intoxication. In those often prolonged phases, the typewriter could have served in precisely its originary function as a supplementary writing machine for the blind, whose coordination between eye and hand is, analogous to inebriation, significantly impaired. Lowry at one point almost certainly envisioned a typing machine in such terms. In his and Margerie's film script of F. Scott Fitzgerald's *Tender Is the Night*, sloshed pianist and composer Abe North during a bar crawl thinks about "making use of hangovers . . . I'm going to invent a machine. . . . A machine for keeping your hand still, so that composers like me can write music" (83–84). The shakes, by some accounts conducive to authentic vision, can be channeled into artistry through a device that bypasses the fine motor skills of traditional handwriting; with the right machine, Lowry seems to say, delirium tremens can yet result in the right text, whether as musical, literary, or other composition. And in fact, presumably unbeknownst to Abe and his creator, composer Arnold Schoenberg (who was, significantly, trained as an engineer) had already invented a "typewriter for music" to speed up the composing process (Everdell 275).

At the same time, overriding this potentially facilitating function, Lowry may have seen the typewriter, like many other communications devices in his life, as yet another infernal machine, the technologized writing demon usurping the writer's hand for its own diabolic purposes. Working on a typewriter meant that the writing process was no longer solely a question of the writer's volition but rather of a machine enforcing its machinic will on willing hands. In Lowry's paranoid way of thinking, the typewriter's mediating function, and seemingly autonomous functioning, may have fed into not one but two of his lifelong anxieties. As a machine conjuring up visions of bureaucratic control (as it did for Franz Kafka), the typewriter suggested official and officious text processing that was at odds with his sustained fear of state power. In addition, instead of exercising agency by determining to write of one's own free will, the typewriter commutes authorial control into a machine-inspired form of predetermination, in effect dictating rather than being dictated (that is, written) on and to; instead of writing oneself, of controlling the machine, one is being written, controlled by the machine.

What is more, in a gendered logic that roughly parallels Norris's two generations earlier, Lowry may have come to associate the typewriter with woman as a reproductive device disciplining chaotic and self-engendering male creativity. Throughout his career Lowry hired female typists to transcribe his texts and apparently felt so intimidated by the prospect of having to type himself at one point that he agreed to pay one lover-typist 25 percent of the future royalties of *Under the Volcano* (Bowker 260). Similarly, both of Lowry's wives worked as secretaries in Hollywood and became the typist and private secretary of their husband until the typewriter morphed from an instrument of transcription to a mediating device for an essentially synergistic creative process. With Lowry drafting longhand and Margerie, his second wife, typing and adding her own suggestions during the various stages of revision, they engaged in a kind of compositional collaboration that complicates the notion of "authorship" (the occupation Margerie and Lowry indicated on their marriage license [Bowker 305]). Work on *Under the Volcano*, in Bowker's words, became a kind of "communal thing," eventually developing into "a pattern of companionate authorship and parallel writing" (292;

see also Day 270–71).[7] Indeed, once that creative synergy had become daily routine, Lowry "could not work without Margerie, who was immeasurably helpful in cutting back his literary excesses" (Bowker 287), certainly in part by streamlining—or, if you will, stripping or denuding—his text during the transcription process from hand-writing to machine-writing. Much in contrast to his own hand-driven compositional eruptions that fired his authorial self, the typewriter seemed to encode the restrictive linearity of a paradoxically female order pruning the male mess.[8] Given these scenarios and this manual-technological division of labor, a self-determined and embodied hand free from machinic and female intervention becomes all the more important.

Lowry defines virtually all major characters in his fiction in manual terms. Dana Hilliot's "bleeding hands enveloped in cloths" suggest, in juvenile dramatic pose, the stigmata of crucifixion (92); Laruelle's "refined nervous fingers on which he was aware he wore too many rings" reveal his anxious vanity (6). He also saw the hands as the elementary human instrument of artistic expression, and hence self-definition. As a young guitarist Hugh in *Under the Volcano* is concerned that "the worst possible thing that could befall me seemed some hand injury," suggesting that any manual incapacitation would no longer allow him to play the guitar and thus deprive him not only of his income but also of his sense of personhood (178). Bill Plantagenet in *Lunar Caustic* ascribes his failure as a pianist to his "small hands" that do not allow him to stretch over an octave (*Psalms and Songs* 266).[9] And the subtext of the *Volcano*'s cinematic leitmotif, *Las Manos de Orlac*, similarly tells of a pianist who, after having lost his hands through a technological mishap—a railway accident—has the hands of a murderer grafted onto him and is no longer fit to express himself artistically but only to commit murder. It is no coincidence that the Chief of Municipality does have "both his trigger finger and his right thumb . . . missing," and eventually collaborates in the murder of Geoffrey (357). Lowry clearly presents the hand as a marker of humanness and *self*-expression—of artistic execution—or, as in the case of a mutilated or "false" hand, as the opposite: a marker of animality or inhumanness. Heidegger observed that "the hand is, together with the word, the essential distinction of man. . . . Man does not 'have' hands, but the hand holds the essence of man, because the word as the essential realm of the hand is the ground of the essence of man" (80). Lowry, who felt a basic congeniality to the philosopher, would have agreed (*Letters* 2:255).[10]

Lowry foregrounds this nexus of hand and word and human self, of manual motion and inscription, particularly in Geoffrey Firmin's handwriting. When Laruelle discovers Geoffrey's famous letter fluttering out of

Geoffrey's book of Elizabethan plays, he is at first unsure as to the identity of its author. Once he sees "the marginless writing in pencil" on both sides, however, "there was no mistaking, . . . the hand, half crabbed, half generous, and wholly drunken, of the Consul himself, the Greek e's, flying buttresses of d's, the t's like lonely wayside crosses save where they crucified an entire word, the words themselves slanting steeply downhill, though the individual characters seemed as if resisting the descent, braced, climbing the other way" (35). Laruelle here recognizes in the idiosyncrasy of Geoffrey's "hand" a window to his soul. He sees Geoffrey's identity encoded in his penmanship; it is transparent in his script. For Laruelle, indeed, as for Lowry, Geoffrey's epistolary characters become, in effect, a shorthand for his character. In what one could call a logocentric fallacy, they see Geoffrey's tragic stature literally inscribed in the morphology of his lettering, and a "graphic investment" standardized type would have effaced (Goldberg 282).

That Lowry was, however, disturbed precisely by the erasure of individualized—and hence individuating—lettering, by the erasure of scriptive difference through the standardized type of a keyboard, is evident. Responding to Christopher Isherwood's handwritten letter praising the *Tender* script, Lowry observes that "I began to write this letter originally, returning the compliment (which I appreciate) in my own handwriting, such as it is . . . taking advantage of this to write outside"; but after their cats had spilled coconut oil and beer on the letter and it had blown into the sea, he continues, "I gave in, temporarily, to the machine age," resigning himself to type the letter (*Letters* 1:250).[11] While other writers of "the machine age," such as Stephen Crane and Stefan George, labored to stylize their handwriting until it became a virtual typeface (Fried 145–47; Kittler, *Discourse Networks* 259–64), Lowry saw his "hand" as an anachronistic alternative to the conformity of printed script. In his handwriting, "such as it is" (meaning: an almost undecipherable manuscript, as any Lowry scholar can confirm), he recognized a countermechanical form of expression that undermined the regularity of print. He cultivated precisely what typewriting was designed to erase: manual illegibility. Indeed, Lowry, no less than Geoffrey in *Under the Volcano*, "worked outside, longhand, as he liked to do," while Margerie "sat typing at the desk by the window—for she would learn to type, and transcribe all his manuscripts from the slanting e's and odd t's into neat clean pages" (271). (The implied division between handwriting/outside and typewriting/inside also suggests the greater "naturalness" of writing by hand.)

Similarly, when Lowry congratulates a yet unknown David Markson on the acceptance of a piece in the *Saturday Evening Post*, he admonishes him "not to lose your style," not to be rewritten by a "magazine noted for 'typing' its authors," and then recommends the cultivation of one's "own self-editorship," so as not to get "caught in a 'type'" occasioned by "the amount of conformity" within the New York magazine industry (UBC SC 3–10). Though he was not directly concerned with the typewriter *an sich*, Lowry's self-conscious linkage between style and "type" here again hints at his belief in the impossibility of locating the self in a keyboard-generated script; "type" is understood as the absence of an authentic style, as the equidistant spacing between uniform signs that is incompatible with individual self-expression. It is no coincidence that Lowry fetishized a quill-like eagle feather as a writing instrument to sign important documents (Day 293), just as it is no coincidence that Geoffrey has consistently refused to engage Quauhnahuac's "little public scribe," whom both he and Yvonne observe "crashing away on a giant typewriter," to answer some of her letters (53). Since Geoffrey's personhood is vested in his expressive handwriting, any typed (and dictated) script would "naturally" efface his writerly individuality and represent an unauthentic self to Yvonne. Whereas in longhand the hand *is* the executive organ in the writerly fluidity between mind, pen, and paper, in typing it is reduced to a transfer point of instantaneous physiological impulses and is completely severed from the production of the letter on the page, and hence from the self-qua-letter.

As it turns out, the value of Geoffrey's life amounts, indeed, to no more than "a mere misprint in a communiqué" (5). It is through a telegram, a machine-produced and ruptured script, that Geoffrey at the end must die. When the Unión Militar fish Hugh's telegram out of Geoffrey's jacket pocket, they see only cryptic, unpunctuated phrases without semantic cohesion: "*mexpress propetition see tee emma mexworkers confederation proexpulsion exmexixo*" (94).[12] Not being able to decipher the print, and over Geoffrey's protestations that his name is Blackstone, they misconstrue the telegram as "a disguise" that leads quickly to Geoffrey's death (370). This is Lowry's most resonant concluding gesture about the metaphysics of scriptive presence. The telegram functions as an extended, that is, truncated, metaphor for the impossibility of machine-generated text to communicate fully—whether information or personal essence—that, in Lowry's logocentric view, handwriting affords.[13]

Added to the commercial penumbra of typing and the self-falsification of typed script, the linearity of machine-produced text fettered Lowry's fundamentally spatial sensibility as well. Scholars of the orality-literacy debate have observed that while "chirographic control of space tends to be ornamental, ornate," "typographic control typically impresses more by its tidiness and inevitability: the lines perfectly regular, all justified on the right side, everything coming out even visually, and without the aid of guidelines" (Ong 122). Such an orderly and linear directness, however, was completely anathema to Lowry's mode of composition, which required, almost simultaneously, the expanse of the whole manuscript page. Unlike in typing, where the sheet is immovably pressed against the platen to ensure linear script, the blank page and the pen afforded Lowry a compositional fluidity roughly analogous to that of a drawing board. His holographs are notably produced on unlined paper in unleveled handwriting and are replete with asterisks, inserts, and marginal additions that suggest the interweaving of textual fragments into a spatial bricolage that composing on a typewriter would not have allowed him to do. To Yvonne, for example, Geoffrey's poem draft on the back of a menu appears in "handwriting at its most chaotic," as a "wavering and collapsed design, and so crossed out and scrawled over and stained, defaced, and surrounded with scratchy drawings—of a club, a wheel, even a long black box like a coffin—as to be almost undecipherable" (330). In Lowry's pictorial logic, the center and the margin become interchangeable sites of composition that merge into a dialogic field of meaning. Unlike the orderly, segmented sheet of typing, Lowry's page is a space of drafting, a zone of delineation with an almost painterly sense of order: a word picture.[14] As he himself put it (anticipating Ong's comment on chirographic control), the "Blank Page . . . exists but to be decorated" (UBC SC 3: 4).[15]

Thus Lowry was resistant to the technology of typing, even as he relied on typists to translate his turbulent manuscripts into orderly—that is, "professional"—type. He felt that the removal of the hand from script and thus from the writing subject negated the possibility of manual self-authentication and that the linearity of typing compromised his spatial sensibility so crucial to his hand-based artistic practice. These objections and contradictions are encoded in the first name of his protagonist, Wilderness: Sigbjørn. Lowry was "infatuated with the line through the O" (*Letters* 2:625), not only because the letter paradigmatically exemplifies his romantic, essentialized conception of character that is inscribable in a character: Sigbjørn—a Norwegian surname meaning "self-Bear"—is both baring and bearing the self and has "a considerable emotive value in print that it lacks without the ø." Lowry was enthralled with this letter also because it hints centrally at his pictorial imagination, because (as double symbol for the wheel and the lowercase zero in European typography) it can represent everything and nothing and, most important, because the letter suggests his desire to transcend the limitations of typing and printing technology: when he notes that he had "no such letter on his typewriter"[16] and that, in a letter to his publisher, "It would be understandable if your printer would resent this ø. . . . I shall under-

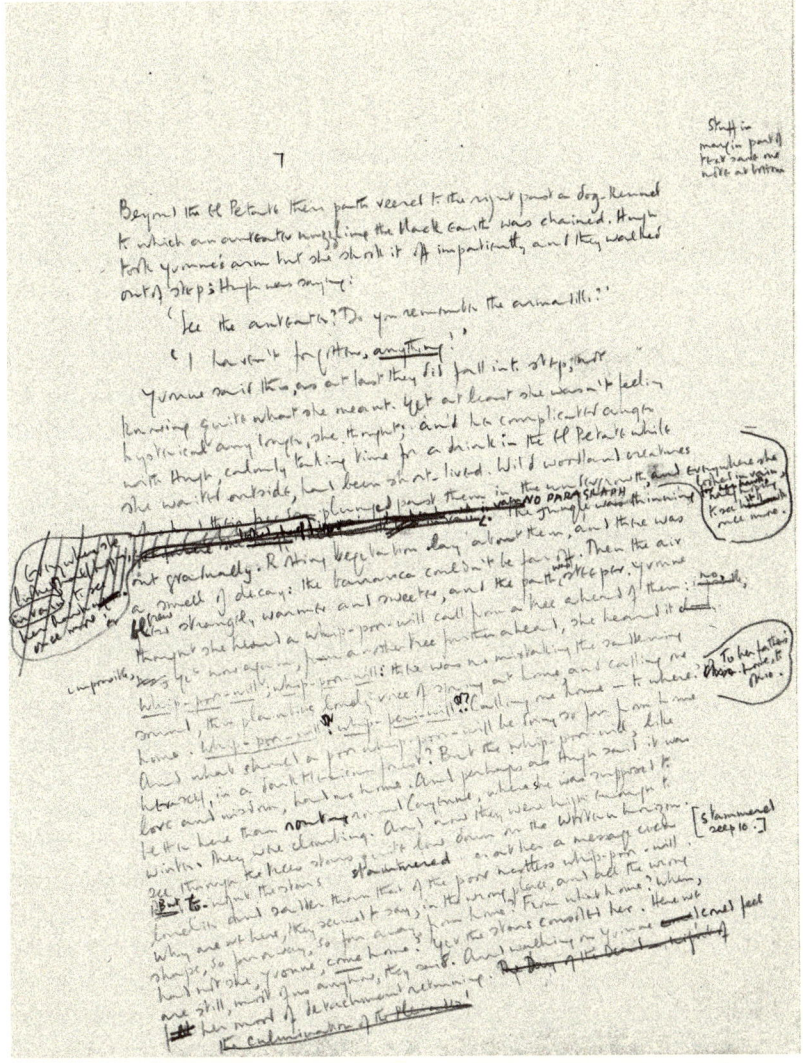

2. A page of a draft of Malcolm Lowry's *Under the Volcano*. Malcolm Lowry Archive, Special Collections, University of British Columbia, Box 31, Folder 10.

stand it if your printer should say, 'To ø with Lowry's ø,'" he mischievously suggests that his manual lettering escapes the standardized signs of the keyboard (*Letters* 2:636).

Narrative Technology: The Myth and the Machine

What is characteristic of the whole sweep of Lowry's mythopoetics is the constant recourse to technological models as structuring devices or narrative engines, what Lowry was fond of calling "design-governing postures" (*Letters* 1:321), and Lowry's setting up of a dialectic between that formal modeling and its investment with mythological content. To balance his real fascination with the aesthetic of technology with his equally real reservations toward technology, he endows his machine models with a mythological flush. By tempering their contemporaneity with a gloss of ancientness, the patina suggests a kind of derealization, a muting of technology's controversial historicity, and hence its ideological liberation for purposes of literary form.

Under the Volcano is engineered around the wheel, one of the most ancient, and hence archetypal, human machines in Lowry's symbolic world. Lowry was explicit about the "very form of the book [which] is to be considered like that of a wheel, with 12 spokes," a wheel he identifies with the Ferris wheel in the square of Quauhnahuac (*Letters* 1:507, 511).[17] Just as Geoffrey comes to see the Ferris wheel as an aesthetically appealing design of component parts—as "an enormously magnified child's structure of girders and angle brackets, nuts and bolts, in Meccano" (190)—so Lowry assembled *Under the Volcano* from a series of prefabricated chapters into a narrative *Gesamtkunstwerk*. The twelve chapters should be considered as "twelve blocks," since each "is a unity in itself," forming self-contained segments within the narrative architecture (*Letters* 1:505–6). While the text is given a kind of superstructural cohesion through a twelve-hour period, the Mexican locale and the texture of the novel's allusive coordinates, Lowry emphasizes the integrity of each chapter through shifting points of view and the absence of connective transitions. *Under the Volcano* was "designed, counter-designed, and interwelded" (*Letters* 1:527); it is like the "new kind of pipe, insanely complicated, that . . . none but [he himself] knew how to put . . . together again" (259). The pipe was assembled from a series of component parts and not perfected until after Armistice Day; Lowry's "insanely complicated" novel was assembled from a series of chapter modules at the end of World War II; both emerged after numerous revisions to a master plan known only to their respective creators. The engineer of the pipe, who in Hawaii attempted to "harness the volcano behind their estate to run a hemp machine" (258), has engineered a smoking mechanism playfully reminiscent of a miniature volcano.

This "static" design of *Under the Volcano* Lowry reproduces in the engineering of the text's "internal" dynamic, the montage of its elementary conceptual units: an aggregate of wheels in simultaneous motion. Lowry appears to have drawn for this design from various heuristic models of ancient mythology and scientific traditions. Scholars have already acknowledged that J. W. Dunne's concept of serial time and the Kabbalah inform Lowry's understanding of the universe (New 11; Ackerley and Clipper 237). Lowry adopted Dunne's notion of layered enclosure (in the manner of a "Chinese box") as his privileged vision of the universe and, it appears, as one of the models of his text-machine: the novel as a series of integrated wheels. Analogously, Lowry intimates an additional origin of his machine design when he has Geoffrey invoke Ezekiel's vision of the Divine Chariot, "The wheels within wheels this is" (174)—the pivotal revelation of the Kabbalah's Merkabah tradition that describes Genesis as a "Mechanism of Creation" (Blumenthal 13–51).

In ways similar to Dunne's model of seriality, the Aztecs as well envisioned time and space as "concrete multiplicities" that were integrated into one another "like so many hollow wooden Russian dolls." In their view, this chronotopic intricacy was sanctioned by divine intervention, as was the individual's birth into any one of these space-time loci. Hence they believed that each human being was, by predestination, inserted into a divine order, "the grasp of the omnipotent machine" (Soustelle 112). This mythological influence is all the more likely, given Lowry's suggestion that Geoffrey can be read as a political allegory of Mexico and that he believes himself to be at the mercy of just such a universal machine, the Máquina Infernal.

Superimposed on Aztec mythology, Newton's idea of a "world machine" also seems to have provided Lowry with a model for his novel machine. Lowry acknowledges Newton's achievement in the marginal gloss of "To the Panama," and in *Under the Volcano* endows Yvonne, a one-time astronomy major with dreams "of becoming the 'Madame de Curie' of astronomy," with the knowledge to explain the Newtonian universe to Geoffrey (as Margerie did, in fact, to Malcolm). In *Principia Mathematica*, Newton proposed his well-known galactic machine in which the "primary planets are revolved about the sun in circles concentric with the sun" (543). And Yvonne, similarly, envisions galaxies as a "sublime celestial machinery," with "the earth itself turning on its axis and revolving around the sun, the sun revolving around the luminous wheel of the galaxy, the countless unmeasured jewelled wheels of countless unmeasured galaxies, turning ... into infinity" (281). As with Aztec mechanics, of course, Lowry envisioned this divine design in its negated form as a set of interlocking congeries grinding down and ticking away a human life.

Thus, Lowry's conception of *Under the Volcano* is informed by machine models from various epistemes of human history that merge into a synchronically existent aesthetic coherence and that make the novel an archaeology of "world machines": a virtual *paideia* of machine models amalgamated into a kind of archetypal machine.[18] In Ezekiel's "wheels within wheels," especially, Lowry appears to have recognized an *Ur*-engine of sorts, whose simplicity was generalized enough to subsume all the other machine models he crammed into his text and a model that allowed him to codify, on the level of form, his fundamental ambivalence toward technology: for when he models his novel machine on the primordial or scriptural mechanics of the Aztecs and Ezekiel, instead of on contemporary machine design, he suggests again his distance from modern civilization while yet ratifying the aesthetic of machine design as such. This dialectic toward modern technology thus makes visible what Fredric Jameson has called "the ideology of form," the political content of narrative reflected in its design (*Political Unconscious* 99). In a sense, this content of form *is* the design of *Under the Volcano*. The schismic bar of Sigbjørn that, Cain-like, marks the halves of Sigbjørn's dual sensibilities, registers in the split of the novel's form: archaic mechanics, but mechanics nevertheless.

Such machine models, as Peter Brooks and Mark Seltzer have argued, begin to emerge in late nineteenth-century European and American fiction as, for example, the steam engines in Dickens, the multiple machines in Zola (*Plot* 43–47), or the miniature machine designs in Stephen Crane (*Bodies* 113–18). More prominently, they figure repeatedly in *Remembrances of Things Past* (a set of books Lowry knew well), in which Proust, similar to Lowry, would create "an almost archetypal view of the emergence of modernity" by juxtaposing old-fashioned technologies to cutting-edge innovations (Danius 121). Their inclusion, indeed, marks the cultural absorption of the machine—its naturalization—for purposes of narrative meditation and historical reflection, and hence indicates the beginning self-consciousness of fiction and its compositional strategies.

As one of the prototypes of Lowry's machine model, the Newtonian "world machine" engendered the visual paradigm of the mechanics of the Enlightenment. Begun as a metaphor in *Principia*, a model of intelligibility to encode the benevolent causalities of divine design, the notion of a world functioning with the precision of clockwork transformed into a "metaphysics of mechanism" that dominated the scientific tradition through much of the eighteenth and nineteenth centuries (Turbayne 5). Geoffrey's belief in such a metaphysics is evident primarily in his political passivity and historical fatalism, his assumption that "there's a sort of determinism about the fate of nations" (309). His own fate appears to be similarly determined by the inexorable logic of his philosophical convictions. Just as the Máquina Infernal spins as one wheel within the wheels of the Plaza, and as such operates as the pivot within Lowry's narrative engine, so Geoffrey, wheeling Ixion-like inside the Infernal Wheel, integrates himself into a negative, mechanical universe. At the end of the day, once he has been deprived of his wristwatch—his portable model of the Newtonian world machine—the effect of what (in his mind) the infernal gods have orchestrated systematically concludes the narrative: his death.

Yet, Lowry's machine model also raises the possibility of construing Geoffrey's death not (only) in terms of necessitous causation but contingency, the coincidental result of multiplying disparate effects. This model has its origins in Hume's skepticism and the emergent philosophy of science in the nineteenth century, before leading turn-of-the-century scientists (such as Karl Pearson in England, Henri Poincaré in France, and Ernst Mach in Germany) variously qualified the Newtonian paradigm by advocating a notion of probability distinct from traceable cause and effect. Witness the following passage from "Ghostkeeper."

> The minute an artist begins to try and shape his materials ... some sort of magic lever is thrown into gear, setting some celestial machinery in motion producing events or coincidences that show him that this shaping of his is absurd, that nothing is static or can be pinned down, that everything is evolving or developing into other meanings, or cancellation of meanings quite beyond his comprehension. There is something mechanical about this process, symbolized by the watch: on the other hand the human mind ... which has a will of its own, becomes automatically at such moments in touch as it were with the control tower of this machinery. (*Psalms and Songs* 223)

Lowry here suggests, following Romantic tradition, that complete and conscious control during the creative process is impossible but that, at the same time, the artist's unconscious appears to enter into a deep level of rapport with the changing raw material of art, enabling the imposition of structure and order anyway, in however preconscious a way, recalling Ortega's premise that a writer "becomes an engineer for the sake of giving [life] form" (223). What is important here is that while Lowry affirms engineering as a traditional activity of systematized and ordered shaping, this shaping can accommodate that which—in a series of imbricated scale levels (as in the self-organizing models of Henri Atlan)—is nonsystemic and unpredictable: the engineering of chaos and coincidence. The unforeseeable and coincidental—that which defies system or order—are as integral to that system as are prediction and causation. Accidence, contingency, disorder, indeterminism, and unpredictability (and along with it the indeterminacy or proliferation of uncontrollable semiosis) fall under the metaphoric orbit of Lowry's machine as much as their systemic absences do.[19]

This second epistemology becomes visible in the synchronization of *Under the Volcano*'s final two chapters when Lowry engineers the convergence of a series of seemingly disparate narrative strands. The virtual simultaneity of both chapters and of the coincidental death of Geoffrey and Yvonne suggest the plotted coordination of the narrative machine. Yvonne, who has haphazardly returned to Quauhnahuac just that morning, dies under the hoofs of the horse released by Geoffrey as she overhears the fatal shots fired at him; and Geoffrey, through Hugh's cryptic telegram and the membership card in his jacket, and his own incriminating pronouncements, becomes the victim of a case of mistaken identity in a politically volatile country. As plot complications thicken and causalities ramify into a diffusive spray of effects, the reader loses sight of the primary, secondary, and tertiary nodes of causation that "determine" the narrative outcomes and contingencies.

Against a background of ticking clocks and "an abysmal mechanic force out of control," a little girl turns "a succession of cartwheels" (347), a level of interlocking alignment that is complicated through images of widening concentric circles: a restaurant menu that features "a design like a small wheel round the inside of which was written 'Lotería Nacional Para La Beneficiencica Pública,' making another circular frame"; the beam of Hugh's electric torch that projects a "luminous target, gliding before them, in sweeping concentric ellipticities"; and Yvonne's concluding re-vision of the cars at the fair as "constellations, in the hub of which, like a great cold eye, burned Polaris, and round and round in here they went" (329–35). These multiple concentricities, moving from a miniature wheel to the wheels of galaxies, suggest not only the reopening of the novel's aperture from the microcosmic to the cosmic (and thus balance the novel's topographic satellite image of the opening before zooming in on human destinies); their oscillating radii also delineate the maelstrom of causalities that are only partly accessible to human observation. Determinism, order, and their respective absences, "two distinct forms of destiny [that] each fractionally assumed the other's field" (*October Ferry* 213), are both engineered into *Under the Volcano*'s narrative engine. Appropriately, Lowry asks his publisher, "Could Thomas Hardy"—that other English Romantic (pre)modernist who negotiates the binary of causality and contingency—"do as much?" (*Letters* 1:83).

The Narrative Engine as Difference Engine

As an instrument of production in a classically Marxist sense, the machine is an ideal figure to suggest the "product" manufactured during the reading process—interpretation—and Lowry himself once remarked that "the wheels within wheels within wheels" keep evolving "newer, yet more wonderful and more meaningless meanings" (*Psalms and Songs* 227). Such hermeneutic proliferation is fully commensurate with a text stuffed with machines and money, billboards and travel guides, menus and price lists—those exemplary icons of a commodity culture that advertise not the novel's autonomy as a modern objet d'art existing in aesthetic suspension but its condition as a postmodern artifact available for consumption. As such a commodity, *Under the Volcano* operates as an exemplary difference engine, as a *perpetuum mobile* of signification that foregrounds the readers' participation in the production of narrative, in effect making them engineers of meaning themselves.

Gilles Deleuze has, indeed, argued that high modernist and postmodern texts operate as a "literary machine," since "the work of art is a form of production" and as such "does not raise the problem of meaning, but rather of use." What is put to use are the readers' interpretive faculties, since each textual sign, "according to its nature awakens one [interpretive] faculty or another, but never all together, impels it to the limits of the voluntary and disjunct exercise by which it produces meaning." In Deleuze's model, a text is always "essentially productive—productive of certain truths" (a term synonymous, for Deleuze, with "'interpreting,' 'deciphering,' and 'translating'"), but since the readers' imagination is always only partially activated by the provocative nature of the sign, they always only produce partial, nontotalizing interpretations (*Proust and Signs* 129–30). The "literary machine" thus enables the making of a product by empowering the reading subject as actual producer to effect a closure of the textual signs.

Under the Volcano is such a "literary machine." The production of meaning in Lowry's text, just as in Deleuze's model, depends on the interaction between text and reader, between the spectrum of interpretations made possible by the text and the reader's signifying practices. Lowry once remarked that *Under the Volcano* was "written on numerous planes with provision made, it was my fond hope, for almost every kind of reader," suggesting that upon each navigation through the textual topography, and each time in a different register, (ideal) readers can assimilate textual signs into a momentarily coherent interpretation (*Letters* 1:506). During each reading loop, they engage not only their idiosyncratic structure of knowledge, their own "text" or *déjà lu*, to speak with Barthes, but also the experience of prior readings of the novel, in turn enlarging "the already read." Each new reading generates, in theory, increasing semantic stratification and is delimited by *Under the Volcano*'s horizons of finality (the interplay of what I like to call the novel's grammar of syntax and grammar of allusion). On the one hand, Lowry's involuted and seemingly never-ending syntax suggests a deferral of closure, a kind of semantic suspension that is reinforced by Lowry's rhetoric of rupture. Sentences trailing off into dots, truncated pieces of writing, and fragments ending in hyphens form a recurrent part of Lowry's syntactic practice and represent, in their elliptic blankness, the text's semantic lacunae, what Wolfgang Iser has called its "gaps" or "elements of indeterminacy" (*Act of Reading* 165–78). Complementing this void of signification, however, is the novel's surplus of signification, the *combinatoire* of mythic and esoteric allusions from which readers are asked to fill the textual blanks, only to experience the text's interpretive inexhaustibility, a plenitude that is as infinite and indeterminate as the causalities of its plot. *Under the Volcano* is, indeed, "a semiotician's dream, or perhaps nightmare," partly because the novel's polyphonic textuality cannot be "activated or apprehended simultaneously" (Asals 105–7).[20]

What sets *Under the Volcano* apart from most other polysemous texts is Lowry's formal self-consciousness about machine-like meaning making. He achieves the novel's circular design through the chronological dislocation of chapter 1 that—seen through the eyes of Laruelle and taking place precisely one year after the main events—functions as a kind of advance epilogue and that, following a reading of the novel proper, has to be reread so as to integrate its cryptic references into a "complete" interpretation. Similarly, Lowry effects a circular reading process through the Ferris wheel at the end of chapter 1, which operates "in an obvious movie sense as the wheel of time whirling backwards until we have reached the year before and Chapter II" (*Letters* 1:511). The reader who has already returned to chapter 1 is thus retransported into the narrative through the Ferris wheel that mediates between advance retrospective and delayed story and that, following a second reading of chapters 2 through 12, makes possible—or better, enforces—a cycle of reading that knows no end, a kind of vicious circle without escape. Even for the reader, it appears, Lowry playfully engineered *Under the Volcano* to be an infernal machine, a conspiracy against the agent whose imagination is required for its coming into being.[21]

More important, Lowry provides a literalization of Deleuze's "literary machine" through the apparatus in the center of his novel machine, the Máquina Infernal. The Máquina operates, as it were, as a mechanism of meaning making whose centrifugal acceleration suggests infinite trajectories of reading: an anarchy of meaning. When the Consul, during his infernal ride, believes he has lost the passport he never appears to have brought along, the absence of this text opens a zone of identifications, and hence a zone of interpretations, that extends from No-man to Everyman and thus allows the writer and reader to affix multiple identities to the legally nameless protagonist. During his rotations, Geoffrey indeed assumes the identity of Prometheus, "that poor fool who was bringing light to the world." He also transforms into Jesus Christ when he sees an inverted, that is, negated, announcement of the coming of the Antichrist ("999") the moment he is crucified on the Machine itself, only to simultaneously be legible as the Antichrist: namely, that while Geoffrey (who has just quoted from Ezekiel) in effect sits on the Divine Chariot, the "wheels within wheels" of the infernal machine convert his seat into an Infernal Chariot. Exceeding these immediate correspondences, Geoffrey here also represents the death figure of the Tarot cards when he hangs "upside down at the top," a Don Quixote gobbled up by a windmill (now that he has escaped the supervision of his Sancho Panza, Laruelle), and numerous other identities such as Sisyphus or Ixion that surround him with various halos of associations. Each loop in the hermeneutic engine puts a new spin on Geoffrey's identity, allowing the loss of his diplomatic—that is, interpretive—immunity to be reinvested with meaning (221–23).

Thus, *Under the Volcano*'s explicitly dialogic relationship between text and reading suggests the self-consciously provisional and interactive quality of much of postmodern fiction—what one could call a hermeneutics of instability. The writing on the wall of Señor Bustamente's movie theater, "the hieroglyphic of the times," projects indeed the fundamental undecipherability of a contemporary world of surfaces, mirrors, and reflections (25). Further, through the infernal machine, Lowry also suggests a meaning-making process akin to the postmodern notion of intertextuality. It is only fitting that a machine that declares itself to be a simulacrum of other literary models and whose constitution from other machine models makes it into a veritable pastiche of engines produces a character as an intertextual composite. While *Under the Volcano* may not perform the postmodern twist "against interpretation, denying either its possibility or its legitimacy" (Spariosu 61), the novel's texture suggests that interpretive allegorical frameworks characteristic of much of "high" modernism are becoming destabilized. Certainly, the novel's stylistic and allusive overloading is in danger of collapsing under its own weight. But Lowry's experimental play with meaning, the writing of a novel in which allusion and cross-reference, depth and surface ("sub"text and "hyper"text), have become the dominating principles of composition, ushers in a carnival of reading that is quintessentially postmodern in character. *Under the Volcano*, in that sense, engages a Derridean grammatology of citation, a heteroglossia in which linguistic signs reverberate with, and indeed draw from, their prior significations.

This threshold postmodernism, as I like to call it, is also evident in Lowry's engagement with technology. While his writings suggest an incipient critique of corporate capitalism, the agent behind the technological exploitation of Canada's natural resources, he also advocates a measured "conquering of wilderness" as part of the human "process of self-determination" (*Hear Us O Lord* 205). As well, his enthusiasm for modern engineering and his design of narrative engines signify the modernist preoccupation with form and an appreciation for the aesthetic of technology, while his presentation of the Machine as a technologized figuration of the Fall reveals a fundamentally romantic ethos at odds with the modernist aesthetic. Indeed, Lowry's conflicting definition as narrative engineer and romantic craftsman, his resistance to a mechanized mode of textual production in an age of commodified print, the patina of myth gilding his modern machines, as well as the archaic design of *Under the Volcano*'s formal machine model, all indicate a vast ideological rift, a personal barranca between allegiance and resistance to the Machine, and a schizophrenia again encoded in the ø of his protagonist, Sigbjørn. The letter centrally illustrates the double consciousness of Lowry's involvement with technology, the multiple negotiations between "Wilderness" and Civilization, between the Garden and the Machine—what Sigbjørn himself describes as "a conservationist divided against himself" (*Hear Us O Lord* 95). It suggests a mind torn between an originary desire to return to a prelapsarian, de-technologized world and the realization that technology is a central constituent of the (post)modern condition. For Lowry, as for the Romantic tradition from which he emerges, the wedding of technology and nature, of the machine and writing, was indeed a marriage of Heaven and Hell.

5

License to Shoot (and Live)
Malcolm Lowry and the Captivity of Cinema

You will see that this little clicking contraption with the revolving handle will make a revolution in our life—in the life of writers. It is a direct attack on the old methods of literary art. We shall have to adapt ourselves to the shadowy screen and to the cold machine. A new form of writing will be necessary. I have thought of that and I can feel what is coming.

But I rather like it. This swift change of scene, this blending of emotion and experience—it is much better than the heavy, long-drawn-out kind of writing to which we are accustomed. It is closer to life. In life, too, changes and transitions flash by before our eyes, and emotions of the soul are like a hurricane. The cinema has divined the mystery of motion. And that is greatness.

—Leo Tolstoy

In a digital world, Tolstoy's ruminations about the advent of cinema sound like the quaint observations of a sage commenting on the obvious.[1] A century ago the new technology quickly captured the imagination of the masses and the intelligentsia alike, but few writers at the time considered film in relation to their medium of expression. Yet Tolstoy's words were, in the first half of the twentieth century, prophetic for no novelist more than Malcolm Lowry. Written a year before Lowry's birth, in 1908, they foreshadow the oscillations between print and film that were to characterize their coexistence in the twentieth century, just as they preview Lowry's meditations on the two media. By then, the Lumières and Edison, among others, had licensed their projectors throughout Europe and America, and when Louis Blériot crossed the Channel the week of Lowry's birth, his flight adumbrated a significant extension of the cinematic apparatus: aerial vision. Technologically, the stage was set for taking the infant medium seriously, just as it was for examining the reciprocities between print-based images in readers' brains and the spectral images dancing on white screens.

Among readers of Lowry, his knowledge of film is legend. He began to haunt the movie houses of Liverpool as a teenager and was exposed to European art film while attending Weber Academy in Bonn and Cambridge University, and during his time in London and Paris.[2] Later, once his marriages to two Hollywood starlets had drawn him to America, he circled on the periphery of Beverly Hills and imbibed the newest productions coming out of the dream factory. Eventually, his never-ending voyage took him to Canada, where he attended the screenings of the Vancouver Film Society. One among dozens of writers with fantasies of landing a job in the industry, he hoped to turn his masterpiece *Under the Volcano* into a film. Nothing "I have read influenced my own writing personally more than the first twenty minutes of Murnau's *Sonnenaufgang* or the first and last shots of Karl Grüne's *The Street*," he observed with regard to the German Expressionist tradition, and he was very pleased when the prospect of making a film in Germany presented itself: "Nothing would make us happier ... than for film to be made of the *Volcano* in Germany, providing it were done in the best tradition of your great films" (*Letters* 2:445–46).[3]

That project remained unrealized, but remarks such as these—and Lowry's writings are peppered with hundreds of them—have served as an invitation to examine the affinities between his fiction and film.[4] Ushering in the cinematic discourse, Stephen Spender observed that "the most direct influence" on *Under the Volcano* came not "from other novelists, but from films, most of all perhaps those of Eisenstein," and he characterized Lowry's narrative techniques as "essentially cinematic," including "flash-backs within flashbacks and abrupt shifts from extended scenes to close-ups" (xiii–xiv). Muriel Bradbrook, Lowry's fellow student at Cambridge, noted that Lowry "learnt from cinema the art of suggestion, of collocation without comment, and transposed it into his own medium" (67). And more recently, as Lowry's writings on film have been released into the scholarly community, Miguel Mota and Paul Tiessen have accorded him "the double role of artist and theoretician with respect to questions of literature and film" (*Cinema* viii).

This chapter continues the focus of such reassessments by taking a close-up look at Lowry's writings on film, especially his work surrounding the screenplay of F. Scott Fitzgerald's novel *Tender Is the Night*. I want to suggest that these writings, coauthored as part of a joint venture with his wife Margerie, not only chart a comprehensive aesthetic of (avant-garde) film but also afford suggestive glimpses into Lowry's divided mind.[5] A novelist if there ever was one, his increasing preoccupation with film late in his career points to a strained double commitment to print and the screen, a media schizophrenia evident early in his work but becoming fully visible in his post-*Volcano* writings. But rather than writing about film from a defensive, writerly point of view, Lowry suggests that film and fiction be viewed in a productive alliance. While delineating the qualities specific to film, and frequently pointing to its effectiveness as medium, Lowry also notes that cinema could benefit from the literary talents of novelists, just as modern narrative could be revitalized through the literary equivalents of filmic technique.

In the second and third parts, I want to reflect on Lowry's gliding allegiance between fiction and film. While Lowry initially saw both writing and film in terms of inevitability and mechanistic constraints—the one rooted in his fear of being locked into textual enclosures of his own making, the other in the mechanical transport of the projector—he eventually began to embrace cinema as a form of art more responsive to the multiple and fluid rhythms of life. The speed, motion, and fluidity of film seemed to hold the promise of undercutting the constricting constructedness of fiction in favor of a more liberatory, less predetermined, and more nuanced mimetic fullness, just as the visual indiscriminacy of the camera allowed for a kind of cinematic unconscious superior to verbal representations. Such a re-viewing of film may be due to Lowry's increasing familiarity with the work of Henri Bergson in the 1940s and 1950s, who saw in the filmic succession of images a contemporary model of cognition. Such a re-viewing is particularly evident in the novel fragment *October Ferry to Gabriola*, in which Lowry uses bus travel as a cinematic device to advance film as an epistemological model more in sync with representing the processes of human knowing and being than print. As such, this work registers not only Lowry's conflicted fealty to the medium of writing (and may help explain why it remained unfinished in the first place) but also his change in philosophy following the *Volcano:* the shift to a series of distinctly affirmative closures in which the protagonists—as in *Tender, Dark as the Grave,* and *October Ferry*—recuperate their agency after prolonged periods of paralysis. Thus, while Lowry originally saw fiction and film as joint expressions of his mythopoetic mastertrope, *la maquina infernal,* unraveling a prescribed fate in immutable succession, he recuperated cinema as an art form that is in keeping with its, quite literally, animating premise—a *maquina viva.*

Inside "the Cabinet of Dr. Caliglowry"

It may be no exaggeration to say that Lowry arrived at his reflections on film by default.[6] As a notoriously fickle writer trying to define the one identity he hoped he had—namely, a *literary* one—he was not about to make grandiose pronouncements about the medium whose mass appeal had left a bad taste in the mouths of the literati. Possessed of qualities ostensibly anathema to print, film was frequently denied artistic legitimacy, and the young writer whose narratives resembled the textured fluidities of the high modernists was not about to commit what he called "heresy to our profession as writers" (*Letters* 2:226). While Lowry enjoyed the screenings of the Cambridge Film Guild in his college years (though occasionally nodding off to recover from the previous night's barhopping), "it simply became less and less respectable for a literary figure to identify openly with the cinema" (*Cinema* ix). Film would preoccupy him for much of the 1930s and 1940s, but it was not until after the publication of *Under the Volcano*—commonly considered "one of this century's most cinematographic novels" (Kilgallin 131)—and the broad cultural acceptance of film that he turned his focus to the medium.

The initial impetus came when one of the American editors of *Under the Volcano*, Frank Taylor, vicariously fulfilled Lowry's lifelong dream to sign on as a producer with MGM. When Margerie, on vacation in southern California, returned to Vancouver with a skeletal script of *Tender Is the Night* Taylor had given her, the stage was set for putting on paper the reflections on film and fiction that had been germinating with him for decades. Over a nine-month period, from July 1949 to April 1950, the Lowrys shelved their "literary" endeavors and (far from making the small improvements they had initially intended) produced a magnum opus of more than 450 pages that included extensive notes and letters replete with technical meditations on film and fiction, and their location in the media ecology of the mid-twentieth century. No doubt, the fact that they were transmuting a novel into film prompted them to toggle imaginatively between print and celluloid. No doubt as well, writing in a new and desirable genre after the verbal cinematography of *Under the Volcano* afforded them a more literal, though no less verbal, opportunity to visualize fiction in filmic terms. Writing a screenplay, after all, might be said to be writing fiction in reverse: beginning with the scenic arrangements of shots, the power of vision, and the speed and mobility of camera, not the evocative power of words, to conjure up scenes in suitably alphabetized readers. As Pier Paolo Pasolini has noted, if "*the primary structural element*" of a screenplay is its "*integrating reference to a potential cinematographic work,*" writers and readers of that screenplay must endow it with a completeness whereby the imagination "enters into a creative phase mechanically much higher and more intense than when [one] reads a novel" (192). More challenging cognitive processing, to put it differently, leads to a greater acuity of consciousness, and hence to a more refined dialogic between print and screen.

In the epistolary "Preface" to their screenplay, for example, Lowry suggests the dialogue of film and fiction as a crossover between cinematic technique in narrative and screenwriting.[7] Acknowledging that "the novel of all the arts, is the one most allied to film," he notes that modern novelists have stuffed their bag of tricks with cinematic procedures without returning the favor: "An enormous number of writers have learned ... from the film: comparatively few have given anything back. It may be that there are some writers who have learned absolutely everything that they know about writing from the film, but who if given a film to do would still turn in a stereotyped job" ("Preface" 4). By breaking the feedback loop between innovative fiction and film, writers not only deny film its self-realization as a medium, they also see it as a devaluation of their craft: "novelists use their talents to complain, and little else. Should their works be bought by the movies, they continue to complain: should they be given a free hand they very often make a mess of it" ("Preface" 4).

Novelists-turned-scriptwriters, in fact, commonly blame their failure on the "ethics of Hollywood" instead of acknowledging that a one-sided commitment to fiction precludes recognition of film's artistic possibilities. Writers import cinematic techniques wholesale but are unwilling to see the two as equals. Far from saluting cinema's formal suggestiveness, "at bottom they feel superior to it—or to everything except the money to be made by it" (*Letters* 2:225). Yet precisely because of Hollywood's global reach, writers ought to have an ethical investment in film. The impact of film "for better or worse ... on the youth of the world has been colossal: and we shall never know how much our own character has been moulded by it"; similarly, Hollywood serves its clientele as "the only Sunday school, college, or military, to say nothing of sexual training they ever get" ("Preface" 7). Film is *the* instrument of modern thought formation and should not be dismissed as a crude medium surrendering art to education and entertainment. "Most everyone has a stake in it," and literature has a critical responsibility to help shape the "formative power" of the burgeoning sister medium: "More depends on the writer than it did" ("Preface" 9).

Contemporaries like Nathanael West and William Faulkner, of course, were notorious for grumbling about Hollywood, but Lowry may also have had in mind the man whose cinematic novel he had just rewritten in even more cinematic terms. In "The Crack-Up," the sobering assessment of his failures, Fitzgerald took the high road of literary traditionalism to argue against the cross-fertilization of film and fiction. Instead of enriching its narrative repertoire through the new art form, the novel found its linguistic resources subsumed by the shiny, yet monochromatic, surface of filmic representation: "People still read . . . but there was a rankling indignity, that to me had almost become an obsession, in seeing the power of the written word subordinated to another power, a more glittering, a grosser power" (*The Crack-Up* 78).

Much of the "Preface" can be seen to respond to these and similar concerns. Lowry did not share the assumption that commercial and political film automatically translates into artistic compromise. As he was to say elsewhere, "good propaganda, I take it, is good art," adding that when he first saw Pudovkin's *The End of St. Petersburg*, he "did not recognize it as propaganda at all. I merely thought . . . that it was marvellous, the best I had ever seen . . . up to that point" (Lowry and Noxon 32). As if to answer Fitzgerald's failure in film (whose years in Hollywood did not yield one significant script) and to counter the myth that good fiction and scriptwriting do not mix, he notes: "perhaps the best thing we could do was to try to write a good film ourselves" (*Letters* 2:224). As well, Lowry laments that if novelists could see virtue in the subordination of word to image and sound, the appropriate "sacrifice of words would not seem so great. These writers cannot make you see and hear in their novels either" ("Preface" 6).[8] Unwilling to translate sight and sound into their scripts, or, for that matter, to allow these senses to come alive in their novels, writers once more refuse to take a cue from the new medium.

For film to reach its full self-realization, it is crucial to subordinate literary conventions to its visual domain. Invoking Charlie Chaplin and D. W. Griffith (who acknowledged the proto-cinematic techniques of Dickens as a major influence), Lowry notes that the director is "a sort of super-writer in whom nearly everything is sublimated or subsumed in the faculty of vision, but he has to depend to some extent on words." As long as he is able to synergize his visual (primary) and literary (secondary) sensibilities, he can transmute "the most absolute tripe . . . onto a higher plane." Even badly scripted Hollywood schlock can be redeemed in the hands, or, rather, eyes, of a director with a vision. More frequently, however, "the words drag [the director] down," and instead of making a properly cinematic film, the result is a flawed work of art untrue to its media-specific possibilities or what Lowry called its "resources of nobility" ("Preface" 9).

As a case in point, Lowry cites developments in cinema after the introduction of sound, following a generation of brilliant silent films. Sound subverted, for a time, not only the primacy of filmic visuality; early talkies were also marred by "the reappearance of the horrible tyranny of the theatre" ("Preface" 9). Instead of combining sounds, words, and images in ways germane to the infant media hybrid, early sound film defined itself in terms of the stage, and what promised to be an innovative conjunction of sound effects, moving mouths, and moving pictures turned into a regression from which film would not recover for a generation: "There is little future for the poetic drama or Shakespeare in the movies, which cannot do much more than make accessible to more people a sort of simulacrum of plays that were otherwise difficult to see" (Lowry and Lowry, *Notes* 51).[9]

For the same reason, Lowry warns against grafting literary conventions onto the fledgling medium. While *Citizen Kane* can sport a narrator because it is integral to its artistry, "there are about fifty reasons" why its usage, "save in rare cases ... is artistically indefensible on the screen." With a further nod to drama's negative effects, Lowry argues that "that sour and much-abused gift of Joseph Conrad, Orson Welles and the radio" is similar to a manager getting up "to make a speech," or as if a novel should be interrupted by a "mysterious gramophone record in the author's voice" giving you "a précis of the next five chapters" (Lowry and Lowry, *Notes* 51). Intrusive rather than conducive, a narrator in film in most cases detracts from cinema's primacy of vision. Similarly, using written words (as in posters or letters) may be "a decidedly unusual function for a talking picture," but their effect—as silent comments on the scene—is solely visual and hence in keeping with the medium's resources. What might otherwise be considered "a liability or weakness, in fact a limitation of the form," Lowry recuperates to serve the apparatus of cinema (Lowry and Lowry, *Notes* 29).[10] Only if film reaches for formal innovation in sync with its potential can it realize itself fully as a medium, and no forms of censorship (of concern through much of the "Preface") or "such limitations as Hollywood provides" can block its evolution.

It is significant that Lowry locates his script of *Tender* within one such limitation of Hollywood: the failure to exploit film's cinematographic plenum. He describes it as "one of the greatest and most moving films of all time" that returns to "a great tradition" and combines "the emotional impact of Griffith's Broken Blossoms and Isn't Life Wonderful with Citizen Kane" (*Letters* 2:171). A missing link between Hollywood's early triumphs and its current dearth, the script marks the "doldrums of the American movie" and a "prophecy of its recovery" (*Letters* 2:756).

And yet, paralleling Lowry's championing of cinematic vision and *Tender*'s filmability, the script also shows the literary impress of Lowry's legacy. *Tender* is a mirror cabinet of Lowry's major themes, reflecting on *Under the Volcano, Lunar Caustic,* and several stories (Mota and Tiessen, *Cinema* 29). Similarly, Lowry's language to describe cinematic form is often distinctly literary. The "grammar of the film has scarcely been used," he notes, speaking instead of the script's "poetic and visual and aural *drang*" (*Letters* 2:217–18); and the director combines elements into "whatever cinematic poetry he may consider negotiable" (*Cinema* 174). Hard-pressed for money, he advertises *Tender* as a work of literature that is "eminently publishable" (*Letters* 2:269), a conclusion supported by one of its first readers: "Quite simply said, it is a masterpiece—a new sort. I wait to see it filmed . . . but equally, I want to see your full script published with all your notes and comments. . . . It *ought* to be printed as well as played, because much of it is for a mental theatre like Hardy's *Dynasts*" (*Selected Letters* 443).

Christopher Isherwood's praise, no less than Lowry's language, suggests why *Tender* remains unproduced to this day. While brilliant by most accounts, the script turned out "quite impractical, both too literary and too detailed, leaving little or no room for directorial contribution. It was the script of a cinema-inspired novelist, not of a film-maker" (Bowker 471). Notwithstanding his sensibilities for film, Lowry's literary origins, combined with his naiveté about Hollywood priorities, weighed too much on his scriptwriting excursion, and what was intended as a "practical basis for film" evolved into a cinematically insightful rewriting of an ambitious novel whose orbit of gravity remained, fundamentally, literary—a sequel in his never-ending voyage (*Letters* 2:217). More important, Isherwood and Lowry's rhetoric also points to the feedback loop between film and literature in the discourse network of the postprint age: for Hardy's "mental theatre" became possible only after several centuries of literacy had conditioned readers to envision black marks as sequential images; Lowry, that perfect subject of the late age of print, understands reading precisely as such filmic seeing: "we have, so to speak, *seen* the film, and you are supposed . . . to see it in a minute or two," he observed to Frank Taylor upon submitting the script (*Letters* 2:218, Lowry's emphasis).[11] Put differently, as media theorists since Benjamin have argued, it was print itself that ushered in the transition from mental theater to filmic theater, for cinema only implemented technologically the desire for the evermore authentic real that novels and newspapers had been instilling in readers. Lowry can run his imaginary film—his mental cinematography of literature—in the dark chamber of his skull only because he has been thoroughly alphabetized. While another Canadian, Marshall McLuhan, would soon be publishing his canonical claim that media bear the imprint of their predecessors, Lowry's *Tender* provides a more practical demonstration of how these issues inform the work of novelists.

Meanwhile, a century and a half before either one of them, one of Lowry's heroes saw it all coming. When Samuel Taylor Coleridge lectured on Shakespeare, the Bard appears as a medionaut of the future whose plays prepared for screenplays, for the real plasticities of reels: his imagination had "the power of so carrying on the eye of the reader as to make him almost lose the consciousness of words; to make him *see* every thing . . . with the sweetness and easy movement of nature" (57). Let us see how the Lowrys achieved such transparency with literary means in their own screenplay.

Trains, Planes, and Automobiles: The Cinematic Real in *Tender Is the Night*

Lowry's sensitivity to the resources of film and fiction is evident in his commentaries on Fitzgerald's *Tender Is the Night*, which he reads as novelist and scriptwriter, author and auteur. Acknowledging that the novel is "a work of genius of importance" and "scarcely more than a quid pro quo of first rate camera work," the text yet falls short of its literary integrity: its "near failure as a novel" was due to the fact that "it was not realised fully as a book" (*Letters* 2:168, 229). *Tender*, in that sense, suffers from a schizophrenia that is analogous to that of its protagonists and cracked-up author, in that literary and (proto)cinematic aspiration coexist in unresolved tension.

Such lack of integration, however, offers the screenwriter suggestive maneuverability. In contrast to *The Great Gatsby*, "whose theatrical perfection was conceivably a filmic liability," *Tender*'s sprawling form "paradoxically saves it for the movies because it gives one more room to move creatively within it . . . without damaging a perfect whole" (*Letters* 2:229). Lowry warns against adhering to the specifically textual logic of causality, which is anathema to film's scenic unfolding (*Letters* 2:230), and he deemphasizes what he considers the unrealized and easily censored motif at the center of the novel—incest—instead shifting attention to the enabling moment of Nicole Diver's Oedipal urge: a car crash involving the death of her father. The film features a symbolic car as "the traumatic precipitate of Nicole's madness," where it "appears not only as a motivation of Nicole's later actions but as a vehicle of her cure—coming in line here with Fitzgerald's intention" (*Letters* 2:232).

In a more general sense, Lowry reenvisions the novel's scenes to stress the audiovisual dimension of the planned film. He imagines sound as part of a synesthetic *Gesamtkunstwerk* drilling itself into the eyes and ears of the spectator-listeners, thus implementing, at least theoretically, Eisenstein's hope for sound film to reconstruct "all phases and all specifics of the course of thought" (105). When Dick, Nicole, and their American set are making whoopee in a Parisian nightclub, Lowry imagines the scene in terms of the frenetic turbulence of the Jazz Age. At the same time, he visualizes the music in a distinctly cinematic mode, whereby syncopated jazz and disorienting shots coalesce in a kind of *bruitisme* that is reminiscent of surrealist film, or perhaps George Antheil's musical score to Fernand Léger's *Ballet mécanique*.[12] Schizophrenic dislocation (one of the central themes of *Tender*) and cultural dissipation (one of Fitzgerald's central themes generally) combine into a mixture of intoxicating sound images.

> At this moment it is as if a cymbal or gong, which fills the whole screen, is struck a tremendous splintering crash. The gong becomes a kind of cornucopia-shaped vortex into which, as if into the screen, or as though it were the centre of a musical tornado that extends into the screen, all the characters and ourselves are sucked. The momentum of the picture violently increases . . . accompanied by unending and relentlessly good hot jazz. . . ; scenes, sometimes linked by hot breaks, are punctuated by shots of the intersecting planes made by lobby lights, of glass doors, of glass doors revolving, buses and taxis rushing by. (*Cinema* 75)

What is important here is Lowry's fine ear for orchestrating the (dis)harmony of sound and image and the subordination of sound to the vision of film. True to his prime directive about film—namely, that it be filmic—forms of music and noise ought, if possible, to have an equivalent in the very texture of the medium. If they do not, they should be relegated to a secondary (though not unimportant) position in the film. For that reason, when Lowry represents Nicole's split mind from within, he favors blurred "time exposures, of half a second and one second" that capture "far better . . . than auditory hallucination" her vertigo, even though the entire scene "is accompanied by a sort of suitable ectoplasmic half-din" (*Cinema* 95). Similarly, to convey the inside passage into Nicole's sundered mind, Lowry once more subordinates sound to image to suggest what one might call his materialist imagination of cinema. Immediately after the diagnosis, when "SCHIZOPHRENIA" fills the screen, "as if struck by lightning, the screen splits apart, there is a ghastly noise, and we enter the terrifying world of schizophrenia itself" (*Cinema* 93). Lowry's scenic imagination has here been framed by the malfunctioning hardware of film itself, just as the use of a linguistic sign as image, reminiscent of silent cinema, foregrounds filmic montage. While written titles, as Ronald Sukenick notes, "remind the audience of the artifice of the medium" and thus, in a Brechtian sense, "break the usually hypnotic relation between medium and viewer," they also invite increased audience participation, unattached as such signs are to any particular character (162). What can be seen in the exploratory intertitles in the work of Jean-Luc Godard, among others, namely the "peculiar identification of the meaning of this language with the visually concretized events of the film," has been anticipated by Lowry in his script (Kluge 140).[13]

This primacy of cinematic vision also governs the scenic directives of the script. It almost seems as if Lowry, in adapting *Tender* (and in keeping with his historical ambitions), were revisiting the traditions of perception specific to cinema itself. Numerous scenes and more theoretical passages comment on the enlarged registration of the camera. Walter Benjamin has designated as "the optical unconscious" film's extraordinary reach for the real, the indiscriminate recording of visual data beyond the threshold of conscious perception: "the sense that a space informed by human consciousness gives way to a space informed by the unconscious" (*Selected Writings* 3:117). Lowry is similarly conscious of the enlarged, unconscious apparatus of cinema. Much of the action in the Parisian nightclub passes "at such great speed it does not have time to sink into our minds ... nonetheless it all contributes to what one might call the subconscious life of the movie itself" (*Cinema* 76). Earlier, in a more explicitly discursive passage, he describes the camera's work in terms of the unconscious precisely because its mode of apprehension is nonverbal; or, rather, he endows the camera's acuity of vision with a suggestiveness far outsourcing the modalities of conscious, human seeing: "The camera's rôle therefore here is of an interpreter whose intensity of awareness is far in excess of anyone's present ... ; perhaps only a fraction of these things could or should emerge into our full consciousness, all one is saying here is that the camera's evocative power is much greater than that of words" (*Cinema* 60). In the script of a book about the unconscious—emphasizing, in contrast to the literary text, the psychological etiology of the characters—it is only proper to stress the optical unconscious of film itself. Lowry may well replicate in his script on the level of cinematic perception (form) what, in the "Preface," he observed apropos its major themes (content): it was necessary for the film "to apply the technique of psychoanalysis or blind analysis to the book itself, to try to see, or imagine, what it had passed through, and might have repressed in its unconscious" (*Letters* 2:233).[14] Or, as Benjamin put it, establishing the general correspondence, "It is through the camera that we first discover the optical unconscious, just as we discover the instinctual unconscious through psychoanalysis" (*Selected Writings* 3:117).

Paralleling the deeper scan of the camera eye, *Tender* also instantiates the mobilized vision of early cinema. Tom Gunning has suggested that, historically, "camera movement began as a display of the camera's ability to mobilize and explore space," usually when film equipment was mounted on moving trolleys, trams, and, most frequently, trains, thus beginning a collusion of railroad and film technology still in evidence today ("Unseen Energy" 362). Arguing that the railroad be understood as "an important *protocinematic* phenomenon," Lynne Kirby highlights the couplings between train and film: "As a machine of vision and an instrument for conquering space and time, the train is a mechanical double for the cinema and for the transport of the spectator into fiction, fantasy, and dreams" (2). Lowry from the very beginning of his career had experimented with these constellations, culminating in the various cinematic panoramas seen from trains and buses and in the eyes of people's minds in *Under the Volcano*.[15] It was, however, not until his work on *Tender* that he could project back into filmic form the cinematic devices he had been exporting into his fiction for decades and thus celebrate (as a flashback, as it were) their medium of origin.

The beginning of *Tender* is framed in terms of fully mobilized railroad vision. Following a shot of clouds enshrouding the ominous moon, "the clouds become smoke coming out of a tunnel from which we see a train emerging into morning sunlight." Installed in its window is a camera whose viewfinder stops abruptly in front of the sign of Antibes—ΑΝΤΙΠΟΛΙΣ— filling the screen. Shortly thereafter, as "the train forges on, the camera . . . takes in a shattering landscape" such as the Alps, "clear and terrible, cutting the suddenly empty sky with lance points and spearheads like uplifted templars' swords" (48–49). Similarly, as Dick Diver is pulling into New York, we see him "alone in a corner Pullman seat by the window. . . . [T]he El can be seen in motion, with skyscrapers between, a ship standing out in the harbour with tugs. New York looks magical, remote, nostalgic, fantastic, as a vision of Troy" (147). Such panoramic shots from railroad windows exemplify Lowry's awareness of the collusion of camera and train in the formation of a filmic point of view, just as their stylized form nicely illustrates Lowry's cinematic heritage. The abstract mapping of the Alps mirrors the nightmarish set designs of some of Lowry's personal blockbusters, such as Wiene's *The Cabinet of Dr. Caligari* or Murnau's *Sunrise,* and as such reflect the contorted souls of the Diver household. The sleek vision of a miniaturized New York has, similarly, touches of Lang's *Metropolis,* in which (anticipating David Lynch) a smooth, public exterior masks the ailing souls of its inhabitants. Not insignificantly, in both scenes (and in much of the script), the tonal atmosphere is one of chiaroscuro, as if Lowry wanted to gesture toward the black-and-white dynamism of Expressionist films. As he noted after reading the original script draft, the film "should not, cannot possibly be, as the present treatment seems to hint, be made in technicolor" (*Letters* 2:168).

Complementing these renditions of mobile vision, Lowry adds metacinematic notes that comment on the link of train and camera and on the genetic progression of filmic perception: aerial vision. *Under the Volcano* opens quite literally with a shot of global topographic satellite imaging, the verbal rendering of an aerial reconnaissance mission, before zooming in on human destinies. In *Tender,* reinserting such a literary application of cinema back into film itself, the train carrying Dick's friend Abe out of Paris apprehends filmic vision in terms of flight: the train "almost immediately is going at tremendous speed which we glimpse from the receding rails. . . . [T]he camera travels obliquely over the flying rails . . . and diagonally back over the fields and vacant lots and appalling suburbs of Paris . . . as if we were abroad [*sic*] a too low flying plane" (87).[16] And as the script steers toward its midway climax, the car crash is framed by "a sort of God's eye view that sees the future. . . . We now see the road from the air, looking down, where we are able to observe not only Nicole's roadster but . . . around the corner and also at a great rate of speed, the huge truck" (91). In "Cinema Isn't I See, It's I Fly," Paul Virilio alludes to what he calls "the logistics of military perception," and while *Tender* is little concerned with warfare—its major combat zones being the anguished self—part of Lowry's cinematic perception, as that of film generally, is linked, if only indirectly, to the military gathering of visual data (*War* 11). After all, Lowry's first essay publication on film (though not concerned with technique) is titled "Hollywood and the War"; cryptic, military messages echo through his chef d'oeuvre, which is thoroughly informed by local and global warfare; and Lowry himself was repeatedly under surveillance and afraid to be spied on (and, indeed, in touch with several informers).[17]

Underlying these semi-theoretical reflections on camera work is a concern central to Lowry's work in both fiction and film: knowledge and point of view. Not only does the camera harvest the subliminal plenitude of the optical unconscious, it also occupies the literary equivalent of narrative omniscience: a panopticism exceeding that of any single character. During the accident, the camera oscillates between an Olympian perspective of the entire (and parallel) action and a restrictive point of view momentarily located in Nicole's mind, much as the refracted perspectives in Lowry's fiction explore the gray zone between unknowing and all-knowing positions. During the fete in the Parisian nightclub, "some characters may get tight as guinea fowl," thus shutting their already limited apertures even more, "but the camera, if none too sober," has a perspective wide enough to compose "a sinister and beautiful little poem full of meaning" (*Cinema* 75). As he puts it at the beginning of *Tender* to differentiate the knowledge gaps between camera, audience, and individual character, here the jejune film star Rosemary Hoyt who has her eyes on Dick: "There is of course a slight division too between the camera and ourselves: we know slightly more than Rosemary, and less than the camera has suggested. But this establishes from the very beginning the right of the camera to see a little more than Rosemary . . . and ourselves to see and hear more . . . : the camera's role is rather that of a sporting clairvoyant" (51). As with his fiction where gaps of indeterminacy coerce readers into becoming interpretive decoders, so the interstices—or, better, blind spots—between camera, viewer, and character in the script open a hermeneutic space that asks audiences to construe their own picture.

Nowhere does Lowry reach such a "complexity of interpretation" better than in the single major reaccentuation he performed in the script: the integration, if not complete substitution, of the incest theme into the motif of the car ride, the most cinematic of early twentieth-century transport technologies that extends the railroad's panoramic sweep into the space of private transportation (*Letters* 2:232). Wolfgang Schivelbusch reminds us that as the railroad shaped cinematic vision, "the outer world beyond the compartment window was mediated to the traveler by the telegraph poles and wires which flashed by" (31). And Lowry, as if rehearsing the genetic affinity between car and train, similarly notes in *Tender* that "a road in bright moonlight stretches before us with telegraph poles flashing by" (72). Since Lowry writes part of film's technological unconscious into the script, largely by marshaling its major forms of vision, it is not surprising that he introduces the train-cum-car motif in the film within the film, *Daddy's Girl.* Not only does the film prepare for the subdued incest motif, as Nicole, upon seeing the accident on the screen within the screen, has a total recall of her own car crash with her father and screams with "not quite hysterical laughter" (73). Equally important, in this film about the unconscious, Lowry embeds—as with the view from the train window—automobilic vision within the deep structure of film itself, as if to emphasize another milestone in the history of cinematic perception.

Thematically, the car, an Isotta roadster, serves as a vehicle for Nicole's complex etiology. Practically an "important character," the car symbolizes Nicole's "neurosis and sickness," as well as "adolescent phantasy, sexual characteristics, father, patricide," among other "psychological implications" (Lowry and Lowry, *Notes* 12). In the cinematic discourse of the "Preface," Lowry describes it as "a multiform visual symbol" that gives Nicole's schizophrenia a "visual backing" and that projects "the madness itself into far sharper visual focus" than any explicit reference to her Oedipal longing ever could (*Letters* 2:232). It provides a visual synecdoche for her troubled conditions without any possibly graphic shots of her sexual fantasies that would invite censorship.[18]

Formally, in sync with film's panoramic enframing, the car extends the mobilized vision of trains by adding speed and shock to the viewing experience. Following a character's escape onto a train, "the quality of the direction ... should be that of a hyperactive Fritz Lang," with the film going "at tremendous speed" (*Cinema* 87). Sitting with Nicole behind the wheel, viewers "see the corn shocks and patches of woodland fly by faster and faster" (90), a sensation of velocity that is prefigured in a suggestive scene from *Daddy's Girl* filmed from the driver's seat. As Nicole and her father are careening down the street, "We get a tremendous horrendous sensation of increasing speed and the exhilaration of being on the road ourselves, which ever recedes beneath our very chairs," eventually surpassing "the breaking point of exhilaration and excitement" (72). But unlike *Daddy's Girl,* whose dizzying frenzy is disrupted by Nicole's cognizant outcry, viewers get to see the crash of Nicole's Isotta and the truck, whose impact is "so sudden and frightful that the spectator feels the shock. The first shock is succeeded by a succession of later shocks, expressed by a series of static, or almost static, instantaneous shots like newspaper pictures, taken from different angles, following in flashes as swiftly as the previous flashes ... we hear a noise like the Blitzkrieg" (92).

By linking the acceleration of motion with the acceleration of visual intake, including stills to accentuate speed *en ralenti,* Lowry maximizes the kinesthetic suggestiveness of the medium. Spender has noted that Lowry "seems to write with every faculty which is active, or observes action: the calf muscles, the throat swallowing, the frank outward-looking eye observing." His writing fuses "muscular mental energies of body and intellect" to engage readers' entire bodily sensorium (xv). Put differently, Lowry's verbal cinematics is fundamentally kinesthetic, and an aesthetic he now writes back into the envisioned film: the audiovisual illusion is meant to be so real as to afford a seemingly fully embodied experience. Series of stilled images put into motion affect equally stilled viewers in a fully visceral way so that they believe they are in motion themselves, with the road "reced[ing] beneath [their] very chairs."[19] Equally important, based on the effectiveness of the illusion, Lowry connects the viewers' sensation to shock as an experience that coincides with the fully mobilized modernity and with the perception of railroad and car travel (Schivelbusch, esp. 157–58). While filmic viewing at high speeds had, by the 1930s, become almost naturalized, Lowry emphasizes their historical convergence as reels on wheels. Through the shocking scene of the accident, he foregrounds what film theorists refer to as early film's "primal scene": its capacity for terror based on the first generation of viewers as yet unhabituated to the two-dimensional dynamics of film. As Tom Gunning has put it, "Far from credulity, it is the incredible nature of the illusion itself that renders the viewer speechless. What is displayed before the audience is less the impending speed of the train [or car] than the force of the cinematic apparatus. Or to put it better, the one demonstrates the other" ("Astonishment" 118).

An earlier generation of writers had already dwelled on this synergy of speeding cars and fleeting vision. In "En Automobile," Maurice Maeterlinck celebrated the recalibrated eye under the influence of speed.[20] In his comments on industrialized perception (anticipating both Benjamin and Schivelbusch and coinciding with Kipling and Wells), Ford Madox Ford distinguished various "psychological effects" of mobilized vision, arguing that "familiar aspects . . . grow unfamiliar on the motor car" (28–29). The Italian Futurists, under the baton of maestro Marinetti, had since 1909 been singing the virtues of a futurist cinema, fueled by the ecstasies of speed and the "famished roar of automobiles" (*Writings* 39). And William Carlos Williams was among the first "to fashion art from the dreaminess of driving a car" (xvi). His early poems celebrate what he called "the inevitable flux of the seeing eye" by arresting fleeting, drive-by moments in verbally cinematic form (105).

What all these writers had in common of course was their driving experience, which they translated into their kinesthetic vision (even as they experienced it vicariously in film). Williams rushed from house call to house call in his Ford; and Ford and his ilk surrendered themselves to the need for speed, as their Austins and Bugattis raced through the countryside and came to a halt in roadside ditches. Lowry, in pursuit of a different rush, also imbibed the thrill of speed and landed off-road. As if rehearsing the complex psychodrama of the novel he was to adapt for the screen two decades later, he stepped into a friend's MG Magna in the spring of 1931, hoping to get killed out of fear of failing his father in his Cambridge finals. Lowry "'sat on the accelerator for about twenty miles till the thing just overturned from sheer vexation,'" and he walked away virtually unscathed (qtd. in Bowker 120). Two years later, after a couple of pints, he overcame his by now deep-seated fear of driving to go barhopping in the same Magna his mother had bought him (or so she thought).[21] Driving under the influence, Lowry "failed to navigate a sharp bend" and, if it had not been for a flat rock, "would have plunged over a two hundred foot drop" (Bowker 164). These shocks (combined with the theft of the *Ultramarine* manuscript out of his editor's sports car the year before) may have cured Lowry of the desire to sit behind the wheel, yet not without instilling in him the panoramas he had been watching on the screen and importing into his fiction and his script. Like writing—affording Lowry, in theory, comfort and relief—a car could easily become another iteration in his trope of the infernal machine.

Lowry never owned a car again after these early experiences with speed, and in *October Ferry*, his protagonists unload his mother's gift before moving to western Canada, "a special 1932 four-seater convertible MG Magna 'University' model" (115)—a sale that may well be the result of Lowry's history of driving and his concurrent work on *Tender* and the novel itself. This ambivalence about driving had profound repercussions for Lowry's fear of agency and control—of steering the course of one's life—just as it contributed, in however serpentine a way, to his remaining career as a fiction writer.

Incarceration and Imaginary Liberation in *October Ferry to Gabriola*

Side by side with *Daddy's Girl*, the film within the film, the script of *Tender* also sports a fiction within the film, *Duel in Dinard*. Written by Dick's friend Albert McKisco, this "Great American Novel. Like Joyce, only Different," earns its author accolades similar to those Lowry received for *Under the Volcano* (158). But unlike *Duel*, *Volcano* never generated the profits for the writer whose self-esteem was tied to earning what proved to be an ever-elusive income. For that reason, Dick's professional observations on fiction writing offer a perspective on Lowry's post- (and pre-) *Volcano* work. Psychiatrists, he notes, "look for the faculty of communication seen as a faculty of social adjustment, measured in dollars and cents; ... a great work of art that was at the same time a commercial flop would be identified with its author from the point of view of that author's maladjustment rather than as art" (180). Such rhetoric may help explain Lowry's precarious psychological balance as well as his anxieties about writer's block.[22] It may also help explain why, of all the projects started after *Under the Volcano* (which itself evolved into a compositional saga of an entire decade), Lowry brought only the film script to a conclusion. *Tender* was not only doubly pre-scripted as a novel and prior screenplay draft; the writing of his own version, while stuffed with the symbolic architecture of his own world, did not invite the sustained identification of its author with his work. In contrast to his "own" fiction, writing a (non-commissioned) film resisted deep self-analysis, the vicious imbrication of the authorial self in his work that typically led to prolonged bouts of self-doubt and that was, frequently, tied to immediate financial concerns.

Nevertheless, the energies and aftereffects of Lowry's screenwriting stint are fully visible in his post-*Volcano* work, and perhaps no more so than in *Oc-*

tober Ferry, the novel that preoccupied him more than any of his other late fiction drafts, expanding from a short story to a voluminous work he repeatedly rewrote.[23] Both texts feature couples in the throes of marital adjustments and relocations, and both male protagonists are caught in a web of guilt, agency, and paralysis—about their own and their wives' mental well-being, their poor professional judgment, and their sense of dislocation, among others. The motif of schizophrenia so prominent in *Tender* resurfaces in *October Ferry* as an almost literal form of homelessness: the Llewelyns replicate the script's shuttling back and forth between American and European domiciles in their repeated migration within eastern Canada and their eventual relocation to the West, where they are faced yet again with having to move. What is true of the divided mind of Dick, a psychiatrist, is also true of the divided mind of Ethan, a lawyer: it was "not because of any professional disgrace that he [was] currently a non-practising doctor of medicine" but rather because of his psychological hang-ups (77). The ocean liner as "the right image for the soul of a man" anticipates the death of Dick (and literalizes Lowry's favorite phrase of Ortega, "Consciousness of Shipwreck"), just as it suggests the symbolic overlays of Ethan's ferry ride into a new, possibly infernal paradise. Dick's vision of the boat's "bridge with no one at the wheel," in fact, expands into a prominent motif of *October Ferry* and highlights the thematic continuities of both texts (172). Lowry, indeed, gives Fitzgerald's *Tender* a life-affirming ending similar to the way *October Ferry* closes on a note of tender, however uncharacteristic, optimism.

Formally as well, *October Ferry* registers the increasingly powerful hold of film on Lowry's imagination. *Tender* opens with the Greek capitals of Antibes, ΑΝΤΙΠΟΛΙΣ, and the arriving steamer Oedipus Tyrannus, ΟΙΔΙΠΙΟΥΣ ΤΥΡΑΝΝΟΣ, eventually closing with the sinking of the steamer Aristotle, ΑΡΙΣΤΟΤΛΕ. Such a visual featuring of disorienting letters, even more so than in the *Volcano*, recurs in *October Ferry*, including a repeat of the (almost) same Greek capitals when Ethan sees the ΑΡΙΣΤΟΤΕΛΗΣ at anchor in Nanaimo and, later, outward-bound from his ferry (249).[24] More important, Victor Doyen has noted that in writing *October Ferry*, Lowry frequently "first sketched the outline in the form of a scenario, a technique he had developed while working on the filmscript of *Tender*." Ethan's flashback to Eridanus, for example, as he sits in a bar, is in the novel's later drafts subdivided into sequenced "shots" that suggest a compositional practice "typical of Lowry's later writing techniques" (173).

Shot 1—The Llewelyns, beyond the light in the sky, see their little house for the first time.

Dissolve to 2 The Llewelyns enter the house
Cut shot 3 The Well....
11 Fade back to the house.... (qtd. in Doyen 173)[25]

What I want to suggest is that in the wake of *Tender*, Lowry envisioned *October Ferry* as a cinematic work in the tradition of mobilized perception. More important—and subsuming any experiments with filmic form—*October Ferry* advances film as an epistemological model more suitable than fiction for representing the cognitive processes of human being, knowing, remembering, just as he empowers his protagonist with renewed volition to become a meaningful agent in a symbolic world of technological paralysis.

Lowry's heroes (and heroines) are typically stuck in a technological apparatus, moving vehicles that allow their riders, almost literally, to take a backseat as they are watching the world go past. Sitting in/on cars and carousels, trains and buses, ships and planes—emblematized in the arch-engine of Lowry's oeuvre, *la maquina infernal*—these prisoners of technology accept their immobility in part because they refuse to take responsibility for the course of their lives. Condemned to a seemingly enforced passivity, controlled by a machine rather than controlling the machine themselves, these captives surrender to the ambiguous anguish of their technological enclosures precisely because they afford a convenient excuse for their own lack of agency, the deterministic logic governing their (non)action. For characters suffering from such compromised autonomy, it is, after all, a good feeling to be able to pass the buck, seemingly to be held hostage, in the diabolical grip of an engine more powerful than one's self.[26]

Not surprisingly, the discourse of incarceration, guilt, and law is a central motif weaving its way through Lowry's work, with references to *Crime and Punishment* arguably leading the list of allusive overlays.[27] Not surprisingly as well, part of Lowry's understanding of film is identical to such notions of imprisonment. In formal terms, the "tyrannically mechanical apparatus" itself—the measured, Fates-like unspooling of a reel—suggests a predetermined conclusion unwinding with uncompromising logic (Mota and Tiessen, *Cinema* 33). Hence in *Ultramarine*, as a love-torn Dana Hilliot is about to ship out, he envisions Liverpool's Mersey River as "a vast camera film, slowly and inexorably winding," a filmic trap unfurling the form of his life: "Soon he will be entangled in her celluloid meshes, and wound out to the open sea" (132). In a more sustained fashion, Sigbjørn in *The Grave* becomes similarly enmeshed in his cinematic projections. Reading the *New Orleans Time Picayune* on the plane to Mexico, he first sinks into the "reality" of newsprint as he identifies with a Canadian "wife-slayer" reported in the paper. Almost immediately, however, this lettered reality gives way to a filmic consciousness when (much like Humphrey Bogart) he "lit another cigarette in such a deliberate way that he saw himself almost doing it in the act of being photographed, his two rather stumpy fingers pressing themselves against the cigarette and almost squeezing the self-conscious cinematic smoke out into a plume" (54). Once in Mexico City, Sigbjørn waits for two hours in the Palacio de Bellas Artes for the screening of a "surrealist movie" that had simultaneously been playing one floor above—a kind of parallel universe from which Sigbjørn appears to be temporarily absent yet which, "in reality," replays the imprisoning (and conveniently disabling) surrealist script of his life (83). That script also plays out in the bitter farewell of Sigbjørn's wife, a "scene that kept repeating itself, over and over again [in his mind], like a disrupted film repeating itself" (88). In each instance, Lowry figures cinema as an imagined and imaginary enclosure, a self-fulfilling prophecy entrapping its actors and resisting what Sigbjørn is in vain trying to accomplish: "to stand right outside himself . . . to see the situation as objectively as if he were watching a film" (166).

In *October Ferry*, too, the Llewelyns are prisoners of the films surrounding them, just as they are prisoners of the bus carrying them through Vancouver Island. Already the sale of their car in Niagara-on-the-Lake grounded them, and "instead of helping to free them . . . neatly imprisoned them" (130); their proclaimed "'independence of the machine'" made them, in fact, "yet more dependent on it in the shape of buses" (154)—buses that similarly engender a sense of stagnation. Notwithstanding "the beauty of swiftness and light" while traveling, their journey "imposed on the senses finally, in spite of the sheer exhilaration of speed, an extremity of motion which was no motion, where past and future were held suspended, and one began thinking of treadmills, or walking down an upward-moving escalator in a department store" (53). Such a journey, indeed, engenders a feeling of "active resignation and relief" (291). Analogously, films suggest enclosure and inflexible prescription. Similar to the Wildernesses, the Llewelyns reflect continuously on "the eerie significance of cinemas in [their] life" (26). Paralleling Sigbjørn, Ethan reflects that "his life had been less a life than a sort of movie, or series of movies" (42), and when he watches *The Wandering Jew* to escape from the pressing realities of self, he finds that they have already caught up with him, been inscribed in the film itself: "when life was going desperately, and you dropped into some lousy movie to get away for an hour from yourself," one discovered that, "lo and behold, this movie might as well have been a sort of symbolic projection, a phantasmagoria, of that life of yours" (132). Films, no less than buses, run their predestined course, which leaves Ethan rattling in his self-constructed cage: "And against such predetermined doom, as against one's fate in the nightmare, finally you rebel! How? When film will always end in the same way anyhow?" (133).

Yet, contained within that peephole of imprisonment is a loophole of liberation. For all the armature encasing Ethan—whether a wound-up film or a road-bound bus—he nourishes visions that transcend technological enclosures. As Michel de Certeau has noted, "there is something at once incarcerational and navigational about railroad [and bus] travel; like Jules Verne's ships and submarines, it combines dreams with technology. The 'speculative' returns, located in the very heart of the mechanical order" (113). Put differently, the enforced idleness of bus or train travel translates physical immobility into an imaginary mobility that—fully paralleling Lowry's protagonists—is orchestrated by that very machine. In de Certeau's words, "as invisible as all theatrical machinery, the locomotive [or bus] organizes from afar all the echoes of its work" (113). A sitting body gazing out of the window becomes, in effect, the enabling condition for an active mind, the releasing of a thought stream that parallels the speed of the moving vehicle: "paradoxically it is the silence of these things put at a distance, behind the windowpane, which, from a great distance, makes our memories speak or draws out of the shadows the dreams of our secrets. . . . This cutting-off is necessary for the birth . . . of unknown landscapes and the strange fables of our private stories" (112).

As Ethan travels through known landscapes and familiar territory, he begins indeed ranging through the unknown landscape of his imagination and developing the strange fables of his private stories. The mysterious conflagrations while living in Niagara-on-the-Lake; the visits of Ethan's esoteric father-in-law; the specter of his school friend Peter Cordwainer's suicide; the encroachment of suburbia on the beauty of British Columbia; and the status of capital punishment in Canada—these are some of Ethan's spots of time around which his mind circulates with frightening constriction and which have been triggered by the immobility of his chauffeured body and the cues brushing past the bus windows. The large poster ads of "Mother Gettle's Soup," in particular, featuring a young boy whom Ethan believes to be a representation of Peter, recalls his anguish over failing to prevent his death. Paralleling the fluid self of Lowry's other protagonists, Ethan constitutes his imaginary world through his observations of the outside as much as the outside imprints itself on his imagination. Lowry, in fact, displays Ethan's sensation of "merging into [the world around him], while equally there was a fading of it into himself" (76), so intensely that both reader and hero—in this novel about sight—lose sight of Ethan's motorized journey. Notwithstanding sudden interruptions from "the outside" that remind the reader that more than two-thirds of *October Ferry* takes place on a moving bus (with Lowry at one point intending to bring the bus onto the ferry), the narrative for long stretches unfolds in the folds of Ethan's mind, to the point of total absorption: the inward journey of Ethan's mental peregrinations clearly surpasses the outward journey he is, simultaneously, traveling on.[28]

Equally important, Lowry engineers Ethan's (doubly) mobilized consciousness in such a way as to achieve a condition of narration that is reminiscent of film. He blends the speeding Greyhound with the flux in Ethan's gray matter so that the bus functions as a driving movie theater whose windows serve as projection screen and shooting frame, as well as a horizon of hope. Not only do they delimit Ethan's vision for a new edenic life; they also encase the impressions rushing past the window to form "exposures" that register in Ethan's consciousness. In their accumulation, these perceptions yield—as with the panoramas in *Tender*—a phenomenological registry of the world (which Ethan then interiorizes to produce, in montage-like fashion, the disjointed film of his private stories that is *October Ferry to Gabriola*). As he reflects, staring out of the speeding bus: "Suddenly the landscape began to take on a sort of reality but it was not its own reality, but the reality of a landscape seen from a train window, in the sunset, in a film" (61). Leaving aside that Lowry here intimates *in nuce* the history of panoramic vision discussed by Schivelbusch, the window here suggests the frame-by-frame perception of the impression, while emphasizing the segmented fluidity of the process. Furthermore, by mobilizing vision so as to produce the illusion of a landscape rushing toward the in fact stationary observer, Lowry employs a syntax of velocity to circumvent language's resistance to the lived experience of speed, instead emphasizing the unceasing flow of perception. And by thus associating the seen-through landscape with filmic vision that regulates *October Ferry*'s narrative flow, he suggests film's increasing attraction as a formal model for printed narrative and perhaps his, however playful, notion that Ethan star in a film-qua-novel in which (in true Lowryesque fashion) he espies infinite iterations of himself.

Psychologists had of course quickly recognized that montage and flashforward and flash-backward are techniques infinitely closer to perception than is printed narrative (and such psychologists, hence, advanced the first theories of film and emerged, not coincidentally, as a profession side by side with early cinema). In 1914, Otto Rank put on the couch what, in a later version, happened to be one of Lowry's favorite films, *The Student of Prague*. Rank observed that while psychoanalysis "generally aims at uncovering deeply buried and significant psychic material," it "need not shy away from even some random and banal subject" such as "film-drama," and concluded that "cinematography . . . in numerous ways reminds us of dreamwork" (3–4). Two years later, Hugo Münsterberg spelled out with impressive insight the correlatives between human cognition and film, suggesting that in contrast to theater, cutbacks and flashbacks are "an objectivation of our memory function" (41). The entire range of montage effects, Münsterberg noted, can in fact be understood as a technological equivalent to "the whole manifoldness of parallel currents with their endless interconnections," including the unconscious (44).

Given Lowry's wide-ranging reading, it is not inconceivable that he encountered the work of Rank and Münsterberg in formulating his own scattered elements of a theory of film and fiction. More likely, ideas such as the broad equivalence between film, dream work, and perception had by the 1940s sufficiently diffused into avant-garde cinema—evidenced, among others, in the oneiric visions of German Expressionist film as well as the dream sequences of surrealist film—to be recognizable more generally. Still, were one to identify a likely source of Lowry's cinematic understanding of mind, I would point to Henri Bergson, whose theories of time charted the modernist experiments of subjective being, including Lowry's. Lowry began rereading Bergson's *Creative Evolution* in the late 1940s while writing the film script and several works in progress, helping himself, as he was wont to do, to the philosopher's repertoire of images. In *Tender*, as the Divers are watching fireworks on the Cannes waterfront (where film would soon be celebrated as an art form), Lowry accentuates the pyrotechnic display to illustrate "the Bergsonian concept of one fundamental process of life itself, . . . that a movement that is beginning to make itself in one direction, has to unmake itself in the other" (225). Through the "rocket slithering up the sky . . . bursting into a thousand stars" and its shower of ashes raining on Dick, Lowry suggests the chiasmic trajectory of hero and heroine: while Nicole recomposes herself to the point of psychological balance, Dick progressively disintegrates as a man wounded in soul and spirit (225).[29]

More to the point, Bergson in *Creative Evolution* relates the nature of cognition to filmic viewing. Observing that the elementary functions of "perception, intellection, language" do not encompass the process of becoming, he notes that humans "take snapshots, as it were, of the passing reality," snapshots that are spliced into a continuity "at the back of the apparatus of knowledge" and that are characteristic of his notion of becoming. "Whether we would think becoming, or express it, or even perceive it," Bergson continues, "we hardly do anything else than set going a kind of cinematograph inside us. We may therefore sum up [and say] that *the mechanism of our ordi-*

nary knowledge is of a cinematographical kind" (306).[30] What is more, Bergson continues, the segmentation of perception and reflection afforded by film resembles epistemologically the very essence of being and cognition: "The application of the cinematographical method . . . leads to a perpetual recommencement, during which the mind, never able to satisfy itself and never finding where to rest, persuades itself . . . that it imitates by its instability the very movement of the real" (307). Film, to put it differently, allows for an infinite number of (regressive) frames to break down the processing of being and seeing, and thus offers a beautifully effective, if illusory, metaphor to describe the flux of apprehension. It offers a technological trope to suggest an authentic rendering of the core of processual Being.

No doubt, to the champion of fluidity, reading such analogies must have gone down like top-grain gin. The writer who had always celebrated organic rhythm and flux saw himself confirmed by a congenial philosopher whose model echoed his own affinity for film. Not coincidentally, therefore, in the most cinematic novel of his thoroughly cinematic oeuvre, Lowry-cum-Ethan offers what may be his most significant statement on the medium. He declares that film's flux approximates the fluidity of human being and processing—and is hence a more precise, more truly mimetic art form—whereas novels, because of their plottedness, "possessed secretly no reality for him at all" (*October Ferry* 61). This line condenses what appears to have been germinating in Lowry since his Cambridge days and what the increasing cinematization of his fiction and the scripting of a novel not his own exemplify.[31]

Extending the formal-epistemological reach of Bergson, *Creative Evolution* might also help account for the fundamentally life-affirming endings of Lowry's post-*Volcano* works. For characters (and authors) unceasingly striving upward, Bergson's notion of exemplary human conduct might have been a behavioral blueprint: "a will which does not try to counterfeit intellect, and which . . . ripens gradually into acts which the intellect will be able to resolve indefinitely into intelligible elements without ever reaching its goal" (47). Dick in the *Tender* script and Llewelyn in *October Ferry*, in particular, pull themselves together to exercise self-restraint and self-sacrifice for the benefit of others and redeem themselves in the process: both enter symbolic voyages of self-discovery; the journey of both is accompanied by a legendary albatross weathering the storms; both assist ailing people in need; and, most important, both resume their agency as ethical human beings by deciding, hesitantly, to take charge of their lives in the face of adversity. Dick and Ethan both step up onto the bridge of their symbolic vessels, with Ethan ruminating whether "he really was standing ... on the bridge of his own life, of their lives, at one of those moments when lack of continued resolution could wreck them both" (298). Indeed, in the same way Dick is told that the ship "has become uncontrollable from this source," leaving the liner doomed to sink and Dick spiritually redeemed, Ethan's skipper returns the storm-beaten ferry safely into the harbor before eventually heading out again, in effect representing Ethan's decision to be the *cybernos* or steerer of his and Jacqueline's life (240). Unlike his earlier reservation (with further echoes of the *Tender* script) that "a car represented a residual responsibility of an alien world best left behind, a world where, with oneself at the wheel, inexplicable disasters might be expected to happen," Ethan is now willing to act, hesitantly, and to embrace a possible relocation to their insular paradise (154).[32]

What is behind these scenarios of redemption, as I've suggested, is Lowry's increasing gravitation toward what he believed to be film's greater mimetic fluidity and fullness that, so he thought, was closer to the actual processes of being. Having suffered through what all his protagonists painfully come to recognize—namely, "the failure of language as a means of salvation," the limits of discursive logic and signification (McCarthy 100)—Lowry shifts allegiance toward cinema without ever giving up the balancing act between the two media on whose twin bosoms he came of age. In contrast to most fiction fragments after *Under the Volcano*, film—or, more properly, the scripting of another's novel and of his own final novel project—held out the hope for spiritual and artistic deliverance, for reframing the prescribed tragedy of literary print in life-affirming terms. In the words of Wilderness, who remembers seeing a redemptive adaptation of *The Fall of the House of Usher*: "Were we not empowered as the director of that film ... to turn the apparent disaster of our lives into triumph?" (*Grave* 249).[33] While continuing to work in print, both the finished (though unproduced) *Tender* and the unfinished (though published) *October Ferry* suggest the shifting media loyalties of a born wordsmith fully aware of the precarious status of fiction in a changing media ecology.[34] Lowry could thus be said not only to replicate the divided minds plaguing his protagonists but also to merge the formal techniques characteristic of both print and film. For, if Ortega gave Lowry the notion of a self-creating engineer, Bergson may have enabled him to see that trope as extending into evolutionary self-improvement and into what he had been doing, in effect, for more than a generation: filmic montage. As Eisenstein reminds us, indeed, not only does montage as the formal principle of film have a literary origin (in writers such as Dickens writing in the shadow of photography), but as a term of construction and design it derives from the profession of engineering at the beginning of the twentieth century (203–4). Conceiving of himself as a engineer, as "a cutter and a shaper" of narrative materials ("Work in Progress" 74), Lowry defines the novelist as cutting across the literary-cinematic divide to capture the quicksilver of being in the verbal cinema of his texts.

6
Literary Narrative and Information Culture
Garbage, Waste, and Residue in the Work of E. L. Doctorow

Those masterful images because complete
Grew in pure mind, but out of what began?
A mound of refuse or the sweepings of a street,
Old kettles, old bottles, and a broken can,
Old iron, old bones, old rags....

—William Butler Yeats, "The Circus Animals' Desertion"

Taking Yeats's cue that "refuse" and "rags" make up the recycled raw materials of "masterful images," this chapter takes a close look at the trope of trash in E. L. Doctorow's fiction. Similar to the Irish poet, Doctorow assembles images into complex narratives that yield a Yeatsian sheen of, however tarnished, mastery and brilliance. Similarly as well, both are concerned about the modes of consumption that have become constitutive of the economic system of the Western industrial complex, be it the modern Anglo-European world or twentieth-century America. Given the epistemological premises of Doctorow's fiction, however, he also (and very much in contrast to most other writers)[1] employs the trope of garbage or waste to demarcate a unique domain of knowledge for the novel in present-day culture—a domain that is outside the boundaries of received disciplinary practices as well as the contemporary media landscape. Doctorow suggests that the serious novel can give itself important cultural legitimacy by locating itself at the interstices of contemporary knowledge and information production. An unending encyclopedia by definition, the novel is poised to assimilate the forms of knowledge that resist integration into the scientific disciplines of late twentieth-century bureaucratized culture. What would go by cultural residue or waste in the established fields of formalized knowledge can be absorbed into the epistemological broth called the novel. While the novelist can, therefore, be understood as a collector of discarded materials, as an archivist or archaeologist of unacknowledged knowledge, of sorts (or, in more senses than one, a refuser), the novel can be seen as transmuting "nondisciplinary" debris or leftovers into forms of telling knowledge that can speak volumes about a culture's historical moment.

In that sense, extending the trope of garbage into narrative function, the novel can itself be seen as a figurative waste product, a node of both discarded and reassembled texts that complicates existent reports on knowledge and that disturbs the reality scenarios of other media; it operates as a form of leftover cultural assembly, a way of exposing the epistemological blind spots of other media and disciplines in their formation of truth, knowledge, and history. Unlike most other forms of inscription, fiction (in the language of information theory) can serve as a "noisy channel," a dense and multiply coded medium whose content does not yield its signifying potential in one cycle of consumption; its semantic residue is such that even repeated readings will never, in their entirety, exhaust the arch of possible meanings. As with the theme, so with the function of Doctorow's novels—as reassimilators of unassimilated and presumed-to-be unassailable knowledge, they figure the tropes of residue, leftover, and garbage to propose themselves as their formal equivalents.

The Stuff Novels Are Made On, or the Artist in Stitches

Cultural theorists and practitioners have paid attention to the status of trash within the changing frameworks of present-day cultures. British "rubbish" sculptor Tony Cragg, for one, has observed that in a climate of global consumerism, visual artists (arguably beginning with Duchamp) are finding "values and meanings for all the population of objects in the world," including Coke bottles, Wendy's cups, and Campbell cans (qtd. in Meijer 3). Harriett Hawkins has addressed the boundary dynamics between literary classics and trash, their appropriation and transvaluation of one another, in the context of postmodern openness and the attendant destabilization of cultural hierarchies. What happens, she asks, when canonized literature comes in contact with Hollywood schlock, when King Kong and King Lear and Batman and Hamlet become not strange but equal and familiar bedfellows in the cradle of contemporary culture (3–13)? And James Clifford has developed a nuanced model in cultural anthropology whereby discarded or unappreciated objects reemerge as fetishes and prized possessions, changing their status from utter worthlessness to ones with extraordinary monetary value depending on historically specific systems of appreciation. What was once fit for the cultural dustbin, including "primitive art," can, under the influence of reconfigured values (such as "authenticity" and "ethnicity"), become prime material for major museums and art galleries (222–26).[2]

Doctorow, for all his impressive range of essays, has not elaborated theoretically on the cultural importance of trash. Always the novelist, he has taken to writing about the United States and the West from the perspective of a narrative practitioner, preferring to let his concerns emerge in the looser fictional form rather than in the rhetorical cogency of the essay. While early commentators have noted the radical distinctness of each of Doctorow's novels, and indeed have seen that distinctness as a sign of genius, Doctorow himself has drawn attention to the networks of issues and concern that bind his oeuvre, strung as they are historically over a period of roughly a century and a half: "For many years people have been telling me that one book is so different from another, and I've always known that wasn't true. I think not only thematic preoccupations, over and over, but I sometimes think that basically I have a repertory of actors, and I give them different names in each book and put different costumes on them, but essentially they are the same spirits over and over who recur and return eternally in my working mind" (*Conversations* 221). I will return to this troupe and costume motif later but note here that the very repetition of characters and their constellations suggests in itself a form of "intertextual recycling," a way of reworking the leftover residue of his prior texts (as well as of those of some literary predecessors) to extract, one might say, new or unfinished dimensions.

Doctorow's most erudite critics have noted the thematic and formal iterations of his work. Arthur M. Saltzman observes that Doctorow's fiction is centrally concerned not with any one interpretation of history but with "the condition of interpretability as a perpetual option" (38). Christopher D. Morris sees in Doctorow's work similar evidence of a "challenge to the validity of hermeneutics" and a Nietzschean awareness that "no new articulation—*of whatever content, even of recurrence in history*—can escape iteration" (6, 9). Christian Moraru, continuing this line of thought, notes that Doctorow's reuse of literary building blocks enables him to put forth "*a critical commentary* on the sociohistorical ambience . . . within which rewriting is undertaken or within which the reworked text was produced" (xii). And Geoffrey Galt Harpham, extending these critical positions, suggests that Doctorow's textured fictions not only define his "central continuing concern, narrative itself and its relation to power, imagination, and belief," but also instantiate "a technology of narrative," a series of technological principles that typify the historical period in which a particular novel is set and that characterize that novel's very mode of representation (81–82).

Harpham's focus on technological models in the rewriting of history parallels my interest in Doctorow's narrative project most closely. But whereas Harpham suggestively emphasizes the figurative and formal capacities of various technologies, such as the electric circuit in *The Book of Daniel* or computer texting in *Loon Lake,* I want to bring to bear upon Doctorow's work fundamental insights of media theory. That is, I want to foreground the location of Doctorow's narrative as a technological medium within an ecology of other contemporary media against which it, like ambitious fiction generally, has to redefine itself. Doctorow writes with an awareness that the production of every reality is always an "effect" of a media representation and that the novel's possible import in today's mediaverse derives from its marginalization as a medium. One point of entry to demonstrate such media sensitivity is the trope of trash and dirt, which marks the archaeological and revisionary dimension of Doctorow's work.[3]

Consider, for example, the sustained political allegory of dirt and dust in *The Book of Daniel* (1971). Centered around the Rosenberg espionage case during the hysteria of McCarthyism, the novel articulates a critique of the discriminatory practices of capitalism through garbage-dweller Williams, the black janitor living in the subterranean catacombs of the Isaacsons' apartment building. Never addressed as "Mr." or known by a first name, Williams is condemned to shovel coal and live amid trash as the material (and color-coded) equivalents of his social standing, a position further epitomized by his, quite literally, subsurface existence. Another invisible and underground man, he embodies not only the failed self-realization of African Americans and other minority groups in the United States but also the explosive potential of a political system of repression (which has been repressed from view itself) underneath a social façade of harmony: "The cellar smelled of ashes, of dust, of garbage, and of the green poison in the corners for the mice and roaches. There was also the smell of Williams, which filled the basement like its weather . . . an overwhelming smell which proved that Williams ruled in the cellar, that even though his family lived in the house, the cellar belonged to Williams. It was the smell of constant anger" (111). What Daniel's father, in his Marxist analysis, had spelled out earlier for his precocious son—namely, that Williams "was destroyed by American society because of his skin and never allowed to develop according to his inner worth" (44)—is here visualized through the trope of a discarded existence. Boiling under the surface in a sea of volcanic trash, Williams is fit only to reside, vermin-like, among the already consumed debris of a user culture and to move the dusty source of energy that, echoing back to the days of slavery, makes capitalist economies go.

Daniel's narrative analysis of the espionage case surrounding his parents is laced with the trope of dust as well. A radio repairman, Daniel's father listened routinely to rigged cold war broadcasts and would poke "his soldering iron into the heart of the radio as if trying to repair the voice, trying to fix the errors of analysis and interpretation"—precisely what Daniel will attempt to do in his later, fictional rendition of his family's history. When Daniel, therefore, becomes "engrossed with the mystery of the problem, the tracking down of the trouble inside the guts of the machine" as he is working on the radios himself, he gestures proleptically toward his project of cultural analysis that is *The Book of Daniel*, the disassembly of the machinery of law and order whose malfunctioning and mass-mediation brought about his parents' death.[4] Cleaning "out the insides, clear[ing] the dust of years out of a chassis with a small powerful vacuum that was like a flashlight," Daniel prefigures his later work as a narrative archaeologist rearranging the shards of history, a cleanup operation lifting the patina of dust that has been encrusted onto the received versions of events (47–48). As with the silenced record of black exploitation that Doctorow has dredged to acknowledge the dignity and contributions of America's repressed other, so he endows Daniel's literary reconstruction with a rummaging quality to bring to light the dark underbelly of American political history.

Rising from the ashes of the Jazz Age, Joe of Paterson in *Loon Lake* (1980) stages his self-invention in terms of waste and, if you will, shed skins. The novel opens with Joe's anger against the numbing mediocrity of his parents and looks toward a trash-collecting bum, a "maniac" "alive" on the street, as a possible model for transformation: "one we called Saint Garbage who went from ash can to ash can collecting what poor people had no use for . . . and whatever he found he put on his cart or on his back, he wore several hats several jackets coats pairs of pants, socks over shoes over slippers" (2). Joe, in fact, remakes himself in the image of successive father figures and traverses the entire social span from rummaging bum to gallivanting nabob, but the idea of an exterior camouflage, frequently in the form of the clothes of others, sticks with him all his life. Saint Garbage, in that sense, functions (quite literally) as a king of the *Lumpenproletariat,* as an archetypal user of discarded materials or camouflage artist of the skin-deep American dream whose layered disguises suggest the potential for infinite sartorial transformations. He is one of several Carlylean puppets in Doctorow's oeuvre, a dummy or shell to be draped for the occasion, and a model Joe, and indeed Doctorow, falls back on repeatedly.

Many of Edgar's clothes in *World's Fair* (1985), his reminiscences of growing up in 1930s New York City, come indeed from "the emporium of rags and seconds," the S. Klein's Department Store on Union Square, while garbageman Williams appears in recycled form as "Mr. Smith," the black janitor shoveling coal in the basement (153, 26–28). Edgar's trusted friend Arnold is likewise redressed as Arnold Garbage in *Billy Bathgate* (1989), the connoisseur of filth singularly suited for the work of refined collecting. In his daily meanderings through the backyards and basements of the Bronx, Arnold "lifted the lids of ashcans and found things," outsmarting fellow rummagers.

> Garbage was a genius, he found things that other junkers discarded, he saw value in stuff the lowest most down-and-out and desperate street bum wouldn't touch. He had some sort of innate mapping facility.... To love what was broken, torn, peeling. To love what didn't work. To love what was twisted and cracked and missing its parts. To love what smelled and what nobody else would scrape away the filth of to identify. To love what was indistinct in shape and undecipherable in purpose and indeterminate in function. To love it and to hold on to it.... [Arnold] was busy adding his newest acquisitions to the great inventory of his life. (31–32)

Even more than the underworldly dwellers of the earlier novels, Garbage (whose real name, like Arnold's, is unknown) "sat in his ashen kingdom and collected everything as it made its way down to us from the higher realms of purposefulness" (249). In the days when "trash was a commodity" (31), he has the gift of seeing residual use value in junk and reenters it into the cycle of consumption once more. While residing at the bottom of the food chain, Garbage supplies Billy with a gun and others with costumes from his "collections of clothing in big cardboard boxes" (98). A hideout, love nest, party lounge, and more, Arnold's basement becomes an inventory of the refused materialities of 1930s consumer culture, in which Billy cached his cash (in a catalogue extending more than a dozen lines) "under carriage parts and old newspapers . . . and machine parts and acetylene torches . . . and shoeboxes of bubble-gum cards . . . and typewriters and parts of saxophones and the bells of trumpets and torn skins of drums and bent kazoos and broken ocarinas . . . and molding stamp collections and tiny flag of toothpicks from all the nations of the world" (318).

Like Arnold, the Little Boy of *Ragtime* (1975) is a gourmet of garbage who "treasured anything discarded.... He had his eye on his father's Arctic journals but would not attempt to read them unless Father no longer cared about them. In his mind the meaning of something was perceived through its neglect" (96). (For that reason, the boy's notion of knowledge is informed by that which is marginal, unnoticed, and out of the ordinary: "He took his education peculiarly and lived an entirely secret intellectual life," alive "not only to discarded materials but to unexpected events and coincidences" [97].) Everett in *City of God* (2000) is similarly preoccupied with waste and filth. Commensurate with his encyclopedic reach, his notes sport "dung beetles" degrading—as they must have on Noah's Ark—digestive surplus (139). Wittgenstein offers himself to scientists as a "guide to the infernal shambles of human reason . . . the dreck of the real" (192). One of Father Pemberton's mentors fears a more-than-literal sailing trip because "there seems . . . more floating garbage, more oil slick and unnameable waste the farther out you go" (165). And birds, contrasting the human fear of trash (and always in the vanguard of evolutionary change), have made the detritus of modern consumer culture—"an enormous garbage dump north of Madrid"—their habitat of urbanity: "Eggs are laid in old Big Mac containers, nests are lined with cassette tape, the songbirds flitter in and out of rusty cans, grackles huddle in TV cabinets, gulls bomb old sofas with the clamshells of paella" (241).

It should be clear by now that these various piles of trash and stuff offer suggestive modelings for Doctorow's formal concerns. *The Book of Daniel* can easily be seen as a narrative receptacle of refuse that affords a revealing glance at the constitutional bedrock of the United States, similar to Williams's garbage cans that Daniel heard "crashing around under his feet . . . like a storm that would raise the foundations of the house" (112). *World's Fair*, like *Billy Bathgate*, is "an emporium of rags and seconds," a personal and punctual memoir of early youth recollected in the tranquillity of age. *Loon Lake* may be read as a carnival of clothes, a carousel of the American Dream in which puppets change into already worn shirts only to slip into already worn selves. *Ragtime* understands itself as a collection of bits and pieces left over from the lives of others, and the deep soundings of *City of God* suggest a secondhand collection of profoundly eclectic texts—some of which lost, retrieved, and reconstructed themselves—recomposed into a firsthand (and first-rate) polyphony.[5] Variously, all novels propose themselves as narrative archaeologies of junk that offer meaning by reading the cultural tea leaves of the historical moments they portray: their very dregs and grounds.

For that very reason, most Doctorow novels contain explicit models of their self-formation in terms of junk and stuff. In *Daniel*, "EVERYTHING THAT CAME BEFORE IS ALL THE SAME" is a pastiche of rubbish echoing the illusion of historical progress, a palimpsest of trash reflecting on the nature of the compositional process: "I go on a collecting binge," the artist observes, "and when I have a lot of stuff I plaster it up there. There is stuff underneath you can't even see anymore" (167–68). At the end of *World's Fair*, Edgar intimates his future book by making a time capsule from leftovers: "a cardboard mailing tube," already used, lined "inside and out with tinfoil methodically collected from the insides of cigarette packs and gum wrappers." Stuffed with sundry boyhood treasures, including "a silk stocking of my mother's, badly run . . . which she had thrown away and I had recovered," and Arnold's cracked "old prescription pair of eyeglasses" to illustrate "our technology," the time capsule encapsulates *in nuce* the assembly of the *Fair* (369–70).[6] *Ragtime*, perhaps Doctorow's most thoroughly self-modeling novel, is laced with the trope of rags to suggest the sartorial fabrication of the book (or, in a complementary reading, a series of silhouette cuts or character schemata spliced together like a film).[7] And *City of God*, continuing the sartorial trope, invites a reading as the "rag bin" of ghetto tailor Srebnitsky (another "emporium of rags and seconds")—its stitching into a narrative texture from shed and shredded textiles. Like the encyclopedic writer's almost random collecting of used materials, and their artistic refabrication, young Blumenthal recalls, none of "the bits of thread and shreds of rag that accumulated . . . could be thrown out, everything went back into the rag bin. The garments brought to the tailor were threadbare coats, dresses, trousers that he would mend and tear down and reconstruct, somehow, with his bits of thread and rags from his rag bin" (63).

Doctorow has indeed observed that the recycled and uncontrolled element of the creative process is captured well in the literal, "private meaning" of the title *Ragtime*, which is "to take bits and scraps of discarded material and sew them together to make something new" (*Conversations* 216). In *City of God*, Yehoshua recalls explicitly in terms of Srebnitsky's sartorial dexterity with scraps a leading member of the ghetto writing his diary—itself a hodgepodge pieced together from shreds of documents and observations: "He used whatever paper he had on hand. . . . Even now I can close my eyes and see Barbanel's handwriting, a neat Yiddish, like stitches sewn into the page, the characters very small, the words flying off his pen line after line" (94). Elsewhere, Doctorow has expressed his fondness for the "image of the writer as a ragpicker, wandering through the streets, his disreputability and insecurity . . . in the sense that the materials of all novels are the lives the writer has lived or observed or heard about, these materials or rags, bits and pieces of thread, notions of stuff that he puts together somehow into something that didn't exist before" (*Conversations* 198). Like the rag men in *Ragtime* sifting through bins, Tateh morphing from silhouette cutter to loom operator to cutting moviemaker, and Srebnitsky sewing and patching, Doctorow, I would suggest, proposes himself as an Edgar Scissorhands of Narrative, a Sartor Resartus gathering, snipping, pasting, and stitching worn materials into novel textures of collage and montage. In the words of Carlyle's Diogenes Teufelsdröckh, the arch-sewer whose very name suggests discarded being and the wisdom of "devil's dirt" (what Wittgenstein called "the dreck of the real"), "the Tailor is not only a Man, but something of a Creator or Divinity.... What too are all Poets and moral Teachers but a species of Metaphorical Tailors?" (231).[8] Or, as Walter Benjamin suggests in the more modernist idiom of cultural critique that points to the marginalized position of art and to Doctorow's animating concerns: "From the *littérateur* to the professional conspirator, everyone who belonged to the *bohème* could recognize a bit of himself in the ragpicker. Each person was in a more or less obscure state of revolt against society and faced a more or less precarious future" (*Baudelaire* 20).

Literary Recycling, Postmodernism, and the Novel Nomad

Doctorow's tailoring of narrative suggests what may well be his overarching formal motivation: the manual scissors-and-paste bricolage of his texts from remainders and remnants in the service of cultural meaning making. Typically, such paste-of-waste takes the form of intertextual recycling, the continual rethinking of Doctorow's own materials within his work, as well as the rethinking of, frequently American, myths and legends written about by earlier writers. Beginning with the very notions of garbage and rags, which Doctorow reworks from novel to novel, thematic motifs and character clusters circulate in his oeuvre and thus afford a glimpse into the cognitive constellations and compositional logic of a working writer. (For that reason, such connections are frequently most visible between two novels written in sequence.)

Albert Einstein, for example, the "Jewish professor in Zurich [who] had published a paper proving that the universe was curved," makes two brief cameo appearances in *Ragtime* (259, 169) but becomes a central figure in *City of God*, suggesting that Doctorow is working out in detail the implications of the science-humanities rift that has been simmering in his fiction for at least twenty-five years (with the important addition of Dr. Wrede Sartorius in *The Waterworks* and *The March*). The father of Joe of Paterson's host in *Loon Lake* is "millionaire Augustus Bennett founder of Union Supply Company major outfitter army uniforms and military accessories" (62), who reappears, in modified form, as Augustus Pemberton in *The Waterworks*, who had "made a fortune in the war supplying the Army of the North" with a host of shoddy goods (5). Echoing this constellation, a version of McIlvaine, the narrator of *The Waterworks,* reappears in *City of God,* where he is visited by "the Reverend Dr. Thomas Pemberton" in a hospice replete with "the generic blank stares of the pre-dead" (244). These might as well have been the glazed dazes of the zombies in Sartorius's shop of immortality in *The Waterworks,* though the historical moment of both novels are separated by several generations, thus arguably making McIlvaine the aged son of the earlier novel's narrator (who is unmarried and childless at the end of his own book) and Pemberton the son of not Augustus but Martin Pemberton. Conversely, given Everett's reflections on composition to "bend time" (48) and the prominent place of Albert Einstein in his notebooks, the texture of *City of God* may enact a novelistic version of the Einsteinian space-time continuum so that both McIlvaine and Pemberton may in fact be aging but identical personalities traveling in the space of narrative relativity.[9] In their entirety, Doctorow's especially encyclopedic novels have elective affinities with what Everett remarks of the Bible: "a scissors-and-paste job," a "hodgepodge of chronicles, verses, songs, relationships, laws of the universe, sins, and days of reckonings," whose scholarly exegesis is close to "the venerable ancestry of hermeneutics" (115).

Paralleling such intimations of an intergenerational saga of character, Doctorow also interrogates the central myths and motifs of writers gone before (and thus suggests an intergenerational, Joycean saga of literary brotherhood). Scholars have identified Doctorow as "a critic of America's failures to fulfill its dreams and founding convictions" (Parks 11), and a simple glance at the titles of his books suggests the serious encounter with prior literary examiners: *Welcome to Hard Times, Lives of the Poets,* and *City of God* echo canonical predecessors, and the allusive fabric spanning his fiction—including Hawthorne, Melville, Fitzgerald, and Steinbeck; Kleist, Doyle, Stoker, and Conrad—has a more compelling purpose than "to confound the Ph.D.s." (*Conversations* 125). More than locating himself within a tradition of dead white males—important as that may be to serious writers of repute—Doctorow above all wants to reconsider the *grand récits* and clichés circulating within the (largely Anglo-American) literary archive for his own historical moment.[10] William R. Paulson has noted that the dialogic structure of literary history ultimately expresses itself in the production of "new literary works, sent forward in time to their virtual audience and not back in a circle to their author's predecessors" (*Noise* 14). Doctorow has similarly observed, "We may be in a period of literary ecology where writers . . . understand their books as answering other books. Every book inevitably is a response to some other book" (*Conversations* 198). Indeed, in the same way Doctorow continually rethinks the undistilled residue of his own earlier work, so he continually visits old stories to re-view their central concerns and claims. Both empty character manikins and literary myths, in that sense, circulate as vacant schemata in his work, as sartorial blueprints or hand-me-downs to be filled, draped, and pasted together for whatever is called for by the fictional occasion. Each operates, as Wolfgang Iser has put it, as a "structured blank that bears all potential realizations within itself and provides the basis for all its own subsequent realizations" (*Act of Reading* 230).

Fredric Jameson, among others, has noted that Doctorow's privileged narrative form—visible, above all, in *Ragtime*—is that of "pastiche," which Jameson sees as an expression of the postmodern "crisis of historicity." Reading narrative as a "socially symbolic act," as punctual expressions of cultural moments (as he had done in *The Political Unconscious*), Jameson suggests that Doctorow is, almost by default, forced to use pastiche, as the preeminent form of artistic production brought about by the "very logic of the postmodern," to express his political sympathies with the left. While Doctorow exhibits a "well-nigh libidinal historicism," as do many postmodern writers, through his fine-tuned attention to historical circumstance, his narrative forms almost unwittingly endorse and reify the cultural practices of capitalism, both early and late, which his fiction seeks to critique. Far from entering a synergy of representation, narrative form and content—pastiche and theme—are diametrically opposed to one another. *Ragtime,* for that reason, is legible as "the most peculiar and stunning monument to the aesthetic situation engendered by the disappearance of the historical referent" (*Postmodernism* 25)—a claim which, in Jameson's logic, would easily encompass much of Doctorow's work.

Techniques such as pastiche are certainly evident in Doctorow's work, and one can easily enlist other artistic forms—including the notion of a character cutout, as well as dislocations, parallel (almost hypertextual) story lines, and a profound sense of intertextuality—to classify Doctorow's work under the general rubric of a postmodern cultural dominant. To suggest, however, that Doctorow's fiction is of nostalgic pseudohistorical depth, condemned to recycle the blank images of a "stereotypical past" and, hence, to endow "present reality and the openness of present history with the spell and distance of a glossy mirage," is to ignore its nuanced historical sensitivity (*Postmodernism* 21).[11] Doctorow's novels invite a continual reinvestigation of the present by their dialectical engagement with the past, when, as in *Daniel,* they juxtapose cold war paranoia with the radicalism of the 1960s and when, as in *The Waterworks,* the postbellum boom of New York City can be seen as an allegorized foil for the dot-com stock market bubble of the 1990s. (The gradual curtailment of the Isaacsons' civil liberties in *Daniel,* silently enhanced by the co-opted media apparatus of the 1950s, gives the novel an almost prophetic flush in the wake of September 11 and, to readers so disposed, invites reflection on the present, almost imperceptible erosion and compression of civil liberties.)[12] "Historiographic metafiction," Linda Hutcheon's trope for an array of postmodern fiction intent on thinking through the consequences of past history, seems to me a concept more apropos to Doctorow, acknowledging as it does that "there seems to be a new desire to think historically, and to think historically these days is to think critically and contextually" (88). Such an approach, contra Jameson, does not dismiss literary re-creation of the past as a bland nostalgic reflex or anesthetic aesthetic effect but validates contextual, that is, intertextual, thinking as a means of working through *critically* what is at stake when "history," as it always must be, is (re)constructed retrospectively.[13]

What is more, such a metafictional approach also assigns a continued central role to literary narrative in present-day culture. Jameson claims that in our postmodernist moment, "the novel is the weakest of the newer cultural areas and is considerably excelled by its narrative counterparts in video and film," further noting that literature is an "archaic holdover," a quaint hobbyhorse or cottage industry left over from a different communicative order (*Postmodernism* 298, 307). Wrapped in a musty smell, of antiquarian interest only to archivists of the past, the novel is out of touch with its time, according to Jameson, a print-based dinosaur all too willing to "retreat before the democracy of the visual and the aural" (318). Yet, if media and systems theory have taught us anything, it is that any surviving medium, however senescent and belated it is perceived to be, performs vital functions within a media ecology, leading not only to medium-specific differentiation but also to a redrawing of its raison d'être, as terrains of representation and critique are enlarged, redrawn, and redistributed (see, for example, Tabbi and Wutz 8–10). Far from being without power of critique, a piece of textual flotsam on the garbage heap of consumable goods, the novel can perform effective cultural work from the very margins to which it has been pressed.

Thus while Jameson is quick to dismiss literary narrative (and related archaic art forms) as engaging in illusory projects of demystification, blind to the fact that their desire for "achieving transparency" is only a second-order "ideological" effect of an omnipresent system of capitalist domination that strategically preempts effective political critique (*Postmodernism* 316), most contemporary writers believe in the cultural work of writing fiction.[14] Doctorow, for one, has always written in full awareness that "we're living in a national ideology that's invisible to us because we are inside it," a political-critical blind spot which it is the writer's job to transcend and illuminate. As well, the power of the serious fiction writer is such that, without any false pieties, "you might inch things along a little bit in a good way towards civility, toward enlightenment, and towards diminishing the suffering" (*Conversations* 151, 155).

Perhaps for that very reason, Doctorow has a great affinity for some of the preeminent raconteurs of the nineteenth and early twentieth centuries and, perhaps for the same reason, he splices in the modernist figure of the literary guerrilla fighter, the ragpicker or *chiffonnier,* to challenge the complacencies of bourgeois thinking. That tradition, from the early Baudelaire onward, does so precisely by adopting the *chiffonnier* as a parasite circulating on the fringes of middle-class culture, from there inserting himself once more into the cycle of consumption. Typically occupying "the lowest rung of the wretched hierarchy of the . . . *Lumpenproletariat,*" as Richard D. E. Burton has noted, he was "a creature of the night, contaminated by filth and detritus from which he eked a living, a taboo figure, *fascinans and tremendus,* utterly alien to the ordered, well-lit world of the . . . bourgeoisie" (222). Working his way through the deserted city streets at night, the *chiffonnier* would sift "through the rubbish left by those who live by day in search of such items as might be kept, sold or pulped down for further use" (222), thus not only recycling the leftovers of leftovers but at the same time questioning the capitalist models of wasteful consumption and class division.[15] Doctorow's garbagemen, certainly, embody this form of cultural critique, as does Doctorow's self-consciously parasitical and recombinant narrative stitching and the very allegory of leftover or garbage as unfinished business to be rethought and rewritten, as already consumed trash to be reused and unrefused.

An alternate theoretical postmodern model more in sync than Jameson's not only with Doctorow's narrative fabrications but also the continued vitality of print and the possibility of (dialectical) historical thinking is Gilles Deleuze and Félix Guattari's notion of "the nomadic" in *A Thousand Plateaus,* the title suggesting their collective term for all the itinerant and mercurial energies that resist submission to the control of modernist state power. As they put it, "History is always written from the sedentary point of view and in the name of a unitary State apparatus. . . . What is lacking is a Nomadology, the opposite of a history" (23).[16] From fugitive ethnic minorities (such as gypsies and Jews) to migrant laborers (such as traveling artisans and carnival workers) to knowledge outside the protocols of emergent disciplines and bureaucracies (such as orally transmitted texts), the nomad comprises all the subversive forces waging war against official dogma (351)—hence Deleuze and Guattari's trope of the "war machine," invented by nomads "in opposition to the state apparatus" (24).[17] Books can operate as such a war machine, "a literary machine" or engine of discourse emerging from within, but fundamentally locating itself outside state power. When they ask "in which other machine the literary machine [can] be plugged into, must be plugged into in order to work" (4), they have in mind the administrative machinations of the nation-states in the nineteenth and twentieth centuries designed to homogenize difference into one vast Orwellian space of uniformity and compliance.

To illustrate the imbrication of the subversive within state power—the one rarely exists without its twin evil—Deleuze and Guattari introduce the notion of "smooth" and "striated" space, the latter figured in the linear symmetries of Euclidean space, the former in the amorphous and multiply enfolded field of a rhizome, with manifold possibilities of connection and iteration. Each point within a rhizomic mesh is a temporary node of convergence and points beyond itself to numerous new lines and trajectories: "A rhizome ceaselessly establishes connections between semiotic chains, organizations of power, and circumstances relative to the arts, sciences, and social struggles" (7). Because literature, like any discursive form, is a node of notions, a mixed bag of ideas and thoughts, Deleuze and Guattari define it as "an assemblage" that operates, as do all "collective assemblages of enunciation," as a rhizome or smooth zone of subversion within the striated space of state power (4, 22). The "technological model" to visualize this interpenetration of smooth/nomadic and striated/"sedentary" space is the patchwork quilt, "[a]n amorphous collection of juxtaposed pieces that can be joined together in an infinite number of ways." The rhizomic, nonmetric quality of the patchwork quilt—involving "leftover fabric, pieces salvaged from used clothes, remnants taken from the 'scrap bag'"—suggests that "a smooth space emanated, sprang from a striated space, but not without a correlation between the two, a recapitulation of one in the other, a furtherance of one through the other" (476–77).

In their search for literary assemblages to illustrate this spatial enfolding, Deleuze and Guattari cite William Faulkner's *Sartoris:* "She had been working on [the quilt] for fifteen years, carrying about with her a shapeless bag of dingy, threadbare brocade containing odds and ends of colored fabric in all possible shapes. She could never bring herself to trim them to any pattern; so she shifted and fitted and mused and fitted and shifted them like pieces of a patient puzzle-picture" (qtd. in *Plateaus* 476). This passage could well have come from Doctorow to demonstrate not only the fabrication of his narratives from leftover patches and rags but also, in Deleuze and

Guattari's terms, the operation of literary war machines, of nomadic writing, within the matrix of state power. Following such pioneers of nomadic writing as Kleist (whom Doctorow considers his literary "brother"), Deleuze and Guattari observe, "American literature . . . manifest[s] this rhizomatic direction to an even greater extent; [American writers] know how to move between things, establish a logic of the AND, overthrow ontology, do away with foundations, nullify endings and beginnings" (25).[18] Perhaps paradoxically, Doctorow's work is such a war machine, a nomadic novel project positioning itself at the crossroads of official narratives of power and disciplinary knowledges typically controlled by the media. If insurgency is only a "supplementary" objective of war machines, "*if they make war only on the condition that they simultaneously create something else*" (423), then Doctorow's oeuvre can be seen to unfold a rhizome, a series of counternarratives threaded into the master text of state power. Like the meandering ragmen and laborers in his fiction, and like "the nomadic and itinerant bodies of the type formed by masons, carpenters, smiths" whose energies the state always seeks to "regulate" and "sedentarize" (368), Doctorow's novels operate within discursive systems of surveillance—interrogating as mutant and uncontainable energies the dogmas of administrative power. Absorbing the cultural debris left out of other disciplines and media, as well as myths spun out by earlier writers, Doctorow's work can be seen as tracing a subversive figure in the carpet of official narratives, what Geoffrey Hartman has termed "the voice of the shuttle."

Doctorow's infusion of "disreputable genres" (*Conversations* 193) into the domain of respected fiction, for example, suggests a deliberate interrogation of the traditional distinctions between high and low art, popular culture and elite practices, as they have been created and upheld by the culture industry. *Welcome to Hard Times* reworks the formula of the Western to probe the founding ideology of the United Sates; *Big as Life* manipulates a science-fiction structure to bring into view the slippery definition of any American identity; and *Billy Bathgate* partakes of "the great operative myth of individualism in this country," which "expresses itself to a degree beyond tolerance in the gangster" (194). All of these novels recycle "popular genres" as a meaningful "source of who we are and what we're doing" (193), and all of them are heterogeneous formal assemblages that include outlawed literary elements once trashed and refused by the critical-literary establishment. In that sense, Doctorow employs what Walter L. Reed has described as the novel's "half-outsiderhood," generically "a type of literature suspicious of its own literariness," designed to question unquestioned convention and practice (4, 24).[19]

Doctorow's narratives interrogate such mythic categories as good and evil, fact and fiction, as they have been used by the powers that be in the service of ideological control. Most prominently, as commentators have noted, Doctorow, in his essay "False Documents," maps out a discursive space between "*the power of the regime*" and "*the power of freedom*," the former dominant in industrial societies that are grounded in "the primacy of fact-reality," the latter associated with the creative space of literature which, "alone among the arts ... confuses fact and fiction" (*Essays* 152–54). Since "the regime of facts is not from God but man-made, and, as such, infinitely inviolable," and is furthermore recognized by scientists, philosophers, and historians alike (who are telling their own factual stories with fictional means), the novelist can legitimately conclude that "there is no fiction or nonfiction as we commonly understand the distinction: There is only narrative." Given that fundamentally epistemological insight, fictional narrative in particular is called upon to mobilize its energies to unmask and destabilize the polarizations and constructs that, as ossified truths (myths), have entered our very definitions of knowledge, power, and worldview: "The novelist's opportunity to do his work today is increased by the power of the regime to which he finds himself in opposition.... [W]e have it in us to compose false documents more valid, more real, more truthful that the 'true' documents of the politicians or the journalists or the psychologists" (*Essays* 163–64).[20]

Indeed, Doctorow's good guys and bad guys are sometimes hard to distinguish. If Srebnitsky in *City of God* is a literal and benevolent Sartor Resartus, a man resewing old rags for the benefit of others, the tailor's "negative print" may well be marked by Dr. Sartorius in *The Waterworks*, that other tailor whose medical cuts and snips, while at times visionary, have the potential for disaster (59). A surgical genius during the Civil War whose cutting-edge techniques "earned him the gratitude of hundreds of soldiers," frequently by defying medical opinion (129), Sartorius acquires overtones of a Frankenstein when, in his more sinister postbellum phase, he refabricates human bodies—with "spare" parts cannibalized from kidnaped orphans—into octogenarian zombies.[21] But while Sartorius's stitchings no doubt prefigure, in their indifference and ethical complexity, the medical experiments in Nazi concentration camps (where Srebnitsky does his reconstructive sewing) and may well anticipate a Josef Mengele, Doctorow is careful not to unequivocally condemn the "marvelous brain," whose "one working principle ... is to connect himself to the amoral energies human life in society generates" (197). Martin Pemberton, the eternal skeptic doubtful of everything thrown his way, is mesmerized by the brilliant doctor; a panel of experts and the district attorney's office, similarly impressed by Sartorius's Faustian feats, refuse to bring charges; and a state-appointed panel charged with determining the legitimacy of Sartorius's commitment to an institution never releases its report—all indications that a clear-cut judgment on the genius on the edge is impossible to arrive at. As McIlvaine ruminates, "[I]t is the nature of villainy to absent itself, even as it stands before you" (213), thus pointing to the murky gray zone of ethics and epistemology, morality and immortality, that defines Sartorius's brilliantly nefarious work—the possibly consciously unconscionable search for knowledge.[22]

Similarly, among the underworld of *Billy Bathgate,* as in the world of law and order, "a strong ethic prevailed, all the normal umbrages and hurts were in operation, all the outraged sensibilities of justice, all the convictions of right and wrong" (64); and when a member of Dutch Schultz's gang kills innocent victims, Dutch vows, "as a matter of restoring the moral world to its rightful position," to punish the culprit. As in the world above, gangsters unbound "by any rules of civilization" must face the judgment of their peers (263–64). As Billy observes about his learning curve in the "shadow world" of crime, which spans the ethical arch of much of Doctorow's work, "the first thing you learn is there are no ordinary rules of the night and day, there are just different kinds of light, granules of degree.... The blackest quietest hour was only a kind of light" (74).

Most important, as one of "a multiplicity of witnesses," literary narrative can collaborate in a "democracy of perception" to complicate the mass-mediated myths of history masquerading as truths (*Conversations* 113). In *The Book of Daniel,* the radio and the press have, under the influence of cold war paranoia, surrendered their agency and become complicit extensions of the state apparatus. Radio Town Meetings are routinely rigged in favor of militant right-wing sensibilities (48); "long before their trial, the Isaacsons were tried and found guilty in the newspapers" (269); the FBI convicts suspects in the same press release that announces their detention (133); and the press willingly exacerbates public hysteria about an impending Russian invasion (29)—all collectively heightening public willingness to abrogate the law in the service of national security. To correct this mass-mediated, ideologized history, and to rescue his parents from the prison house of prisms—the flat sheen of photographs and screens—Daniel writes his own counter-narrative, a "novel as a sequence of analysis" (341), and a novel that tries to fill the blind spots or knowledge gaps of other media.[23] Similarly, Billy presents his story as a personal account of the Great Depression, and while the police make a stenographic report of Dutch Schultz's final babble (which "made its way into the newspapers" to create the gangster's public image), Billy's parallel record of the same delirium tells a different story. Noting that "there was no truth of history in it," that "my own version doesn't always match the official transcript," it being "more selective" and "in longhand," it stands as an alternate account of Dutch's cryptic mutterings that were partly discarded from the public record (307–13). For that reason, the boy in touch with the dark side does the nomadic work of cultural critique, seeing in "public monuments" the effects of a false consciousness, "stupid lies" that erase agony and suffering in favor of national mythologies of self-aggrandizement, with "soldiers standing in aesthetic hills of dying comrades and lifting their arms and holding their rifles up to the sky" (39). For that reason as well, when Billy throws his criminal clothes "in a trash basket" to don his role as unofficial historian, he stores his record (in a valise) in the "deepest darkest bin" of Arnold's cave of scrap, thus suggesting once again the expository need of the novel medium to unearth the muted data—the leftovers of other media—of public history (311).

And *City of God*, as if to work through the intermedial boundary conflicts suggested in the preceding novels, not only contains a sustained dialogue with storage and information technologies but raises that dialogue to the level of philosophical reflection. In his search for the authentic real, Everett eventually gives up using a tape deck to record the spoken word (248), acknowledging, in contrast to other media, what Pem takes as an epistemological a priori, "that no writer can reproduce the actual texture of living life" (47). For that very reason, Everett comes to rely on verbal recollection as he feels the memory of his parents, imperfectly textured as it always must be, slipping away. Images and photographs, "taken with one of those folded Leicas at the time," to him become reminders not of complexed being but of the "sad truth of the characterless soul ... for the failure of brilliant life to maintain its rich specificity" (129). As a writer, not only is he thus critical of the "simple waxworks melodrama" of film (85) and the "system of social archetypes" that projects hollow holograms, but he articulates—in this novel about the limits of all discourse—what is no doubt Doctorow's own meditation on the epistemological trajectories of film and fiction: "The term *film language* is an oxymoron. The literary experience extends impression into discourse. It flowers to thought with nouns, verbs, objects. It thinks. Film implodes discourse, it de-literates thought, it shrinks it to the compacted meaning of the preverbal impression or intuition or understanding.... In the profoundest sense, films are illiterate events" (214).[24] Even as literary narrative is cognizant of its own limits, Doctorow suggests, it continues to hold out the possibility (without presumption of pietistic superiority) of fostering genuine intellectual thought and of enabling communication, particularly in a world where the Clancys and Crichtons, the Stallones and the

Schwarzeneggers—the icons of "the power of the regime"—have been taken to be the coin of the realm. As he himself put it in a memorable, that is, word-affirming, phrase: "That pictograms, whether corporately or privately produced, may eventually unseat linguistic composition as the major communicative act of our culture is a prospect I find only slightly less dire than global warming" ("Quick Cuts").[25]

Half-Life, Shelf-Life, and Literary Fallout, or Waste Making Noise

No less than journalism, radio, and film, of course, fiction is an always constructed, and hence provisional, form sharing similar narrative conventions. But while literary narrative acknowledges its "inventedness" as composition by a human subject with his or her system of beliefs, other media and discourses tend to erase their human processors. Instead of a visible and erratic narrator or a self-conscious or stylized page design in fiction, the reader-viewer of, say, a feature film typically encounters a fully realized world in which the cinematic framing and behind-the-scenes choreography are part of the overall effect of illusion: the work of camera and editing, among other things, is invisibly visible (if not erased altogether) to produce the appearance of a smooth and complete naturalness. Thus Hollywood, as Everett notes, is financed by conglomerates of "banks and business companies" that leave no room for directing talent, instead producing cookie-cutter schlock (237).[26] The televised and published images of Daniel's parents become vacuous snapshots of history, "soft, sheer flesh shimmering in the air, like the rainbowed slick of a bubble" (88), partly because they erase the agents behind lens and camera. Billy notes that "reporters . . . never wrote about themselves, they were just these bodiless words of witness composing for you the sights you would see and the opinions you would have without giving themselves away" (*Billy Bathgate* 212). And McIlvaine more pointedly observes that late nineteenth-century journalism acknowledged its affinities with storytelling: "We did not feel it so necessary to assume an objective tone in our reporting then. We were more honest and straightforward and did not make such a sanctimonious thing of objectivity, which is finally a way of constructing an opinion for the reader without letting him know that you are" (*The Waterworks* 29). More so than most other media and discourses, the serious novel freely acknowledges its subjective rhetorical assembly and, as such, is well equipped to undo the dirty work of mystification done by (seemingly unauthored) other media, and done (unwittingly, or not) in the service of the state.[27] Telling a story in the first person, in that sense, and telling it in style, as do many of Doctorow's narrators, is more than a convention of fiction: it is both a recognition of the ineluctable provisionality of each record as well as the self-conscious insertion of another narrative into the narratives of other media and discourses.[28]

Locating fiction in such a provisional and inquisitive way goes to the heart of Doctorow's notion of narrative as "a system of knowledge" exceeding those of other media and disciplines. Since journalism and fiction, pace McIlvaine, are basic to human understanding, Doctorow points to an originary primacy of narrative: a way to comprehend meaning and relay experience (what Hayden White has called translating "knowing into telling") without distinguishing ontological categories of more recent date, such as fact and fiction, truth and falsehood.[29] With Roland Barthes, he would agree that "narrative is international, transhistorical, transcultural: it is simply there, like life itself" (251). For that very reason, for Doctorow, fiction is "more capacious as to truth, reality, than any other discipline.... [I]t is the discipline that includes all the others. Its language is indiscriminate, it accepts the diction of science, theology, journalism, poetry, myth, history, everything" (*Conversations* 172). Frequently polyphonic and encyclopedic, his novels transcend boundaries, subsume local knowledge, and offer perspective amid competing accounts of reality. Fundamentally oral without presuming to be oracular, fiction for Doctorow is "an ancient way of knowing, the first science" (*Conversations* 181)—and a science that, like Walter Benjamin's memorable storyteller, offers "counsel for readers" to contain what is the hallmark of modern consumer and media culture: the shrinking "communicability of experience" (*Selected Writings* 3:145).[30]

For that reason, Doctorow sees in "the first science" not a form of data pooling, in the manner of a conventional science or realism, but a metaphoric discourse with multiple semantic vectors opposed to what the regimes of science and the media have introduced into modernity: the category of information. "Hawthorne's idea of romance," Doctorow notes, always had a special appeal for him because it suggests "a curing up of life into meaning. The gamier taste, somehow, than you get in a realistic novel of accumulated data" (*Conversations* 169). Unlike the fiction(s) of verisimilitude (working, by definition, within the protocols of empiricism), with their prescribed levels of representation, Doctorow's novels have the qualities of romance and offer a wider swath of signification. If information ultimately serves the *power of the regime* by circulating discrete units of data in the interest of ideological and/or economic control, the novel's carefully capacious reach beyond disciplinary bounds can destabilize such monologic reality. Opposed to the management of short-lived bits, Doctorow's narratives release aggregates of fact and fable, lore and legend, into the data streams of industrial media culture—sedimentations of human experience that have accumulated over centuries, condensed into what goes by the name of knowledge, and assumed a penumbra of indeterminacy, while drawing on the immediacy of their historical moment. Symptomatically, while the police at the Dutchman's deathbed hope for facts and information, Billy "listens to the wisdom of a lifetime" (307), thus bringing to a point the luminous elusiveness Benjamin has identified as central to good storytelling: "narrative achieves an amplitude that information lacks" because, unlike information, a story "does not expend itself. It preserves and concentrates its energy and is capable of releasing it even after a long time" (*Selected Writings* 3:148).

Doctorow's fiction is of course not uninformed, uninformative, or resolutely opposed to the by now proverbial postmodern culture of information. On the contrary, as Tom LeClair has argued beautifully, novels of high literary seriousness can be seen "as systems of information" that try to accommodate the "scale of information" that is consistent with the contemporary culture of data overload (20).[31] Such novels, including those of Doctorow, commonly "synthesize various aspects of realism and postmodernism," such as traditional plot and narrative fragmentation, and such novels frequently avail themselves of the "full advantage of the scale of information storage that textuality provides." Instead of retreating "from the capabilities of the book," novels of this sort focus on their own medium by foregrounding "the technology of textuality, collecting and testing stores of information, often from nontextual cultures" (23), and, I would add, information or discourses considered unworthy of storage in other disciplines, venues, or media. Indeed, as LeClair notes, such narratives "proceed from, include, and frame information that most novels ignore" (15), thus mapping a space for themselves even within the domain of narrative literature, marshaling their often "thick and profound information" against the "mass media's thin layer of superficial information" (16). Thus, rather than celebrating information for the sake of information, these novelists, including Doctorow (and very much in keeping with Deleuze and Guattari's nomad), could be said to be supra-informational, in that they incorporate numerous data streams to analyze the anesthetizing effects of contemporary media culture, "the master ideologies of American and multinational cultures," such as "statist imperialism and totalitarianism, monopolistic capitalism, consensus politics, industrial growth, and an alienated consumerism of objects, entertainments, and information—a cultural system of waste" (16).[32]

LeClair's notion of information qua waste also usefully returns our discussion to the significance of trash in Doctorow's work. As Benjamin notes, not only does information lay claim to "prompt verifiability"; it also "does not survive the moment in which it was new" (*Selected Writings* 3:148). Immediately consumable, it can be seen as a kind of data junk with only ephemeral use value, while literary narrative, with a wider signifying swing, has a more enduring life span, or shelf life, available as it is for consumption without ever fully yielding its hermeneutic potential. Put differently, fiction (like literature more generally) can be seen to distinguish itself from other forms of text precisely by its communicative unfinality or indeterminacy to produce "noise in the channel"; that is, it sacrifices communicative transparency for a unique mixture of codes that harbors a built-in residue of inexhaustible meaning. In the words of William R. Paulson, "[I]f literature is to deviate from the utilitarian task of communication, it must be an imperfect process of communication . . . in which what is received is not exactly what was sent. Rather than attempting to reduce noise to a minimum, literary communication *assumes* its noise as a constitutive factor of itself" (*Noise* 83). Such noise is the stuff the literature is made on, an informational density or surplus that may produce single-reading closures or temporary interpretative constructs but no conclusive master readings that put an end to all readings. With literature, absolute noise reductions are not possible, only short-lived orchestrations of dissonances into unstable harmonies. To put it differently (and to recap LeClair), the kind of information that literature communicates is not discrete, superficial, and single-planed, as that of the mass media tends to be, but infinite, local, and dispersive. Precisely as such, it complicates and distorts, in a productive way, the single-dimensioned messaging systems of the AOLs and CNNs of the world.[33] For that same reason, such more properly literary information is arguably more enduring.

The trope of trash, therefore, circumscribes not only the gargantuan capaciousness of Doctorow's novels. As I have been urging here, the narrative reach of Doctorow's fiction frequently centers on the residue or discursive leftover of other media and disciplines to bring to the surface, contrapuntally, in the manner of the carnivalesque, their blind spots of mediation; hence, it produces noise, discordant sounds, where other media broadcast in (often conforming) harmony. Locating itself at these interstices of knowledge is fully in keeping with the novel's senescence in an electronic global hamlet; it also—and again in sync with Doctorovian fiction qua cultural critique—relegitimates itself as a medium capable of interrogating, from the margin, the susceptibility of other media to partisan and/or national ideologies. Figurative ash or trash cans, Doctorow's novels invite a reading as productive literary scavengers transvaluating trash into treasures and waste into worth. For the collection of refuse into literary garbage cans, or novels, proceeds from a fundamentally conservative or preservative, not dissipative or dispensive, impulse by giving trash a new lease on life. Edgar, Arnold, the Little Boy and all the other connoisseurs of trash are, at bottom, keepers and recyclers, not disposers, and their collections accumulate never in the attic, there to remain invisible, but in the underground—the locus classicus of the repressed, a culture's seething dirt pressing upward from below. As with Victor Hugo's anatomy of the sewers in *Les Misérables*—"the ditch of truth" harboring "every foulness of civilization, fallen into disuse"— Doctorow's work can be understood as "the conscience of the town" dredging up buried fragments of cultural unhistory (Hugo 2:369). The debris and residue he brings to the surface signify the dark mirror image of official culture pushed into the muck of invisibility, the return of the repressed seeking release through narrative exposure. As such, his novels function as what Peter Stallybrass and Allon White have termed "a poetics of transgression," in which "what is *socially* peripheral is often *symbolically* central" (5). Incidentally, as we know at least since Fyodor Dostoyevsky and Ralph Ellison (the latter's invisible man, like Doctorow's, literally residing in a subterranean hole in New York City filled with trash), the underground is the site not only of decomposition but of composition as well. In notes from the underground making visible the dark underbelly of U.S. history, Doctorow offers his culture what it refuses to smell and see, while simultaneously validating the novel's alterity within the contemporary media ecology.

Ultimately, therefore, the discourse of dirt and dust in Doctorow's fiction may well circumscribe what he sees as the role of print narrative in a world governed by electronic networks. Shortly before the end of *City of God*, Everett notes that "at the moment the last remaining piece of the world is lit and shot for a movie" (257), thus completing the visual storage of the globe into "an arrangement of downloaded ones and zeroes" (110). With the stage set for the corporate-industrial hegemony of film to project a monological, not meta- but megahistory on a Big Screen, Film is about to propose itself as "a form of life," the only form of life, "to which life must aspire, as it has now shown every sign of doing" (238). Then, as Friedrich Kittler has put it, "absolute knowledge will run as an endless loop" (*Gramophone* 2). To absorb what is left out of these digitized images—the waste and residue of industrialized cinema and image production—to wedge itself, with its own sign system, into the interstices of downloaded ones and zeroes, and thus to function as a platform for alternate versions of reality, may well be the (future) task of the novel.

7
The Waterworks
Knowledge and Cognition in the Early Age of Data Storage

When it comes to molecules and cranial pathways, we automatically think of a process similar to that of Edison's phonograph.
—Georg Hirth

Man was created by Nature in order to explore it. As he approaches Truth, he is fated to Knowledge. All the rest is bullshit.
—Dr. Sartorius, astrobiologist, in Stanislaw Lem, *Solaris*

The literary broth of *The Waterworks* is simple enough: Sarah, a beautiful young widow left penniless by her aged robber baron husband, Augustus; Martin, a caustic young ingenue in search of his deceased father's mysterious whereabouts; innocent children at the mercy of the Faustian Dr. Sartorius in obsessive pursuit of an elixir of life; exhumed bodies and brutal murders in the foggy back alleys of Gotham; and the list goes on. We have all the classic ingredients of a detective and science-fiction thriller with their requisite echoes of Dickens, Doyle, and Hawthorne, among others. The madly brilliant scientist is German, of course, and might well hearken back to any number of brainy villains that have stalked the (alternately, urban or lunar) back lots of Hollywood. Welcome to the *Night of the Living Dead*, or, as the case may be, to *Frankenstein, Dracula,* or *Invasion of the Body Snatchers*.[1]

The point here is as simple and obvious as the formula above: in a series of self-conscious maneuvers, Doctorow dips into the reservoir of literary and cinematic narratives that make up *The Waterworks*. Similar to Dr. Sartorius's constructive sewing of old bodies into new ones through forced organ transplants and fluid exchanges, Doctorow doctors with the narrative spare parts of his predecessors to stitch together a new novel that understands itself as a high-and-low and cut-and-paste composite of leftovers. The spirit of thievish recycling is so evident that one reviewer described the book as "a terrific piece of literary larceny" (Jones)—but it is larceny with a twist, of course. For Doctorow, literary and cinematic reappropriations are not self-serving props but time-tested building blocks flexible enough to be updated with a contemporary flush.[2] Thus, the standard chase through the streets of New York, when the police keep bludgeoning a perpetrator already incapacitated, reads like a déjà vu of the Rodney King incident, a historical reflection of police brutality evident in 1992 no less than in 1871, the year the novel is set.[3] The strangling grip of Boss Tweed and his Ring over the municipality of New York City, including the press and the police, "like a vampire's arterial suck," evokes the modern specter of repressive regimes throughout the world. And the medical experiments of Dr. Sartorius himself, of course—involving blood transfusions and the injection of "cellular matter" with hypodermic needles—anticipate not only the inhumanly human cruelties of Auschwitz but, in contemporary terms, also the ethical dilemmas of medical advances and the dubious cultural authority of science.[4] In more senses than one, as the novel's narrator McIlvaine puts it, *The Waterworks* depicts "a panoramic negative print" of our contemporary condition (59), and as such it mirrors one of Doctorow's central concerns: the illusory progress of history, the Nietzschean notion of "eternal recurrence" as the apparently ineluctable course of human and institutional degeneration.[5]

Paralleling such large historical resonances, *The Waterworks* also stages retrospectively the building crisis in information processing and knowledge production following a booming postbellum economy. While Doctorow's late nineteenth-century predecessors were acutely sensitive to the emerging media ecology, especially the growing fissure between the ethos of journalism and fiction writing and the emergence of new data streams, only a writer looking back on such a medial juncture from the late twentieth century can offer sustained reflections (in, significantly, fictional form) on the continued epistemological role of narrative. Through the quixotic figures of a maverick detective and a fictionalizing newspaper editor, not only does Doctorow open a space that interrogates the slippery distinction between knowledge and information in a predominantly empirical culture; he also retraces the cognitive recalibrations of the human mind as effects of an urban data surplus, evident above all in the various forms of personal information processing and the novel's sustained discourse of the brain.

Stars at War, or Data in Gotham

In his study of the technological and economic origins of the information society, James R. Beniger has pointed to the synergy of energy consumption, transportation technologies, and the desire for the fast distribution of industrial output. Their collective effect on the American economy, particularly from the 1850s through the 1880s, was "to speed up society's entire material processing system, thereby precipitating a crisis of control, a period in which innovations in information-processing and communication technologies lagged behind those of energy and its application to manufacturing and transportation" (427). While the pre- and postbellum American industry developed forms of high-speed production and efficient distribution networks to reach consumers, its communicational infrastructure was playing catch-up with a burgeoning economy, having fallen behind by "perhaps ten to twenty years" (432). As a snapshot of New York's exploding economy following the Civil War, *The Waterworks* registers such a crisis of control on a number of levels, just as it registers the cultural pressures of the new economy on the development of communication and information-processing systems. In a Whitmanesque panegyric to Manhattan (similar to Norris's on Chicago), McIlvaine celebrates "the telegraphy singing through the wires. Toward the end of the trading day on the Exchange the sound of the ticker tapes filled the air like crickets at twilight" (6). Later he rhapsodizes that "our city is lit in gaslight, we have transcontinental railroads, I can send a message by cable under the ocean" (105). Telegraphs, tracks, and ticker tapes are the enabling conditions to accelerate the new economic dynamo, just as they facilitate the corrupt business ventures of Pemberton & Tweed, Inc., such as their ongoing slave-running operation and the delivery of shoddy supplies to the Union Army.[6]

What is more, *The Waterworks* also retraces the feedback loop between improved information-processing technologies, historical junctures, and their secondary and tertiary effects, particularly in the area of McIlvaine's profession: journalism. Beniger has shown that "except for the linotype, ... the technological revolution in power mass printing had been essentially completed in 1883, when Joseph Pulitzer took over the New York *World* and transformed it into what most newspaper historians consider America's first modern newspaper" (359). Correspondingly, McIlvaine's paper, the *Telegram*, along with other New York dailies, is in the vanguard of printing technology and data storage: "Our high-speed rotaries had come along around 1845, and from that moment the amount of news a paper could print, and the numbers of papers competing, suggested the need for a self-history of sorts" (28). To have within easy reach "a library of our past inventions," and hence to avoid having to "spin our words out of nothing," the *Telegram* began to archive the stories it had published in previous issues—what McIlvaine calls a "a memory file of our work" (28), or what Roland Barthes a century later would call *le déjà lu*. A simple operation at first, when an old man in the basement "lay one day's edition on top of another, flat, in wide oak cabinet drawer," story processing intensified significantly during the Civil War, as it "became apparent . . . that salable books could be made of collections of war pieces from the paper." At that point, mere collecting ballooned into an entire archival apparatus that occupied several young men equipped with "scissors and paste pots." Their job was to cut up and sort by topics the "fifteen New York dailies a day [that] were dropped on their tables," thus creating a citywide information network or system of "cross-reference filing," an indexed form of data management containing all the published narratives of New York (28).

Even more important, perhaps, *The Waterworks* also records the beginning of new disciplinary practices and their attendant data streams which, in turn, require new modes of processing. While phrenology, as McIlvaine notes, was a pseudo-scientific rage in the 1870s, it can be understood as a "system for organizing perceptions" that mapped the fledgling theories of human behavior onto the topology of the brain and displaced the Renaissance theory of humors (46).[7] In a position worthy of a Bartleby, officer Donne is originally in charge of the "Bureau for the Recovery of Lost Persons" before being promoted to another dead-end assignment tracking urban mortality rates: "the office that certified deaths in the city by age, sex, race, nativity, and cause . . . and recorded them in an annual table for the city atlas that nobody ever read" (86). Donne is also, in McIlvaine's view, responsible for developing the first system of "description-based portraiture for police purposes," whereby a tentative pencil sketch, "composed from the combined words" of eyewitnesses, yields an image of the perpetrator, thus establishing a visual archive for future crime detection (121).[8] Conversely, complementing these forms of administrative logistics, Donne's opponent on the dark side develops innovative medical technologies to allow for data gathering on the human body, such as "apparatus for the transfusion of blood. . . . Apparatus to measure brain activity. Diagnostic uses of fluid drawn from the spine," among others (232). Submitting himself to analysis, Martin in fact recalls the cerebral wave recorder as "a remarkable picturing device" that yields "a graphic representation of the electric impulsings of my brain" (196). Collectively, Sartorius's instruments are part of what Stanley Reiser has called "the translation of physiological actions into the languages of machines," when the subjective character of an examination is transcribed into "an objective, graphic representation that was a permanent record of a transient event, amenable to study and criticism alone or by a group of physicians" (104).[9] Contemporary physicians reverently referred to their ostensibly infallible data-gathering registers as "'the graphic age'" (Reiser 109), and Sartorius, as if to confirm future medical practice, indeed compares Martin's electroencephalic record with that of a man suffering from "a defect of brain tissue" (196).

The presentation of characters as operators in an information-driven culture is hence commensurate with the novel's attention to emerging disciplines and their data-processing systems. Bad guy Knucks, a one-time career criminal with an outstanding record of murder and mayhem, "makes his living no longer with his muscles but by his faculties of observation and deceit" (91), supplying Donne with crucial information from the city's dark side. He is an agent worthy of Tom Clancy, an informer swapping not classified codes about nuclear warheads or submarines but the dealings of Sartorius in subterranean New York. Similarly, as Martin recounts his observations about the doctor, McIlvaine sees him as "a carrier of essential information," "the messenger" returning from reconnaissance to deliver critical intelligence about Sartorius's whereabouts (142). More important, it is Donne and Sartorius themselves—the detective and his nemesis—whom the novel juxtaposes as two Lords of Information, gifted data processors whose capabilities reflect their location within the urban data grid. For that reason, *The Waterworks* reads like an up-to-date retro version of Sherlock Holmes or *Dracula*, a rematch of the cerebral parrying of a Holmes with Moriarty or the Count with van Helsing, whose stories are told by the figures in their shadow: Watson, Harker, McIlvaine. In each case, the masterminds operate as "perfect living encyclopedia[s]" and engage in a kind of data duel where access to information (both arcane and public) is trump.[10] The difference between these true late nineteenth-century arch-villains and their contemporary reembodiment is that, unlike Moriarty and Dracula, Dr. Sartorius is not an unequivocal allegory of the dark side (a critical point to be raised below) consciously working against his detective twin, even as he is networked into a mesh of crime.

Consider, for example, Sartorius's encyclopedic reach for knowledge. Martin notes that the doctor was "fluent in several languages" and "knows everything going on in the sciences," but "reads impatiently, looking always for something he doesn't know." Propelled by a search for instrumental knowledge, he studied "the philosophers, the historians, the natural scientists, and even the novelists, without differentiating their disciplines in his mind. Looking, always looking, for what he would recognize as true and useful to him" (186). Also, as one of the expert witnesses during the Sartorius hearings notes, while the doctor's brilliant procedures would have revolutionized the field of medical technology, he deigns to join the New York Medical Association and demonstrate his expertise: "We have conferences, symposia, we share our knowledge," Dr. Mott observes, "but Sartorius had no regard for any of that" (125). Instead, the doctor exhibits "a terrible intolerance for opposing points of view" and relishes his role as a medical recluse hoarding knowledge for himself (126). Even his meticulous records—withheld from public view by the commission because of their visionary content—were written in Latin, an Old World practice with a quasi-cryptic flush, to bar their immediate, wider circulation (231).[11]

In that sense, Sartorius is very much like the syndicate he is working for, preferring to work in secretive isolation rather than cooperative sharing. August Pemberton, whose capital helps fund the doctor's doctorings, "did not carry on his ledgers a large complement of employees." Instead, "'It's all up here anyhow,' was his famous line, delivered as he pointed his index finger at his head. 'My own mind is my office, my warehouse, and my account book'" (32). Even when required to involve others, his wife recalls, "my husband was a very secretive man. For different matters he hired different attorneys. In that way no one would know more than a part of his business" (80). Pemberton's executor, similarly, managed the Home for Little Wanderers in a way that separated lines of communication to disperse control save for the mastermind: "[T]he division of responsibility among the staff, the teachers and dormitory monitors, was such that only Simmons would have known that anything was out of the ordinary" (174). And Sartorius himself unwittingly describes his own practice and complicity when characterizing his experimental subjects: "each one of my gentlemen was given by nature to secrecy ... they not only wanted what I offered, they wanted it only for themselves" (229). Each in their own way is preoccupied with the exclusive control of data, their synchronized flow within restricted channels, and their use for specific and secretive operations.

Paralleling Sartorius, Donne was a "lonely eminence," a rare breed of a detective living in monkish seclusion "like someone who has taken holy orders" (85). Like the doctor, he is ensconced amid "stacks of loose pages" and "glass-covered book cases [that] were bowed with the weight of law books, manuals of municipal regulations, and volumes of papers in their folders," much like "a scholar working in the silence of a library" (88). For that very reason, Donne, like Sartorius, is a multitasking operator with an awesome capacity for filtering and synchronizing various channels of information. McIlvaine describes him repeatedly as "a walking newspaper who could carry the stories simultaneously in their parallel descents" (116). But while the doctor is trying to master (godlike) virtually all fields of knowledge indiscriminately, Donne only sorts and selects the data necessary to do his job. While Sartorius seems to aspire to become a medical-scientific polymath, perhaps in the Old World tradition of the French *encyclopédistes*, Donne is a more focused knowledge worker. Systematically, beginning with "the hardly likely" (111), Donne sifts through various public and private documents, such as Pemberton's dubious "medical history" and the contracts in "the Hall of Records" suggesting the gradual liquidation of his assets (189); as he combs through a duplicate of the Ring's ledgers, "what he found meaningful was not the usually inflated sums" but "the occasional entries that seemed legitimate in their accounting," eventually identifying a fictitious bond issue for the improvement of the Croton Aqueduct in the accounts of the city's Water Department (152). Assembling these various bits of information, in turn, allows Donne to have "his brilliant and culminating insight" about the site of Sartorius's factory of immortality and, more important, to exhibit a combinatory power uncanny in its precision (208). Donne's instinctual advance knowledge of the coach driver's identity heading out of the orphanage, for example, prompts McIlvaine to rhapsodize about "the conjunctions of which Edmund Donne was capable. What information did he depend on? I can never know. But at this moment the shock to my system was stunning" (159).

Such deductive brilliance is worthy of a Holmes, and the two are indeed blood brothers: both are socially awkward; both operate on the fringes of official crime detection; and both operate with the knowledge that individual brain capacity is indirectly proportional to the exploding data flow of nineteenth-century urban life. As Holmes put it (in his very first appearance): "I consider that a man's brain originally is like a little empty attic, and you have to stock it with such furniture as you choose. A fool takes in all the lumber of every sort that he comes across, so that the knowledge which might be useful to him gets crowded out, or at best is jumbled up with lots of other things, so that he has difficulties in laying his hands upon it.... It is a mistake to think that that little room has elastic walls and can distend to any extent" (Doyle 25).[12] Rather than cramming their gray matter with irritating surplus matter, Holmes and Donne accrue cognitive power precisely to the degree that they are able to filter that which is insignificant or peripheral to their case. To become an efficient information processor in the new economy, the brain must pre-process data prior to, as it were, putting it in storage: only that which is absolutely essential must be committed to memory; the rest, as with Donne's arcane resources, need only be retrievable from other data banks and not block the human data bank, a.k.a. the brain. Postbellum software efficiency is a question of cerebral sorting, storing, and discarding.[13]

Significantly, while one Lord of Information is fully networked into the fellowship of the Ring, and circulates his research exclusively through its closed circuit, the other is out of the loop even while in the employ of the Municipal Police, not only not having paid for his commission but "remaining always outside the order of connived loyalties that passes for brotherhood among policemen" (86). He makes his critical breakthroughs once he is twice removed from the Ring—that is, when his enforced suspension makes him a doubly independent operator—and he does so by both analyzing arcane data ("which nobody ever read") and by repeatedly circumventing the law, as when he enters the orphanage without a warrant (173). The man who is seen as the poster child for the integrity of a corrupt police force thus in reality operates as a self-incriminating maverick pursuing the criminal superstructure of postbellum New York, ironically upholding the law by breaking it himself. Most important, he lets himself be guided as much by rational analysis as by intuitive guesswork, achieving his greatest moments when his dazzling deductions are tempered by daring hunches, when head and gut combine to filter esoteric bits. His unorthodox methods of inquiry make him into a subversive knowledge producer within the system of lawlessness by bringing into play that very system's practices and by inserting himself into its own channels of information.

As such, Donne can be seen as an ideal, particularly urban "nomad" in the sense of Deleuze and Guattari, a viral defector or informational guerilla fighter operating on the margins of official power. Even more appropriately, perhaps, he evolves into the "intellectual operator" Michel Serres has designated as *le parasite,* a term combining the fields of biology, anthropology, and communications theory and suggesting, in William Paulson's gloss, that "the parasite always *interrupts,* be it the circulation of nutritive elements, the service of food, or the transmission of signals" (*Noise* 37). By uncovering Sartorius's lab inside the waterworks, Donne indeed pulls the plug on various types of both life-sustaining and life-withdrawing circulation. What is more, the parasite has "a parallel relation to order and disorder": it places itself in relation to order it has not produced, and its presence brings disorder to the system in which it appears (*Noise* 37). Donne of course is such a disorderly (and disheveled) agent. By intercepting and decoding the signals running through the networks of the Ring, he becomes in effect a circuit breaker in that he destabilizes the data flow and creates a kind of counterorder, a systemic disorder emerging from the corrupt, exclusionary, and monopolistic order of secretive information.

Thus, what may appear to be Donne's initially anachronistic mode of processing is, in fact, highly futuristic in the sense that he implements a politics of informational hygiene (not unlike today's hackers) that questions the exclusionary and dubious machinations of the Tweed Ring. It is forward looking in that he complements his analytical skill with instinctive reaction to allow for a synergy of mind and body; cerebral efficiency and embodied response surmount the rigid "project of Cartesian rationalism, of a knowledge committed to maximal clarity and maximal efficacy," which is a "project of violent domination" akin to the dictatorial rule of Tweed (*Noise* 36). Most important, even as Donne relies on a union of head and gut, his processing is highly selective and relies on both internal and external storage technologies so as to free the brain for higher-function processing operations. Beniger indeed noted that brains had to be synchronized with the increased flow of goods, people, and data in an industrial economy: the use of human beings "for the more objective capacity of their brains to store and process information, would become over the next century a dominant feature of employment in the Information Society" (225). Donne is such a cerebral sorter, a preprocessor fully adapted to the data streams of postbellum urban America, or what the late Peter Drucker, writing about the twentieth century, has called an "emerging knowledge society" (64). Highly refined powers of selection and combination and a memory storing only crucial data make up the essential software protocols of his brain. Everything else, as it were, is at his fingertips in the archival hardware surrounding him.

When Donne is done, of course, the novelist has only received his Jamesian *donnée,* the raw materials of his narrative, but not the story itself. When *E*d *D*octorow lends *E*d *D*onne his initials (and furthermore suggests their joint heritage in America's literary mastermind, Edgar Allen Poe), he may well point to the occupational hazards of both: detectives, no less than novelists, are professional mosaicists composing their stories from events and evidence.[14] But it is significantly from McIlvaine's perspective, not from Donne's, that the story is eventually reconstructed two generations later. Living in an apartment close to Doctorow's former Manhattan office, "three stories up in Bleecker Street," the man of letters attempts to transmute Donne's evidence into epistemology (178). His narrative perambulations probe the slippery boundaries that Donne's hunt for data is unable to engage: what is the difference between data and knowledge, information and wisdom, sanity and insanity, and, finally, what is the place of narrative in a time of exploding data streams?

Brains, Waves, and Recording Machines

In the tradition of thrillers and films like *Frankenstein* and *The Cabinet of Dr. Caligari,* whose gothic conventions the novel reworks, and in the tradition of epistemological science fiction like *Solaris, The Waterworks* interrogates the ethical consequences of human being and creation. If humankind is, by some accounts, considered the brainchild of evolution, what are we to make of the ultimate fruit of this brainchild: the achievements of human intellect? While Tweed's dealings are indisputably illegal and corrupt on a large scale, the "Commissio de Lunatico Inquirendo" evaluating Sartorius's mind is less sure about a judgment. It ultimately decides to put the doctor into the state's Institution for the Criminally Insane, but when McIlvaine interviews the commission's chair, his responses are one long exercise in waffling and sidestepping, alternately acknowledging the doctor's visionary brilliance and genius yet unable to certify any mental instability. Dr. Hamilton suggests that Sartorius "kept going ... through, beyond ... sanity, whatever that is. Or morality, whatever that is. But in perfect line with everything he'd done before," especially his cutting-edge work as a surgeon during the Civil War that earned him the gratitude of hundreds of soldiers. Most symptomatically, in response to McIlvaine's query that Dr. Sartorius wasn't "truly insane," he simply responds, "No. Yes"—giving expression not only to the commission's ambiguous verdict but also to the gray zones produced by the gray matter that lie outside neat binaries: the imponderables of truth, justice, and the human mind itself (231).

Doctorow's narrative symbology tells a similar story: all the bad guys die from a sustained injury to the head or brain. Informer Knucks, a "brainlessly amoral charmer," has his neck wrung by Sartorius's willing executioner, Wrangel (115), who, in turn, not only gets his noggin smashed by overzealous troopers (prompting McIlvaine to ponder "the effects of the blow on the encased brain" [158]) but dies from "bruises on the ... skull" followed by a hanging (206). Pemberton's right-hand man, Simmons, falls off a cliff and has "his head almost entirely pounded into the sandbank," with "a great mess of blood matter around the head" and thus prefigures the death of his boss (226). An institutionalized inmate, Sartorius is one day found—in a replay of his henchman's feats—with his head "smashed against the asylum stone floor with such force ... that the skull caved in like an eggshell and the brain ... there is no other word for it ... ran" (246). Together with Boss Tweed, who, on the lam, stumbles like a delirious "madman" through the Cuban jungle (244), these more than literal deaths suggest not only ambiguous poetic justice but also a possibly catastrophic disconnect between body and brain, matter and mind. Ubiquitous corruption and unrestrained scientific practice are seen as diseased outgrowths of the human brain, fantasies of godlike power born of an organ that has gone postal.

Such a rhetoric of skulls and brains is of course part of the cultural imaginary of nineteenth-century America. In 1871, the year of the novel's events, McIlvaine's paper reports that scientists discovered "the skull of a Neanderthal," with the "cranium severed from the jaw and brow" to serve as "a drinking bowl" (46). During the same decade, a faddish phrenology assumed that "configurations of the skull" allowed for a mental typology of human beings, as with Martin's "high brainy brow," and raised the issue of whether female heads require their own "special skull reading" (46). Such news fillers suggest not only a kind of evolutionary self-distancing of the brain from its primordial functions—thought and survival—but also its versatility for projections of various sorts, dependent only on the imaginative (that is, cerebral) reach of the mind. This is also true of the evolutionary (that is, imaginative) discourse that entered mainstream America. When Sartorius, once incarcerated with the criminally insane, sees in the motley crew surrounding him evidence of a nature "always willing to transform, to experiment, to propose itself into a new shape, a new way of being, a new mind," he also comments on the questionable achievements of his own brain, as well as the mutations of cerebral effort and endeavor more generally (240).

Most important, perhaps, the novel foregrounds the discourse of the mind, and its (in)ability to process and remember, in the context of Dr. Sartorius's pioneering work on brain research.[15] In their entirety, his contributions read like samples, both actual and visionary, of the work of some of the pioneering (experimental) psychologists of the day. Similar to Paul Broca's groundbreaking autopsy in 1861, which located the speech center in the brain (appropriately called Broca's area since), Sartorius dissects the corpse of one of his patients whose epileptic seizures he had earlier attributed to degenerative brain disease: syphilis. Opening the skull, Sartorius gives Martin a walking tour of the brain, pointing to cranial depressions that correspond to "three hard and irregular coral-like growths on the surface of the brain—as if the brain itself had absorbed the bony material." Noting that "these adhesions about the fissure of Silvius" bind "the anterior and middle into one mass" and that "the dura mater in this area adheres to the brain tissue," he extracts and weighs the diseased portion of the brain—"a suppurating, yellowish cheesy deposit, shaped like a pyramid"—only to confirm the findings of Philippe Ricord's 1838 groundbreaking study, *Treatise on the Venereal,* about degenerative brain disease (194).[16]

Similarly, Sartorius uses the electroencephalic record of a certain Monsieur (a "tic-ridden, stuttering spastic") to diagnose his cognitive disorder: the "compulsive imitation" to return "every fleeting expression on your face." He observes that such behavior had to arise from "a defect of the brain tissue" because the cerebral graph—a "wild disarray of peaks and valleys, irregular, jagged, profuse"—indicates "merely an acceleration and intensification of normal human activity" (196).[17] Such medical practice not only looks forward to contemporary clinical methods, in which EEG is used to determine brain wave activity in obsessive-compulsive patients, but may also suggest the external origin of such disorder: overstimulation. Michael Gazzaniga notes that current cognitive research "points to one overall picture of the essential nature of obsessives. They are overaroused by events that nonobsessive people find easily manageable" and "do not adapt or become habituated to repeated occurrences of an event that has excited them" (132–35). Monsieur may well be such a casualty of overload, an urban data victim unable to process the information streams washing over him. Unlike more fully conditioned modern subjects, who have learned to raise their cognitive shields so as to avoid shock, Monsieur responds to the "*intensification of nervous stimulation*" with a short circuit in his brain (Simmel 175). In a city unmatched in its "acceleration of energies" (13), it was certainly not difficult to develop the disorder New York physician George Miller Beard had unleashed on America in the 1860s and which matched Monsieur's diagnostic profile: neurasthenia, a disease designating "all the forms and types of nervous exhaustion coming from the brain and from the spinal cord" and originating in a civilization-induced "overpressure of the higher nerve centers" (qtd. in Rabinbach 153).[18]

Thus, when Martin sees the doctor "inject cellular matter in deadened brains," his therapy is one of bio-rejuvenation (198). The aim is not just to offset syphilitic degeneracy or cerebral overload but more generally to kickstart dormant minds back into being. His club of immortals, in fact, does recover enough to allow for a kind of vegetative ambling in their subterranean hydrocloche, an Atlantis-like pseudo-Eden without genuine life. Brain cells taken from children allow them to exist as a gang of zombies eating, breathing, and occasionally (with the help of suggestive statues) blinking an eye. More advanced, more properly human functions such as thinking or self-reflection, however, are beyond their cerebral reach and highlight not just quality-of-life issues in the current debate about health care reform but, more important, the ethical and epistemological limits of medical intervention and what it means to live humanely. The very fact that the doctor's "marvelous brain" is thoroughly "lacking in self-consciousness" suggests, in microcosmic form, a cerebral disconnect that the comatose octogenarians play out on a larger scale (198).

Exceeding these cognitive pathologies and therapies, which allegorize once more the mutations of Sartorius's own brain, the doctor also explains the current theory of nervous electricity as a precondition for his work on brains. Alluding to early work in physiology, experimental psychology, and electromagnetic field theory, Sartorius notes that "our bodies have tides, and flow with measurable impulses of electric magnetism." To visualize biological information transmission, he suggests, in a common trope, that we may "live strung like our telegraph wires in fields of waves of all kinds and lengths, waves we can see and hear and waves we cannot, and the life we feel . . . is what is shaken through us by these waves" (216).[19] Much like the water flowing through the waterworks (in whose catacombs his lab is housed), from where it is routed to replenish the vital fluids circulating through individual bodies, the body generates an electrical field even as it is embedded in larger ambient fields. That electric premise, in turn, allows the doctor to construct a diagnostic apparatus to measure cranial currents. Martin recalls how the doctor attached "two anodes of a small magneto to my head, one at each temple," which were "connected by wires to a pair of needles with their points resting against a revolving wax cylinder." That cylinder, in turn, was propelled by a "gearshaft attached to a small brass steam engine" and traced "the electric impulsings of [Martin's] brain," or what we now call electroencephalic currents: the first data of a domain yet to be called cognitive science (196).

Similar machines of inscription had, in fact, been invented by enterprising doctors at about the same time. The kymographion (1847) developed by the German physiologist Karl Ludwig, for example, visualized direct arterial pulsations through a U-shaped mercury-filled tube that—with a pen mounted on a float—"traced the motions communicated to it . . . via a strip of paper stretched around a revolving drum" (Reiser 100). Upgraded by his countryman Karl Vierodt into a sphygmograph (1854), "which connected Ludwig's pen and revolving drum to an artery indirectly, by means of a spring pressed on the artery," it was simplified and made clinically workable by Étienne-Jules Marey's machine of the same name.[20] His invention (1860) "had a lever, one end resting on a pulsating artery and the other connected to a pen. A clockwork mechanism moved a strip of smoked paper under the pen at uniform speed, converting the pulsations into a pictorial form" (Reiser 101).[21] As the pioneer of modern medical notation, Marey, in particular, developed numerous inscriptive devices such as a myograph (improving on Hermann von Helmholtz's muscle-meter), a cardiograph, a pneumograph, and a thermograph, among others.

The point here is not simply that Sartorius's brain-wave meter is part of an emergent data recording regime (and echoes the encephalograph of his futuristic doppelgänger in *Solaris*), a form of automatic writing translating physical signs into technological inscription. Nor is it that such machines signaled the shift from empirical forms of scientific inquiry toward a more clinical, Sartorian form of laboratory research, reinforcing a "conception of the body as a field of forces to be investigated and measured by medical technologies designed for that purpose" (Rabinbach 66). Sartorius's steam-driven apparatus measuring cerebral electricity, in fact, ingeniously unites the two predominant paradigms of late nineteenth-century science—thermodynamics and electromagnetic field theory—and symbolically inscribes the dangerous background noise otherwise rendered inaudible by the waterworks' churning masses of water: the transfer and circulation of energy from young to old bodies, and hence a kind of entropic reversal of the natural order of things.[22] Most important for the argument at hand is that the machine Sartorius's device resembles most closely is Edison's phonograph of 1877 (developed for serial production by about 1888). While Edison's voice recorder had a crankshaft, not a steam engine hookup, to propel its drum, the encoding of electroencephalic waves is identical to Edison's engraving of sound waves onto (first tin foil, then waxen) grooves. Both operate as drum-based, analogical inscription systems for the storage of vital signs or embodied data streams.

Following the discovery of the X-ray in 1896, Edison announced his attempt to photograph a living human brain, one of his many publicity stunts. Challenged by a man who might easily have been one of Sartorius's well-heeled patients—William Randolph Hearst—to produce a cerebral "'cathodograph'" (Baldwin 253), Edison claimed, in a rare moment of modesty, that "[Roentgen] needs men like myself, whose chief aim is to turn the great discoveries of science to practical use and adapt them" (qtd. in Reiser 60). Once word got out, the leading neurological publication in America, the *Journal of Nervous and Mental Disease*, requested that "a repro of Brain Photography" appear in its pages, but the experiment in what would have been an early form of tomography proved unsuccessful because the human skull was, as it were, too thick for present-day cathode rays to penetrate (Edison Papers, D-96–310).[23] Edison also received thousands of "idea letters" from an enthused public urging him to think of machines the inventor was too busy to invent. One such letter noted that "the convolutions of the human brain are largely though not entirely a Phonograph," observing further that the "grey matter acts ... after a manner of the wax-cylinder." Suggesting further research, the letter writer outlined the benefit of postmortem cranial readings in the case of murder victims or Egyptian mummies that would reveal intriguing data (qtd. in Gitelman 88).[24]

But while Edison never appears to have contemplated engineering a brain-wave recorder, it was precisely his phonograph that provided an imaginative model for human memory and cognition. Not just an eager public but literary and philosophical figures as well saw in the sound recorder a technological equivalent of human processing. Rainer Maria Rilke recognized in "the coronal suture of the skull" sitting on his desk "a similarity to the close wavy line which the needle of a phonograph engraves on the receiving, rotating cylinder of the apparatus." He frequently wondered what kind of "primal sound" would be audible "if one changed the needle and directed it on its return journey along a tracing which was not derived from the graphic translation of sound but existed of itself naturally ... along the coronal suture" (*Selected Works* 1:54). Similarly, like Edison's correspondent, the philosopher Jean-Marie Guyau suggested in 1880 that "the most refined instrument ... with which the human brain may be compared is perhaps Edison's recently invented phonograph." Analogous to the engraving of sound waves onto a rotating cylinder, and their subsequent replay, "invisible lines are incessantly carved into the brain cells, which provide a channel for nerve streams. If, after some time, the stream encounters a channel it has already passed through, it will once again proceed along the same path," causing the cells to vibrate "in the same way they vibrated the first time; psychologically, these similar vibrations correspond to an emotion or a thought analogous to the forgotten emotion or thought" (qtd. in Kittler, *Gramophone* 30).

Such a structural analogy of course presupposes not only the actual existence of the phonograph but also its physiological a priori, such as the conception of the nervous system—following the neurophysiologist Sigmund Exner—as an aggregate of conduits (*Bahnen*) and engrams channeling what Sartorius calls "impulses of electric magnetism." What is more, such an analogy also presupposes a virtual equality between the body and the machines invented for its physiological and electrical mapping, which is precisely how psychotechnology in the late nineteenth century came to see the body. For researchers intent on measuring sensory and cognitive deficiencies—often brought on through strokes, gunshot wounds, or industrial accidents—the body that once housed a metaphysical and transcendent Hegelian spirit was reduced to a series of electric (and increasingly disembodied) signals susceptible to mathematical measurement; and such signals, in turn, in effect, constitute an electronic form of the soul or cognition. If humans had, in the well-known Renaissance dictum, been the measure of all things, now they were measured by machines that suggested that the cascade of neurological impulses jumping from relay to relay made humans into information-processing machines themselves.[25] Freud, for one, in both his case studies and lectures repeatedly refers to his "phonographic memory," and hence suggests the evacuation of the traditional notion of the soul from the humanities (22:5). Thanks to the combined work of Edison and psychotechnology, the phonograph can thus be seen to both operate as and *be* a model of a materialized consciousness. As Kittler puts it in the general technospeak of media theory, "All questions concerning thought as thought have been abandoned, for it is now a question of implementation of hardware" (*Gramophone* 33).

It is precisely such a mechanistic model of cognition—a precursor to today's cybernetic (and tomorrow's positronic) brain models—that Doctorow is interrogating. While Sartorius's medical achievements per se are not in doubt, Doctorow questions what is at the very heart of his creation: a single-minded belief in physiological processes blind to the ethical and epistemological ramifications of such processes. It is for that very reason, I would suggest, that Doctorow's doctor (unlike Lem's) invents a machine in the 1870s that was not to see its technological reality until fifty years later, when the German physiologist Hans Berger developed an encephalograph that "measured the electrical activity of the brain graphically" (Reiser 218). Sartorius's visionary brain-wave recorder is not only unable to store a precise analogical record of an individual's memory and cognitive processes (which is what the technological model underlying it, Edison's phonograph, is assumed to be able do to), generating instead only a general graphic representation of microelectric cerebral impulses; it is also unable to record such more traditional yet crucial brain output as cognition, reflection, and knowledge: cerebral activities that may well be unwritable in mathematical (that is, analogical and digital) terms and hence defy belonging to any more technically prescribed notion of *data* altogether. With a head start of two generations, Sartorius's futuristic machine thus charts through its very existence its own limitations as a recorder of vital signs whose humanistic, as opposed to biological, heartbeat goes unrecorded. It inscribes a reductive, physiological conception of cognition and memory, but is unable to document and capture brain work not amenable to technical forms of quantification or measurement.[26]

Equally important, Doctorow takes issue with a relay model of cognition that reduces (a Heideggerian form of) human being to binary signal sets and that defines agency in terms of electric impulse switches. Much like the disjointed necks and brains in *The Waterworks*, whose unlinking from the body suggests interrupted circuits, cognitive processing in mechanistic forms severs instantaneous high-speed decision making from more long-term and wide-ranging ethical considerations, in effect positing "an identity between signal and act and an identity between communication and execution" (Seltzer 11). Instead of inviting reflection on emergent, and hence unpredictable, consequences, such a processing model encourages a slippery autonomy that, again much like the severed heads and brains, can lead to a kind of cruise control or practice unchecked by more nuanced and sustained, fluid and open-ended cogitation. If the doctor's surgical hands (perhaps in a gesture toward *Las Manos de Orlac* and similar genre films) quite literally embody a body gone autopilot—at moments appearing as if it were not the doctor but "the hands that were speaking" (195)—Dr. Sumner's digital answer ("No. Yes") may well circumscribe the reductivism of any binary mode of cognition. Sartorius's work on undead bodies, indeed, is just one step away from delirious fantasies of weightless being that ignore the complexities of a body-in-the-mind "too unruly to fit into disembodied ones and zeros" (Hayles, *Posthuman* 13).

As a traditionally more human and embodied storage technology, literary (and oral) narrative, by contrast, can negotiate such divides and binaries. Fiction, in Doctorow and McIlvaine's view, has the quality of a ruminating and reconstructive retrospectivity to tell its tale. Unlike film and sound storage, which record physiological effects of the real, narrative can enact a form of more conventionally mimetic memorization by sorting through, and distilling, real history into a verbal account cognizant of its symbolic artifice; unlike a futuristic electroencephalograph, which registers cerebral tremors in generalized graphic form, the novel is a more effective brain-wave recorder, the "printed circuit" whose alphabetic software is best equipped to record the vicissitudes of thought (*Essays* 151).[27] McIlvaine offers such an account and suggests a definition of narrative as a form of collective information processing or cultural substrate taking stock of events in hindsight and sorting meaningful from meaningless noise. In the process, he raises critical questions about the (nonphysiological) memory function of literature and, very much in sync with Holmes, Donne, and Edison, about the cognitive distance necessary to pre-process and condense history into the limited storage container of a book.

Meanwhile, the wizened Wizard of Menlo Park sensed it all. While, in the spirit of the media theorists co-opting him, conceiving of his own brain in material terms as a "plate on a record or a receiving apparatus," a more spiritual notion of cerebration crept into his thinking (Baldwin 376). Mystic extraordinaire Madame Blavatsky had instilled in the inventor extraordinary ideas about cosmic matter and energy, and Edison, in a synthesis of technology and mysticism all his own, set out to record the most elusive of all: the human personality. Positing that the Broca fold in the brain housed memory cells capable of storing a person's assimilated lifetime experiences, perhaps even, as he put it, "the subconscious mind so-called," he concluded that such cells would float freely through space once a person had died.[28] To access such knowledge banks, he set to work on a "sensitive apparatus" with which to detect and unlock lifetimes of unmoored information cells "prowling through the ether of space" (qtd. in Baldwin 377). If this sounds like the Houdini of *Ragtime* trying to make contact with his deceased mother, and uncannily prefigures cyberpunk fiction and current fantasies of downloading human consciousness into a computer, it also suggests the project of McIlvaine's novel: the retrospective storage of a historical moment in the medium of alphabetic print as seen through an individual human consciousness, after having accrued a lifetime of knowledge and experience.[29]

Modularity, Information, Narrative Knowledge

It is no coincidence that the emergent cognitive rhetoric of the later nineteenth century spills over into the brain work of *The Waterworks'* major actors and tellers. Following their body-snatching heist, artist Harry Wheelright is haunted by the "image of that dead boy [sitting] in my brain," unable to paint and, hence, release it into artistic form (109).[30] Mesmerized by the ingenuity of the doctor, Martin is similarly aghast at his seeming complicity, "as if I had performed on myself some excision of a portion of the brain" (203). While his stepmother counsels Martin against retelling his experiences, for fear of "leaving them to swell the brain," Donne urges a total recall, aware that mental buildup might require psychological release. McIlvaine too suggests that the best therapy for diseased minds is "getting the story told, turning it into an object made of language" (201). Years after the events, in the throes of composition, he notes that the events have "grown into the physical dimensions of my brain," so "however the mind works . . . that is the way the story gets told" (219). How that mind works is of course part of the very story: a story about the act of re-cognition and re-memorization. *The Waterworks* indeed proposes itself as an extended discourse on literary narrative in relation to print and journalism, memory and morality, and the very idea of cognitive modularity itself.

As part of its cognitive mapping of postbellum America, *The Waterworks* draws attention to the nineteenth-century precursor of the modular mind: phrenology. McIlvaine is quick to dismiss it as another newspaper filler, a science on the cusp of discreditation postulating a veritable bumpology along gendered lines, but the three basic Temperaments he describes—Mental, Motives, and Vitals—already look forward to contemporary descriptions of cerebral domains as "mental organs," as in Steven Pinker's evolutionary models (46).[31] Such a tripartite cranial economy was even then crude and fantastic in the extreme, but the understanding of the brain's subdivision into localized departments, each with a specified range of tasks, was in effect a simplified model of the cerebral modules of the late twentieth century.[32] Sartorius's work on the brain, in that sense, is a pioneering effort to chart the claims of phrenology in experimental and physiological terms. When McIlvaine describes knowledge of noggins as "a system for organizing perceptions," he may have in mind what Orson and Lorenzo Fowler—the cranial connoisseurs with a U.S. corner on all things phrenological—saw as central to their beliefs (46). The publishers of Walt Whitman's first volume of poetry (a fellow Fowlerian who is suitably quoted in *The Waterworks*), the brothers claimed that "the mind is a plurality of innate and independent faculties—a congregate of distinct and separate powers," which fully corresponds to the premise of distributed cognition in present-day modularity (qtd. in Cooter 291). Similarly, their handbills claimed that phrenology can be an aid in cognitive muscle flexing and lead to "a retentive memory," so that "a lawyer or *literati*" could be "enabled to recall all he ever knew"—issues at the center of modern-day cognitive science no less than at the center of McIlvaine's recollective project (qtd. in Cooter 118).

As a novel that self-consciously engages the work of brains, *The Waterworks* indeed displays numerous correspondences between theories of modularity and its narrative mode. Recognizing print narrative's minority report within the contemporary field of representation, Doctorow has always favored a "multiplicity of witness" or "democracy of perception"—a novelist's version of distributed cognition within media culture (*Conversations* 113). Literalizing such representational diversity in *The Waterworks*, Doctorow empowers a de facto decentered narrator to assemble a retrospective narrative from a series of eyewitness reports, surmises, and speculations, to which that narrator adds his own interpretive overlays from a distance of roughly two generations. All the major players lend their perceptions to the story in the making that, in its entirety, makes up a series of micro-narratives orchestrated into a putative master-narrative by "the intrusive factor of an organized consciousness," namely, McIlvaine himself (*Essays* 160). Observations such as, "all of this is filtered through the brain of Dr. Grimshaw and after many years in my own mind," indicate *in nuce* the layered cognitive refractions operative in the novel (40). And while his distanced and seemingly impartial story, from the voice of an octogenarian, has the aura of authority, McIlvaine, no less than the reader, is cognizant that his final version of events is by definition unstable and inconclusive, much as distributed networks "don't quite so much compute a solution as they settle into it" (Pagels, qtd. in Spolsky 33). In McIlvaine's own words, even the tales told by best-intentioned people "must go spiraling off in the resolution of things" (250).

Similarly, in the same way McIlvaine's role as a Jamesian "central intelligence" is complicated through the accounts of others, his position as a narrative processing conduit exemplifies breakthrough innovations in modular theory. For once, his decentered role as switch point or node for the convergence of parallel narrative strands not only gives him greater responsiveness than a traditional, however sophisticated, consciousness. More important, as Ellen Spolsky has noted, distributed cognition allows for the modeling of a "processor that is highly tolerant of error," much like McIlvaine's own thinking is, at virtually every step, recalibrated, refined, and thickened as other narratives are traveling through his neuropathways (34). Donne's criminal insights, in particular, as well as Martin's more philosophical recollections, add narrative loops to an already complicated meshwork of story lines. What is more, the scatterbrained mode of McIlvaine's re-memorization—with competing stories morphing and adjusting in interplay with one another—suggests the cognitive model of Gerald Edelman, in which neurons form clusters and connections based on competing fields of stimuli, eventually producing consciousness and thought, much like the mechanisms of Darwinian selection at work in biological populations. Just as McIlvaine evolves a forever preliminarily final version of the Pemberton story that builds on the cumulative gathering of directive evidence, but shuts out numerous others *in potentiae,* so neuron podding in the brain depends on epigenesis, the often accidental, and hence un(pre)determined, adaptation to environmental pressures. Indeed, as Spolsky notes, in view of Edelman's close attention to the actual physiology of brains, his model contains within itself "a theory of a fragmented, contingent, necessarily opportunistic or pragmatic postmodern consciousness" (37).

Such a consciousness is McIlvaine's indeed, and its refractive quality is signaled not only in his self-acknowledged memory gaps—his repeated recognition that "what you remember as having happened and what truly did happen are no less and no more than ... visions" (59)—but also in his literally elliptical story: the narrative's virtually ubiquitous perforation with the three dots of ellipsis. Indicative, perhaps, of a mentally challenged old man whose speech and thinking patterns are stalling—alternating between bursts of recall and re-memorative dry spells—such gaps also mark the signifying rupture to be closed by the reader's hermeneutic collaboration.[33] As well, such lacunae suggest points of cognitive blindness opening up when communication between (and within) the representation of various modules is suspended, faults that point toward a temporary processing impasse of information in need of neurological rerouting. As Daniel Dennett has noted, while consciousness appears to be fluid and continuous, it is in fact "gappy and sparse, and doesn't contain half of what people think is there" (366). Replacing a materialist biology of the brain with a phenomenologist's penchant for metaphor, he observes that at "any point in time, there are multiple drafts of narrative fragments at various stages of editing in various places in the brain" (135). If this reads like a literal version of what amounts to McIlvaine's progressive chapter drafts in *The Waterworks,* it also describes McIlvaine's own philosophical distancing, through the act of writing, from the cognitive materialism of Dr. Sartorius. The seeming fullness of consciousness is belied by the short-lived and always-about-to-be-bridged breaches in neural connections, outwardly manifest in McIlvaine's disjointed narrative fractals. In the words of Spolsky, "the gaps in the interpretive system, far from being accidental, are necessary and innate aspects of our generally inherited epistemological equipment" (192).[34]

Significantly, as if to rehearse the gappy and multiply spatial nature of cognition, McIlvaine offers a model of meaning making that is akin to the spatial model of modularity. With an eye toward his own discombobulated narrative and as a warning to his readers that "linear thinking" is anathema to sense and thinking—that "knowing in advance the whole conclusive order [of things] makes narration suspect" (123)—he describes the material layout of nineteenth-century "vertical" newspapers as a network of seven descending lines of text (115). In their parallel synchronicity, these text lines require sustained cognitive oscillation to yield meaning: "Now we ran off eight pages of seven columns, and only if you stretched out your arms wide could you hold the paper taut to its full width. And we had readers of the city accustomed to this . . . who scanned our columns the instant they got them . . . as if our stories were projections of the multiple souls of man . . . and no meaning was possible from any one column without the sense of all of them in . . . simultaneous descent" (115). Only the capacity of thoroughly alphabetized readers for parallel processing makes it possible to synthesize disparate narrative elements into the big picture; only the sustained filling of gaps and interstitial voids (of, almost literally, reading between the lines) allows for the coordination of semes into a coherent semantic whole. Similar to the data juggling of Donne, and similar to the composite criminal sketches of Wheelwright—whereby eyewitness accounts yield a kind of pictorial group memory or cognitive abstraction (121)—sense is the result of unparalleled intellectual work: the ramified combination of clues, criminal, hermeneutic, or otherwise.

By advancing such a parallel model of computational processing, McIlvaine of course anticipates in informational terms something akin to the spatial novel of literary modernism, novels whose rearranged chronology is meant to create the illusion of simultaneity within the reader.[35] In contrast to spatial narratives, however, which silently assume that readers synthesize disjointed fragments into a phenomenological gestalt, McIlvaine's model suggests the parallel brain work underlying such apprehension. The synchronous descent of news columns, in that sense, could be seen to look forward to hypertext as not only the mode of industrialized informational retrieval but also the narrative form closest to the vicissitudes of the processes of reading and thinking. George Landow has noted that "in contrast to the rigidity and difficulty of access produced by present means of managing information based on print and other physical records, one needs an information medium that better accommodates to the way the mind works" (14). For Doctorow, by contrast, narrative spatialization appears to be nothing new. While columned news distribution may indeed be a response to modern-day information growth, cognitive synchronicity has evolved as a hardwired feature in the human brain. Parallel processing, he seems to suggest, has long been part and parcel of cognitive, and hence narrative, conventions, and readers of serious fiction have long felt drawn to the nonlinear and multidirectional vectors of literary narrative. When McIlvaine describes his model of parallel descent as "cuneiform carved across the stele" (146), he indeed suggests the ancient, evolutionary character of modular thinking (just as he points to the always already cryptic form of any act of coding).

Thus, while the brain solving the crime is that of a brilliant detective, the brain telling the story is that of ruminating journalist increasingly at odds with the data-based, and hence quickly dated, discourse of his former profession. The prism of McIlvaine not only both refracts and bundles the narrative strands of *The Waterworks* but also illustrates the inadequacy of the informational discourse of journalism. Consider McIlvaine's shift in allegiance from news to novel. A full-blooded journalist since his teens, he believes that newspapers function as *the* stabilizing epistemology of a chaotic world: "If journalism were a philosophy rather than a trade, it would say there is no order in the universe, no discernible meaning, without . . . the daily paper" (14). Such oft-repeated reportorial absoluteness, however, reaches its limits when trying to offer sustained reflections on past events. While McIlvaine's credo anchors journalism in "the social and political urgencies" of the day, his "newspaperman's metaphysics" is under siege once confronted with Martin's "philosophical meditation" on his near-fatal experiences (166). Martin's morose brooding gives McIlvaine "considerable misgiving in [his] newspaperman's soul" about, fundamentally, not going "out to the edges of . . . whatever was possible" (166), culminating in his insight that, even once ostensibly completed, historical events are not "reportorially possible": "there are limits to the use of words in a newspaper" (207–8).

What is behind this schism is the generic oscillation between the late nineteenth-century discourses of journalism and literary narrative, the former gravitating toward an information-based economy of immediately newsworthy information, the latter insisting on reflective discursivity exceeding the regime of data and instantaneous reportability. While McIlvaine is, initially, fully vested in the presumption of reportorial fullness, his probes into the doctor's ethical responsibility make him realize the myth of the narrative totality of any experience. Instead, through a kind of professional crossover, he reorients himself toward the retrospective form of fiction and thus signals his acceptance of the forever elliptical representation of any event. "Whoever tells our moral history . . . must run behind, not ahead of it" (207), he notes, and he thus reprises not only Doctorow's claim about fiction as "a kind of speculative history" filling the gaps left by other discourses and Benjamin's observation about the quick dissipation of newsworthiness (*Essays* 162);[36] he also instantiates—in narrative terms—areas that have defined much of the field of cognitive science: how to distinguish between short- and long-term reflection (formerly known as *cogitation*) and between information and knowledge.

One way to understand these distinctions is to import Freud's notion of *condensation* into this discussion. Freud noted that while human memories are notoriously erratic, they rarely forget experiences altogether. Rather, memories tend to leave traces in a subject's psychic apparatus, configuring and tilting that apparatus to frame future experiences in a similar way. (In evolutionary terms, the human brain can thus be seen as the result of such collective forms of condensation.) Building on Freud, Hartmut Winkler has observed that language, too, in its entirety can "be seen as a product of 'condensation.'" Just as psychological sedimentation always leaves trace deposits in the individual human mind, or, in evolutionary terms, in the human cognitive apparatus, so language is an act of compaction so extraordinary as "to fit into puny human skulls" ("Discourses" 104). While memories and speech acts are often fleeting and forgotten, both lead, over time, to a gradual buildup and increasing concentration on both an ontogenetic and a phylogenetic level. Memories, no less than linguistic symbol systems, are compressed and infinitely coded in cerebral folds.

Analogously, one might say, journalism and literary narrative can be seen in terms of their cognitive longevity and compression. Just as memories and language diachronically commute experiences and speech acts into highly condensed "semantic-mental structures," so literature can be seen as a process of cultural concentration, transforming—through retrospection, that is, time—ephemeral data and short-lived fact into insight with the presumption of (more) enduring value (Winkler, "Discourses" 104). By looking backward, or running behind the times, rather than ahead of them, as McIlvaine says, the novel can submit data to a winnowing or filtering process separating the wheat from the chaff, or the flotsam from the jetsam. Journalism, by contrast, bound to report on the world of verifiable fact and to the protocols of quick information delivery, engages with the immediate present, without the privilege of retrospection and ripening reflection. Instead of substantive reconsideration, the work of reporting virtually coincides with the daily unfolding of history, without temporal space or distance for a sustained critical and imaginative review—documentary, profound, and resistant to prevailing power structures as it often is. If journalism informs in a mode that is almost coterminous with emergent events, literature adds a more distanced and speculative version to these events once they have crystallized into stacked interpretive overlays.

Thus, what goes by the old-fashioned terms of counsel, wisdom, or knowledge—those musty words long mothballed by the postmodern border patrol—can be understood as literature's cultural offering: the cognitive substrate of a historical moment, the dust that has settled into a deposit. If "the true name of the press is oblivion" indeed, as Emile de Girardin, the inventor of the penny press, once famously put it, the true name of the novel might be remembrance or memory working through unresolvable imponderables one more time (qtd. in de la Motte and Przyblyski 4). Significantly, Freud's psychological notion of condensation derives from the poetic notion of *(Ver) dichtung,* suggesting verbal and narrative processes of concentration or, better, densification. Significantly as well, Doctorow in *The Waterworks* repeatedly draws attention to this cognitive (both synchronic and diachronic) compression of language. The reader learns that Sartorius's name evolved during the German Middle Ages, when tradespeople in the process of social elevation "took the Latin form of their names. The miller became Molitor, the pastor became Pastorius, and the tailor became Sartorius" (128).[37] To Sartorius's demand for an abolition of "poetic . . . conceits" (242), Doctorow responds that discourse is conceptual, and hence a mostly verbal substrate—the result of semantic compression. And, perhaps most dramatically, when McIlvaine interviews Sartorius in the insane asylum, his learned answers rise amid a "symphony of shrieks, cries, caterwaulings, trills, shouts, and pealing laughter," sounds that are echoed in the delirious "tweet, tweet" of Tweed, the skilled verbal manipulator now "impoverished of language" (242–44). Nonsense and full sense, non-language and highly evolved discourse are here immediately juxtaposed to illustrate the gamut of cognitive yield, a self-organizing system extending from noise and verbal chaos to coherent speech and sophisticated communicative order.

Mapping the signifying range of language within the space of just a couple of lines is of course part of the power of literary narrative. It draws from the very *Verdichtung* of discourse as a veritable archaeology of semantic strata and, precisely because of its density, always produces noise as a constitutive byproduct; its very concentration forbids transparency even as it invites reflection. "The literary experience extends impression into discourse. It flowers to thought with nouns, verbs, objects," as Doctorow puts it in his next novel, foreshadowing his increasing interest in the imbrication of language and cognition (*God* 214). As long as readers meet the cognitive densities of literary narratives halfway with their own cognitive resources—sharing as they do language as the medium circulating through both cerebral currents and the "printed circuit" of a book—the novel will remain a constructive player in the formation of a culture's intellectual landscape. As long as a culture has enough appreciation for language as its major vehicle of expression and intellectual exchange, it can counteract the danger of cognitive flatlining brought about by a shrinkage in communicative nuance and breadth, be it through tabloid journalism or the visual and electronic media of today. Otherwise, as Doctorow once put it, "If there was a way of taking a national EEG, you'd find that the brain waves have gone flat" (*Conversations* 71).

8
By Way of a Conclusion
City of God, Galatea 2.2, and the Case of No Body in Vain

Why wouldn't a literary scholar want to know everything that neurologists are discovering about the way the brain works?
 —Richard Powers in Jeffrey Williams, "The Last Generalist"

Cognition in Circuit City, or City of Circuits

As a composite of literary and filmic types, Dr. Sartorius has more than a passing resemblance to history's medical arch-villains, just as his genius, however compromised and ethically tainted, parallels pioneering efforts in protocognitive research. Paul Broca, Karl Ludwig, and Étienne Jules-Marey, among others, may have served Doctorow as models from which he composed his experimental researcher (just as the Dr. Sartorius of Lem's *Solaris*, one of the literary predecessors of Doctorow's doctor, may himself be a composite of some of these very scientists). At the same time, the work of the doctor also points to a tradition of cognitive research that saw promise and medical gain in the autopsy of the brains of leading thinkers and luminaries. Thus, upon the death of Lenin in 1924, the Soviet government commissioned Dr. Karl Vogt, the eminent German neuroscientist and founder of the Institute of Brain Research in Moscow, to perform an autopsy of Lenin's brain (affected by "progressive cerebrovascular disease") in hopes of finding the genius residing in the gray matter.[1] Similarly, in what may be one of the most controversial brain heists of the past century, Dr. Thomas Harvey of Princeton University in 1955 took Einstein's brain from the body before the latter's cremation. Removing the brain, it seems, without explicit authorization, Harvey bagged the brain, stored it in two jars (in a box labeled "Costa Cider"), and—before returning it to Princeton in 1996—occasionally showed it off to interested parties the way other people "'show off a rare edition of Shakespeare,'" as a contemporary observer put it (qtd. in Paterniti 45). A friend of another advanced brain researcher, William S. Burroughs, Harvey, like Sartorius, eventually clashed with the medical community in refusing to release the brain and, like Sartorius, lost his medical license (Paterniti, 46–47).[2]

These parallels are suggestive but point to more than the correspondence of Sartorius with his later, real-life incarnations. The removal of, in particular, Einstein's brain coincides with the "intellectual origins" of cognitive science "in the mid-1950s, when researchers in several fields began to develop theories of mind" (Thagard ix). If the hoopla surrounding Einstein's brain was, no doubt, a curiously grotesque expression of his pop star status—of a slightly tubby, disheveled Mensch endowed with the cult proportions of an action hero—the opening of his skull also crystallized emerging cognitive efforts to locate genius in the matter of the mind. At the same time, while the urge for a peek under Einstein's hood was almost certainly fueled by the naive cold war assumption that dissecting this smaller-than-average brain of a larger-than-life pacifist might yield insight into subatomic energies and the ultimate nature of the universe, the equally naive belief underlying it was the presumption of a coherent self residing in the housing of a protective skull.[3] The man who, throughout his life, was careful to acknowledge the contributions of his predecessors and contemporaries was, in death, enlisted to help keep alive the fiction of an autonomous self that cognitive science was soon to reformulate into the notion of distributed cognition. If the autopsy in its search for genius removed the brain from the synergy of its corporeal home, and hence instantiated a literal version of the Cartesian body-mind split, emergent theories of mind were soon to acknowledge that the Cartesian leftover may be in dire need of healing.

For these very reasons, Doctorow may feature Einstein as one of his historical protagonists in *City of God*, a complex philosophical novel trying to engage the imponderables of twentieth-century thought, such as agency and cognition, ethics and intent, science and theology—what it means to be human, in short—in the face of the grisly record of modern-day warfare. Einstein had made two cameo appearances in *Ragtime*, a novel working with turn-of-the-century clichés circulating in U.S. culture in which he is, fittingly, identified as the Brain "proving that the universe was curved" (259, 169). In *City of God*, by contrast, Einstein appears as a flesh-and-blood being by drawing attention to his body not as an index of cryptic genius but as affirming his fellowship with the common run of humanity. "Funny hair . . . sticking up in every direction," "unpressed trousers," and a clumsy way of writing at a blackboard, with chalk bursting into pieces—all these, he thinks, should be seen as forms of common, embodied being, but have been misconstrued by "the press and the radio people" to relieve the public "of thinking about what I have to say. It is an insult not only to me but to you, because the human mind can always find out the truth" (38).[4] The feedback loop of living in and acting with a body is here significantly linked to thought, just as it reaches toward the theological enigma of what may well be the ultimate hope of embodied being: the leap from physics to metaphysics, from mortality to possible eternity. Einstein himself discarded traditional theology, offering his body to science and calling his God "the Old One," whose presence he saw manifest in "certain irreducible laws of the universe" (53). At the same time, he was well aware, as the bloody history of humanity amply testifies, that "the pious brainwork of Christian priests and kings" had over centuries "demonized and racialized the Jewish people in Europe" (52), very much at odds with the presence of any putative divinity.

Nested both within and outside these epistemological fields of tension, and evident in the sustained rhetoric of brains, *City of God* reflects on various models of selfhood and cognition. Observing that "this is my laboratory, here, in my skull" (a phrase tellingly echoed by Everett, arguably the central consciousness orchestrating the narratives of *City of God* [52]), Einstein declares thinking to be largely a matter of creating a *cranium rasa,* of emptying "my laboratory of my furniture there, the beakers, measuring scales, cabinets, old books" (36).[5] Cognitive housecleaning, he suggests, is necessary to do the work of theoretical physics, to reinvent the universe free from the baggage of dominant scientific (Newtonian) paradigms. At the same time, "the entire problem of mind" demands "superhuman courage" to dwell on because it is "too vast, a space without dimension, filled with cosmic events that are silent and immaterial." In lieu of recursive self-reflection, the scientist suggests that "for one's sanity it is preferable to track God in the external world" (44), opting for the material stability of (a quasi-theological) physics, instead of the intangible non-space of imaginative activity.

This incommensurability of outside and inside is precisely what Ludwig Wittgenstein, Einstein's analytical, rationalist counterfigure in *City of God,* seeks to rectify. Surmising that "The I or self can theoretically ascertain everything about the world except who and what it itself is" (125), he anticipates the work of recent cognitive models that suggest the self to be the dissimulating effect of coherent self-construction, and that this construction is always at one remove from analysis since consciousness cannot be conscious of itself in the act of thinking, that is, during cognition itself. Then, postulating the self to be no more than "a presumption of the faculty of language, a syntactical conceit"—a linguistic construct without body—he yet concedes that this self is the constructive agent bringing the world into being. Wittgenstein speaks of a "solipsistic consciousness" that grounds the world even as it is grounded by it and proposes a paradoxical "merger of the real world that exists apart from my perception of it and the world that cannot exist except for my mind's perception of it" (125). This feedback loop, too, points forward to contemporary models of cognition that see the development of the mind as an evolutionary interplay of the environment with an embodied brain, but Wittgenstein is more concerned with philosophical puzzle than biological theorizing.[6] Granting that each human being is the engineer of his or her own world and that "none of us [is] able to discernibly exist except as subject of others' consciousness," he is led into a kind of phenomenological hamster wheel whereby humans run the risk of infinite monadic self-enclosure. That this impasse is a "paradox of three dimensions" at least implies the embodiment of mind in the materialities of organic being (125) and points to Wittgenstein's eventual preoccupation with the body as an epistemological a priori. While the body in his early work is a virtual absence—typically reduced to a play of language—the Wittgenstein of *On Certainty* considers embodiment the precondition for cognition, the incorporated ground of being without which thought would not be. Knowledge in the older Wittgenstein, as Gunter Gebauer has noted, emerges from the "certainties of one's own body, that is, of the body in its given, material form, with a mouth, feet, hands, and fingers on each hand" (240, my translation). Similar to the way grammar determines the structures of human thinking, so the topography of language and thought, as with Heidegger, are "cast" in the structures of our body (*On Certainty* § 558). Significantly, the very fact that Wittgenstein, in both *Philosophical Investigations* and *On Certainty*, comes back time and again to the hand as the primary (both literal and figurative) organ of apprehension already points to the almost coincident theories of André Leroi-Gourhan about the reciprocities of manual and cognitive evolution and, eventually, the emergence of language.[7]

Exceeding these proleptic but nevertheless clearly modernist meditations on (and by) the cognitive self, *City of God*'s narrating consciousness Everett directly engages contemporary models of cognition. In (presumably) his notebooks, Everett writes about a resigned ex-*Times* reporter turned Nazi hunter, who accidentally runs into his victim with a bicycle, resulting (appropriately, given our context) in a fatal brain injury (197). Reviewing the situation, the reporter insists on the agency of his autonomous self by reasoning that, after all, he had seen the killer "from the corner of his eye and recognized him before he lost control of his bicycle." Reversing the traditional logic of cause and effect, he persuades himself that "the body took control of his mind, there was a conflict resolved by the reversal of control systems wherein not his conscious thought was the directing intelligence but the electric buildup of intent in his skeletal and musculature systems" (233). Conscious decision and subsequent action have here traded places—the real, initial action being the cognitive processing of stimuli in the pathways of the nervous system. Rationalizing the accident to himself as an, in essence, unconsciously conscious and at least half-willed act, the reporter denies his loss of intent, even as he invokes the language of electric excitation and transmission that relocates agency away from Enlightenment constructs of the self to the cascading effect of neuropathways. Almost unwittingly, he describes a familiar model of cognitive impulse traveling only to bend it to his need for independent selfhood. His own realizations notwithstanding, it is precisely his need for autonomy (and his sense of disempowerment in the face of professional mediocrity) that does not allow him to view the mind, in posthuman terms, "as a disunified, heterogeneous, collection of networks of processes" (Varela, Thompson, and Rosch 107).

Complicating such illusory visions of agency, Everett's thoughts on an ant colony in Central Park redistribute cognition outside the individual organism into a kind of dispersed knowledge aggregate. Communicating "chemical messages [that] were synapsed back and forth," and furthermore lacking brains and memory, ants "make do with genetically programmed little nervous sympathies." In their operative unity, they function "almost like parallel processors, or in fact our own cortical structure of neurons," each made up of "one cell of a group brain, . . . an invisible organ of thought that is beyond the capacity of any one of them to understand" (241–42).[8] Such parceled information sharing is a biological case study of distributed cognition that echoes, for example, Gregory Bateson's notion in *Steps to an Ecology of Mind* that organic forms ineluctably participate in "pathways and messages outside the body," which then accumulate into a kind of expanded consciousness but "of which the individual mind is only a subsystem" (467).

The point is that Everett, as a novelist engaging the problem of cognition, sees in such collective thinking in the "underground city" an invitation to theorize about parallel circuits in the city above. He speculates that "the ants' invisible organ of aggregate thought" may be reflected in the communication among the members of a crowd, each equipped with "the integrity of the individual will," yet reacting in both sequential and parallel unison if necessary. In a trope reminiscent of the autopoietic processes of a gargantuan cell, and echoing the models of system theory deriving from biology, he suggests that objects or behaviors alien to a crowd, such as a "purse snatcher" or "gun wielder," are "isolated, surrounded, ejected, carried off as waste," so that the system can restore itself to functional integrity. Asserting that humans are "individually and privately dyssynchronous" and at the same time participate in "the pulsing communicating cells of an urban over-brain," he suggests that the (neo-Emersonian) exchange of signals in large spaces, such as a park, illustrates both the dispersed autonomy and cognition of human aggregates. While, "in the comparative blindness of [their] personal selfhood," individual humans may flow "as synaptic impulses in the metropolitan brain," their urge for independent agency is subsumed into "one multicellular culture of thought that is always there" and coordinates interaction (242–43). Distributed cognition literally organizes the city of bits.[9]

Not coincidentally, as if exemplifying the subject of his own discourse and his own perceptual responsiveness, Everett leaps immediately from these larger-scale systemic considerations to the openness and reactive speed of the singular human mind. Amazed by how all stimuli taken in through the portals of the body are "in your mind's possession in the moment's firing of a neuron," he concludes that "the permeable mind, contingently disposed for invasion, can be totally overrun and occupied by all the characteristics of the world, by everything that is the case" (242). Succeeding this nod toward Wittgenstein, and the ineluctable loop between embodied being and its lifeworld, he also ascribes an Einsteinian "kind of quantum weirdness" to human cognition, thus synthesizing in his own mind and in his own way the two thinkers who appear in his fiction as meditators on self, mind, and thought fusing various domains of knowledge. Cognizant of the intellectual achievements of these brilliant minds, he parallels their abstract philosophical and scientific pronouncements with the narrativized version of two embodied humans each with their own fragile ego and idiosyncrasies. Furthermore, while Everett is quick to acknowledge that humans can, by virtue of their body, avail themselves of various processing channels, he draws attention to the mode that comes most natural to him, just as it does—in this nesting game of Russian dolls—to Doctorow, and indeed the mode thinkers of all stripes often find themselves falling back to: narrative. "Think of how the first line of a story yokes the mind into a place, a time, in the time it takes to read it" (243).

Doctorow has always insisted, as we have seen, that narrative has been humanity's primordial way of knowing, a total mode of discourse antedating the specialized vocabularies of narrow disciplines (without presuming of course to be totalizing in the manner of what Jean-Francois Lyotard famously called the *grand récits* of modernity). In his more recent work, particularly *City of God* and *The Waterworks*, he gives this emphasis a strongly cognitive dimension by developing a veritable genealogy of modern, biological forms of agency and selfhood at odds with traditional narratives of individual autonomy and by foregrounding the extraordinary (linguistic) capacities, whether for good or for ill, of the human brain. "Literary practitioners are conservatives who cherish the ultimate structures of the human mind," he once noted, a mind "structured for storytelling" and proceeding from "a confidence of narrative that must belong to us and to our brains as surely as we are predisposed to the protocols of grammar" (*Universe* 52, 24–25). Recognizing this hardwiring of language as a cognitive instrument in the human brain—the way in which Noam Chomsky and Steven Pinker, among others, have maintained for decades—fundamentally underlies Doctorow's repeated insistence on the superiority of print over film in his media ecological considerations, just as it reflects current accounts in linguistics and evolutionary biology that stress "the cognition-enhancing and cognitive-transforming powers of public language itself." The daily recursive work with language, understood as a recent evolutionary development, may well have equipped humans "to think such an open-ended variety of thoughts and hence that cognitive systematicity may be . . . rather closely tied to our linguistic abilities themselves" (Clark 78–79).

If this bio-linguistic version of cognition is close to "the slowly evolving consciousness" of Murray Seligman in *City of God*, the novel's second Nobel Prize winner reconciling cutting-edge physics with metaphysics (253), it also registers in *City of God*'s narrative form. A "printed circuit" with multiple points of view, numerous discontinuous passages and encompassing virtually everything under the sun, all the major characters of this encyclopedic novel become expert decoders of mystic and cryptic, electric and electronic signs and signals, ranging from radio frequencies in ghettos and communications during both world wars to secret letters and several codes, among many, many others (181). One could easily make the case that the novel authorizes its own tortured search for a divine Presence out of the paradox between the extraordinary sophistication of twentieth-century communication and information technologies and their fundamental inability to avoid the carnage of the modern world; instead of facilitating global understanding and tribal communion (à la McLuhan), new media seem to lead to atavistic regressions at odds with the evolutionary cerebration of human being. The point here is that readers, like the novel's major players, become (as they always must) co-creators in the process of decoding and that this process is intimately linked to the dislocations of the narrative itself. Doctorow has said that his rationale for the form of *City of God* was to see "our minds as clusters of web sites" so that the novel's structure can serve as "a template for our discontinuous minds" swimming in an "overabundance of stimuli" and suffering from "cultural ADD" ("On *City*").[10] Just as readers are called upon to engage the full resources of their cognitive horizons to initiate decryption, without ever reaching signifying closure, so the novel's inchoate form itself points to the chaotic dynamics and emergent structures of self-organizing systems (such as the sign system novel), engaged by the very activity of reading, without ever reaching a state of permanent equilibrium. Narrative structure represents the aleatory, convergent process of distributed cognition itself, its synchrony as a clustering cascade of processing knots (similar to *Under the Volcano*'s meaning machine, now with a cognitive twist). At the same time, the density of that narrative structure, its multileveled and multistranded texture, points to the dialectic between the (over)determination of form and the signifying process, that is, the catch-up game of the brain forever running behind in the challenge of decoding and evolving its synaptic firings to ever new levels of complexity and speed—what Hubert Dreyfus has called the "thickness" of cognitive processing (198). In the long, evolutionary run, cultural ADD translates into not only additive but exponential pathway combinations.[11] In the sign system novel, indeed, "the venerable science of hermeneutics" is always at work (115).

Like Doctorow, Richard Powers developed an interest in the relays between narrative and cognition in the 1980s when the modularity of mind began to circulate in the society of mind, and, like Doctorow, Powers has emphasized "the bidirectional relation between narrative and cognition," the process of "fabulation, inference, and situational tale-spinning that consciousness uses to situate itself and make a continuity out of the interruptive fragments of perception." He has also emphasized the circularity between perception and story, noting that "the actively narrating conscious brain is not arbitrary; it is itself the evolutionary product of several billion years of bumping up against the world" (qtd. in Neilson 2–3). Thus acknowledging the interplay of external reality with a decentered narrative collaborator living in that reality, Powers has made cognition as, of, and in narrative his subject of choice, not only mastering with baffling erudition "entire disciplinary knowledges at a rate of a new book every three years" but also writing about cognition in embodied and artificial forms, as in *Galatea 2.2* (Tabbi, *Fictions* 59).[12] Unlike the more punctual cognitive references in Doctorow's fiction, *Galatea* systematically illustrates the full spectrum of first- through third-generation cognitive research, including its disciplinary camps, as readers witness the evolution of a fledgling database into a large-scale distributed network designed to pass a master's exam in English. (That Powers does so in narrative form testifies in itself to one cognitive dimension of the novel in that it affords passage of a narrowly prescribed discourse into the wider public domain.) Rather than offering a full cognitive reading of *Galatea*, however, which would carry the risk of redundancy (and involve the question of memory, brain malfunction, and the condition of literary criticism at a time of science), I want to conclude by looking briefly at the novel's relays between language and cognition, and at the interplay of embodiment, the materialities of writing, and the (posthuman) notion of agency that have been of concern in much of this book.[13]

Language and (Narrative) Cognition in *Galatea 2.2*

Linguists have often expressed awe at the nuanced range of linguistic expression. Zellig Harris, for one, claimed that "language was much more powerful than humans recognized or, in general had need of. He compared it to a dynamo used to operate a door bell" (qtd. in Spolsky 16). Powers too revels in the powers of language, cultivating a register of style that is as awesome as language itself is resilient in its reach. Readers of his fiction enter a dense thicket of tropes and metaphors, and a concomitant luxuriance of thought, that illuminates in surprising ways specialized knowledge in disciplines such as genetics, evolutionary paleontology, and molecular biology. As well, in what amounts to a version of distributed cognition, Powers often alternates dramatic revelation with a more essay-like, discursive rhetoric "because that's how the human organism works. We employ all sorts of intelligences, from low-level bodily intuitions to high-level, syllogistic rationalism" (qtd. in J. Williams 12). Such an infusion of realist modes with hybrid innovations have often identified Powers as a literary egghead, instead of seeing his, in effect, cerebral dance as an expression of both linguistic *jouissance* in the service of illumination and a reaffirmation of his ongoing experiment with narrative cognition.[14]

For that reason, Powers rejuvenates the much-maligned notion of organicism, a leftover of the New Criticism, to suggest the integral reciprocities between form and content. Observing that "in its true sense, 'organic' form is by far the most complex and ingenious of any form imaginable," he notes that style and subject matter form an indivisible, evolutionary whole much like the scale levels of a chaotic system: "When a story 'lives,' I think it generally has all the breathtaking, indescribable complexity of a living hierarchy. Organism, organ, cell—novel, scene, sentence: form shades off into the same particulars that evade and inscribe it" ("Dialogue" 2). Echoing his belief in the merger of narrative and expository rhetoric as complementary cognitive forms, and gesturing toward autopoietic models of self-organization, Powers acknowledges that his writing ideally instantiates such a model of biological organicism: "Successful writing advances as its own, complex, living hierarchy, one that mirrors the kind of complex hierarchy that we living beings are.... You could look at a sentence of a well-made story and see it as a fractal microcosm of the entire working of the story" (qtd. in J. Williams 8).

Thus, *The Gold Bug Variations* is a book "about linguistic mutation and wordplay" in which Powers tries to replicate his "vision of the genetic code as a punning, runaway fecundity in the book's prose," while "the transparent style of [*Galatea*] tries to recapitulate the child Helen learning how to read" (qtd. in Neilson).[15] Indeed, a novel that seeks to model the process of English-language acquisition by an AI—which is paralleled by the narrator's struggle with Dutch—cannot but gesture at the lexical density which it is the brain's job to unravel and group into semantic units with lightning speed. Thus, when the narrator's cognitive tutor, Lentz, offers a burlesque of Dutch syntax, his verbal contortions point to the incredible complexities of language and, in a recursive loop, to the processural challenges such complexity poses to the weighted weaves of neuropathways: "An even by native speakers not until the ultimate grammatical arrival capable of being unraveled word order that one's brain in ever more excruciatingly elaborate cortical knots trivially can tie" (18). Similarly, when the narrator notes that "something had slipped 'twixt cortex and lips," as he chronicles his hilarious faux pas in Dutch, he illustrates in twisted proverbial form the density of utterance as well as his at least retrospective, and notably cognitive, wit, let alone his cultural-linguistic illiteracy (187). (It may well be for this reason that he is then, at this cross-linguistic stage of his life, writing "his most American book" [189].) In a different vein, when an early neural net does its first linguistic steps, it eventually learns by itself how to "plough through tough dough," thus signaling not only Powers's verbal exuberance once again but, more important, the phonemic sequence of sounds whose phonetic sequence is truly mind-boggling, yet which it is the job of brain or network to sort into discrete units of meaning (30).[16] Each of these sentences or phrases stands as a pars pro toto for the immense cognitive effort involved in making speech (or writing) into sense; each operates as a cryptogram encoding the decoding operations at the center of the novel.

Similarly, as Lentz and Powers are reaching a new level of network complexity (Imp F), the narrator celebrates the unfathomed processing capabilities of the human brain that enable him to rise to the rhetorical occasion deserving of the moment. Matching verbal brilliance with the networking brilliance he seeks to sing, his prose becomes as soaring and scintillating as the biological pyrotechnics of firing pathways which, it is implied, no digital network could assemble: "Every neuron formed a middle term in a continuous, elaborate, brain-wide pun. With a rash of dendrite inputs and handfuls of axon outs, each cell served as enharmonic point in countless constellations, shifting configurations of light, each circuit standing in for some new sense. To fire or not to fire meant different things, depending on how the registers aligned at a given instant and which other alignments read the standing sum. Each node was an entire computer, a comprehensive comparison. And the way they fit together was a cupola itself" (154). In this rhapsodic blueprint of connectionism, which reads like a microgalactic weave, knowledge and thought are metaphorized as a decentered dance of nerves, an interplanetary play of circuits that is as textured and beautiful as the language attempting to celebrate it. On a small scale that mirrors the larger narrative architecture, the grace and density of style and subject matter once more line up to go beyond even the most sophisticated composition software and furthermore, in the recursive loop characteristic of Powers, reflect on cognition itself.

Such microstructural nesting (which is also visible in Lowry's writing to sustain narrative momentum and defer closure) registers in *Galatea 2.2* also on two larger and interrelated levels: canonicity and narrative form. Powers has repeatedly said that *Galatea* afforded him a collective look back at all his work written up to this point, so that each preceding novel is reflected upon (by a distributed self different from the composite self-aggregates that had written them). Just as a sentence, scene, or chapter in Powers's poetics can operate as corresponding scale levels within a novel, so each previous novel functions as a building block or narrative nucleus in *Galatea;* each operates as a memory cell in what amounts to a collective narrative deposit, and recursive references to all of his earlier novels abound. In that sense alone, literary narrative can be understood as "a supreme connection machine," as Powers puts it (qtd. in J. Williams 7). Thus, the narrator of *Galatea* notes that in *Prisoner's Dilemma,* he "meant to reverse-engineer experience" into what "shaped itself as a set of nested Russian dolls" (160); similarly, of *The Gold Bug Variations* he notes that he "tried to code into its paragraph cells" private experiences to provide "some fossil record" of lived life; his metaphors were meant to capture "the way the genome carries along in time's wake all the residue of bygone experiments and hypotheses, from bacteria on" (256). The point here is that this archaeology of personal remembrances is paralleled both by the engineering of the successive neural networks and by the canonical compression evident in the layered texture of *Galatea.* Just as the novel is the most recent depositing site for (its) previous textual memes, so Helen contains all of its previous implementations and *Galatea* itself trace elements of much of the canon of English and American literature. This convergence is made explicit when Lentz describes the memory loss of his wife, Audrey, following a brain aneurism: "Each machine life lived inside the others—nested generations of 'remember this.' We did not start from scratch with each revision. We took what we had and cobbled on to it.... E's weights and contours lived inside F's lived inside G's, the way Homer lives on in Swift and Joyce, or Job in Candide or the Invisible Man" (170), or, one might add, the way they all live on in Powers.

However, while Helen amasses digitized literary bits into a synchronic database, and while her neural net at times vaguely resembles the complexity of the cerebral weave, she is without the embodied awareness that comes with organic being. The diachronic and dialectic layering of language and the canon as the joint expressions of evolutionary condensation, as well as the understanding of what Powers has called "the archive of literature as the race's high-level genome" as a grown structure over time, are sensibilities that do not seem emergent in her silicon pathways (qtd. in Neilson). Helen *does* have a mind-boggling database of hundreds of years of literary production contained within her, but she cannot develop the embodied, historical sense that these works have been authored, often laboriously and under great physical strain, by human bodies in time, nor can she vicariously experience the actions of literary characters grounded as they are in physical experience. Her *information* about these works is accessible virtually instantaneously, but *knowledge* about the embodied conditions of both literary production and imaginative being she has none.[17] Similarly, while her incessant accumulation of experience will change her processing matrices for future input—and hence any new "reading" experience—that experience only comes in highly mediated bits divorced from a body and is thus always limited to computerized channels.

Yet, it is precisely these embodied conditions of reading and print, coupled with the awareness of the canon as a literary archive of cognition, that *Galatea* itself demonstrates. While Powers and his narrative self are clearly in awe of neural network capability, the novel emphasizes the mental practices fostered by attention to a core of printed texts (as does its own artifactuality). In contrast to Helen's instant retrieval system (and much as in *City of God, Under the Volcano,* and nearly every literary text with a layered thickness), the reader has to work *through* the text of *Galatea* itself and integrate, in a massively diachronic parallel operation, numerous allusive commentaries into the ongoing narrative. The intertwining of this double bildungsroman—that of the Powers-narrator and that of Helen—offers, or requires of, the reader a further intertwining with the allusive structures lacing the narrative texture. The surface unfolding of the text—the parallel yet parallaxed stories of the narrator's involvement with C. and H—is imbricated with the text's deep structure, its fossil record of literary allusions, which the reader's cognitive effort and cultural knowledge combine into an oscillating constellation whereby textual synchrony and literary diachrony (e)merge into a kind of narrative origami or double helix. Thus, just as Lentz's ironic appellation of the Powers-narrator as "Marcel" multiply resonates with Proust's prodigious effort to remember things past in all their writerly immediacy (and hence echoes the narrator's own recollective project), the allusions to literary oddballs—from Frankenstein to Tarzan to Kaspar Hauser, among many others—echo the vicissitudes of linguistic acculturation, with their obvious reference to Helen. Similarly, in a particularly concentrated form, when the narrator explains to Helen that literature is "inductive proof of thought's infinitude," he offers a small-scale archive of canonical quotations that readers can combine with the running narrative surface in ways a disembodied neural network is hard-pressed to do: "She wanted to know whether a person could die by spontaneous combustion. The odds against a letter slipped under the door slipping under the carpet as well. Ishmael's real name. Who this 'Reader' was. . . . Whether single men with fortunes really needed wives. What home would be without Plumtree's Potted Meats" (292). This allusive sequencing, continuing for almost half a page, is grounded in bodily experience and throws into relief the difference in cognitive performance between Helen and humans. Embodied experience, as Antonio Damasio and others have argued, can supply answers to these questions no amount of digitized analytical reasoning or combinatorial capacity can, and the constant back and forth between *Galatea*'s allusive layers and textual surface in the act of reading (involving irony, parody, and subversive commentary, among many others) can assume numerously unpredictable, slippery, and shifting constellations not readily available to computational algorithms.

At the same time, *Galatea*'s double helical interlocking of surface and depth also recuperates literary thinking at a time of postliterary information flow. If the authorial messages contained within a literary canon, as William Paulson has argued, were and still are "part of strategies of social and intellectual control," they may "nonetheless interfere with the newer cybernetic loops in which we are more immediately and pressingly caught up" ("Canon" 243). Opposing or relativizing forms of computerized information processing, old works "provide a space of freedom away from the most immediate and contemporary of the cognitive and discursive constraints acting upon us" ("Canon" 246). Put differently, by implanting an entire matrix of canonical allusions into a narrative about high-speed and high-level computation, and a computation that fundamentally involves the recognition of literary passages, Powers juxtaposes the algorithmic, high-volume, and virtually indiscriminate processing of a neural net with the more measured, reflectively selective, and qualitatively different sorting operations of a human brain geared toward the slower decoding processes of alphabetic reading; these decoding processes, in turn, are partly instantiated by the changing oscillations between textual surface and depth that the novel brings into being. Contained within the old-fashioned form of a print narrative, the textured canonical layers in *Galatea* not only cater to literary knowledge and connoisseurship but also invite reflection, amusement, and a form of cognitive labor straining against the technological and economic modes of processing built into Helen itself: the electronic accumulation, manipulation, and exchange of bits of information.

Significantly, the very title of the novel, *Galatea 2.2*, indicates this fissured fusion of canonicity with the reading process in terms of a software upgrade. An obvious allusion to Pygmalion and his sculpting of a lifelike ivory statue named Galatea, the sleeping beauty of Greek mythology, it is also a recursive and multiply shaded reference to the activities in the novel in which male egos—like Pygmalion, often distrustful of women—try to create a virtually lifelike neural network gendered as female to compensate for their (failed) engagements with real women, even as they are looking toward these women for their models of Helen. Diana Hartrick, the one female among an otherwise male cadre of cognitive researchers, agrees with the narrator's assessment that their monthly book club is "for the men who need to play Pygmalion" (183), and the narrator himself at one point observes that he "wanted to write the story of a man who made a living by imitating a statue," no doubt aware that he is now engaged in a cybernetic mutant of that very story (35). If Helen's hardware is, indeed, the brainchild of Lentz's almost Mephistophelian ingenuity, the deposits in her data banks are largely those of the narrator's literary feeds, thus making Helen the sp(l)it image, if you will, of an all-male literary-scientific parenting couple. These and repeated other allusions to and inversions of the Pygmalion myth, often involving the narrator's love interests as well as Lentz's wife, point to the multiply folded rewritings of the "original" myth and are encoded in the title's digital iteration. Not only is there no "real" original (in fact, two complementary versions of the Galatea myth exist), that very original has been, like a software program, upgraded and enriched with present-day overtones to yield a repeatedly modified story platform that is recognizable in its iterative refraction (and thus adds to the allusive density of literary discourse challenging even to the reading abilities of a Helen). As the narrator puts it in the novel's cryptic opening: "It was like so, but wasn't" (3).[18]

What is more, the title's digital refraction also expresses the novel's central concern with embodiment and cognition generally. The complementary and reversible mirroring of 2.2 suggests the synergy of mind and body as one indivisible unit of being, the organic integration of the brain within its corporeal housing, as well as that body's environmental context. That kind of organic reciprocity is what Helen perpetually falls short of, simply because her experience is fully mediated by digitized portals, but never embodied. The 2.2, in that sense, is also legible as a sensuous-sinuous palindrome, an almost feminine curvature forever one step shy of embodiment. A digitized, "material theory of mind" in itself, Powers maintains, is not enough (297)—leading Helen herself to eventually pull the plug and commit cybersuicide. At the same time, the title's *2.2* encodes the notion of a fluid and perpetually decentered selfhood at the heart of cognitive science. The narrator of Powers's first novel, *Three Farmers*, already reflects that he molds his past decisions and experiences "into some biographical whole, inventing for myself a theme and a continuity" (206). In the more cognitive *Galatea*, the narrator similarly comes to accept the incessant reconstitution of the self based on all of his prior reading, his *déjà lu* accruing in the skull. A "coauthored" essay by Diana (that is, an essay growing out of collaborative, distributed cognition) convinces him that "[e]very sentence, every word I'd ever stored had changed the physical structure of my brain," leading him to abandon the fiction of the coherent self: "The writer who had signed on to the reckless bet [of creating a neural network] was dead" (56). Conversely, he comes to realize that while consciousness is always at one remove from observation because it itself cannot be observed at the moment of reflection, its function yet must be "in part to dummy up and shape a coherence from all the competing, conflicting subsystems that processed experience. By nature, it lied" (217). Every act of cognition is, fundamentally, a fissured process projecting a coherent self that is de facto always refracted and continuously refracting at every moment of consciousness—a schism indicated by the number 2 and the dot between 2 and 2.[19]

In that sense, the split doubling of 2 also points to the cognitive gap or slippage occurring during every process of reading and meaning making, done as it always is by a distributed self that is different from its earlier self-aggregates. Just as every self is continuously rearranging itself into a quasi-fictional composite whole, so the constellations of sense change with every run through a text—as in the case of *Galatea*'s oscillation between narrative surface and allusive depth. Indicating this slippage of self, Powers has noted that "every first-person story," as is *Galatea*, "is a constant recursive revision (hence 2.2, and not 2.0). I can no more read my work twice than I can see the same thing in any work that I go back to in the run of time" (qtd. in Kiteley). Similarly, indicating the slippage of sense, he observes that any portion of text "*means* by setting up expectations and then not quite fulfilling them, leaving the slightly rearranged expecter to do a calculus on the gap opened up between the expected trajectory and the resultant one" ("Dialogue" 4).[20] Put differently, and in the cognitive context of *Galatea,* the "weird parallaxes of framing" in the brain's architecture "must be why the mind opened out on meaning at all. Meaning was not a pitch but an interval. It sprang from the depth of disjunction, the distance between one circuit's center and the edge of another" (154). This amounts not only to a recasting of the sense-making models of reader-response theory, such as Wolfgang Iser's notion of gaps, in cognitive terms, as in the work of Daniel Dennett (whose "gappy" consciousness model is similarly phenomenological);[21] the interval between processual nodal points also models biologically what the gap or deferral between 2.0 and 2.2 signifies in its iterated sequence. While the computer and the human brain may well both work through similar principles of back-propagation, it is only the embodied brain—and the self generated in that brain—that can register, and conceive of, the full weight of this difference. The brain is more than a version of software, after all, as the narrator slowly comes to realize. That his anthropomorphic urge (which culminates in his erotic attachment to a machine gendered and named by himself) does, at the beginning, not quite allow him to do so is nicely captured in a reflective moment regarding the naming of the neural nets: "We called that first filial generation B, but it would, perhaps, have been better named A2" (170). Instead of acknowledging the concentric articulation of the successive Imps, with one growing out of and superseding the other, in the language of software upgrades, each implementation is given a separate, lettered identity as if indicating its progressive proximity to the humans who serve as its cognitive models and competitors: C. and A. Rarely has the point after a letter made more of a difference.[22]

Posthuman Embodiment, Writing, and Print

The links between (dis)embodiment, agency, and authorship are fully evident in Powers's novels. The narrator of *Three Farmers,* a tech writer in the computer industry, is being told that "I was one of the few who carried my weight in the office," adding that "I've always been rather light for my weight" (79). The Dutch immigrant woman befriending him in the office, indeed, leaves chocolate bonbons on his desk "because she had seen my photo in the . . . company newsletter and had vowed to save me from terminal thinness" (127);

then, on the last day of the year, in keeping with Dutch custom, he finds "the chocolate letter P, my last initial" (203), arranged on his desk, indicating an almost literal filling out, a compensatory way of giving weight and body to a narrative center on the verge of anorexia. Similarly in *Galatea,* the narrator feels the danger of dematerialization when, as humanist-in-residence at the Center for the Study of Advanced Sciences, he begins to think of himself "in the virtual third person, as that disembodied World Wide Web address: rsp@center.visitor.edu" (9).[23] The doubly generic letter sequence, barely individualized by the lowercase initials at the beginning, suggests anxiousness about dispersion into a network and about shrinking to a digitized pattern, even as the central female figures populating his narrative are literally made up of "characters" and are thus curiously reduced to hollow markers stripped of any embodiment. While the focalizing figure is fearful of losing his own weighted presence, he yet deflates the (often threatening) bodies of women to the materiality of a single letter—and is hence not entirely unhappy that Helen, as the virtual doppelgänger of C., is a disembodied and multiply distributed terminal without sexual needs.[24]

Yet, like the return of the repressed, embodiment pushes through the textual surface in numerous ways. For one, the abbreviated narrators of Powers's oeuvre for the first time fill out into "Richard Powers," as if balancing the threat of erasure and self-effacement. Paralleling their role as carriers of Powers's own cumulative research, they shoulder "a weight of information that would overwhelm conventional characters" (Tabbi, *Fictions* 60), and a weight that is, in *Galatea,* given material expression in the full spelling of the name. The novel's informational density, particularly its front-loadedness about cognitive science readers have to work through before entering lighter narrative stretches, is replicated in the lettered materiality of the narrator's name, a kind of a concentration that corresponds to *Galatea*'s ongoing self-reflection about Powers's preceding work. It may well be for that very reason that the narrator, in his dalliance with A., takes issue with the poststructural notion of the "author function" (286), as it would reduce the embodied knowledge base of authorial agency to an, at best, half-intentional network of impulses or codes divorced from more traditional matters of intention and craftsmanship. Although the Powers-narrator accepts a fluid notion of selfhood, he is unwilling to surrender his creative artistry, particularly in matters of language, to airy theoretical constructs. What is more, precisely because Helen's output port (a loudspeaker) does not lend itself to erotic fixation, the narrator yields, against his better judgment, to A.'s postcolonial musings because they came "from A.'s mouth. She convinced me at blood-sugar level, deep down, below words. In the layer of body's idea" (286). Embodied being, as a subject of a sexualized fetish and over against computerized voice production, once again carries the day.[25]

Most important, however, it is in the materiality of print (not the intangibility of voice) that the narrator figure vests his weighted sense of agency and authorship. He is aware that "like the human body, the book is a form of information transmission and storage, and like the human body, the book incorporates its encodings in a durable material substrate." He similarly knows that books and humans have a "resistant materiality that has traditionally marked the durable inscription of books no less than it has marked our experiences of living as embodied creatures" (Hayles, *Posthuman* 28–29). Embodiment and print, and the link between signal and heft, are part of a large synergy that allows the narrator to secure his own materiality against dissolution into data patterns, particularly in a project that involves him, above all, as an ephemeral voice converted into digitized bits. He appreciates the solidity of books, particularly the great guns of the Western canon, as a venerable expression of print-based stability, as a congealed form of distributed cognition over time. As Helen is "thinking the unthinkable: the disappearance of books from all but the peripheries of life," he counters that "the archive is permanent" and that "it does for the species what associative memory fails to do for the individual" (290–91). Similarly, even as some of Powers's essays and interviews have appeared online, and his deep interest in cutting-edge science would make him a "natural" for hypertext and electronic publishing formats, his novels only appear in print form and insist on their bound and unalterable durability, as material objects resistant to the sudden erasure or manipulation of a digitized database. Exercising control over the design of his books, such as redoubling August Sander's animating photograph both on the front cover and the flyleaf of *Three Farmers* (not a cheap proposition for any publisher), he has refused to allow a picture of himself on a book jacket until *Galatea*, fully aware that his very first novel was prompted by that very medium (in Keller 4). Indeed, the positioning of his work from the start in the contact zones between various disciplines and media highlights, in the recursion characteristic of Powers, the noteworthy qualities of books and the qualities that make print-based embodiment possible.

Thus, while all previous novels get their share in *Galatea*, the Powers-narrator draws particular attention to the surcharged materialities of *The Gold Bug Variations*. With a manuscript length of "thirteen hundred pages," the narrator imagines his publisher asking to "free the skinny book hiding inside this sumo," thus suggesting not only proportionality between material heft and intellectual ambition (in danger of being unrecognized or misunderstood) but also that weight extends into cognitive reach: thought is the result of embodied being. Deciding to send the work in "a small crate" and "by boat" (not the faster option of airmail), he "cradled the box, with its long customs form marked *Drukwerk*. Printed Matter. Several kilos of story, an attempt to feel, in music, life's first principles and to hear, in those genetic principles, living tune" (256–57). The heft of printed type is once more figured as a live body, an intellectual offspring whose durable materiality encodes live matter resistant to easy manipulation: proteins and print are possessed of a quickening inertia that makes them ideal vehicles of embodied storage, including the senses of touch and (aesthetic, appreciative) hearing. The compressed density of verbal composition and DNA encoding are suggested to be complementary acts of inscription and culminate in the emphatic foregrounding of "*Drukwerk*. Printed Matter"—the weighted work of print harboring the code of life.

Helen, by contrast, can feel no such materiality. Not only is she a neural network without a human body, heavy as her dispersed hardware is; much unlike the compounded reading experience of *Galatea*'s narrator, she cannot physically register the "crucial" peripheral sensory impressions such as "the smell of the cover, the color and cream resistance of the pages" as well as "the bed, the lamp, the room where I read." Self-conscious as she may be, Helen is congenitally unable "to associate the meaning inherent in the words of a story with the heft and weight and bruise of the story's own existence" (229). "Reading knowledge," as the narrator puts it earlier, "is the smell of the bookbinding paste. The crinkle of thick stock as the pages turn. Paper the color of aged ivory" (148). These materialities of print, in which Powers and his narrative personae partly vest their selves, are beyond her digitized reach.

And yet, if taking into account Powers's own practices of writing, it becomes apparent that the (authorial) self emerging from his fiction straddles the fence between traditional subjecthood vested in the materialities of print and a more posthuman notion of authorship in which embodiment becomes increasingly light and lithe. As if going through most stages of late nineteenth- and twentieth-century textual production, Powers wrote his first few novels longhand and then typed his revisions using a computer. At the same time, the one-time programmer also developed a specific software application for *Three Farmers* to refine and check the patterns of his style (in Neilson 6–8). More recently, Powers has been experimenting with a wireless keyboard to beam his prose onto a giant computer screen across the room in which he writes (often in a bedroom). Noting that "typing is a very artificial thing," that "we've gotten good at it, but basically it means breaking down the whole semantic phrase into individual letters—which is not the way we think and compose" (qtd. in Keller), he has also started to work with voice-activated software to dictate into a headset: "I can lie in bed, stretch out or walk around. My goal for technology has always been to reach a point where the technological mediation becomes invisible. Now I can compose the way Wordsworth used to, wandering around the Lake District" (qtd. in Eakin).[26]

As classical, embodied forms of textual production, hand- and typewriting require physical effort and suggest long hours of often laborious work, even though the use of pen or typewriter already removes the body from what still goes by the name of manuscript. Walking and speaking are, similarly, physical activities, and while their kind of exertion is not comparable to the traditional scene of writing, they are both tied to the body and, each in their own way, conducive to composition. As complementary activities that can induce in the writer a measured sense of steadiness, with voice and step begetting word after word, they enable writing through the fundamentally embodied rhythms of physical movement and aural cadence. At the same time, writing for Powers is also a matter of physical ease, of composing out loud into a voice-activated recorder, much like modern authors (such as the late James, or the Lowry who also envisioned himself as a meandering Wordsworth) dictated to their (classically female) secretaries. Developing a software code that automatically scans his work for stylistic features similarly suggests a way of refining text separate from sustained physical action. This dimension of Powers's writing—a progressive removal of the body, and particularly the digits, from the physical act of writing—puts him close to Helen's digitized modes of operation, and only confirms the erroneous assumptions of those Powers detractors who see in him a novelist of head, not heart, a brain unable to let the language(s) of the body come forth. It may also invite speculation that Powers, for all his resistance to corporate practices, has succumbed to the high-speed textual processing characteristic of postindustrial culture. Caught in the vicious circle of editorial policies demanding more and more (of the best) in ever-shortening cycles of consumption, he has surrendered his earlier modes of writing in favor of text-generating media designed to increase his output as a writer.

I prefer to see Powers's shifting writing practice in more media-theoretical terms, as does Powers himself. He knows that no matter how transparent any writing technology purports to be, it is fundamentally always an embodied and mediated process; and he similarly knows that any change in the synergy of body and inscription system will, in effect, redefine the conditions of embodiment. Thus, as his (Kittlerian) observations on the typewriter show, any hand-based form of inscription is fundamentally at odds with "the way we think and compose." Breaking down the "whole semantic phrase into individual letters" interrupts the fluidity of ideas emerging in the mind, a fluidity that is captured more readily by speaking into a recording device. Composing in such a way not only shortens the distance between conception and its materialization as text; while reduced in physical effort (in the classical sense of manual labor), such a way of composing is, fundamentally, also still an embodied process and closer to the human dream of an invisible, interfaceless interface. As Powers puts it, "I want to feel as if there isn't any mediation between me and the words as they come out" (qtd. in Keller). It is almost a way of writing, not *against* but *with* the body. This is of course an insight known already to Dr. Seward in *Dracula*, the first doctor in literature to speak his medical records onto a phonographic roll. As the technological link between thought and writing reduces in distance, so increases the immediacy between cognitive and physical work to the point where emergent thought in the mind is, if not coterminous with its voice-activated transcription, a step closer to what we could call inscription in real time: the dizzying speed of thinking, as it forms and crystallizes into discrete (verbal) units, can be more easily recorded in a medium that can bypass the resistant materiality of the body, such as the heavy-handedness of the writing hand.

Thus, while Powers (and his narrative incarnations), much like his modernist predecessors, seeks to embody himself in the materialities of print, he also strives for a, in theory, frictionless and virtually disembodied mode of composition that can keep pace with the rush and lightness of cognitive work. While he insists on a version of literary craft that is close to the classical agency of autonomy, his writing practices also suggest the acceptance of a posthuman view of control that comes about "through chaotic dynamics and emergent structures" (Hayles, *Posthuman* 288). For if his dictations resemble modernist forms of "automatic writing," they do so by acknowledging the slips 'twixt cortex and lips: the synergy of conscious and unconscious creativity to be edited and revised upon printing. As he put it in a recent essay, notwithstanding the precision of his speech software to transcribe voice into word, "my software's recognition engine doesn't model meaning. So where my fingers might stop at changing 'sign' to 'sing,' my [PC] tablet can turn my words hallucinatory without limit" ("How to Speak"). Artistic craft and subliminal work, purposeful word choice and verbal autosuggestion, oscillate in a kind of distributed creativity recordable by the phonograph and its present-day implementations. Powers's mode of composing is certainly no direct transcript of neuronal activity in the cerebral cortex—the unspoken fantasy of many a science-fiction story—but the recording of voice and its subsequent translation into text may give Powers the kind of (posthuman) embodiment older forms of mediation were not capable of producing: presence through the virtual simultaneity of enunciation—ephemeral, but coming from a body—and its digital imprint, amenable to subsequent correction.

Of course, more so than his earlier colleagues, Powers is well aware that mediation without resistance is impossible, noting that "the more advanced the media, the higher the level of mediation," which is to say, the promise of transparency means just the opposite, an impenetrable thicket of code: "the digital age has completely reversed the sense of the word transparent. We speak of transparent applications, of transparent operating systems, of transparent interfaces, when what we really mean, here, is *opaque*. We want these new, active, symbol-like actants of ours to hide from us everything that is under the hood" ("Representation"). Powers, in that sense, shares some of Sven Birkerts's (and Jean-François Lyotard's) concerns about the hegemony of the bit and its deleterious effects on language and print culture. As if illustrating Powers's feminized database in *Galatea,* Birkerts famously (and elegiacally) noted that "once the materials of the past are unhoused from their pages, they will surely *mean* differently," meaning that the sense of chronology enshrined in books and libraries will yield to a depthless informational order—a *"flattening of historical perspectives"*—as humans come to rely increasingly on computerized retrieval systems. For Birkerts and Powers both, the book embodies history "as a growing deposit of sediment" (*Gutenberg* 129).

Birkerts similarly prophesies the gradual erosion of the private self as "the process of social collectivization" accelerates in the face of global connectivity. For humans becoming increasingly enmeshed in networks of information and power, "the expansion of electronic options is always at the cost of contractions in the private sphere" (*Gutenberg* 131). Powers, it would seem, agrees with this view, as he understands reading—and along with it, the cultivation of productive solitude—as a counterweight to the energies pulling on the networked self of tomorrow. Reading, for Powers, is "the last act of secular prayer," a way of "making a womb unto yourself" during which the reader is "blocking the end results of information and communication long enough to be in a kind of stationary, meditative aspect" (qtd. in Berger). As a slow and singular cottage industry in the age of industrial information, reading is out of sync with networked being, a private and silent activity shoring up the self in danger of dissolving into electronic circuits.

But where Birkerts sees a large-scale erosion of language as a result of digitization, Powers sees an opportunity for creative intervention. While "a more telegraphic sort of 'plainspeak'" and "simple linguistic prefab" are no doubt widely in evidence (*Gutenberg* 28)—and in fact have been for a while, especially in instrumental forms of communication—Powers, like the writers we have looked at previously in this book, reclaims the province of print literature as a medium reasserting its literariness once more or, to put it differently, its function as a zone for the fullest possible marshaling of verbal and imaginary resources.[27] Powers, like Doctorow, Lowry, and Norris, as we have seen, all in their own way understand the novel as a medium whose very marginality in the postprint mediascape invites the fullest verbal suppleness, elegance, and intelligence, and a swath of signification and articulation that make it unique from other, later media.

This reassertion of print literature is of course intimately connected to the shifts in the relation between bodies and media this study has been tracing and which always bring about a different configuration of inscription. As Powers puts it, "I'm like a guitarist who wants to play in a different style, one with very fast action, one with nylon strings. Each arrangement produces a different physical relationship to the medium." His use of voice-activated software, he notes, may indeed lead to "a kind of fundamental shift in my style" (in Eakin), much like earlier media constellations produced literary forms and scenes of writing that are historically specific. Norris wrote against the regime of photographic surface by probing the invisible forces of human agency, and his conflicted position toward the typewriter expresses itself in a handwriting aesthetic and a fixation on manual mutilation that codifies his fear of lost agency and of a body severed from machine-mediated writing. Lowry saw in film a mimetic art form superior to print, which resulted in a prolonged writer's block and incomplete narrative forms whose fluidity is fundamentally cinematic, and despite an aesthetic appreciation for modernist technology, Lowry, like Norris, resisted the typewriter as an instrument of manual disembodiment and, conversely, romanticized handwriting as a form of unmediated naturalness. Doctorow, by contrast, has become thoroughly habituated to the dislocations between body and keyboard and, like Powers, sees his work in part as a corrective response to the flattening effects of mass mediation and the possibilities of digital manipulation that threaten to reassemble bodies and selves into flickering data patterns. While all the writers discussed in this study variously reflect on reflection and think about thinking, Doctorow and Powers in particular carry embodiment into the more contemporary domain of cognition to suggest that the Cartesian dream of severing the mind from the body is, for the foreseeable time at least, indeed only a pipe dream. In order to be human, in order to think and communicate—no matter how far removed from the technology of mediation—no body is in vain.

Notes

Chapter 1

1. The phrase is of course Marjorie Perloff's in *The Futurist Moment* passim.
2. In a contradictory, and hence self-de(con)structive, gesture that indicates the intellectual heritage of Bergson, Marinetti urges the cohabitation of "metallic discipline" with "the constant interchange of intuition, rhythm, instinct" (*Writings* 91)—organic attributes that are, of course, a far cry from today's hard-core hardware enthusiasts such as Friedrich Kittler and Hans Moravec.
3. See Haraway, "A Manifesto for Cyborgs," and the works of Paul Virilio, esp. *War and Cinema*.
4. Both Flusser and Kittler are responding to Jameson's lament that the "displacement of literary terminology by an emergent mediatic conceptuality" occurs at the historical moment when "the philosophical priority of language" has become "dominant and well-nigh universal" (*Postmodernism* 68). Thus Flusser, articulating a theory of posthistorical mediation, distinguishes between "conceptual codes" and "imaginal codes" that separate the waning order of alphabetic and linear—that is, historical and elitist—writing from the culturally ascending, spatial, and non-linear order of posthistorical images, such as photography, film, and virtual reality (*Writings* 28).
5. See, for example, Derrida, "Freud and the Scene of Writing," and, in a specifically Anglo-American context, Fried.
6. Emerging from a late modernist background, William Gaddis was among the few (in fact, *literary*) theorists to have taken stock of the player piano. His posthumous novella *Agapē Agape* is, among other things, a media-technological study of the impact of the player piano on American culture, as are several of his posthumously published essays (which served him as collection sites for a never realized, longer novel on the same subject). Observes Gaddis: "Analysis, measure, prediction and control, the elimination of failure through programmed organization, the player

emerged as a distillation of the goals that had surrounded its gestation in an orgy of fragmented talents seeking after the useful" (*Second Place* 13). For a fuller discussion of this issue, see my essay "Writing from between the Gaps."

7. For a similar argument, see Tabbi and Wutz, introduction to *Reading Matters*, esp. 3–6.

8. Self-conscious twentieth-century fiction generally subscribes to "a theory of prose style as radical artifice rather than native transparency," never denying, as Richard Lanham suggests, that print is "an act of extraordinary stylization" (9). More generally, as David Thorburn and Henry Jenkins have noted, the introduction of new media technologies engenders a "self-awareness" and "reassessment of established media forms, whose basic elements may now achieve a new visibility [and] become a source of historical research and renewed theoretical speculation. What is felt to be endangered and precarious becomes more visible and more highly valued" (4).

9. For critiques of the notion of technological determinism (including Marshall McLuhan's largely formalist media theory), see R. Williams, *Television*, and "Culture and Technology," esp. 119–23, as well as Latour and Gitelman.

10. See also LeClair: "Systems novels work the two extremes of low and high information, redundancy and overload, to register the contemporary significance of information" (14).

11. For Kittler's indebtedness to Foucault, including his inheritance of a "proclivity for unexplained epistemological ruptures," see Winthrop-Young, "Sociology," esp. 393–94 and 401–02.

12. With regard to the tension between liberal market culture (where locomotion signifies agency) and machine culture (where locomotion suggests automatism) characteristic of naturalism, Seltzer observes that "the uncertain status of the principle of locomotion precipitates the melodramas of uncertain agency" (17).

13. Shortly before his death, Norris and the widow of his friend Robert Louis Stevenson were apparently "persuaded to record their voices in a phonograph" (Van de Grift Sanchez 278), but I have been unable to locate the roll.

14. Fredric Jameson dates the "virtually fullblown emergence of filmic point of view" with Dreiser's *Sister Carrie* (*Unconscious* 160), the novel Norris's editorial advocacy at Doubleday and McLure helped usher into print one year after publishing *McTeague*. In "The Metropolis and Mental Life," Georg Simmel (soon to be followed by Walter Benjamin) noted that the intensity of urban life, threatening the integrity of a stable (really, premodern) self, can be met only by processing such stimuli in "the transparent, conscious, higher layers of the psyche" (175–76).

15. As Miles Orvell notes, in late nineteenth-century photography, "the pictured subject, with all its concrete particularity, *stands* for a more general class of like subjects. The individuality of the subject is thus presented on its own terms while it simultaneously serves the larger purpose of representing a general category" (88).

16. Auerbach had in mind the novels of Virginia Woolf and the emergent stream-of-consciousness tradition. Woolf, for her part, distinguished the representational

capacities particular to each medium: "All this, which is accessible to words, and to words alone, the cinema must avoid" (qtd. in Bluestone 21).

17. For Lowry's anxieties about writer's block, see McCarthy, esp. 133–40. In "Blocked," Joan Acocella provides a recent assessment of why modern (American) writers stop writing (without, however, discussing the possibly debilitating pressure from non-print media).

18. The novel of information multiplicity that most resembles *Under the Volcano* is, perhaps not surprisingly, Gaddis's *The Recognitions*, and both writers agreed, Lowry noting that Gaddis's novel is "a truly fabulous creation, a Super Byzantine Gazebo...funnier than Burton [his *Anatomy of Melancholy*] though Burton is a good parallel" (letter to David Markson, qtd. in Moore 9). Furthermore, Lowry's chaotic semiotics is close to Gaddis's own, as are their joint fixations on manual incapacitation and their belief in a creative trance or quasi-romantic possession (often with the help of spirits).

19. In a review of *The March* (2005), Vince Passaro nicely articulates the "distinct generational split" between Doctorow's (and Roth's and Updike's) not-quite-postmodern sensibilities, as opposed to those of his slightly younger contemporaries, such as Joan Didion and Don DeLillo (32). Born of the belief in a fundamentally idealized and hopeful understanding of the United States that originates in the judicial, labor, and military history of the 1930s and 1940s, Doctorow's vision (however complex) is "without the cold contempt of DeLillo" and "utterly lacks the ambivalence, paralysis and psychosis of postmodern fiction" (33). For Doctorow's initial reaction to television, see his *Conversations* (esp. 199–200); seeing the first "flat, hermetic, oppressive" picture became a kind of primal scene for him, as it did for Gaddis (199).

20. Doctorow's resistance parallels that of Jean-François Lyotard, who is similarly concerned that the introduction of (and possible domination by) "bits" as the elementary "units of information" could easily eliminate "any question of free forms given here and now to sensibility and the imagination" (*Inhuman* 34).

21. E. L. Doctorow to the author, 7 November 2005.

22. See Lanham for a scathing critique of Postman's reductive duality between print and television (236–46), with which Doctorow would not agree in such stark simplicity. Postman does not acknowledge evolutionary changes in brain processing, noting that "at no point do I care to claim that changes in media bring about changes in the structure of people's minds or changes in their cognitive capacities" (27).

23. Jay David Bolter similarly notes that the computer is another instance "of the metaphor of writing in the mind. With the aid of the computer, the writer constructs the text as a dynamic network of verbal and visual symbols. These electronic symbols in the machine seem to be an extension of a network of ideas in the mind itself. More effectively than the codex or the printed book, the computer reflects the mind as a web of verbal and visual elements in a conceptual space" (207–8).

24. In *The Second Self* and *Life on the Screen*, Sherry Turkle has shown how no-

tions of authorial and readerly selfhood have changed under the influence of the computer and the Internet, as "*we have learned to take things at interface value*" (*Screen* 23). Noting that in the "real-time communities of cyberspace, we are dwellers on the threshold between the real and the virtual . . . inventing ourselves as we go along," she shows that digital environments facilitate thinking of "identity as multiplicity" that extend Freud's model of a decentered self into the contemporary technological domain (*Screen* 10, 178).

25. See, for example, Heise; Winthrop-Young, "Sociology," esp. 410.

26. Tom LeClair observes, "Many, perhaps most, of our cognitive operations are analog in nature. Most of our storage of information is digital. . . . The artistic achievement of systems novelists is deforming synecdochic conventions of the fictional text—employing excess—to press a digital technology toward analog communication" (24).

27. See Virilio, *The Art of the Motor*, and de Kerckhove, *The Skin of Culture*, esp. "The Stress of Speed" (chap. 6, 65–75) and "Mass, Speed and Cyberculture" (chap. 12, 123–40). Michael Joyce calls this accelerating condition "an anticipatory state of constant nextness" ("Forms" 227), almost amounting to a form of virtual amnesia.

28. See the works by Postman and Kernan.

29. Murphy gives a succinct overview over the various theories of media change, including their shortcomings, noting that "If one would predict the death of books, one must understand how they live" (92).

30. In a further gesture of remediation, Joyce likens his narrative threads to "William Burroughs's compositional cuts," which, in turn, have their immediate origin in the montage and segmentation of film ("Forms" 234).

31. As the foremost American author of hypertext fiction, Joyce has, significantly, returned to print-based hypertextual narratives, as in *Liam's Going* (2002) and *Was* (2007), thus suggesting once more the cross-fertilizing reciprocity between these different media.

Chapter 2

1. As Ronald E. Martin has put it, Norris could "supply for his narrative an awesome cosmic background, a scientifically accredited set of causal explanations and a deep and abiding sense of either menace or reassurance, depending on what was called for by the fictional occasion" (148).

2. Thorstein Veblen in *The Theory of the Leisure Class* may have been among the first to recognize fluid divisions between "the animate and the inanimate" (qtd. in Seltzer 3). Tichi similarly notes that at the turn of the century, a "mix of American flora and fauna with pistons and gears, and engines indicates that the perceptual boundary between what is considered to be natural, and what technological, is disappearing" (34).

3. James develops a nuanced hierarchy of the poetics of print, ranging from tabloid journalism and magazines to the novel of artistic ambition. His journalists are

often caricatures of their "profession" at the expense of literary work. In *The Reverberator*, in response to a call for novels instead of magazines, journalist Flack whitewashes it all: "Well, it's all literature; it's all the press, the great institution of our time. Some of the finest books have come out first in the papers. It's the history of the age" (258). James's work provides a fine instance of how writers reflect on the tectonic tremors within the ecology of print. For analyses of these tensions, see Anesko and my essay "The Word and the Self in *The Ambassadors*."

4. Together with the sciences and manufacturing, journalism was one of the "great and highly developed phases of nineteenth-century intelligence" (Norris, *A Man's Woman* 268).

5. Barbara Hochman notes that "even at the level of explicit formulation, Norris was essentially committed to the aesthetic effect of truth, rather than to scientific or philosophical demonstration" (6).

6. See Norris's almost William Jamesian formulation about the fluidity of being: "[The artist's] personality is one thing today and another thing tomorrow; is one thing before dinner and another thing after it. How then to determine what life actually is?" (*Criticism* 57).

7. In a letter offering one of his articles on Cuba to *The Youth's Companion*, Norris states, "I took some dozen photographs to go with this article wh. I could forward you with the M.S. (typewritten)" (*Letters* 66).

8. This understanding of photography may have prompted William Dean Howells to describe Norris's work as approximating "the impartial fidelity of the photograph." He misunderstood Norris's fundamental sensibilities and sanctioned what was the reigning sensibility in the late nineteenth century: the conflation of photographic and literary "realism" as among the highest forms of contemporary art (242).

9. According to Scharf, the blurred image common in early photographs "is one of the innovations attributable to Impressionist paintings" (170). He also notes that "the uncompromising naturalism to which [Impressionists] aspired . . . their dedication to painting only before nature; the great emphasis on the objective eye; their desire to record the transitory character of natural light and shade, amounted to a kind of perceptual extremism which was germane to photography itself" (166). In media-theoretical terms that anticipate Scharf, Benjamin states, "With the increasing scope of communications and transport, the informational value of painting diminishes. In reaction to photography, painting begins to stress the elements of color in the picture. By the time Impressionism yields to Cubism, painting has created for itself a broader domain into which, for the time being, photography cannot follow" (*Selected Writings* 3:36).

10. "Salt and Sincerity" (V, June 1902), Frank Norris Collection, Bancroft Library, University of California, Berkeley (hereafter FNC, followed by box and folder number, if possible). Pizer's useful edition, *The Literary Criticism of Frank Norris*, reprints most of the "Salt and Sincerity" series but does not reproduce its page design (so important to Norris). The series' title is framed by a decorative flourish suggest-

ing Norris's fondness for medieval motifs, while the text is laced with boldface keyword inserts that gloss the gist of the article. The second insert, commenting on literary imitations, reads "chromoliterature."

11. Otto Glasser's classic history recounts how news of the rays was heard around the world within days (1–28). Musser notes that "the greatest photographic novelty during much of 1896 was not moving pictures but the x-ray. This newest discovery received constant newspaper attention [in San Francisco]." Early film "was outclassed by this impressive scientific discovery," because "Americans were even more impressed by the ability to reveal something no one could see than to capture and 'reproduce' what could be seen every day" (*Nickelodeon* 79–80). In one of his essays, Norris speaks of "the blonde, whiskered German Herr Doktor—Roentgen it is" (*Apprenticeship* 1:192).

12. The first apartment of Norris's parents in Chicago was located "above a photographer's shop" (Walker, *Norris* 9).

13. Green-Lewis notes that in nineteenth-century fiction, photographers are routinely "affirmed and controlled by their relegation to the fringes of novelistic action" (7). See her chapter, "Fiction's Photographers and Their Works," for a fuller discussion of the narrative treatment of photography (65–94).

14. Sekula similarly observes that evidentiary photographs at the time defined "both the generalized look . . . and the contingent instance" ("Body" 7).

15. Even less-developed figures, such as Old Grannis in *McTeague*, may owe their literary existence to Lombroso, who discusses a pensioner with a "pathological penchant for newspaper reading" (qtd. in Stingelin 65, my translation). See Bower for a recent reading on how Norris "racialize[s] the language of naturalism" (33).

16. "We understand the culture of the photographic portrait only dimly if we fail to recognize the enormous prestige and popularity of a general physiognomic paradigm in the 1840s and 1850s. Especially in the United States, the proliferation of photography and that of phrenology were quite coincident" (Sekula, "Body" 12). Green-Lewis provides a detailed analysis of the reciprocities between photography and facial readings (145–86).

17. The sudden interest in the artistic sketch by such artists as Honoré Daumier and Constantin Guys is intimately tied to photography. What the photographic apparatus could do by definition, that is, capture the fleeting moment, was done by hand in quickly executed drawings. As Benjamin put it, in his analogy between artist and detective, "He develops forms of reaction that are in keeping with the pace of a big city. He catches things in flight. . . . Everybody praises the swift crayon of the graphic artist" (*Selected Writings* 4:328).

18. A generation later Gertrude Stein would observe that literary portraiture, as in her composite sketches of Cézanne, Mabel Dodge, and Picasso, evolved from the "period of the cinema and series production" that typified her time (qtd. in Crunden xiv).

19. Francis Ford Coppola's *Bram Stoker's Dracula* (1992) provides a suggestive

complication of these reciprocities. Not only does the film reflect "the beginning of its craft by using early special effects that movies inherited from stage illusions and parlor tricks popular in Stoker's day" (Winthrop-Young, "Undead Networks" 108), it also features a cinematograph not in Stoker's novel (1897) to suggest the historical coincidence of film and its cultural pressure on print. For a beautiful, media-centered reading of *Dracula*, see Winthrop-Young, "Undead Networks."

20. Estelle Jussim has noted that "while it is customary to equate the study of Remington with the study of the horse, it is much more true to say that to study Remington is to study the rise of instantaneous photography and the perfection of photographic technologies for the illustrated press" (41). Aside from Muybridge, Remington also availed himself of the work of frontier photographer Laton Alton Huffman (51).

21. Here and in the following, I am indebted to Rabinbach's fine account of Marey and Muybridge's work (esp. 88–108), as well as to Haas's biographical study, *Muybridge*.

22. Norris almost certainly echoed contemporary descriptions of the vitascope. Gustave Walter, the owner of Orpheum vaudeville theaters in San Francisco and Los Angeles, announced it in ads as the "Sensation of the 19th Century," and the *San Francisco Examiner* noted the Orpheum's "engagement of Edison's latest wonder, the vitascope" (qtd. in Musser, *Nickelodeon* 78). A June 1896 program of the Orpheum reads, "Edison's Latest Marvel: The Vitascope: The Photo-Electric Sensation of the Day" (qtd. in Graham, *Fiction* 49).

23. Musser notes that several "rival forms of screen entertainment . . . converged on the West Coast in the Spring of 1896," such as the "picture play" (photographic slides), "the illustrated song" (lantern slides projected onto a screen), and the Lathams' "eidoloscope," among others, against which the vitascope had to compete (*Nickelodeon* 77–79). This may be another reason for Norris's mix-up. As well, given that the kinetoscope, like its aural predecessor, the nickel-in-the-slot phonographs, carried "suggestions of private desire and forbidden pleasures," it might (for Norris) have been a perfect analogue for a lascivious McTeague getting his sexual highs from the peepholes, a cinematic voyeurism in sync with his instinctual psyche (Musser and Nelson 39).

24. Danius has noted that Proust included a kinetoscope roughly ten years later in *Remembrances of Things Past*, with allusive overtones of Muybridge's work on running horses (95–97). However, unlike for Norris, for whom cinematography was largely an analogy of mechanical precision and for the unself-conscious processing of visual data, Proust (following Bergson) saw in the kinetoscope a model of elusive memory, whose flow of images "is impossible to scrutinize the way one would inspect individual frames on a film strip" (97).

25. Similarly, Paul Young has recently (though with different emphases) noted that Norris risked "the novel's singularity as a medium by adapting aspects of new representational strategies," and he does so "in a form that speaks directly to the

cinema's challenge to the cultural authority of the novel: a narrative of intermedia mutiny in which the incorporated medium surreptitiously turns the tables on its elder" (646).

26. McTeague and Trina's notorious kiss at B Street Station may well have been prompted by *The May Irwin Kiss,* kinetographed in April 1896, the first screen kiss in history showing the climax of the Broadway farce, *The Widow Jones* (see Musser, *Nickelodeon* 65). The film and its hundreds of remakes was a nationwide success and illustrated naturalism's repressed desire. In addition, while the sources for *McTeague* in San Francisco's history have been well established, Norris (while in Paris) may also have heard or read about the case of a dentist named Lévy who hypnotized a female patient before abusing her. Jean-Martin Charcot discussed such cases in his public demonstrations, and Norris may well have been aware of the proceedings in the Salpêtrière (see Gauld, esp. 495–99).

27. Parallel montage to foreground economic disparity does not appear in *McTeague* because the novel centers on San Francisco's lower-class population. *The Octopus,* by contrast, casts a wider spectrum and concludes with a parallel montage that contrasts the lavish dinner at the Gerards' with the starving Hoovens (590–613). Norris uses the serial simultaneity peculiar to print to substitute for explicit narrative commentary, in the process replicating what Eisenstein described as the typical form of montage in D. W. Griffith: the dialectic "structure of bourgeois society" (234).

28. See Buck-Morss, esp. 16–18, for a discussion of Benjamin's notion of shock.

29. Schivelbusch also comments on the coincidence of slide shows and railroad travel: "What the opening of major railroads provided in reality . . . was attempted in illusion . . . by the 'panoramic' and 'dioramic' shows and gadgets. These were designed to provide, by showing views of distant landscapes, cities and exotic scenes, 'a substitute for those still expensive and onerous journeys'" (Buddemeier, qtd. on p. 62). By the end of the century, such shows were no longer meant to replace but stimulate railroad travel. In Norris's "She and the Other Fellow," the audience is treated to a series of lectures on "European travel, illustrated by lantern-slide photographs of all points of interest" (243). Norris's attention to the fluid transitions between slides is also noteworthy and may point to the cinematic effect of his jump cuts: The presenter "pressed a little tick-tack between his fingers, and the picture of the omnibus seemed in a manner to dissolve into a view of the square. He paused a moment for effect, and then proceeded" (244).

30. While the routine of Polk Street, as Warren French has noted, is "a source of McTeague's security," he functions more as a panning camera eye rather than a subject drawing sustenance from city life (64). His fleeting moments of awareness are not enough to make fine emotional discriminations. Ron Mottram correctly observes that McTeague's vision is "generally without thought, perhaps approximating the objectivity of the camera lens" (578).

31. The erasure of McTeague's body thus complicates Jonathan Crary's general argument that the nineteenth century moved away from a non-corporeal, transcen-

dental, Cartesian, or Newtonian mode of vision toward the immanence of the individual body and the "interrogation of the physiological makeup of the human subject" (70). While artists in other domains (from the Impressionists to the high modernists) reaffirmed a highly particularized point of view that is grounded in bodily being, Norris seems to align his character with the vision of a camera eye (see Danius 55–57).

32. Much has been written about Trina's delirious intercourse with gold. Norris's interest in contact between skin and metal may also derive from his sojourn in Paris, where Charcot was then, briefly, one of the most vocal advocates of a practice called metallotherapy. Supporters of the therapy claimed that "contact of the skin with metals could relieve hysterical anaesthesias, and also . . . paralyses and contractures" (Gauld 310). While Trina may, in a strictly clinical sense, not be diseased, Norris's instinct of fiction may have recognized the dramatic possibilities inherent in such a bath in metal.

33. Significantly, while *McTeague* formally replicates the increase in cinematic processing speed, McTeague himself is always ahead of new technologies. Telegraph lines are strung along the railroad tracks McTeague walks, and the Big Dipper Mine has a "telephone on the wall" (210). But rather than catching up with him, their disembodied messages are no match for McTeague's "sixth sense"—his instinctual equivalent of telegraphy. Only when the novel's other telepathic figure, Marcus Schouler, hears of his blood brother's deed is McTeague finally caught.

34. A generation later Zelda Fitzgerald observed that "authors who want to make things true to life make them smell bad—like McTeague's room" (*Correspondence* 52), and her husband noted that "by appealing to the sense of smell . . . rather than the commoner form of word painting," Norris in *McTeague* had produced a sense of authentic sensory reality (*Miscellany* 127). Both acknowledge Norris's synaesthetic range within an enlarged media ecology.

35. Seltzer has noted that the idea of the brute is "at once a principle of dissipation and of generation" in naturalist fiction (38). Amy Kaplan has observed that "the culture at large was in the process of redefining white middle class masculinity from a republican quality of character based on self-control and social responsibility to a corporeal essence identified with the vigor and prowess of the individual male body" ("Romancing" 662).

36. The locus classicus for this redistribution of "sense ratios" is of course McLuhan's *Understanding Media*, 18.

37. In yet another, and very recent, cinematic circularity, Manohla Dargis, in her review of *There Will Be Blood* (2007), has pointed to the affinities between *McTeague* and Paul Thomas Anderson's epic film, which is based on Upton Sinclair's novel *Oil!* Daniel Plainview, the film's protagonist, "is an American primitive. He's more articulate and civilized than the crude, brutal title character in Frank Norris's 1899 novel 'McTeague,' and Erich von Stroheim's masterly version of the same, 'Greed.' But the two characters are brothers under the hide, coarse and animalistic, sentimental

in matters of love and ruthless in matters of avarice." She also notes that Anderson "opens his story in 1898, closer to Norris's novel than Sinclair's, which begins in the years leading up to World War I."

38. On Norris's ambivalent attitude toward the various forms of professionalization, particularly with regard to his own status as a writing professional, see Heddendorf.

39. The quote is from the Franklin Walker Collection, Bancroft Library, University of California, Berkeley (hereafter FWC), 30 April 1931. Invented in 1884, the fountain pen freed writers from the "spatial and temporal limitations that the study and the inkwell imposed" and provided "ease of transport and the permanency of ink," thus making it "superior to the quill and the pencil" (Borus 74). During his illness while on assignment in South Africa, Norris, as he told his brother, "was so weak . . . that he could not remove the cap from his fountain pen" (Walker, *Norris* 123).

40. The editors of Norris's *Apprenticeship Writings* suggest that he produced "personally-generated typescripts" but "never became a proficient typist" (McElrath and Burgess 2:266, 269). For reasons just elaborated, I suggest otherwise, though it is of course possible that a techno-savvy Norris tried his, as it were, hand at the new machine.

41. In his study of American "ideologies of manhood," David Leverenz distinguishes among artisanal, patrician, and entrepreneurial models of authorship. The artisanal writer understood manhood "as autonomous self-sufficiency," while the patrician writer emphasized "property, patriarchy, and citizenship" (78–80). While both assumed writing to be "a model of industry and honesty," the entrepreneurial writer "made competition and power dynamics in the workplace the only source of valuing and measuring oneself," emerging as one does in "a marketplace emphasizing competition, risk, and calculation" (85). Norris embodies a hybrid of the artisanal and entrepreneurial models, sharing a dual commitment to hand-based autonomy and professional authorship. For that reason, he can aspire to typed or printed forms of public authorship without seeing his private identity as writer of manuscripts compromised.

42. See also Hartman Strom, "'Light Manufacturing': The Feminization of Clerical Work," in *Beyond the Typewriter*, 172–226.

43. I would add the exercise of authorial power to Den Tandt's fine description of Norris's style as "a mannerist form of discourse that the writer seems to pursue for his own writing pleasure" (*Urban Sublime* 201).

44. Fried also notes a tendency "toward miniaturization and the other toward monstrosity" in Crane, which is visible in *McTeague* in the small scale of the dental instruments counterpointed by the monstrous mining drills: "I think of the second tendency as expressing (and repressing) a subliminal awareness of the nearness of the writer's hand, and more broadly of the role of that hand—of the writer as corporeal being—in the production of writing" (141).

45. Kolodny has demonstrated that "America's oldest and most cherished fantasy: a daily reality of harmony between man and nature based on an experience of the land as essentially feminine," succeeded to fantasies of male domination. The "passive filial stance appropriate to a maternal pastoral matrix" has given way to a notion of the landscape as "The Ravished" (4, 146). For a more historically and ecologically located inquiry into the tropes of exploitation of a gendered nature, see Carolyn Merchant's classic, *The Death of Nature,* esp. chap. 1, "Nature as Female."

46. Fried has observed that the upturned and blank faces in Crane evoke "the special blankness of the as yet unwritten page" (100); Seltzer has suggested that the abstract white spaces in Jack London might "emblematize the practice of writing" (224). Beyond the examples cited in the text, "the immense salt flats" in *McTeague* (that are "broken by winding streams of black water," perhaps denoting the writer's ink), as well as Death Valley's "horrible vast sink of white sand and salt," possibly suggest Norris's anxieties about an empty writing pad (46, 234). As well, in *Vandover and the Brute,* Vandover never starts on his chef d'oeuvre, "The Last Enemy," the canvas for which remains as threatening to him as was Norris's own, which "stared down at him in its blankness" (Walker, *Norris* 40).

47. Jonathan Goldberg has observed that "human evolution, from the point of emergence of the human-in-the-hand, has taken place through the labor of the hand, through the extension of the hand into the world through the instrument, the tool, the machine." Goldberg also usefully reminds us that "graphesis and incision," writing and inscribing, "are etymologically one" (312–13).

48. Alfred Habegger has argued that the origins of American realism and naturalism are deeply enmeshed in the "basic significance of women's fiction," which had become the major "live tradition at the end of the American Renaissance" (65). Nevertheless, as Jane Tompkins has noted, male critics (generally more receptive to the conventions of realism and naturalism) rewrote literary tradition by culling the writers of the "American Renaissance" at the expense of women's literature and domestic fiction.

49. Norris was principally supportive of women entering the professions, and he encouraged his bride to become a nurse. In "Evolution of a Nurse"—almost certainly an impetus for *Blix* and *A Man's Woman*—Norris suggests that a nurse "is on the road to prosperity . . . a great deal faster . . . than either the school teacher or the female journalist or the typewriter" (*Apprenticeship* 1:132). Conceivably, Norris encouraged his future spouse to enter a line more in tune with the tradition of female nurture instead of joining him as a (re)producer of texts, thus bringing out once again, as is evident in the essay itself, his anxieties about women entering his own terrain.

50. Goldberg notes that in logocentric thinking, women and machines signify simulation and reproduction, so that the typewritten page—copied from the originary male script by the reproductive hands of Woman—figures as "a space of representations," intimating "the secondariness of all origins, including the origin of life" (301).

51. Seltzer reads such handwriting as "an inexhaustible masturbator" that allows the male self to propagate itself against the pressures of naturalism's fertile mothers and Mother Earth (31; see also Den Tandt, *Urban Sublime* 83–96).

Chapter 3

1. Katz, for example, observes that "like all of Norris's novels, [*The Pit*'s] direction is to support middle class values. Extremes of any kind are intolerable to that value system" ("Eroticism" 164).

2. McElrath notes that around 1900, "Norris seems to have been beginning a change of perspective and life-style" that lead to an aesthetic reorientation (229). Hochman observes that in *The Pit*, "Norris was perhaps preparing to leave his entire 'Naturalistic' armature behind," instead turning toward the "psychological drama of urban, educated, middle-class characters, characters more like himself" (37).

3. Pizer argues that Norris does not participate in the romantic "nature-machine conflict" but instead "substitutes for the machine the contemporary aesthetic movement" (Norris, *Criticism* 20). I would suggest that Norris's critique of aestheticism is not a displacement as much as an extension of that binary. As was widely perceived at the time, technological advancements reduced physical labor and could easily lead to physical degeneration and emasculation of the American and European male—in short, to the aestheticization of the male body. The Boy Scout movement and the emergence of an entire industry of health clubs are intimately connected to the Decadence and form part of the modernist history of the body, its physical restoration, and its maintenance in the service of national productivity and identities. For a recent discussion of some of these reciprocities, see Seltzer, esp. 149–72.

4. As Christophe den Tandt has argued, "[B]y virtue of an ingenious strategy of containment, the masculinized heroines are commissioned to implement a reinscription of the patriarchy: they shame their male companions into living up to masculine standards they, as amazon figures, have partially appropriated" ("Amazons" 653). See also den Tandt's "Overcivilization and the Crisis of Civilized Manhood" in *Urban Sublime*, 189–94.

5. The Poundian "Men of 1914," as Peter Nicholls observes, were concerned with "developing models of psychic order, which reinstate the divide between art and life, frequently in terms of a parallel re-fixing of sexual difference" (167).

6. Den Tandt has noted that post–World War I writers inherited from turn-of-the-century novelists not the transgression of gender boundaries "but the reinscription of masculinity; the direct legacy of London's and Dreiser's gender discourse to modernism was not a further development of androgynous types but rather Ernest Hemingway's or D. H. Lawrence's paeans to bohemian machismo" ("Amazons" 660). For a useful overview of male writers and their anxieties about a beleaguered masculinity, see Shi, esp. 214–22.

7. Norris inscribes the consuming/nonproducing attitude of Woman also in Page's writing desk, which "was a miracle of neatness, everything in its precise place,

the writing-paper in geometrical parallelograms, the pen tray neatly polished" (150). Writing is here a matter of keeping up appearances, of indulging in idle introspection (Page rereads her journal with "vague thrills of emotion and mystery" [147]), much in contrast to what Christopher Wilson has described as "the labor of words," the male project of making an onerous and strenuous living with one's pen.

8. *Madame Bovary* was one of Norris's "favorite books," which he "read and reread," notwithstanding that he "evinced throughout his writing an insensitivity to and lack of care for stylistic artistry that would have made Flaubert writhe" (Walker, *Norris* 233). While Flaubert claimed that "I spent *5 days writing one page*" (qtd. in Nicholls 19, Flaubert's emphasis), Norris's writing practice was in inverse proportion to Flaubert's, easily equaling five pages per day.

9. Following Darwin's claim in *The Descent of Man* that in women, the self-protective "power of intuition ... and perhaps of imitation, are more strongly marked than in man" (vol. 2, chap. 19, p. 326), the patriarchal logic of Woman as copycat became enshrined in the widely read work of Remy de Gourmont. In "Woman and Language," an essay codifying the attitude of an entire generation of male modernists, Gourmont observed that "the art of mime is the art of women" (136), which could (pace Nietzsche) easily be manipulated to suggest that Woman is synonymous with duplicity, evident in the sustained association of women with the stage in (male) modern fiction.

10. Though Herf focuses on the evolution of fascism in Germany, coming as it does out of the Enlightenment, he does identify concurrent tendencies in England and literary figures such as Lewis and Pound (12). For a useful summary of the reactionary tendencies in late nineteenth-century France beyond the literary, culminating in the fascist Action Française, see Antliff, esp. 11–38.

11. As Robert Henri, an American contemporary of Norris and a member of several prominent artistic groups (such as those of Paul Sérusier and Maurice Denis), put it, "among the great number of students [at the Académie Julian] there were those who searched each other out and formed little groups which met independently of the school, and with art as a central interest, talked and developed ideas about everything under the sun" (qtd. in Chipp 101).

12. Letter to Franklin Walker, FNC, Box 1, Maurice V. Samuels, 20 May 1930.

13. Nobody less than Baudelaire spoke of the modernist disease as "Americanization." Witnessing the first avalanche of well-to-do Americans on the Continent (of which Norris was a part) and the transformation of Paris into a playground for innocents abroad, he described the onset of commodity capitalism as "the period we shall next be entering, of which the beginning is marked by the supremacy of America and industry" (*Oeuvres* 2:603).

14. As a system circulating theories of production and consumption, *The Pit* would lend itself to a "chaos theoretical" reading. The famed "Butterfly Effect," which theorizes the large-scale effects produced by minuscule changes and which illustrates what expert parlance refers to as a system's "sensitive dependence on initial conditions," is nicely encapsulated in the warning of Jadwin's business partner, Gretry:

"If you run [the price of wheat] up to two dollars . . . it will be that top-heavy, that the littlest kick in the world will knock it over" (304). James Gleick notes that beginning with the weather, dynamical systems theory soon recognized (trans)national economies as models for complex systems, and "by the seventies and eighties, economic forecasting by computer bore a real resemblance to global weather forecasting" (20; see also 92–93). Evident in the murky explanations of the novel's economics, Norris never claimed to have mastered the intricacies of market fluctuations; instead of a computer model, he used the insights of a young broker who demonstrated price variations with a model of his own: "a wire was run from the radiator grate in the floor to a hook in the ceiling, and upon this wire was threaded a float which rose and fell with the fluctuations of heat from the furnace" (Walker, *Norris* 278).

15. Norris modeled Corthell on his friend stained-glass artist Bruce Porter (1865–1953). Norris's wife recalled that throughout his life he "remained fond of" his San Franciscan brotherhood, "Ernest Peixotto, Gelett Burgess, and Bruce Porter, especially the last" (interview with Franklin Walker, 8 May 1930, FNC).

16. For Norris's life at the Julian, see his "Student Life in Paris," and "The Animal of a Buldy Jones" (*Apprenticeship* 2:28–36). Norris's assessment of the Julian as a zoo for American art students is confirmed by his contemporary Henri: "Julian's Academy . . . was a great cabaret with singing and huge practical jokes" (qtd. in Chipp 103). For the truly international student mix of the Julian, see Weisberg 159–84.

17. D'Emilio and Freedman note that lithographs and reprints of numerous Bouguereau canvases, such as *Nymphs and Satyrs* (1873), "hung over the bars of men's saloons throughout the country" (plate 23). Paradoxically, Bouguereau was widely sought by American collectors, notwithstanding that in his paintings eroticism often masqueraded as high art. Sherwood Anderson's comment that "in spite of his skill, Bouguereau gave away his own inner nastiness" by painting childlike nudes, is typical of the widespread critical reaction to Bouguereau's work in America (28). Anderson's artistic tastes were closely tied to those of his brother Karl, a distinguished American Impressionist painter (and later a member of the National Academy) who was one of the organizers of the Chicago Armory Show in 1913.

18. As Jesse Crisler and Joseph R. McElrath Jr. have recently pointed out, the painting in question is most likely Bouguereau's *The Nymphaeum* (1878), now on display at the Haggin Museum in Stockton, California (87). Unlike their expansive understanding of Norris's artistic sensibilities, which seem to accept competing traditions and modes of presentation (such as academic and Impressionist models) on an equal footing, I see a distinct hierarchy in Norris's thinking about art for reasons elaborated in this chapter (esp. 84–99).

19. In his essays on art, Norris's portrayal of Bouguereau and his work is similarly unflattering. In "Student Life in Paris," Bouguereau "looks more like a well-to-do butcher than like the painter of Aphrodites and Cupids. He is very fat, very red as to the face, very loud as to the breath, very wheezy as to the voice"; in "Western Types," Norris belittles the provincial horizon and training methods of the aspiring West Coast artist, for whom "Bouguereau is his enthusiasm; he can rise no higher than that" (*Apprenticeship* 1:48).

20. See esp. chapter 4 of *The Theory of the Leisure Class*, "Conspicuous Consumption," for a differentiation of consumer items to indicate social status (68–101). "In the process of the gradual amelioration which takes place in the articles of . . . consumption," the "canon of reputability" will begin to factor in: "Since the consumption of . . . more excellent goods is an evidence of wealth, it becomes honorific; and conversely, the failure to consume in due quantity and quality becomes a mark of inferiority and demerit" (74).

21. See, for example, "An Opening for Novelists" (*Criticism* 28–30). In several of his other essays on art, esp. "The Sketch Club Exhibit" (*Apprenticeship* 1:188–89), "The Winter Exhibition" (1:198–99), "Charles Peter Rollo" (1:246–49), and "The Hopkins Institute: Art Education in San Francisco" (2:146–48), Norris speaks of artists who have returned to the West with sensibilities developed in Europe, and particularly the Académie Julian, but also of emerging painters who, conversely, are leaving their mark on the European art scene: "It is rather surprising and gratifying to know that their average work in drawings from the nude is quite as good as the average work turned out in Julian's. . . . Students leave from the Art Institute of this city every year whose names figure afterwards on the walls of the *Salon* or on the pages of the great illustrated magazines of this country" (2:146).

22. See, for example, http://www.cahier-naturalistes.com/pages/Bouguereau.html.

23. Seurat's most generous critic, Félix Fénéon, described the "optical vibration" effect in 1886 in his review of *La Grande Jatte* (that foreshadows Norris's observation): "The atmosphere is transparent and singularly vibrant; the surface seems to flicker. Perhaps this sensation . . . can be explained by the theory of [the German physicist] Dove: the retina, expecting distinct groups of light rays to act upon it, perceives in very rapid alternation both the disassociated color elements and their resultant color" (qtd. in Broude 5).

24. Critics hostile to Seurat and his followers described their stippling technique (*peinture au point*) as "mechanical" and "scientifically detached." Meyer Schapiro, following Fénéon, has, however, drawn attention to Seurat's "intensely personal" technique; his "touch . . . is never mechanical, in spite of what many have said" (qtd. in Broude 6).

25. Corthell observes that the opera at the novel's beginning is appropriately middlebrow and made for bourgeois consumption: "this music seems to be just the right medium between the naïve melody of the Italian school and the elaborate complexity of Wagner" (26). Later, he associates Wagner's difficulty with his own performance of Liszt's *Mephisto Walzer* (221)—perhaps partly because Liszt married Wagner's daughter Cosima. Norris's stay in Paris coincides with the Wagner frenzy, "the object of cultic fascination in France between 1885–1888," which produced the short-lived *Revue Wagnérienne* (edited, among others, by Éduard Dujardin) that "placed the composer at the centre of the French literary avant-garde" (Nicholls 49). No doubt many of Corthell's judgments about classical music derive from Norris's bohemian days in Paris (see also Walker, *Norris* 27).

26. Given Norris's attentiveness to the pianist's hands and Sheldon's climactic rendering of Franz Liszt's *Mephisto Walzer*, Norris may well have modeled Sheldon

partly on Liszt himself. Liszt was a household name in Paris at the time, especially during the Wagner craze, and the Chopin-Liszt rivalry was legend. The artists even going so far as to require different instruments for their techniques and approaches. Chopin played a Pleyel piano known for its soft touch, while Liszt preferred the heavier Erard that was known for its faster action, which was necessary for some of his innovations on the instrument. Liszt also had long slender fingers, which helped create the myth that having such fingers is a requirement for virtuosity, and was the first who "faced the piano sideways to enhance the audience's visual and acoustic experience" (DiSilvio). Norris may consciously echo Liszt's repositioning of the piano—with its consequent foregrounding of the pianist's hands—as he frames Sheldon's performance in *The Pit*.

27. Norris's essay "Inside an Organ," based on the newly installed electric organ in San Francisco's Church of St. Ignatius, is almost certainly the fieldwork for the organ in *The Pit*: "The great advantage of the use of electricity in connection with organs is that it insures a perfection of touch and an absolute promptness of response.... [The isolation of the bellows plant] does away with all the noise and creaking of the bellows machinery, so disturbing in the musical performance of the organ itself" (*Apprenticeship* 1:219). The modernist schism between machine- and handmade art is, as elsewhere in Norris, reproduced in his distinction between journalism and fiction. While Norris the reporter, in the spirit of public education, was almost indiscriminate in his support of new technologies, his literary treatment of the same issue is far more nuanced and critical, suggesting that embodied agency is central for the production of more challenging art (as opposed to utilitarian reporting).

28. Reginald Pound observes that *Tit-Bits* (1881), for the first time in the history of industrialized publishing, expressed "the common banality of broad layers of society" by capitalizing on "insignificant news item[s]" (11). In concert with Baudelaire, contemporary observers were concerned that this shift in mass audience (partly engendered by the 1870 Education Act) dramatized serious literature's increasingly marginal position in an emergent information culture.

29. Scholars have gone to great lengths to document Norris's sources. For *The Pit*, see, in particular, C. Kaplan. Norris also had a personal encounter with Leiter in Chicago (*Letters* 148). The stationery of Norris's father reads, "B. F. Norris & Co., Wholesale Jewelers, Corner State and Washington Streets, opposite Field, Leiter & Co.'s, Chicago" (FNC 1, no date). Given their proximity, Norris may also have associated his father's business bravado with Leiter's.

30. In *Blix*, Condy similarly entertains his disapproving beloved by telling her "stories about society reporters, and how they got inside news by listening to telephone party wires for days at a time" (16).

31. In one of his brief notes on *The Pit* (which are similar to Zola's *carnets*), Norris writes, "Jadwin at lunch/telephone on table," to suggest Jadwin's thoroughgoing immersion in communications technologies (FNC 3).

32. Den Tandt similarly notes that while Norris was a keen advocate of Anglo-Saxon masculinity, he does "not seem to be able to shed his belief that the writing of fiction belongs to the sphere of women and genteel aesthetes" (*Urban Sublime* 193).

Chapter 4

1. Malcolm Lowry Archive, Special Collections, University of British Columbia, Vancouver, Box 12, Folder 13, page 3 (Lowry's emphasis). Further references to the archive appear as UBC SC in the text, followed by box, folder, and page number, if possible.

2. In *Hear Us O Lord,* Lowry suggests that "everybody on this earth is a writer, [in] the sense in which Ortega ... means it. Ortega has it that man's life is like a fiction that he makes up as he goes along. He becomes an engineer and converts it into reality" (271; see also *Psalms and Songs,* 223).

3. In a letter to Harold Matson, Lowry notes that "curiously on my father's side, many of my forebears were ... either architects or engineers, one was Stephenson's chief on The Rocket, that old steam engine" (*Letters* 2:475). Lowry's brother Russell has confirmed that a Lowry grandfather once apparently worked for Stephenson. A version of The Rocket, of course, occurs in *Under the Volcano.*

4. Cecelia Tichi has observed that in "an age in which machine manufacture took precedence over handicrafts and artisanry, the engineer was the new kind of author.... He set a new example for the twentieth-century artist, no longer a craftsman fashioning unique objects from raw materials, but a designer committed to the functional, efficient arrangement of prefabricated components into a total design" (99).

5. The proto-Marxist attitude behind this hand-machine division, and the resistance to the mechanization of the body more generally, is reminiscent of the left-wing politics of the Pylon poets, of which Isherwood was a member, together with W. H. Auden and Stephen Spender, among others. To the bureaucratic structures of capitalist modernity—which they understood as the enabling condition of fascism and individual alienation—they juxtaposed the self-conscious politicism of their art and actions (and the typewriter, not surprisingly, became an easy symbol of bureaucratic control and "official" textual processing). Moving among intellectual circles in Cambridge in the late 1920s and early 1930s, Lowry was well aware of the Pylon group. Like his mentor Conrad Aiken, he too was heavily influenced by the "Complex Boys," the "adolescent audens spenders with all their pretty little dexterities, their negative safety, their indoor marxmanship" (Aiken qtd. in Bowker 281; see also Spender, esp. xxv–xxvii). But "whereas writers like Orwell, Spender and Auden set out to find the alternative society through organized political action, Lowry embarked on a lonely and seemingly undirected search for an alternative identity in and through literature" (Bowker xvii). Indeed, while Hugh in *Under the Volcano* might well have been modeled on Auden or Spender, who both participated on the Republican side during the Spanish Civil War, the "professional indoor Marxman" (8) is the only one of his Cambridge circle who does not, instead allaying his guilt by helping smuggle a shipload of dynamite to the Spanish Loyalist forces.

6. Lowry's first biographer, Douglas Day, explains that Lowry's obsession with hands stems largely from his reputedly small, ugly, and clumsy hands that were "a source of shame and frustration to Lowry all his life" (90). Day also suggests

that the repeated accusation of being a masturbator (evident in *Ultramarine* and Lowry's Haiti notebook [UBC SC 7: 9]) could also be an "important causative factor in [Lowry's] continuing preoccupation with the *hands* of his various protagonists" (130). Within the framework of deconstruction, it would be interesting to investigate the relays between writing and masturbation, what Derrida calls "that dangerous supplement" (*Of Grammatology* 141–63). Rather than seeing in Lowry's focus on the hand a repressed masturbation complex, I see it within the framework of Lowry's philosophical definition of humanness and technology that is more prominent in his texts. Such a framework also explains Lowry's concern with injured and mutilated hands.

7. The de-individuation of typed script coproduced by Malcolm and Margerie (M & M) makes individual contributions virtually impossible to distinguish. The Lowrys, therefore, are an important addition to Kittler's "register" of "literary typewriting couples of this century" (*Gramophone* 214–27). "Word processing these days," he notes, "is the business of couples who write, instead of sleep, with one another" (214). The Lowrys did not have children (Margerie had a hysterectomy), but they engendered a brainchild that, in true romantic fashion, assures their literary immortality. Similarly, Jan Gabrial described her childless marriage to Lowry as "our writing-paper love" and the publication of her very first story (following the couple's separation) as "my small first-born" (197–98). In more senses than one, it appears, love may have been mediated by the typewriter.

8. The relays between (male) modernism and the production of discourse are beyond the reach of this chapter. Let me note, however, that similar to Lowry, writers like John Dos Passos and D. H. Lawrence came to frame typing technology in strongly gendered terms. For Dos Passos's alter ego in *Manhattan Transfer,* Jimmy Herf, the linotype, in a nightmare, morphs into a veritable *vagina dentata* threatening male literary production: "The arm of the linotype was a woman's hand in a long white glove.... [It] was a gulping mouth with nickelbright rows of teeth" (329). Lawrence came to associate typewriting, similarly, with a female labor force invading the, for him, exclusively male terrain of writing. Women "settle like silly locusts on all the jobs, they occupy the offices ... like immensely active ants ... and the rather dazed young male is naturally a bit scared ... by her devouring energy" (549). Ostensibly wounded, he continues, "Men really care still about engineering and mechanical pursuits, so there is very little intrusion of women there. But men are sadly indifferent to clerking pursuits, and journalistic pursuits.... So women flood in to fill the vacuums" (547).

9. Hugh's hand injury may well be modeled on that of guitarist Django Reinhardt (one of Lowry's favorite jazz musicians mentioned in the *Tender Is the Night* script [77]). Reinhardt developed a highly celebrated idiosyncratic technique as a result of having two burn-induced disfigured fingers on his left hand. Bill Plantagenet may recall the genius of jazz pianist Bud Powell who, like Lowry, was (repeatedly) hospitalized in New York City's Bellevue Hospital (see Bowker 198–99). These musicians, unlike Lowry himself, were able to exercise their agency despite

manual injuries—perhaps another (more philosophical) reason for Lowry's affinity for jazz.

10. Eventually, Lowry was to tell a friend that he was "'driven nuts' by discovering that much of Heidegger's thought paralleled what he was doing in *Dark as the Grave*" (Bowker 423). Katherine Rowe has noted that stories of dismembered hands, especially in the nineteenth century, ought to be seen against the background of the Marxist insistence on the embodiment of labor, as they often "literalize the popular synecdoche for labor and the ghostly forces that possess it" (15). While Lowry's dismembered and mutilated hands are not primarily expressions of the labor history of modernity, the hands in his fiction are often inhabited by demonic forces or threaten to become autonomous, much like the typewriter itself. In a larger political sense, then, Lowry's manual preoccupation *does* draw attention to the historical moment when mass-industrial processes severed the link (but not necessarily the hand from the body) between body and self-expression.

11. The handwriting/typewriting binary would also pursue Lowry into the film script of *Tender Is the Night*. While Dick Diver sojourns in New York, a letter (in "Gothic handwriting") from his mentor, Dr. Dohmler, reminds him "to exclude all emotional element from your letters." Immediately thereafter, in the next shot, "the camera picks out another piece of notepaper on Dick's desk on which Dick has written: Dearest Nicole, my girl, my sweetheart"—a note he scratches out and crumples up, only to pick it up from the floor "with a gesture of love as if to undesecrate it." Dohmler's "Gothic handwriting" and his own reaffirm the link between handwriting, personal essence, and emotional expression. Yet simultaneously, interspersed into these logocentric associations, Dick tries to work on his professional manuscripts "on a typewriter, but his hand is trembling and it is difficult for him to type," suggesting that even his usually prolific and distanced production of text is momentarily blocked by the short circuit between impassioned/private urge and depersonalized/public script, the need to communicate intimate thoughts by hand and the professorial caveat not to do so (*Tender* 156–57). It is also noteworthy that Dick, like many of Lowry's alter egos, is at one point also identified as an engineer and bridge builder (*Tender* 129).

12. Similarly, for Dick Diver in *Tender Is the Night*, "the whole condensed telegram" he receives from his sister suddenly "becomes subject to a sea-change of meanings" (125).

13. In an early draft of *Under the Volcano* Lowry identifies his protagonist (then named "William Ames") with a passport. A marginal note reads "telegram," thus suggesting that Lowry saw the potential for miscommunication through the telegram's ruptured text (UBC SC 27-5: 396, D-draft). It is noteworthy that Theodore Dreiser's visionary electrical engineer in *Sister Carrie* (commonly seen as a mix of his mother's ideals and Thomas Edison, whom Dreiser interviewed for *Success* magazine) is named Robert Ames.

14. Even in "Through the Panama," where Lowry breaks open the scriptive cohesion of the printed page to establish a fluid dialogue between margin, marginal gloss,

and "actual" text, he achieves "an amalgam of fragments and typographical dynamics" that complicates the structured rationality of print (Grace, "Intertextuality" 192).

15. In a September 1952 letter to David Markson, Margerie similarly noted that "I don't know anything more sickening, wildly exciting, despairing and generally frantic than the Battle of the Blank Page" (qtd. in Doyen 180; see also *Letters* 2:604).

16. Letter to A. Porter, UBC SC 3: 5.

17. Scholars have frequently drawn attention to the centrality of the wheel in Lowry's oeuvre. Grace, for example, has observed that "the narrative strategy of *Under the Volcano* is best approached through the symbol of the circle or wheel which whirls on forever in the same place" (*Voyage* 43).

18. Lowry's narrative machine assembly could even be said to look forward to J. T. Fraser's "new theory of time," as he articulated it in *The Genesis and Evolution of Time* (1982). The founder of the International Society for the Study of Time (ISST) in 1966—seven years after C. P. Snow had announced the hermetic existence of the humanities and the sciences in *The Two Cultures*—Fraser was seeking synergy and connections, and he did so by distinguishing between "six major integrative levels" that "bear a hierarchical, nested relationship to each other (28–29). The principal idea in Fraser's model, which extends from the atemporal world of electronic radiation to the time frame of human institutions, and which takes into account their interrelationships, is to establish truly interdisciplinary relationships between various conceptions of time and knowledge production.

19. See Ackerley, "'Well, of course, if we knew all the things,'" esp. 52–56, for a useful discussion of Lowry's "chaotic" sensibilities.

20. As R. M. Albérès observes, "For Joyce, for Butor, for Malcolm Lowry, it is necessary in effect that the reader be invited to *decipher* the novel, to see in it a palimpsest or a labyrinth, whereas the traditional novel, where everything is explained, transformed into descriptions and masterly analyses, does not demand the same effort in reading, holds no mystery, and does not correspond to real life, in which we must also *decipher* reality" (124, qtd. in McCarthy and Tiessen 6).

21. In a review of *Under the Volcano* for the *Saturday Review*, John Woodburn, one of the book's first perceptive readers, similarly noted that "you are this book's fool, it has stolen you and mastered you by some trickery, and you cannot appraise it tranquilly until it leaves you alone. It has not let me alone.... I have now read it twice, and the second time has bound me to it more tightly than before" (qtd. in Bowker 398).

Chapter 5

1. Tolstoy's quote can be found in Leyda 410. Leyda himself also wrote to Lowry, noting that in writing a screen adaptation of *Tender* he had "put an amazing film on paper" (*Selected Letters* 442).

2. The influence of German Expressionist film on Lowry has been discussed most prominently by Grace in *Regression and Apocalypse* (163–84) and "Midsummer Madness." Spender has identified Russian films, particularly those of Eisen-

stein, as central to Lowry's work, and Mota and Tiessen have pointed to the tradition of Hollywood. Mota and Tiessen's introduction to *The Cinema of Malcolm Lowry* must certainly be the starting point for anyone interested in Lowry's affinity for film. An elaboration of their previous publications, the essay weaves together many of Lowry's significant pronouncements on cinema.

3. In keeping with many unorthodoxies Lowry cultivated about himself, he was inconsistent about underlining or italicizing film and book titles in his correspondence.

4. John Huston's 1984 realistic adaptation of the novel is largely a failure because Lowry's general aesthetic is distinctly nonmimetic. Grace notes that to provide authenticity for the film's brothel scene, "Huston imported real prostitutes from Mexico. Such realism, however, supplants and displaces Lowry's far more important symbolic and visionary intentions" (*Regression and Apocalypse* 282). Prior to Huston, sixty-six screenwriters had tried their hand at the novel, and directors interested in doing the film included Luis Buñuel and Ken Russell (Wieland). Gabriel Garcia Màrquez, not surprisingly, wrote a script from Lowry's magical realist novel, an interest confirmed by Carlos Fuentes (who also attests to Lowry's expressionist sensibilities): "I consider [*Under the Volcano*] one of the best Mexican novels.... The way Lowry fuses the Mexican landscape with the soul of the Consul, that is unique. You cannot disassociate the Consul and his troubles from the Mexican landscape. You cannot, in any way. They are wedded, as wedded can be" (qtd. in Wutz, "*Reality*" 18).

5. I have retained the scholarly convention of focusing on Lowry "proper," rather than the duo of Malcolm Lowry and Margerie Bonner Lowry, well aware, as I indicated in the previous chapter, that they formed a productive synergy. As Fredrick Asals notes, "from her entry in Malcolm's life, Margerie became not simply his personal partner but his writing cohort, and even the latter function, deeply involving her in his work, was multiple. She very quickly became his muse, sounding board, editor, critic, and codrafter as well as typist" (*Making* 12). For a recent assessment of this synergistic authorship, see D. T. Max, "Day of the Dead: Malcolm Lowry's Mysterious Demons," *The New Yorker*, 17 December 2007.

6. Lowry and Noxon 34.

7. Lowry's long cover letter accompanying the manuscript is known as the "Preface." Prior to its inclusion in *Sursum Corda!* (2:224–46), it was edited by Paul Tiessen and appeared, with expanded fragments, in *White Pelican*. I quote from the expanded version ("Preface") except when indicated.

8. Lowry's "Preface" here echoes Joseph Conrad's better-known preface to *The Nigger of the "Narcissus,"* in which he urged writers, "by the power of the written word," to engage readers' full sensory spectrum: "to make you hear, to make you feel—it is, before all, to make you *see*" (52). What new frontiers, Conrad asked, can narrative reach for in the context of the cinema's competing presence? Lowry, two generations later and with allegiances to both media, would see film and fiction in more complementary terms.

9. Marinetti similarly notes that film in both its early silent *and* sound stages

defined itself in terms of stage conventions. While "appearing in the guise of theater without words, [silent film] had inherited all the most traditional sweepings of the literary theater" (131). Many of Lowry's ideas parallel those of his countryman William Somerset Maugham: "I venture to insist that the technique of writing for the pictures is not that of writing for the stage nor that of writing a novel. It is something betwixt and between. It has not quite the freedom of the novel, but it certainly has not the fetters of the stage" (186).

10. Tiessen notes that such a visual use of words for film was akin to "bringing a 'cinematic' literary device into film" ("Statements" 127).

11. William Burroughs would concur: "When you read a novel—that is, if the writer is good—you *are* seeing a 'film,' but you are seeing it in your own mind" (63).

12. One of the carnival rides in *Under the Volcano* may have derived from Léger's *Ballet mécanique:* "the machine itself was feminine, graceful as a ballet dancer, its iron skirts of gondolas whirling higher and higher" (217). While Lowry himself does not seem to have met Antheil, Jan Gabrial in Hollywood went to the movies with the composer on Lowry's twenty-ninth birthday (Bowker 243). Lowry also refers to "the ballet mécanique of the raindrops on Great Howe Sound" in *La Mordida* (265).

13. The tearing of the screen is the cinematic equivalent to Lowry's verbal signifier to indicate a split personality: the ø, as in Sigbjørn. Both *Ultramarine* and *Under the Volcano* contain significant scenes involving a filmic blackout, and in the *Tender* script, Lowry's scenic imagination is similarly informed by the materialities of film. As Dick and his set are watching a screening of *Daddy's Girl,* Lowry notes, "We hear the flickering noise of the projector.... [W]e have become aware that the silence—the sudden total absence of music with nothing to be heard save the whining projector—constitutes a dramatic element in itself" (*Cinema* 72).

14. The *Tender* script also anticipates Alain Robbe-Grillet's call for a new cinema in the decade to follow. Similar to the Lowrys, but more rigorously, Robbe-Grillet redefines reality along the lines of the unconscious. If, in film, "it should be necessary to seek a resemblance with the world, let this be a resemblance with what is real—that is, the universe of dreams, sexual fantasies, and nocturnal anxieties simultaneously confronted and produced by our unconscious" (118).

15. The story "A Rainy Night" (1925) takes place in a railway carriage, "a narrative setting [Lowry] found useful," with the narrator enjoying "the cinematic view from the window, like a tracking camera." As with film, "being 'on the move'... gives a narrative the impression of movement even when it is standing still" (Bowker 41). For an exemplary confluence of these devices, see the short story "June the 30th, 1934" (*Psalms and Songs* 36–48).

16. Similarly, when Dick returns to Europe on a freighter, we get "a shot looking down through the open skylight—as if the lid of a box of toys had been lifted—into the firemen's foc's'le" (183).

17. Lowry's Kafkaesque fear of surveillance is well-known, including his reluctance to enter the United States during the McCarthy era (see Bowker 232, 476). Not just his father but several governments kept a close eye on him. Lowry was seen

in the company of "Douglas Maclean, later to distinguish himself as a Russian spy," and Maurice Sachs from *Nouvelle Revue Française,* who held out the promise of getting *Ultramarine* published in France and eventually became "an informer for the Gestapo" (Bowker 135, 180).

18. In a letter to Lowry, Isherwood notes that Lowry's scripting of Fitzgerald's novel "was a complete revelation of new meanings and of greatness which was certainly in the book somewhere, but which you made evident. . . . [A]ll your changes and developments on Fitzgerald fill it out and add significance to it" (*Selected Letters* 443).

19. See also Mota and Tiessen, *Cinema* 30.

20. See Danius 124–26 for a reading of the essay. Grace notes that Lowry was interested in Maeterlinck as a forerunner of Expressionism (*Regression and Apocalypse* 167).

21. In an early story ("Bulls of Resurrection") that uncannily prefigures Lowry's "Preface," one of the protagonists in pursuit of sexual exploits has the advantage of "a damned little secondary characteristic of a car," which he stole from his mother (qtd. in Bowker 182). Lowry's doting mother promised to buy her darling son a "Morning Roundabout," a then popular small roadster, Morgan Runabout, if he managed to graduate from Cambridge. When, after graduation, Evelyn forked over £200 to buy the Magna from a friend of Malcolm's (which, as it turned out, he got for free), he pocketed the cash as liquor money (Bowker 132, 138).

22. For Lowry's anxieties about writer's block, see McCarthy, esp. 133–40. Regarding the autobiographical nature of Lowry's fiction, esp. in the case of the mythogenic Lowry, I hold it as a self-evident truth that "the biography that is useful to the literary historian is not the author's curriculum vitae or the investigator's account of his life. What the literary historian really needs is the biographical legend created by the author himself. Only such a legend is a *literary fact*" (Tomashevsky 55).

23. Victor Doyen's "From Innocent Story to Charon's Boat" remains the most authoritative essay on the genesis of *October Ferry*.

24. See Lowry's letter to his friend Downie Kirk for the "visual" and "dramatic effect" of Greek letters (*Letters* 2:203). The variant in the spelling of the ship probably derives from the different English (*Aristotle*) and German (*Aristoteles*) spellings of the philosopher's name. (Lowry could not have slept at Weber Academy all the time.)

25. Grace similarly notes that Lowry "appears to have considered writing in terms of shots and cuts" and quotes a reference to "visual Murnau-like" techniques from his notes (*Voyage* 88).

26. See McCarthy, esp. 161–64, for Lowry's various infernal machines.

27. See, for example, *The Grave* 136; *October Ferry* 8, 20, 137; *La Mordida* 97, 199, 210, 252, 254 (including references to the French film *Crime et Chatiment*).

28. Lowry broaches this indistinguishability of outside/inside in a chapter draft of *October Ferry* titled "Plato's Cave," in which film is given philosophical priority over human reality. While the narrator sees cinemas initially as modern allegories of

Plato's cave (as second-order shadows of the real), that priority begins to shift after their departure from their cabin: "Now it was the other way round. They lived in the cave ... and yet, if poetry was life, life was art too, what they saw in the film was life" (UBC SC 17–13: 4–5).

29. See Ackerley, "Lowry's Screenplay," who traces this reference to Bergson to Lowry's copy of *Creative Evolution* (47). For additional allusions to Bergson's rocket image, see *La Mordida* 126 and *Letters* 2:328.

30. Juxtaposing Münsterberg to Bergson, Kittler notes that "for Münsterberg, a sequence of stills, that is, Bergson's cinematographic illusion of consciousness, is by no means capable of evoking the impressions of movement.... Rather, a series of experimental and Gestalt-psychological findings demonstrates—contra Bergson—that the perception of movement takes place as 'an independent experience'" (*Gramophone* 161).

31. For the same reason, Lowry in his letters and "Preface" notes that their script is not prescriptive but suggestive—an "adjustable blueprint" (*Notes* 4) awaiting its cinematic realization by a director and/or producer.

32. Living with the "impression of self-mastery" (307), Ethan does what critics have described as the primary urge of Lowry's optimistic rewritings: "the autobiographical impulse toward self-mastery" to escape the doomsday scenarios of his earlier fiction (Mota and Tiessen, "Re-Writing" 32; Falk 209). What remains to be explored are the reciprocities between cars in the film script and in *Gabriola*, particularly in relation to Lowry's concerns with human hands and their executive role in asserting agency.

33. The film (1928) was made by Jean Epstein, one of the "French Impressionist" directors specializing in "interior states and oneiric visions" (Cohen 8). In Sigbjørn's estimate, the film has "a happy, or a hopeful ending," because the "entombed was Usher's wife and not his sister, she came back in time, as it were with the doctor's help, to save him: they went out into the thunderstorm, but into a new life" (*Grave* 248–49). Ironically, as McCarthy has noted, Wilderness does not seem to turn around his life, unlike his later incarnations (150–53).

34. Lowry is, not surprisingly, sensitive to technological changes in other domains. Repeatedly in *Tender* he notes the gradual displacement of steam trains by electric trains and trolleys (113), and Dohmler, the old-school humanitarian psychologist treating Nicole, is associated with "an older order," like "some dignified and magnificent older locomotive about to be supplanted by an automatic electric trolley system" (142).

Chapter 6

1. The most notable exceptions are the work of William Gaddis, in particular *JR* and *Agapē Agape*, and Don DeLillo, reaching from the recent massive *Underworld* to *White Noise*. Symptomatically, in search for the remnants of his wife's death-defying Dylar, Jack Gladney sifts through the evidence of the trash compactor like an ar-

chaeologist, in the process pondering the epistemological dimension of trash: "Is garbage so private? Does it glow at the core with personal heat, with signs of one's deepest nature, clues to secret yearnings, humiliating flaws? What habits, fetishes, addictions, inclinations? . . . I found crayon drawings of a figure with full breasts and male genitals. . . . I found a banana skin with a tampon inside. Was this the dark underside of consumer consciousness?" (258–59). For Donald Barthelme's use of trash, see William Gass.

2. Michael Thompson's distinction between the categories of the durable, the transient, and rubbish in *Rubbish Theory* is similarly grounded in structural anthropology.

3. Incidentally, Agnès Varda's acclaimed 2001 documentary *The Gleaners and I* strikingly parallels Doctorow's focus on how trash, castoffs, and leftovers can be meaningfully reused and reconsumed in the capitalist throwaway cultures of today. The film offers an archaeology of (long-standing) practices of recycling and re(f)using in France and is often similar to Doctorow's narrative project.

4. Doctorow's use of radio signals in his work is beyond the reach of this chapter. Let me note, however, that particularly in the recent *City of God*, Doctorow establishes the large equivalencies between print and postprint media, and particularly radio, as forms of communication emerging from different technological orders. Following his grandfather, who took up "the printer's trade" upon his emigration to the United States, Everett's father was, during World War I, "a signal officer . . . communication was his speciality as it has been the speciality of all men in my family" (130). And while Everett's father would eventually own a "record player business" (thus echoing the shop of Daniel's father), Everett's older brother Ronald—in turn, following in his father's footsteps—becomes a World War II "radio man" deriving comfort from "the reliable glow of the radio tubes" (169). Ronald, in fact, is not the only one to see stability in electric signals. In the chaotic world of the Kovno ghetto, young Yehoshua "Mendelsohn" too listens to the radio frequencies of a Grundig shortwave radio and believes that numbers "were the imperishably true handiwork of God," in fact enabling him to "perceive the Messiah when he came" (97). The larger point here is that systems of signs and signals—including the sign system novel, "a printed circuit" (181)—await decoding of their deceptively simple—that is, cryptic—messages, whether communication be understood in secular or theological, scientific or mystical, material or immaterial terms.

5. As Doctorow's most ambitious novel, *City of God* has received mixed reviews. A. O. Scott finds Doctorow's "anticinematic" (which is to say, cerebral and lyrical) style worthy of note, just as he acknowledges the novel's commitment to thought, "both as a subject and as a mode of literary experience." However, the book's cosmological reach makes for a series of frayed narratives that, ultimately, do not cohere: "To call this a novel of ideas would be half accurate. The ideas are certainly there— the idea of New York, the idea of God, the idea of literature. But where is the novel?" (7). Jonathan Alter takes issue with Doctorow's flat rendition of American historical moments (an almost Jamesonian point) and his "odd lack of style" (27–28). He sees

in *City of God* a book of "overweening ambition that leads into a long series of embarrassments" (28). If the novel is conceived as "a key to all mythologies, and theologies, and histories, and sciences," it is "an undertaking that tests the limits of [Doctorow's] abilities as a writer and finds them sadly wanting" (30). From a more religious perspective, Bruce Bawer has taken issue with the representation of Episcopalianism in the book, calling it Doctorow's "most abhorrent work and his most conspicuous failure" (402). Needless to say, engaging with these judgments would require a separate chapter.

6. As with Arnold Garbage's junk, Edgar and Arnold's becomes an almost epic catalogue of leftovers. As well, after already having slipped the tube into the ground, Edgar reopens it to retrieve his "Little Blue Book, *Ventriloquism Self-Taught*," which seemed to him "a waste of a book to bury it like that" (370–71). Edgar reuses the manual to develop his own self-speaking voice as a writer, thus figuratively ushering into the series of narrative recyclings that make up Edgar Lawrence Doctorow's work.

7. See Dawson for a fine reading along cinematic lines.

8. For another American writer similarly influenced by *Sartor Resartus*, see *The Education of Henry Adams*. Not only does the name of Adams's hero echo Carlyle's Goethean philosopher Diogenes Teufelsdröckh (401–15), Adams's very notion of education is Carlylean as well. "For purposes of model," he envisions the ego as "a manikin on which the toilet of education is to be draped in order to show the fit or misfit of clothes. . . . The tailor adapts the manikin as well as the clothes to his patron's wants" (xxx). *Teufelsdröckh* is a compound of the (archaic) German "devil's dirt" or "devil's dung" and thus resonates with overtones of garbage and residue.

9. Again, this chapter is not the place to elaborate on the many-layered interactions between science and narrative that are central to *City of God*. But an ambitious novel that attempts to remember the very act of remembrance may well have bent Einstein's space-time continuum to its own chronotopic needs. When Sarah Blumenthal first glances at the list of ghetto victims retrieved from her father's diary, her memorization conflates the past into a moment of immediate reenvisioning (further accentuated, as in Thomas Pynchon's *Gravity's Rainbow*, by the use of the present tense) that suggests a form of unruptured continuity: "There is no time or distance in Sarah's apprehension of these pages, they are not historical but, in their simple exact notation, a curve of the universe's light flashing through her, lasing her consciousness into these leaves of paper, letter by letter, as if the newly dead are being written down as she reads" (205). Thus, what could otherwise be seen as a (by now trite) staple of "magical realism" is here given quasi-scientific theorizing to bend the contours of imaginable fiction.

10. I would, hence, not at all want to suggest that Doctorow "kills," in however symbolic a way, male predecessors on his way toward literary authenticity, as Harold Bloom has advanced of the British romantics in *The Anxiety of Influence*. Given the intense search for fatherhood of many of Doctorow's young, male writer-artists,

however, it may be plausible to note that lineage, in literary and other terms, is an important concept for Doctorow.

11. Theoretically arresting as *Postmodernism* is, some readers of Doctorow may be hard-pressed to accept, among others, Jameson's reading of *Ragtime* as "white writing." The effect of the novel's self-consciously simple style is not "one of condescending simplification and symbolic carefulness of children's literature, but rather something more disturbing, the sense of some profound subterranean violence done to American English" (24).

12. For Doctorow's outrage and commitment to historical change, see his *Lamentation 9/11*, the profits from which will be donated to Seeds of Peace, a nonprofit, nonpolitical organization designed to bring American and Arab teenagers together to create a common understanding between their two cultures.

13. For a similar critique of Jameson's "pseudohistorical" reading of Doctorow, see Moraru 41–53.

14. For a helpful explanation of Jameson's tricky notion of erroneous "transparency" as the blinding effects of "ideology," see Helmling, esp. 122–25.

15. Burton has noted that "[e]ssentially apolitical himself," the *chiffonnier* had, by the mid-nineteenth century, "been transformed into a political 'myth' of considerable potency for Left and Right alike" (229).

16. See Marks, esp. 123–39, "The Literary Machine," for a helpful summary of the centrality of literature in Deleuze's philosophy.

17. Not surprisingly, while the myth of the ragpicker was his radical otherness, making him a generic marker for all kinds of social outcasts, "the most common, indeed, virtually automatic, assimilations are ... with the two great 'outside groups' of European society: Jews and gypsies" (Burton 225).

18. A tribute to Kleist, in which Doctorow notes that Kleist's "chronicle fiction ... to this day dazzles me as no other," ends with, "when I first read Kleist I recognized a brother" (*Conversations* 123). Doctorow has written a foreword to an American edition of Kleist's plays, and Deleuze and Guattari's description of *Michael Kohlhaas* might well serve as a gloss on Doctorow's motivations for reappropriating Kleist's novella for *Ragtime*: "Throughout his work, Kleist celebrates the war machine, setting it against the State apparatus in a struggle that is lost from the start. Doubtless Arminius heralds a Germanic war machine that breaks with the imperial order of alliances and armies, and stands forever opposed to the Roman State. But the Prince of Homburg lives only in a dream and stands condemned for having reached victory in disobedience of the law of the State. As for Kohlhaas, his war machine can no longer be anything more than banditry" (355).

19. Doctorow's work thus illustrates the dynamics of literary evolution through what the Russian formalists have termed "the refunctionalization" of formal elements. Observes Jurij Tynjanov: "If we agree that evolution is the change of interrelationships between the elements of a system ... then evolution may be seen as the 'mutation' of systems.... They do not entail the sudden and complete renovation or

the replacement of formal elements, but rather *the new function of these formal elements*" (76–77).

20. Doctorow's notion of a false document (a term borrowed from Kenneth Rexroth) is strikingly similar to Meir Sternberg's distinction between "truth value" and "truth claim." That "history-writing is frequently wedded to and fiction-writing opposed to factual truth," notes Sternberg, is "a category-mistake of the first order. For history-writing is not a record of fact—of what 'really happened'—but a discourse that claims to be a record of fact. Nor is fiction-writing a tissue of free inventions but a discourse that claims freedom of invention. The antithesis lies not in the presence or absence of truth value but in the commitment to truth value" (25). Much in contrast to recent narrative theorizing, Marie-Laure Ryan has argued in favor of upholding the "fiction/non-fiction distinction" because "it provides our only protection against the 'hyperreality syndrome' (to borrow Baudrillard's concept): the replacement of reality . . . by the simulacra thrown at us by culture and the media" (180).

21. Sartorius, as Simon Schama has noted, here reinterprets Carlyle's central claim "that the tailored garment of our bodies is but a fabric for our divine spark" into an understanding of the body as "biological matter" or an organ supply bank ready to be harvested (31). Such issues of course resonate in today's climate of stem cell research and organ transplants (Wutz, "*The Waterworks*" 178). Sartorius's surgical feats recall Jean Baudrillard's notion of "anthropological deregulation," whereby the scientific and medical developments that lead to an increasingly more complex synergy of body and machine go hand in hand with the "simultaneous deregulation of ethics, of all the moral, judicial and symbolic rules" (*End* 97).

22. To argue, as Theodora Tsimpouki does, that "[u]nlike in [Doctorow's] earlier novels, in *The Waterworks* it is innate depravity rather than social conditioning that is considered the cause of evil" (187) is to diminish the nuanced ethical complexity of Doctorow's fiction. Moraru provides a more science-based contextualized account of Doctorow's ethical complexity in *The Waterworks* (137–48).

23. Doctorow has spoken about "the vulnerability of people to television" (*Conversations* 158). Distinguishing the imaginative richness of radio from television, Doctorow recalls his first reaction to the medium: "The picture was flat, hermetic, oppressive. . . . It was all there and it was one dimension and it was constrictive . . . the flatness and the almost claustrophobic nature of the image pressed up against the screen" (*Conversations* 199).

24. Doctorow published many of Everett's ruminations on film verbatim in an essay for the *New York Times*. After a discussion of prominent cinematic codes, he notes, "In some of today's film dramas 95 percent of a scene's meaning is conveyed before a word is uttered; 98 percent if you add music" ("Quick Cuts").

25. In *Reporting the Universe*, Doctorow similarly noted that "[w]e writers are exemplars of print culture, one of the minor forms of modern communication. We are a cottage industry in a post-industrial world. Our voices are constricted by the censorship of the marketplace. The entertainment behemoths that finance us are finding us

a bad investment. The public libraries that stock our work have given over rooms to the Internet, videotapes, audiotapes, and music CDs" (4).

26. As Doctorow puts it in "Quick Cuts," "one can imagine a merger of film esthetics and profit-making incentives that, apart from the efforts of this or that serious principled filmmaker, effects a culture of large, beautifully dressed, tactically pigmented, stimulating and only incidentally verbal movies that excite predetermined market tastes and offer societal myths that slightly vary with each recycling: films composed artfully from the palette of such basic elements as car drive-ups, interiors, exteriors, faces, chases and explosions" (7).

27. Doctorow's war machine, in that sense, is radically different from the pro-military techno-fiction of the likes of Tom Clancy, Larry Bond, and others. As the Polish novelist Piotr Siemion has noted, "by putting political and social discourses to the fore and subordinating them to all individual voices," techno-thrillers legitimize not only the military but, more broadly, "the modern primacy of institutions over the individual subject" (197).

28. As Hayden White has noted, "[H]istorians usually work with much less *linguistic* (and therefore less *poetic*) self-consciousness than writers of fiction do. They tend to treat language as a transparent vehicle of representation that brings no cognitive baggage of its own into the discourse" ("Fictions" 127).

29. In a theoretical argument paralleling Doctorow's, Lennard J. Davis has argued that in sixteenth-century England, all printed prose narratives circulated in what he calls a "news/novel discourse," a muddled soup of tropes without distinctions of veracity and truthfulness. Through "news ballads," which were known as "novels" and reported on public matters, "narrative was given the ability to embody recentness, hence to record that which was novel, that is, to be a 'novel'" (48). Only as these ballads developed into "partisan notebooks" with distinct political inflections did it become necessary for "journalism and history [to be] distinguished from novels—that is, factual narratives [had to] be clearly differentiated from fictional ones" (67). Under siege by the slant of such ballads, regimes saw fit to provide legal frameworks distinguishing "factual news" from "fictional narrative" so that news critical of the regime could be banned or censored, while fiction—generally not considered harmful to the power structure—was allowed to flourish.

30. Doctorow has repeatedly associated his work with Benjamin's notion of storytelling as an "ancient craft," while disagreeing with Benjamin's account of print culture as a superstructural reflex of capitalism isolating the novelist, as opposed to the storyteller, from communal experience: "Benjamin . . . said the era of storytelling was over because we had now only the individual writers who could offer us no counsel nor wisdom as the ancient story tellers could. I don't happen to subscribe to that part of the essay" (*Conversations* 188). For an insightful discussion of Benjamin's historically contingent notion of information, see Johnston 34–38.

31. Doctorow is part owner of "Booknet, a 24-hour-a-day, books-only cable TV service" (Morris xxx), thus further suggesting that he seeks to establish synergies

between print narrative and electronic media. Similarly, Doctorow's publication of *Three Screenplays*—the film version of *Daniel*, an unproduced version of *Ragtime* (very much unlike the Milos Forman film), and an unproduced script of *Loon Lake*—suggests his involvement in making his own novels into films, as well as his recognition of intermedial dialogue. The very fact that two of the three scripts have not yet been produced in their original form also points (as with Lowry's adaptation of *Tender Is the Night*) to their distinctly verbal literariness that is not easily amenable to the visual codes of cinema.

32. Various theorists have of course noted the disproportion between informational overload and significance. Doctorow would agree with fellow novelist Carlos Fuentes that "true writers are offering the other avenues of sensibility [and] imagination that are constantly being restricted by the abundance of information, which is really a posited information because of the lack of significance" (Wutz, "*Reality*" 9). Let me also add that I do not want to make Doctorow into a "systems novelist" in LeClair's terms, even though I would submit that *The Book of Daniel*, *The Waterworks*, and certainly *City of God* have the qualities of systems novels.

33. Beyond the inherent instability of language to signify, LeClair has also noted—wonderfully—that serious novelists are leaving "spare parts lying around the book, parts that imply a plenitude resistant to any ordering, including the author's" (23). Similarly, John Johnston: "[W]hat is noise, detritus, or waste on one discursive channel may be meaningful—or made meaningful, by rewriting, translating, or recoding—on another" (50).

Chapter 7

1. Given Doctorow's affinity for Hawthorne, the following entry in *American Notebooks* (about an idea for a short story) is particularly uncanny and could serve as a gloss on much of *The Waterworks:* "To represent the influence which Dead Men have among living affairs;—for instance, a Dead Man controls the disposition of wealth; a Dead Man sits on the judgment-seat, and the living judges do but repeat his decisions; Dead Men's opinions in all things control the living truth.... Everywhere and in all matters, Dead Men tyrannize inexorably over us" (252). Doctorow himself, of course, has noted that the novel is partly an homage to the dark visions of his namesake and contemporary of Hawthorne, Edgar Allen Poe.

2. Christian Moraru notes that such reappropriations put forth "*a critical commentary* on the sociohistorical ambience ... within which rewriting is undertaken or within which the reworked text was produced" (xii).

3. In his informal history of the New York underworld, Herbert Ashbury notes that police brutality has also been a staple of nineteenth-century crime fighting: "organized gangs have been clubbed out of existence by the police, who have always been prompt to inaugurate repressive campaigns when permitted to do so by their political masters. Inspector Alexander S. Williams ... enunciated and put into prac-

tice his famous dictum that 'there is more law in the end of a policeman's nightstick than in a decision by the Supreme Court" (xvi; see also 217–19).

4. *The Waterworks* also contains suggestive conceptual and structural affinities to Stanislaw Lem's science-fiction novel *Solaris*, which similarly interrogates the authoritative pronouncements of science and the limits of knowledge. While *Solaris* (adapted for the screen in 1972 by Andrei Tarkovsky, and again in 2003 by Steven Soderbergh) is set in a space station in an undefined future, Doctorow's uncanny parallels (unwittingly) gesture toward the scientific tradition from which *The Waterworks* emerges. Both novels feature scientists named Sartorius with Faustian overlays, and both are in search of what one of Lem's characters calls "an immortality agent"; both scientists work with human brains and conduct experiments with encephalography; and both novels offer an epistemological meditation on the question of (in)sanity. In a more abstract way, Lem's churning oceanic soup on the planet Solaris, which engenders the mind-bending changes on the space station as if it were a fluid capable of cognition and mind control, parallels the postbellum version of a waterworks housing a scientist's lab that is seemingly propelled by the water masses rushing through its pipes and channels. Even the fact that the "visitor" of Lem's Sartorius is a little child (presumably a materialization of his memory brought about by the planet's "intelligent" fluid) may be replayed in the children of *The Waterworks*, where they serve Doctorow's Sartorius as organic farms to replenish the failing bodies of his wealthy patrons. Similarly, the fact that these "visitors"—as quasi-organic life-forms similar to yet different from human beings—can exist only in the space station parallels the comatose state of Doctorow's zombies quarantined in the sealed-off waterworks. *The Waterworks* invites a reading as a late nineteenth-century version of a *Solaris*-like science fiction, with numerous additional parallelisms too numerous to develop here.

5. For a Nietzschean reading of Doctorow, see, for example, King. Christopher D. Morris's approach to Doctorow focuses more on the deconstructive side of Nietzsche—the postmodern "crisis in articulation" (5) that is evident in Doctorow's work.

6. The media-technological focus of this chapter makes the important discussion of gender in relation to the novel impossible. For a sustained focus on gender in *The Waterworks* (and Doctorow's work in general), see Gentry. Gentry argues that while "Doctorow generally treats women and children, not adult males, as tuned in to the forces that direct the course of events," *The Waterworks* is "narrated by a character villainously capable of persuading us that women and children are powerless to do anything but build illusions in opposition to the evil mechanisms of men" (63–64).

7. On its way to cultural respectability (and "medical" data management), phrenology quickly acquired a quasi-scientific cachet: while in early diagrams, "the head was portrayed in a natural lumpy manner and the countenance was of a real person, by the 1820s the head had become a stylized sphere.... The image of scientific precision, authority, and definitiveness that this allowed was further enhanced by the re-

drawing of the lines demarcating the mental faculties. The cranial topography that had appeared . . . 'like the maps of revolutionized France' or 'like the scales of a salmon magnified' was thereby rendered into something far more reminiscent of an illustration from physics or mechanics" (Cooter 75). The most popular rendition of phrenology in 1870s America was of course L. N. Fowler's minutely mapped cranial bust, to which, among others, Walt Whitman pledged allegiance.

8. Donne's system coincides with Alphonse Bertillon's anthropometric method in 1870s Paris, which relies on precise bodily measurements recorded on a personal file. See, for example, Ginzburg, esp. 119–21.

9. For these medical relays between bodies and technologies, see also Tim Armstrong's fine study, *Modernism, Technology and the Body,* esp. 1–10.

10. The phrase is Poe's to describe the arguably first modern information processor, detective Dupin: "From Homer to Rousseau, from the Bible to the civil code, from the laws of the twelve tables to the Koran, he has read every thing, retained every thing" (qtd. in Barbara Johnson, "The Frame of Reference: Poe, Lacan, Derrida," in *The Purloined Poe,* 245).

11. While it would have been common to do a Ph.D. thesis defense in Latin in nineteenth-century Germany (see, for example, Popplestone and McPherson 9), scholarly notes and articles were typically done in German (or any other modern language). Sartorius's records hence suggest a level of secrecy at odds with the profession.

12. Gian Paolo Caprettini notes that Holmes's mental space can be compared "to an encyclopedia, not only for its variety and vastness of knowledge, but also for the impossibility of having them all under control to the same degree, from the mnemonic point of view" (328).

13. See Winthrop-Young, "Informatics," for a beautiful analysis along similar lines.

14. Edgar Lawrence Doctorow has often noted that he is named after Edgar Allan Poe and D. H. Lawrence (see, for example, *Conversations* 96).

15. In a kind of advance retrospective, Dr. Sartorius also appears as a Civil War doctor in *The March* (2005), about a half-dozen years before the events in *The Waterworks*. In the later, but chronologically earlier, novel, Sartorius already intimates an interest in cognition and (biological) information distribution. Responding to another character's description of General Sherman as the "small brain" and of his march as "an immense organism," Sartorius notes that "[a]ll the orders for our vast movements issue forth from that brain. . . . They are carried via the generals and colonels and field officers for distribution to the body of us. This is the creature's nervous system. And any one of the sixty thousand of us has no identity but as a cell in the body of this giant creature's function" (62).

16. A celebrated authority of his time, and widely known for his innovative treatments, Ricord was among the first to distinguish a third stage of syphilis involving "nodules . . . necrosis, syphilitics tubercles of the brain," as well as certain "internal affections" (qtd. in Dracobly 541).

17. The fact that some of Sartorius's experimental (and aphasic) subjects go by the designation "Monsieur" may point to the doctor's partly French origins. Broca's famous diagnosis, in which he posited the correlation of a speech deficit with a lesion in the left frontal lobe of the cortex, was made as a result of the autopsy of the brain of a certain "Monsieur Lebornge" (Harnish 64).

18. Evolutionary brain discourse is also at the heart of *Dracula* (and would require a separate essay). The parallels between Sartorius and Abraham van Helsing, M.D., D.Ph., D.Lit., J.D., are many, culminating in their joint interest in "the continuous evolution of brain matter" (*Dracula* 295). The allegorical battle between Dracula and van Helsing pits, as Dracula puts it to Mina Harker, "your brains against mine" (343), and Mina, in van Helsing's left-thinking mind, is fortunately endowed with a "great brain that is trained like a man's brain but is of sweet woman" (401). Van Helsing repeatedly distinguishes between the evolutionary bifurcation of Dracula's "man-brain" and "child-brain" (401) and sees clear evidence of his increasing intellection (380). Again similar to *The Waterworks*, the brain lesion of Renfield ("a depressed fracture of the skull, extending right up to the motor area" [330]), and the consequent trephining operation, echoes Broca's early surgeries and Monsieur's cerebral short circuit. The very fact that Renfield can only speak in conscious moments while "his poor injured brain had been working in the interval" leads to a highly discontinuous account of his experiences (332–34), inviting a media-technological Lacanian reading. Kittler sees in Lacan's theoretical register of the real a "historical effect" of the advent of phonography that stores (unlike print and film) all the voices and utterances produced by bodies, regardless of meaning or intent, in the process separating the signifying function of words from noises that cannot be seen and written. Renfield's ruptured conscious narrative, even as his unconscious narrative is automatically unwinding itself, thus suggests a modeling of his memory along the lines of Edison's phonograph, a "mechanist model of cognition" (Gitelman 88) similar to other (literary) memory-fantasies of the time.

19. Following Galvani's work on the electrical nature of nerve impulses, by the middle of the nineteenth century it was generally accepted that "the nervous system was essentially a conductor of electrical impulses and that the nervous system functioned much like a switching station, shunting the impulses onto either sensory or motor nerve fibers" (Schultz 39). In his *Untersuchungen über thierische Elektrizität* (1848), for example, the French physiologist Du-Bois-Raymond demonstrated "the existence of independent electrical properties in the muscles and the nerves and postulated the presence of a 'general muscular current' to replace the [Cartesian] theory of nerve substance and fluid" (Rabinbach 6).

20. Reiser notes that in 1807 the English physician-scientist Thomas Young was probably the first to conceive of a device based on "a rotating cylinder" for recording "the continuous motions of events" but did not develop it (100). Reiser also notes that unlike Vierodt and Marey's sphygmographs, Ludwig's had to be inserted directly into a pulsating artery, thus making it obviously unusable for diagnoses on human bodies (101).

21. After Marey had presented his instrument to the Académie des Sciences in 1860, he became famous instantly when Napoleon III requested a demonstration at court: "A few days after Marey's instrument detected irregularities in the pulse rate of a courtier, the unfortunate fellow was found dead in his bed, and Marey's prestige in royal and political circles was greatly enhanced" (Rabinbach 89).

22. Sartorius's cerebrograph, in that sense, much like the recorded narratives of *Dracula*'s Renfield (see note 19 above), invites a Kittlerian reading as a recorder of the Lacanian real, inscribing as it does, "the physiological accidents and stochastic disorder of bodies" (*Gramophone* 16).

23. See the Thomas A. Edison Papers at http://edison.rutgers.edu/. The journal's editor indicated that the shot of gray matter preferably be taken "immediately upon removal from the body" because of its continued presumed vitality at this point. Apparently Edison abandoned the idea of photographing the brain through the skull, settling instead for X-ray photographs of the exposed brain itself. Sartorius in his chronologically first appearance in *The March* also does not photograph the brain, but he rightly predicts the day when humans "will photograph through the body to the bones" (59).

24. Edison might have also been prompted to conduct this experiment upon receiving an "idea letter," whose author spoke "of an English scientist who was experimenting in the new X-ray. The account stated that this scientist took a picture of his own brain while thinking of a little child who was dead. When he developed the plate he found that there was a faint impression of the child of whom he was thinking when he took the picture" (qtd. in Gitelman 88). See Baldwin for the technicalities of the failed experiments (253).

25. I want to thank Geoffrey Winthrop-Young for suggesting the link of Sartorius with the psychotechnological work done in German labs in the late nineteenth century (see *Friedrich Kittler,* esp. 93–96).

26. In her sketch of the history of information theory, Hayles shows how British researcher Donald MacKay, in contrast to Claude Shannon's model, "linked information with change in a receiver's mindset, and thus with meaning. To be workable, MacKay's definition required that psychological states be quantifiable and measurable—an accomplishment that only now appears distantly possible with such imaging technologies as positron-emission tomography" (*Posthuman* 18). This is of course precisely what Sartorius's machine is incapable of performing.

27. Appearing first in Doctorow's important essay "False Documents" (*Essays* 151), the phrase recurs twenty-five years later in *City of God* (181).

28. Stephen Kern traces this notion of organic memory to Henry Maudsley, who argued in 1867 that the cumulative residue of memory is dispersed and stored in living tissue, even in "the nervous cells which lie scattered in the heart and in the intestinal wall" (40). Later psychologists and writers, among them Ewald Hering, Samuel Butler, Bram Stoker, and Henri Bergson, would advance their own version of memory encoded in cellular forms.

29. See, for example, William Gibson's classic *Neuromancer,* in which a lifetime

aggregate of consciousness and memory is stored as a "construct," "a hardwired ROM cassette replicating a dead man's skills, obsessions, knee-jerk responses" (76). The most prominent scholarly fantasy of such cerebral downloading is Hans Moravec's *Mind Children,* in which "a robot surgeon purees the human brain in a kind of cranial liposuction, reading the information in each molecular layer as it is stripped away and transferring the information into a computer" (Hayles, *Posthuman* 1). Hayles also cites computer scientist Marvin Minsky, who suggested that "it will soon be possible to extract memories from the brain and import them, intact and unchanged, to computer disks" (13).

30. Body snatching, including "selling the bodies to doctors and medical students," was a common gang practice in nineteenth-century New York, including the famous case of Alexander T. Stewart, whose body was exhumed and sold back to his wife. Reminiscent of Pemberton, Stewart acted "as his own bookkeeper, salesman, porter, and errand boy, but by the exercise of vast industry and excessive shrewdness he died the foremost storekeeper of his age" (Ashbury 200).

31. Pinker passim. For a brief and accessible account of the current schools of thought regarding brain science, see Blakeslee.

32. As early as 1929 Harvard psychologist Edwin G. Boring noted that "it is almost correct to say that scientific psychology was born of phrenology, out of wedlock with science" (qtd. in Morse 27).

33. See Iser, *Reader* 230. In that sense, such gaps are more than McIlvaine's "romantic predilection for the three dots of ellipsis" (*New Yorker,* 27 June/4 July 1994, 195) but closer to what "[Toni] Morrison calls the 'unspeakable' breaking into, disrupting, the smooth prose surface we would otherwise expect, marking the place of an absented . . . but nonetheless utopian desire" (DeKoven 124). Tokarczyk has similarly noted that the ellipses "moderate the certainty of the tale's moral by underscoring the incompleteness of memory, leaving readers to ponder an alternate tale left out in the elliptical spaces" (182).

34. Spolsky also notes that Dennett's "theory scans the territory that modernist literature has been exploring for almost a century now: it confirms the realism of those representations of mental life found in the stream of consciousness writing of James Joyce and Virginia Woolf" (38).

35. For a discussion of the spatial novel, especially in relation to cinema, see Tabbi and Wutz 14–16.

36. Notes Nancy Peterson: "The conventions of history do not allow imaginative speculation to restore the record, and so literary texts are essential, if not to restore the record through speculation, to mark the spaces, gaps, aporias that cannot be filled" (9).

37. In contemporary medical terminology, *Sartorius* also describes the longest muscle in the body that aids in flexing the knee and derives from tailors crossing their legs to assume their traditional working posture. Thus, while Sartorius's medical stitching does honor to his name, the name also inverts what its medical designation implies: echoing the body's longest muscle, a small and diminutive Sartorius dem-

onstrates that he may well be short on brawn but long—perhaps overextended—on brain.

Chapter 8

1. Similarly, in terms of popular culture, Mr. Memory (Wylie Watson) in Alfred Hitchcock's *The 39 Steps* (1935)—"one of the most remarkable men in the world"—"has left his brain to the British Museum" in an effort to put on display a specimen of gray matter capable of committing to memory "50 new facts a day."

2. For a useful and reader-friendly overview of the research histories of Lenin's and Einstein's brains, including links to the scientific papers published on the findings, see http://faculty.washington.edu/chudler/ein.html. Steven Levy recounts his original chase of the brain at http://www.echonyc.com/~steven/einstein.html. The odyssey of Einstein's brain is of course variously covered in all of the recent biographies published on the occasion of the Einstein centenary and has received wide circulation in Michael Paterniti's "Driving Mr. Albert," recently expanded into a road trip memoir by the same title (2000). A recent TV series, under the auspices of University College London, profiles the individuals involved in the peregrinations of Einstein's brain. That Paramount Pictures has already purchased film rights to Paterniti's book suggests where the odyssey of Einstein's gray matter is ultimately headed.

3. Einstein's brain weighed in at about 1,230 grams, about 200 grams less than the average adult brain. However, Einstein's brain differed in neuron density, particularly in the area of the parietal cortex, which may help explain "highly developed mathematical skill and visuospatial processing." See the column by neuroscientist Mark Lythgoe at http://www.physorg.com for an accessible and brief description of the peculiarities of Einstein's brain.

4. See also Doctorow's appreciative essay, "Einstein: Seeing the Unseen," in *Creationists,* 151–63.

5. The trope of the skull qua laboratory echoes Augustus Pemberton in *The Waterworks* (32), and the elaborate description of a Neanderthal skull converted into a drinking bowl appears, at different historical moments, almost verbatim in both novels (*City of God* 25; *The Waterworks* 46–47). These and other echoes, such as various brain injuries, suggest the development of both novels, written consecutively, out of the same evolutionary and cognitive context, just as they point to Doctorow's practice of narrative recycling (or cognitive efficiency).

6. This fundamental circularity anticipates the constructive loop between perception and the world, as in the work of Maurice Merleau-Ponty. In *A Phenomenology of Perception* he wrote, "The world is inseparable from the subject, but from a subject which is nothing but a project of the world, and the subject is inseparable from the world, but from a world which the subject itself projects" (qtd. in Varela, Thompson, and Rosch 4).

7. In my view, Wittgenstein's preoccupation with manual embodiment and expressiveness is, most likely, intimately connected to his older brother Paul, a concert

pianist who lost his right arm during military service in World War I. Paul resolved to continue performing with the left hand only (like the pianists Leon Fleisher and Joao Martins) and eventually became a celebrated pianist, often playing works composed specifically for him by the likes of Maurice Ravel, Benjamin Britten, and Richard Strauss. (For a contemporary variation of this theme—in this case, a pianist with two six-fingered hands—see Andrew Niccol's 1997 film *Gattaca*.)

Echoing Heidegger's observation on manual embodiment, Hans-Georg Gadamer notes that the hand "in itself is not a tool, that is, it doesn't serve specific needs but is, instead, capable of working on things so that, as a hand-tool, it serves the purposes for which it was selected. In that sense, the hand is also a mental organ, a link with multiple purposes and submitting other tools to its uses.—For that reason, that organ is intimately connected with language. The hand is not only a hand which makes and grasps something, but also the hand that points to something" (18, my translation).

8. Andy Clark has shown how termite nest building (a low-level form of distributed cognition) could be seen as a model for work in artificial life, "emphasizing the importance of factors other than rich, individual computation and cogitation." Involving the interplay of mudballing, chemical tracing, and the, at least initially, aleatory accumulation of mudballs, nest building—an apparently complex and highly negotiated skill—does not depend on "coordinated activity," a "central plan," or "a designated 'leader.'" "No termite knows much at all," he concludes, "the collective activity is not even orchestrated by regular signaling or communication" (108).

9. The phrase is William J. Mitchell's (*City of Bits*). In a more theological and evolutionary framework (that is never far from *City of God*), such an overbrain also recalls Teilhard de Chardin's notion of the noosphere. An evolutionary biologist and Jesuit priest (whose work fell under Catholic censorship and was published only posthumously), Teilhard posited the emergence of what he called a "'thinking layer'" or "noosphere" stretching over the biosphere, a global membrane of mentality that coincides with "the sudden deluge of cerebralisation" brought on by humans (182–83). Eventually, in Teilhard's view, the harmonized synergy of individual minds yields "a sort of super-consciousness. The idea is that of the earth not only becoming covered by myriads of grains of thought, but becoming enclosed in a single thinking envelope so as to form, functionally, no more than a single vast grain of thought on the sidereal scale" (251). While this gradual thickening of cognition expresses itself, in part, in new technologies (such as cars and the modern media), for Teilhard such concentration is fundamentally mystical (and hence viewed with suspicion by the scientific establishment). Nevertheless, both Bateson and McLuhan (e.g., *Gutenberg* 32) drew on Teilhard in formulating some of their groundbreaking ideas.

10. The very fact that "first you write the book, then you find a rationale for it," as Doctorow put it further, not only echoes the thought processes of the self-deluding ex-*Times* reporter in his attempt to explain his accidental murder of the Nazi criminal but also acknowledges the interplay of pre- and unconscious thought that relinquishes full agency in favor of distributed cognition ("On *City*").

11. The debate between Louis O. Mink and Hayden White on the intersection of cognition and ethics provides further perspective on Doctorow's (and Powers's) work. Mink contests White's repeated association of narrative with the Law, arguing that such linkage discredits narrative as a cognitive domain: "White's thesis is not just that narratives *may* express the need to moralize but that narrativizing is uniquely and necessarily the instrument of that need. And this means that narrativizing is never in the first instance cognitive and never a primary and irreducible human capacity but a creature of something more primary—the 'moral impulse'" ("Annalist" 239). In response, White notes that "[i]t is only by virtue of what it teaches about moral wisdom, or rather about the irreducible moralism of a life lived under the conditions of culture rather than nature, that narrative can claim cognitive authority at all" ("Narrativization" 253). For White, as for Doctorow and Powers, narrative is certainly moral, ineluctably imbricated in the network of primary ethical questions that define a culture at its historical moment. At the same time, in order for literature to be literature, and hence a cognitive instrument, it must be fundamentally non-moralizing in a narrowly prescribed sense and eschew degenerating into political or religious dogma. Says Powers: fiction provides "a forum for the awakening of conscience. Social conscience and moral conscience" (qtd. in Tortello).

12. Tabbi has, appropriately, called Powers "our time's most systematic literary researcher of cognition" (*Fictions* 59).

13. The thoroughness with which Powers orchestrated the discourse of cognitive science is well expressed in "the eight-page fan letter" Daniel Dennett wrote him upon the publication of *Galatea*. Says Dennett: "I found myself wondering who Powers' informants in the field were" (qtd. in Eakin).

14. See, for a recent example, William Deresiewicz's review of Powers's most recent novel, *The Echo Maker*, in *The Nation*, 9 October 2006, available at http://www.thenation.com/doc/20061009/deresiewicz (30 November 2007).

15. I would add that especially in its often discursive, pre-Helen portion, *Galatea* is initially top-heavy and requires sustained cognitive effort before increasing in facility.

16. The playful plosive sequence of letters may allude to the famous song "The Rain in Spain" from the musical *My Fair Lady* (1956) based on George Bernard Shaw's *Pygmalion* (1913). In the musical, Professor Higgins and Colonel Pickering take flower girl Eliza Doolittle through numerous speech exercises in an attempt to break her Cockney accent speech pattern. When she properly enunciates, "The rain in Spain stays mainly in the plain," they believe to have been successful in their, in effect, linguistic reprogramming efforts.

17. Helen's information-based language processing appears to be similar to recent innovations in translation software, which has moved from rule-based programming to statistical analyses aimed at recognizing word patterns and cross-linguistic matching probabilities. Franz Och, chief engineer of Google's development division (aiming at translating from Arabic or Chinese into English), acknowledged that "feeding the machine-translation software with text that equated to one million books was key to performance improvements" (qtd. in Stix 95), which of course parallels Helen's own linguistic computing power. For all its algorithmic reach, however,

machine translation (MT), like Helen, brushes up against the semantic density of language that is impossible to compute—impossible, that is, unless one is a human being. While advocates of what is known as FAHQT (fully automatic high-quality translation) point to the progress in statistical algorithms made over the past decade, the chorus of skeptics currently seems to outweigh MT zealots. Even when statistical techniques will "work tolerably well in many situations," as Keith Devlin, executive director of Stanford's Center for the Study of Language and Information, put it, "fluent translation, as a human expert can do, is, in my view, not achievable" (qtd. in Stix 95). For recent assessments of algorithm-based translation techniques, see Stix; "How to Build a Babel Fish."

18. I would add the female robot in Fritz Lang's *Metropolis* (1927) to this iteration of mythological Galateas, which Powers may well have had in mind. The robot is constructed by the scientist Rotwang (Rudolf Klein-Rogge) and was originally modeled on his former love interest and the now deceased wife of "Joh" Fredersen (Alfred Abel), the mastermind of the futuristic city. This erotic doubling of origins is redoubled in the Wellsian division of the city itself into the affluent planners and thinkers living high above the earth and the workers toiling in underground seclusion, and is redoubled further in the bifurcated function of the robot itself. At the behest of Fredersen, Rotwang gives the robot the appearance of beautiful Maria (Brigitte Helm), who has joined the cause of the workers, but reprograms her so as to sabotage, not enable, an emerging uprising, thus switching her from good to evil and from demure to erotic—an oscillation between the Victorian binary of virgin and/or whore. At the same time, Rotwang also programs the robot not only as a Golem-like secret operative against the workers but also as a weapon of personal revenge against Fredersen for losing his former lover, thus not only reinscribing the social divisions and the marginal status of the (occult) sciences in an engineered world but also adding another layer of bifurcated function to the male-controlled robot. Sexual, emotional, and scientific control over a female body and mind enter into a complicated synergy throughout the film. The robot is named Hel (an abbreviated form of Helen and an allusion, among others, to Helen of Troy and the female goddess Hel presiding over the Norse underworld also called Hel); she/it has been bifurcated—2.2'ed, if you will—in more senses than one.

19. The instability of the self and consciousness's task to forge a semblance of self-continuity and self-possession are reprised and expanded upon in Powers's more recent *The Echo Maker*. As neuroscientist Weber (the German word for *weaver* to suggest the infinitesimally networked process of each cognitive activity) puts it in his newest book, *The Country of Surprise*, each of his case studies of brain-damaged patients "called into question the solidity of self. We were not one, continuous, indivisible whole, but instead hundreds of separate subsystems, with changes in any one sufficient to disperse the provisional confederation into unrecognizable new countries" (171). Needless to say, *The Echo Maker* is the next installment in Powers's ongoing interrogation of the final (interior) frontier and too complex to give it adequate treatment in the conclusion to this study.

20. This perpetual splitting and reconstitution of both the self and verbal mean-

ing also holds true for the way in which the brain is making sense out of music, which is one of the dominant tropes in Powers's *The Gold Bug Variations*. As Jonah Lehrer put it in *Proust Was a Neuroscientist*, his insightful study of the ways in which modern art anticipates the findings of contemporary advances in brain research: "Music is the playful overflow of information." If the level of noise exceeds the processing capabilities of the brain, the human auditory cortex tries to establish relationships between individual notes by uncovering "patterns at the larger level of the phrase, motif, and movement." This sorting operation, in turn, lets the brain "extract *order* from all these notes haphazardly flying through space, and the brain is obsessed with order" (130). We are hardwired for sense, structure, and meaning making on many levels of cognitive work, it seems.

21. See Dennett, esp. 253–82.

22. For a beautiful reading of the title's *2.2* along the lines of her argument about presence and absence, pattern and randomness, including the significance of dots separating numerals, see Hayles, *Posthuman* 261–72.

23. Bolter and Grusin note that when "the self is expressed in its email affiliations," it is not "disembodied but . . . embodied in a particular mediated form (as electronic text, with a return address, a user ID, a signature, and so forth)" (234). This is certainly true, but I would add that the mediated form of such a self could be seen to be close to an erasure of embodiment precisely because of its flickering, electronic constitution.

24. That Helen is without body also expresses the males' fear of their own corporeality, given that Lentz's body, in particular, "had been nothing but a nuisance to him" for many years (93). The novel's lettered shrinkage of women is also strongly reminiscent of the classically male modernist fear of Woman, as in the case of Ezra Pound, who urged his one-time imagist companion Hilda Doolittle to reduce her name to the pictorial "H. D.," thus in effect erasing her female authorship.

25. As one in a series of erotic displacements, A.'s mouth is ultimately linked to "The Mother's Mouth," the oracular origin of print discourse which, as Kittler has argued, "freed children from books. Her voice substituted sounds for letters," and thus rendered invisible a material medium that alphabetized children into readers (*Discourse Networks* 34). The Powers-narrator, indeed, repeatedly connects the readings of his mother to his own development of literacy (26, 55, 147), and he further notes that the language relays in early neural networks were reinforced when "sounds that coincided with mother speech were praised" (30). Of course, when the narrator himself feeds Helen his own literary knowledge by reading into her microphone, he serves precisely in the capacity as a mother's mouth, but unlike the narrator, whose fetish derives from his own embodiment, Helen's disembodied functioning makes her incapable of this kind of erotic rerouting. For a suggestive reading of the scene of writing in Powers's work along the lines of Kittler, see Tabbi, *Fictions,* esp. 72–76.

26. See Powers's recent essay in the *New York Times,* "How to Speak a Book" (7 January 2007), for an update on his shift from typewriting to voice dictation (http://www.nytimes.com/2007/01/07/books/review/Powers2.t.html). Incidentally,

as if echoing the argument about the fissure between 2.2, Powers extends the cognitive gap between reading and rereading to the compositional process itself: "Writing is the act of accepting the huge shortfalls between the story in the mind and what hits the page.... Everything we write—through any medium—is lost in translation. But something new is always found again, in their eager years. In Derrida's fears. Make that: in the reader's ears."

27. Asked by Birkerts in an interview whether he wishes to put "the genie of the binary back into the bottle" if he could, Powers—while acknowledging the concern of digitalization—noted that "you can learn more by examining that desire than by acting on it." For Powers, "writing is a far more dangerous, destabilizing, and catastrophic technology than anything digital. The impact that it's had on the way we live will never be exceeded by the technologies that derive from it" (*Bomb* 63).

Bibliography

Ackerley, Chris. "Notes towards Lowry's Screenplay of *Tender Is the Night*." *Malcolm Lowry Review* 29/30 (Fall 1991–Spring 1992): 41–50.

———. "'Well, of course, if we knew all the things': Coincidence and Design in *Ulysses* and *Under the Volcano*." In *Joyce/Lowry*, 41–62.

Ackerley, Chris, and Lawrence J. Clipper. *A Companion to "Under the Volcano."* Vancouver: University of British Columbia Press, 1984.

Acocella, Joan. "Blocked: Why Do Writers Stop Writing?" *New Yorker*, 14 and 21 June 2004, 110–16, 127–29.

Adams, Henry. *The Education of Henry Adams*. Ed. and intro. Ernest Samuels. Boston: Houghton Mifflin, 1973.

Albérès, R. M. *Métamorphoses du Roman*. Paris: Éditions Albin Michel, 1966.

Alter, Jonathan. "Cosmosity." Review of *City of God*. *New Republic*, 6 March 2000, 27–30.

Anderson, Gregory, ed. *The White-Blouse Revolution: Female Office Workers since 1870*. Manchester: Manchester University Press, 1988.

Anderson, Sherwood. "Form, Not Plot, in the Short Story." In *The Portable Sherwood Anderson*, ed. Horace Gregory. New York: Viking, 1972.

Anesko, Michael W. *"Friction within the Market": Henry James and the Profession of Authorship*. New York: Oxford University Press, 1986.

Antliff, Mark. *Inventing Bergson: Cultural Politics and the Parisian Avant-Garde*. Princeton: Princeton University Press, 1993.

Apollinaire, Guillaume. *Calligrammes: Poems of Peace and War (1913–1916)*. Trans. Anne Hyde Greet. Intro. S. I. Lockerbie. Berkeley: University of California Press, 1980.

———. "The New Spirit and the New Poets." In *Apollinaire*, 333–44.

———. *Selected Writings*. Trans. and intro. Roger Shattuck. New York: New Directions, 1971.

Armstrong, Tim. *Modernism, Technology and the Body*. Cambridge: Cambridge University Press, 1998.

Ärztekammer, Berlin. *The Value of the Human Being: Medicine in Germany, 1918–1945*. Berlin: Hentrich, 1991.

Asals, Frederick. *The Making of Malcolm Lowry's "Under the Volcano."* Athens: University of Georgia Press, 1997.

———. "Revision and Illusion in *Under the Volcano*." In *Maelstrom*, 93–111.

Ashbury, Herbert. *The Gangs of New York: An Informal History of the Underworld*. New York: Thunder's Mouth Press, 1998.

Auerbach, Erich. *Mimesis: The Representation of Reality in Western Literature* (1946). Trans. Willard R. Trask. Princeton: Princeton University Press, 1953.

Baldwin, Neil. *Edison, Inventing the Century*. Chicago: University of Chicago Press, 2001.

Barthelme, Donald. "The Leading Edge of the Trash Phenomenon." In *Fiction and the Figures of Life*, ed. William H. Gass. Boston: David R. Godine, 1979: 97-103.

Barthes, Roland. "Introduction to the Structural Analysis of Narratives." In *A Barthes Reader*, ed. and intro. Susan Sontag. New York: Hill and Wang, 1982. 251–95.

Bateson, Gregory. *Steps to an Ecology of Mind*. New York: Ballantine, 1972.

Baudelaire, Charles. *Art in Paris*. Ed. and trans. Jonathan Mayne. London: Phaidon Press, 1965.

———. *Oeuvres complètes*. 2 vols. Ed. Claude Pichois. Paris: Pléiade, 1975.

———. *The Painter of Modern Life and Other Essays*. Ed. and trans. Jonathan Mayne. London: Phaidon Press, 1964.

———. "The Salon of 1846." In *Art in Paris*, 116–20.

———. "The Salon of 1859." In *Art in Paris*, 149–55.

Baudelaire as a Literary Critic: Selected Essays. Intro. and trans. Lois Boe Hyslop and Francis E. Hyslop Jr. University Park: University of Pennsylvania Press, 1964.

Baudrillard, Jean. *The Illusion of the End*. Trans. Chris Turner. Cambridge: Polity Press, 1994.

———. "The Implosion of Meaning in the Media and the Implosion of the Social in the Masses." In *The Myths of Information: Technology and Postindustrial Culture*, ed. Kathleen Woodward. Madison, WI: Coda Press, 1980. 137–48.

Bawer, Bruce. "The Faith of E. L. Doctorow." *Hudson Review* 53, no. 3 (2000): 391–402.

Beard, George M. *American Nervousness: Its Causes and Consequences*. New York: G. Putnam's Sons, 1881.

Bell, Michael Davitt. *The Problem of American Realism: Studies in the Cultural History of a Literary Idea*. Chicago: University of Chicago Press, 1993.

Beniger, James R. *The Control Revolution: Technological and Economic Origins of the Information Society*. Cambridge, MA: Harvard University Press, 1986.

Benjamin, Walter. *Charles Baudelaire: A Lyric Poet in the Era of High Capitalism*. Trans. Harry Zohn. London: Verso, 1983.

———. "On Some Motifs in Baudelaire." Trans. Harry Zohn. In *Selected Writings*, 4:313–55.

———. "Paris, the Capital of the Nineteenth-Century." Trans. Howard Eiland. In *Selected Writings*, 3:32–49.

———. *Selected Writings*. Vols. 1–6. Ed. Howard Eiland and Michael W. Jennings. Trans. Edmund Jephcott, Howard Eiland, et al. Cambridge, MA: Belknap Press of Harvard University Press, 1996–2004.

———. "The Storyteller: Observations on the Works of Nikolai Leskov." In *Selected Writings*, 3:143–66.

———. "Unpacking My Library: A Talk about Collecting." Trans. Harry Zohn. In *Selected Writings*, 2:486–93.

———. "The Work of Art in the Age of Its Mechanical Reproducibility." In *Selected Writings*, 3:101–33.

Berger, Kevin. "Art of Fiction CLXXV: An Interview with Richard Powers." *Paris Review* 164 (Winter 2003). http://www.theparisreview.org/viewissue.php/prmIID/164 (15 April 2004).

Bergson, Henri. *Creative Evolution*. Trans. Arthur Mitchell. London: Macmillan, 1911.

Birkerts, Sven. *The Gutenberg Elegies: The Fate of Reading in an Electronic Age*. London: Faber and Faber, 1994.

———. "Richard Powers." Interview. *BOMB* (Summer 1998): 58–63.

Blakeslee, Sandra. "Recipe for a Brain: Cups of Genes and Dash of Experience?" *New York Times*, 4 November 1997.

Bloom, Harold E. *The Anxiety of Influence*. New York: Oxford University Press, 1973.

Bluestone, George. *Novels into Film*. Berkeley: University of California Press, 1961.

Blume, Harvey. "Two Greeks on Their Way to Byzantium: A Conversation with Richard Powers." *Atlantic Unbound*, 28 June 2000. http://www.theatlantic.com/unbound/interviews/ba2000-06-28.htm (18 April 2004).

Blumenthal, David R. *Understanding Jewish Mysticism*. New York: KTAV Publishing House, 1978.

Bolter, Jay David. *Writing Space: The Computer, Hypertext, and the History of Writing*. Hillsdale, NJ: Erlbaum, 1991.

Bolter, Jay David, and Richard Grusin. *Remediation: Understanding New Media*. Cambridge, MA: MIT Press, 1999.

Borus, Daniel. *Writing Realism: Howells, James, and Norris in the Mass Market*. Chapel Hill: University of North Carolina Press, 1989.

Bower, Stephanie. "Dangerous Liaisons: Prostitution, Disease, and Race in Frank Norris's Fiction." *Modern Fiction Studies* 42, no. 1 (1996): 31–60.

Bowker, Gordon. *Pursued by Furies: A Life of Malcolm Lowry*. London: HarperCollins, 1993.

Bradbrook, Muriel C. *Malcolm Lowry: His Art and Early Life—A Study in Transformation*. London: Cambridge University Press, 1974.

Brockes, Emma. "Magic Powers." *Guardian Unlimited*, 14 March 2003. http://

books.guardian.co.uk/departments/generalfiction/story/0,6000,913903,00.html (18 April 2004).
Brooks, Peter. *Reading for the Plot: Design and Intention in Narrative.* New York: Viking, 1986.
Broude, Norma. *Seurat in Perspective.* Englewood Cliffs, NJ: Prentice-Hall, 1978.
Buck-Morss, Susan. "Aesthetics and Anaesthetics: Walter Benjamin's Artwork Essay Reconsidered." *October* 62 (Fall 1992): 3–41.
Burroughs, William S. "Screenwriting and the Potentials of Cinema." In *Writing in a Film Age,* 53–86.
Burton, Richard D. E. *Baudelaire and the Second Republic: Writing and Revolution.* Oxford: Clarendon Press, 1991.
Cain, William. "Presence and Power in *McTeague.*" In *American Realism: New Essays,* ed. Eric J. Sundquist. Baltimore: Johns Hopkins University Press, 1982.
Calvino, Italo. *Six Memos for the Next Millennium.* Trans. Patrick Creagh. Cambridge, MA: Harvard University Press, 1988.
Campbell, Donna. *Resisting Regionalism: Gender and Naturalism in American Fiction, 1885–1915.* Athens: Ohio State University Press, 1997.
Campbell, Miranda. "Probing the Posthuman: Richard Powers' *Galatea 2.2* and the Mind-Body Problem." *Reconstruction* 4, no. 3 (2004). http://www.reconstruction.ws/043/campbell.htm (14 April 2005).
Caponegro, Mary. "Impressions of a Paranoid Optimist." *Review of Contemporary Fiction* 16 (Spring 1996): 23–27.
Caprettini, Gian Paolo. "Sherlock Holmes: Ethics, Logic, and the Mask." In *Sherlock Holmes,* 328–34.
Carey, John. *The Intellectuals and the Masses: Pride and Prejudice among the Literary Intelligentsia, 1880–1939.* New York: St. Martin's Press, 1992.
Carlyle, Thomas. *Sartor Resartus: The Life and Opinions of Herr Teufeldröckh, in Three Books.* New York: Scribners, 1903.
Caruth, Cathy. *Unclaimed Experience: Trauma, Narrative, and History.* Baltimore: Johns Hopkins University Press, 1996.
Cendrars, Blaise. *Complete Poems.* Trans. Ron Padgett. Intro. Jay Bochner. Berkeley: University of California Press, 1992.
Chipp, Herschel B., ed. *Theories of Modern Art: A Source Book by Artists and Critics.* With contributions by Peter Selz and Joshua C. Taylor. Berkeley: University of California Press, 1968.
Chudler, Eric H. "What Became of Albert Einstein's Brain?" http://faculty.washington.edu/chudler/ein.html (17 February 2005).
Clark, Andy. *Mindware: An Introduction to the Philosophy of Cognitive Science.* New York: Oxford University Press, 2001.
Clifford, James. *The Predicament of Culture: Twentieth-Century Ethnography, Literature, and Art.* Cambridge, MA: Harvard University Press, 1988.
Cohen, Keith, ed. *Writing in a Film Age: Essays by Contemporary Novelists.* Denver: University Press of Colorado, 1991.

Coleridge, Samuel Taylor. *Coleridge's Writings on Shakespeare*. Ed. Terence Hawkes. Intro. Alfred Harbage. New York: Capricorn, 1959.

Conrad, Joseph. *Conrad's Prefaces to His Works*. Intro. Edward Garnett. London: J. M. Dent and Sons, 1937.

Cooter, Roger. *The Cultural Meaning of Popular Science: Phrenology and the Organization of Consent in Nineteenth-Century Britain*. Cambridge: Cambridge University Press, 1984.

Corkin, Stanley. *Realism and the Birth of the Modern United States: Cinema, Literature, Culture*. Athens: University of Georgia Press, 1996.

Crary, Jonathan. *Techniques of the Observer: On Vision and Modernity in the Nineteenth Century*. Cambridge, MA: MIT Press, 1990.

Crisler, Jesse S., and Joseph R. McElrath Jr. *Frank Norris: A Reference Guide*. Boston: G. K. Hall, 1974.

Cross, Richard K. *Malcolm Lowry: A Preface to His Fiction*. Chicago: University of Chicago Press, 1980.

Crunden, Robert M. *Body and Soul: The Making of American Modernism*. New York: Basic Books, 2000.

Danius, Sara. *The Senses of Modernism: Technology, Perception, and Aesthetics*. Ithaca: Cornell University Press, 2002.

Dargis, Manohla. "An American Primitive, Forged in a Crucible of Blood and Oil." *New York Times*, 26 December 2007. http://movies.nytimes.com/2007/12/26/movies/26bloo.html (28 December 2007).

Darwin, Charles. *The Descent of Man, and Selection in Relation to Sex*. Intro. John Tyler Bonner and Robert M. May. 1872. Princeton: Princeton University Press, 1981.

Davis, Lennard J. *Factual Fictions: The Origins of the English Novel*. New York: Columbia University Press, 1983.

Dawson, Anthony B. "*Ragtime* and the Movies: The Aura of the Duplicable." *Mosaic* 16, no. 4 (1983): 205–14.

Day, Douglas. *Malcolm Lowry: A Biography*. Oxford: Oxford University Press, 1973.

De Certeau, Michel. "Railway Navigation and Incarceration." In *The Practice of Everyday Life*. Trans. Steven Rendall. Berkeley: University of California Press, 1988. 111–14.

de Chardin, Pierre Teilhard. *The Phenomenon of Man*. Intro. Sir Julian Huxley. Trans. Bernard Wall. New York: Harper and Row, 1959.

De Kerckhove, Derrick. *The Skin of Culture: Investigating the New Electronic Reality*. Ed. Christopher Dewdney. Toronto: Somerville, 1995.

DeKoven, Marianne. "Postmodernism and Post-Utopian Desire in Toni Morrison and E. L. Doctorow." In *Toni Morrison: Critical and Theoretical Approaches*, ed. Nancy Peterson. Baltimore: Johns Hopkins University Press, 1997. 111–30.

De la Motte, Dean, and Jeannene M. Przyblyski, eds. Introduction to *Making the News: Modernity and the Mass Press in 19th-Century France*. Amherst: University of Massachusetts Press, 1999. 1–13.

Deleuze, Gilles. *Foucault*. Trans. Séan Hand. Minneapolis: University of Minnesota Press, 1988.

———. *Proust and Signs*. Trans. Richard Howard. New York: George Braziller, 1972.

Deleuze, Gilles, and Félix Guattari. *A Thousand Plateaus: Capitalism & Schizophrenia*. Trans. and foreword Brian Massumi. Minneapolis: University of Minnesota Press, 1987.

DeLillo, Don. *White Noise*. Rev. ed. New York: Penguin, 1987.

D'Emilio, John, and Estelle B. Freedman. *Intimate Matters: A History of Sexuality in America*. New York: Harper and Row, 1988.

Dennett, Daniel. *Consciousness Explained*. London: Penguin, 1991.

Den Tandt, Christophe. "Amazons and Androgynes: Overcivilization and the Redefinition of Gender Roles at the Turn of the Century." *American Literary History* 8 (1996): 639–64.

———. *The Urban Sublime in American Literary Naturalism*. Urbana: University of Illinois Press, 1998.

Deresjewicz, William, "Science Fiction." Review of *The Echo Maker*. *The Nation*, 9 October 2006.

Derrida, Jacques. "Freud and the Scene of Writing." *Writing and Difference*. Trans. and intro. Alan Bass. Chicago: University of Chicago Press, 1978. 196–231.

———. *Of Grammatology*. Trans. Gayatri Chakravorty Spivak. Baltimore: Johns Hopkins University Press, 1976.

———. "The Question of Style." In *The New Nietzsche*, ed. David Allison. New York: Dell, 1977. 176–80.

Dillingham, William B. *Frank Norris: Instinct and Art*. Lincoln: University of Nebraska Press, 1969.

DiSilvio, Rich. "Commentary and Bio on Liszt." http://www.d-vista.com/OTHER/franzliszt2.html (28 May 2009)

Doctorow, Edgar Lawrence. *Billy Bathgate*. 1989. Reprint, New York: Harper, 1994.

———. *The Book of Daniel*. 1971. Reprint, New York: Ballantine, 1987.

———. *City of God*. New York: Random House, 2000.

———. *Conversations with E. L. Doctorow*. Ed. and intro. Christopher D. Morris. Jackson: University Press of Mississippi, 1999.

———. *Creationists: Selected Essays, 1993–2006*. New York: Random House, 2006.

———. Foreword to *Heinrich von Kleist: Plays*. German Library Series. Ed. Walter Hinderer. New York: Continuum, 1982.

———. *Jack London, Hemingway, and the Constitution: Selected Essays, 1977–1992*. New York: Harper, 1994.

———. *Lamentation 9/11*. Preface by Kofi Annan. Photographs by David Finn. New York: Ruder Finn Press, 2002.

———. "Left Out by Edith Wharton." Interview with Laurel Graeber. *New York Times Book Review*, 19 June 1994, 31.

———. *Loon Lake*. 1980. Reprint, New York: Ballantine, 1988.

———. "On *City of God*." Talk given at Judge Memorial High School in Salt Lake City, Utah, 10 March 2000.

———. "Quick Cuts: The Novel Follows Film into a World of Fewer Words." *New York Times*, 15 March 1999, E1+.

———. *Ragtime*. 1975. Reprint, New York: Vintage, 1991.

———. *Reporting the Universe*. Cambridge, MA: Harvard University Press, 2003.

———. *Three Screenplays*. Intro. Paul Levine. Baltimore: Johns Hopkins University Press, 2003.

———. *The Waterworks*. New York: Random House, 1994.

———. *World's Fair*. 1985. Reprint, New York: Ballantine 1986.

Doezma, Herman P. "An Interview with Carlos Fuentes." *Modern Fiction Studies* 18 (1972): 491–503.

Dos Passos, John. *Manhattan Transfer*. 1925. Boston: Houghton Mifflin, 1953.

Doyen, Victor. "From Innocent Story to Charon's Boat: Reading the 'October Ferry' Manuscripts." In *Maelstrom*, 163–208.

Doyle, Sir Arthur Conan. *Sherlock Holmes: The Major Stories with Contemporary Essays*. Ed. John A Hodgson. Boston: Bedford St. Martin's, 1994.

Dracobly, Alex. "Theoretical Changes and Therapeutic Innovation in the Treatment of Syphilis in Mid-Nineteenth-Century France." *Journal of the History of Medicine and Allied Sciences* 59, no. 4 (2004): 522–54.

Dreyfus, Hubert. *What Computers Can't Do: The Limits of Artificial Intelligence*. Rev. ed. New York: Harper and Row, 1979.

Drucker, Peter. "The Age of Social Transformation." *Atlantic Monthly* 94 (November 1994): 53–80.

Eakin, Emily. "The Author as Science Guy." *New York Times*, 18 February 2003. http://www.nytimes.com/2003/02/18/books/18POWE.htm 1 (14 April 2005).

Eggum, Arne, Gerd Woll, and Marit Lande. *Munch at the Munch Museum*. Oslo: Scala Books, 1998.

Eisenstein, Sergei. *Film Form: Essays in Film Theory*. Ed. and trans. Jay Leyda. 1949. New York: Harcourt Brace, 1977.

Ellison, Ralph. *Invisible Man*. New York: Vintage, 1972.

Epstein, Jean, dir. *The Fall of the House of Usher*. 1928.

Everdell, William R. *The First Moderns: Profiles in the Origins of Twentieth-Century Thought*. Chicago: University of Chicago Press, 1997.

Falk, David. "Self and Shadow: The Brothers Firmin in *Under the Volcano*." *Texas Studies in Language and Literature* 27, no. 2 (1985): 209–23.

Fanning, Michael, ed. *France & Sherwood Anderson: Paris Notebook, 1921*. Baton Rouge: Louisiana State University Press, 1976.

Fitzgerald, F. Scott. *Correspondence of F. Scott Fitzgerald*. Ed. Matthew Joseph Bruccoli, Margaret M. Duggan, and Susan Walker. New York: Random House, 1980.

———. *The Crack-Up*. Ed. Edmund Wilson. New York: New Directions, 1945.

———. *F. Scott Fitzgerald in His Own Time: A Miscellany*. Ed. Matthew J. Bruccoli and Jackson R. Bryer. Kent: Kent State University Press, 1971.

———. *The Letters of F. Scott Fitzgerald*. Ed. Andrew Turnbull. New York: Scribners, 1963.

———. *Letters to His Daughter*. Ed. Andrew Turnbull. New York: Scribners, 1963.

Flusser, Vilém. *Nachgeschichten: Essays, Vorträge, Glossen.* Ed. Volker Rapsch. Düsseldorf: Bollmann Verlag, 1990.

———. "Taking Leave of Literature." *Senses of Science.* European Association for the Study of Science. Ed. B. Jurdant. Strasbourg, 1986. (Abstract).

———. *Writings.* Ed. and intro. Andreas Ströhl. Trans. Erik Eisel. Minneapolis: University of Minnesota Press, 2002.

Ford, Ford Madox. *The Soul of London: A Survey of a Modern City.* Ed. and intro. Alan G. Hill. London: Everyman, 1995.

Fraser, Julius Thomas. *The Genesis and Evolution of Time: A Critique of Interpretation in Physics.* Amherst: University of Massachusetts Press, 1982.

French, Warren. *Frank Norris.* New York: Twayne, 1962.

Freud, Sigmund. *The Standard Edition of the Complete Psychological Works of Sigmund Freud.* Ed. James Strachey. 23 vols. London: Hogarth, 1953–74.

Fried, Michael. *Realism, Writing, Disfiguration: On Thomas Eakins and Stephen Crane.* Chicago: University of Chicago Press, 1987.

Friedl, Herwig, and Dieter Schulz, eds. *E. L. Doctorow: A Democracy of Perception.* Essen: Blaue Eule, 1988.

Gabrial, Jan. *Inside the Volcano: My Life with Malcolm Lowry.* New York: St. Martin's, 2000.

Gadamer, Hans-Georg. "Verlust der sinnlichen Bildung als Ursache des Verlustes von Wertmaßstäben." In *Der Mensch ohne Hand,* 15–28.

Gaddis, William. *Agapē Agape.* Afterword by Joseph Tabbi. New York: Viking, 2002.

———. *The Rush for Second Place: Essays and Occasional Writings.* Ed. and intro. Joseph Tabbi. New York: Penguin, 2002.

Gardels, Nathan. "Neural Darwinism." *New Perspectives Quarterly* 21, no. 3 (Summer 2004). http://digitalnpq.org/archive/2004_summer/edelman.html (14 April 2005).

Garelick, Rhonda K. *Rising Star: Dandyism, Gender, and Performance in the Fin de Siècle.* Princeton: Princeton University Press, 1998.

Gass, William H. *Fiction and the Figures of Life.* Boston: David R. Godine, 1979.

Gauld, Alan. *A History of Hypnotism.* New York: Cambridge University Press, 1992.

Gazzaniga, Michael S. *Mind Matters: How Mind and Brain Interact to Create Our Conscious Lives.* Boston: Houghton Mifflin, 1988.

Gebauer, Gunter. "Hand und Gewißheit." In *Das Schwinden der Sinne,* ed. Dietmar Kamper and Christoph Wulf. Frankfurt: Suhrkamp, 1984. 234–60.

Gediman, Paul. "*Galatea 2.2.*" *Boston Review.* http://bostonreview.net/BR20.3/fiction.html (14 April 2005).

Geduld, Harry M., ed. *Authors on Film.* Bloomington: Indiana University Press, 1972.

Gentry, Bruce Marshall. "*The Waterworks* as Doctorow's Poesque Preface." *South Atlantic Review* 67, no. 1 (2002): 63–90.

Gibson, William. *Neuromancer.* New York: Ace Books, 1984.

Giedion, Siegfried. *Mechanization Takes Command: A Contribution to Anonymous History.* Oxford: Oxford University Press, 1948.

Ginzburg, Carlo. "Clues: Roots of an Evidential Paradigm." In *Clues, Myths, and the Historical Method*. Trans. Johan and Anne C. Tedeschi. Baltimore: Johns Hopkins University Press, 1986.

Girard, René. *Deceit, Desire and the Novel: Self and Other in Literary Structure*. Trans. Yvonne Freccero. Baltimore: Johns Hopkins University Press, 1966.

Gitelman, Lisa. *Scripts, Grooves, and Writing Machines: Representing Technology in the Edison Era*. Stanford: Stanford University Press, 1999.

Glasser, Otto. *Wilhelm Conrad Röntgen and the Early History of the Roentgen Rays*. Springfield, IL: Charles C. Thomas, 1934.

Gleick, James. *Chaos: Making a New Science*. New York: Penguin, 1987.

Goldberg, Jonathan. "The Hand in Theory." In *Writing Matter: From the Hands of the English Renaissance*. Stanford: Stanford University Press, 1990. 279–318.

Gourmont, Remy de. *Selected Writings*. Trans., ed., and intro. Glenn S. Burne. Ann Arbor: University of Michigan Press, 1966.

Grace, Sherrill E. "'Consciousness of Shipwreck': Ortega y Gasset and Malcolm Lowry's Concept of the Artist." In *Proceedings of the Espectador Universal International Interdisciplinary Conference*, ed. Nore de Marval-McNair. New York: Greenwood Press, 1987. 137–42.

———. "The Creative Process: An Introduction to Time and Space in Malcolm Lowry's Fiction." *Studies in Canadian Literature* 2, no. 1 (1977): 61–68.

———. "Malcolm Lowry and the Expressionist Vision." In *The Art of Malcolm Lowry*, ed. Anne Smith. London: Vision Press, 1978. 93–111.

———. "Midsummer Madness and the Day of the Dead: Joyce, Lowry, and Expressionism." In *Joyce/Lowry*, 9–20.

———. *Regression and Apocalypse: Studies in North American Literary Expressionism*. Toronto: University of Toronto Press, 1989.

———. "'A strange assembly of apparently incongruous parts': Intertextuality in Malcolm Lowry's 'Through the Panama.'" In *Incongruous Parts*, 187–228.

———, ed. *Swinging the Maelstrom: New Perspectives on Malcolm Lowry*. Montreal: McGill-Queen's University Press, 1992.

———. *The Voyage That Never Ends: Malcolm Lowry's Fiction*. Vancouver: University of British Columbia Press, 1982.

Graham, Don, ed. *Critical Essays on Frank Norris*. Boston: G. K. Hall, 1980.

———. *The Fiction of Frank Norris: The Aesthetic Context*. Columbia: University of Missouri Press, 1978.

Green-Lewis, Jennifer. *Framing the Victorians: Photography and the Culture of Realism*. Ithaca: Cornell University Press, 1996.

Gunning, Tom. "An Aesthetics of Astonishment: Early Film and the (In)Credulous Spectator." In *Viewing Positions: Ways of Seeing Film*, ed. Linda Williams. New Brunswick: Rutgers University Press, 1994. 114–33.

———. "An Unseen Energy Swallows Space: The Space in Early Film and Its Relation to American Avant-Garde Film." In *Film before Griffith*, ed. John L. Fell. Berkeley: University of California Press, 1983. 355–66.

Haas, Robert Bartlett. *Muybridge: Man in Motion.* Berkeley: University of California Press, 1976.

Habegger, Alfred. *Gender, Fantasy and Realism in American Literature.* New York: Columbia University Press, 1982.

Haraway, Donna. "A Manifesto for Cyborgs." In *Simians, Cyborgs, and Women: The Reinvention of Nature.* New York: Routledge, 1991.

———. "Teddy Bear Patriarchy: Taxidermy in the Garden of Eden, New York City, 1908–1936." In *Cultures of United States Imperialism,* ed. Amy Kaplan and Donald Pease. Durham: Duke University Press, 1993. 237–91.

Harnish, Robert M. *Minds, Brains, Computers: An Historical Introduction to the Foundations of Cognitive Science.* Boston: Blackwell, 2002.

Harpham, Geoffrey Galt. "E. L. Doctorow and the Technology of Narrative." *PMLA* 100 (1985): 81–95.

Hart, James D., ed. *Frank Norris: A Novelist in the Making.* Cambridge, MA: Harvard University Press, 1970.

Hartman, Geoffrey. "The Voice of the Shuttle: Language from the Point of View of Literature." In *Beyond Formalism: Literary Essays, 1958–1970.* New Haven: Yale University Press, 1970. 337–55.

Hartman Strom, Sharon. *Beyond the Typewriter: Gender, Class and the Origins of American Office Work, 1900–1930.* Urbana: University of Illinois Press, 1992.

Hawkins, Harriett. *Classics and Trash: Traditions and Taboos in High Literature and Popular Modern Genres.* Toronto: University of Toronto Press, 1990.

Hawthorne, Nathaniel. *The American Notebooks.* Ed. Claude M. Simpson. *The Centenary Edition of the Works of Nathaniel Hawthorne.* Vol. 8. Columbus: Ohio State University Press, 1972.

Hayles, N. Katherine. *How We Became Posthuman: Virtual Bodies in Cybernetics, Literature, and Informatics.* Chicago: University of Chicago Press, 1999.

———. *My Mother Was a Computer: Digital Subjects and Literary Texts.* Chicago: University of Chicago Press, 2005.

———. *Writing Machines.* Cambridge, MA: MIT Press, 2002.

Healy, Jane. *Endangered Minds: Why Our Children Don't Think.* New York: Simon and Schuster, 1990.

Heddendorf, David. "The 'Octopus' in *McTeague:* Frank Norris and Professionalism." *Modern Fiction Studies* 37, no. 4 (1991): 677–88.

Heidegger, Martin. *Parmenides.* Trans. André Schuwer and Richard Rojcewicz. Bloomington: Indiana University Press, 1992.

Heim, Michael. *Electric Language: A Philosophical Study of Wordprocessing.* New Haven: Yale University Press, 1987.

Heise, Ursula. http://www.heise.de/tp/deutsch/inhalt/buch/1271/2.html (12 April 1999).

Helmling, Steven. *The Success and Failure of Fredric Jameson: Writing the Sublime, and the Dialectic of Critique.* Albany: State University of New York Press, 2001.

Herbert, Robert L. *Impressionism: Art, Leisure, & Parisian Society*. New Haven: Yale University Press, 1988.
Herf, Geoffrey. *Reactionary Modernism: Technology, Culture, and Politics in Weimar and the Third Reich*. New York: Cambridge University Press, 1984.
Hitchcock, Alfred, dir. *The 39 Steps*. DVD. Screenplay by Charles Bennett. Gaumont British, 1935.
Hochman, Barbara. *The Art of Frank Norris, Storyteller*. Columbia: University of Missouri Press, 1988.
Horwitz, Howard. "To Find the Value of X: *The Pit* as a Renunciation of Romance." In *American Realism, New Essays*, ed. Eric Sundquist. Baltimore: Johns Hopkins University Press, 1982. 215–37.
"How to Build a Babel Fish: Progress in Translation Software." *Economist Technological Quarterly* (10 June 2006): 20–23.
Howard, June. *Form and History in American Literary Naturalism*. Chapel Hill: University of North Carolina Press, 1985.
Howells, William Dean. "A Case in Point." *Literature*, n.s., 1 (24 March 1899): 241–42.
Hugo, Victor. *Les Misérables*. 2 vols. Trans. N. Denny. London: Penguin, 1980.
Hutcheon, Linda. *A Poetics of Postmodernism: History, Theory, Fiction*. London: Routledge, 1988.
Hutchins, Edwin. *Cognition in the Wild*. Cambridge, MA: MIT Press, 1995.
Huyssen, Andreas. "Mass Culture as Woman: Modernism's Other." In *After the Great Divide: Modernism, Mass Culture, Postmodernism*. Bloomington: Indiana University Press, 1986. 44–63.
———. *Twilight Memories: Marking Time in a Culture of Amnesia*. New York: Routledge, 1995.
Iser, Wolfgang. *The Act of Reading: A Theory of Aesthetic Response*. Baltimore: Johns Hopkins University Press, 1978.
———. *The Implied Reader: Patterns of Communication in Prose Fiction from Bunyan to Beckett*. Baltimore: Johns Hopkins University Press, 1974.
James, Henry. *A London Life and The Reverberator*. Ed. and intro. Philip Horne. Oxford: Oxford University Press, 1989.
———. *The Novels and Tales of Henry James*. 26 vols. New York: Scribners, 1909.
Jameson, Fredric. *Marxism and Form: Twentieth-Century Dialectical Theories of Literature*. Princeton: Princeton University Press, 1974.
———. *The Political Unconscious: Narrative as a Socially Symbolic Act*. Ithaca: Cornell University Press, 1981.
———. *Postmodernism, or, the Cultural Logic of Late Capitalism*. Durham: Duke University Press, 1991.
Johnston, John. *Information Multiplicity*. Baltimore: Johns Hopkins University Press, 1998.
Jones, Malcolm Jr. "A Gothic Tale of Horror in Old New York." *Newsweek*, 27 June 1994, 53.

Joyce, James. *Finnegans Wake.* New York: Viking, 1939.
Joyce, Michael. "Forms of Future." In *Rethinking Media Change,* 227–38.
———. *Liam's Going.* Kingston, NY: McPherson and Company, 2002.
———. *Was: Annales nomadiques: A Novel of Internet.* Fiction Collective 2. Tuscaloosa: The University of Alabama Press, 2007.
Jussim, Estelle. *Fredric Remington, the Camera & the Old West.* Fort Worth, TX: Amon Carter Museum, 1983.
Kahn, Douglas, and Gregory Whitehead. *Wireless Imagination: Sound, Radio, and the Avant-Garde.* Cambridge, MA: MIT Press, 1992.
Kaplan, Amy. "Romancing the Empire: The Embodiment of American Masculinity in the Popular Historical Novel in the 1890s." *American Literary History* 2 (1990): 659–90.
———. *The Social Construction of American Realism.* Chicago: University of Chicago Press, 1988.
Kaplan, Charles. "Norris's Use of Sources in *The Pit.*" *American Literature* 25, no. 1 (1953): 75–84.
Katz, Joseph. "Eroticism in American Literary Realism." In *Critical Essays on Frank Norris,* 163–68.
———. "The Shorter Publications of Frank Norris." *Proof* 3 (1973): 155–220.
Keller, Julia. "Illinois Author Richard Powers Speaks Softly But Carries a Big Idea." *Chicago Tribune,* 4 March 2004. http://www.chicagotribune.com/features/lifestyle/chi-0403040026mar04 (18 April 2004).
Keny, James M. "Ohio Impressionists and Post-Impressionists." http://www.tfaoi.com/aa/5aa/5aa280b.htm (27 March 2006).
Kern, Stephen. *The Culture of Time and Space, 1880–1920.* Cambridge, MA: Harvard University Press, 1983.
Kernan, Alvin. *The Death of Literature.* New Haven: Yale University Press, 1990.
Kilgallin, Tony. *Lowry.* Erin, Ontario: Press Porcépic, 1973.
King, Richard. "Between Simultaneity and Sequence." In *E. L. Doctorow: A Democracy of Perception,* 45–60.
Kirby, Lynn. *Parallel Tracks: The Railroad and Silent Cinema.* Durham: Duke University Press, 1997.
Kiteley, Brian. "A Brief Interview with Richard Powers Concerning *Galatea 2.2.*" http://www.du/edu/~bkiteley/powers.htm (14 April 2005).
Kittler, Friedrich A. "Benn's Poetry—'A Hit in the Charts': Song under Conditions of Media Technologies." *SubStance* 19, no. 1 (1990): 5–20.
———. *Discourse Networks 1800/1900.* Foreword by David E. Wellbery. Trans. Michael Metteer, with Chris Cullens. Stanford: Stanford University Press, 1990.
———. *Gramophone, Film, Typewriter.* Trans. and intro. Geoffrey Winthrop-Young and Michael Wutz. Stanford: Stanford University Press, 1999.
Kittler, Friedrich A., and Georg Christoph Tholen, eds. *Arsenale der Seele.* München: Wilhelm Fink, 1989.
Kluge, Alexander. "Word and Film." In *Writing in a Film Age,* 130–48.

Kolodny, Annette. *The Lay of the Land: Metaphor as Experience and History in American Life and Letters.* Chapel Hill: University of North Carolina Press, 1975.

Koszarski, Richard. *The Man You Loved to Hate: Erich von Stroheim and Hollywood.* Oxford: Oxford University Press, 1983.

Kracauer, Siegfried. *Theory of Film: The Redemption of Physical Reality.* Intro. Miriam Bratu Hansen. Princeton: Princeton University Press, 1997.

Lack, Richard. "Bouguereau, William-Adolphe." *Grove Dictionary of Art On-line.* http://www.groveart.com/tdaonline (16 June 2003).

Landow, George P. *Hyper/Text/Theory.* Baltimore: Johns Hopkins University Press, 1994.

Lanham, Richard A. *The Electronic Word: Democracy, Technology, and the Arts.* Chicago: University of Chicago Press, 1993.

Lang, Fritz, dir. *Metropolis.* DVD. Screenplay Fritz Lang and Thea von Harbou. Universum Film A.G./Paramount, 1927.

Latour, Bruno. *Science in Action: How to Follow Scientists and Engineers through Society.* Cambridge, MA: Harvard University Press, 1987.

Lawlor, Mary. "Naturalism in the Cinema: Erich von Stroheim's Reading of *McTeague*." *Frank Norris Studies* 8 (Autumn 1989): 6–8.

Lawrence, D. H. *Phoenix II: Uncollected Writings.* Ed. and intro. Warren Roberts and Harry T. Moore. New York: Viking, 1973.

Lears, F. Jackson. *No Place of Grace: Antimodernism and the Transformation of American Culture, 1880–1920.* New York: Pantheon, 1981.

LeClair, Tom. *The Art of Excess: Mastery in Contemporary American Fiction.* Urbana: University of Illinois Press, 1989.

Lehan, Richard. "American Literary Naturalism: The French Connection." *Nineteenth-Century Fiction* 38, no. 4 (1984): 529–57.

———. *The City in Literature: An Intellectual and Cultural History.* Berkeley: University of California Press, 1998.

Lehrer, Jonah. *Proust Was a Neuroscientist.* Boston: Houghton Mifflin Co., 2007.

Lem, Stanislaw. *Solaris.* Trans. (from the French) Joanna Kilmartin and Steve Cox. Afterword by Darko Suvin. 1961. Reprint, New York: Walker, 1970.

Leroi-Gourhan, André. *Gesture and Speech.* Intro. Randall White. Trans. Anna Bostock Berger. 1964. Reprint, Cambridge, MA: MIT Press, 1993.

Leverenz, David. *Manhood and the American Renaissance.* Ithaca: Cornell University Press, 1989.

Levinson, Paul. *The Soft Edge: A Natural History and Future of the Information Revolution.* London: Routledge, 1997.

Levy, Steven. "I Found Einstein's Brain." http://www.echonyc.com/~steven/einstein.html (17 February 2005).

Lewis, Wyndham. *The Art of Being Ruled.* Ed. Reed Way Dasenbrock. Santa Rosa: Black Sparrow Press, 1989.

Leyda, Jay. *Kino: A History of the Russian and Soviet Film.* Princeton: Princeton University Press, 1983.

Lowry, Malcolm. *The Cinema of Malcolm Lowry: A Scholarly Edition of Lowry's "Tender Is the Night."* Ed. and intro. Miguel Mota and Paul Tiessen. Vancouver: University of British Columbia Press, 1990.

———. *Dark As the Grave Wherein My Friend Is Laid.* Ed. Douglas Day and Margerie Lowry. New York: World Publishing, 1968.

———. *Hear Us O Lord from Heaven Thy Dwelling Place.* New York: Carroll and Graff, 1986.

———. *Malcolm Lowry: Psalms and Songs.* Ed. Margerie Lowry. New York: New American Library, 1975.

———. Malcolm Lowry Archive. Special Collections, University of British Columbia, Vancouver.

———. *Malcolm Lowry's "La Mordida": A Scholarly Edition.* Ed. Patrick A. McCarthy. Athens: University of Georgia Press, 1996.

———. *October Ferry to Gabriola.* Ed. Margerie Lowry. New York: World Publishing Company, 1970.

———. *Selected Letters of Malcolm Lowry.* Ed. Harvey Breit and Margerie Bonner Lowry. Philadelphia: Lippincott, 1965.

———. *Sursum Corda! The Collected Letters of Malcolm Lowry.* Vols. 1 (1926–46) and 2 (1947–57). Ed. Sherrill E. Grace, with Kathy K. Y. Chung (vol. 2). London and Toronto: Jonathan Cape and University of Toronto Press, 1995–96.

———. *Ultramarine.* New York: Carroll and Graff, 1986.

———. *Under the Volcano.* Intro. Stephen Spender. New York: Lippincott, 1965.

———. "Work in Progress: *The Voyage That Never Ends.*" *Malcolm Lowry Review* 21, 22 (Fall 1987, Spring 1988): 72–99.

Lowry, Malcolm, and Margerie Bonner Lowry. *Notes on a Screenplay for F. Scott Fitzgerald's "Tender Is the Night."* Ed. Matthew J. Bruccoli. Intro. Paul Tiessen. Bloomfield Hills, MI: Bruccoli Clark, 1976. v–xix.

Lowry, Malcolm, and Margerie Lowry. "A few items culled from what started out to be a sort of preface to a film-script." Ed. Paul Tiessen. *White Pelican* 4, no. 2 (1974): 2–20.

Lowry, Malcolm, and Gerald Noxon. *The Letters of Malcolm Lowry and Gerald Noxon, 1940–1952.* Ed. and intro. Paul Tiessen, with Nancy Strobel. Vancouver: University of British Columbia Press, 1988.

Lutz, Tom. *American Nervousness, 1903: An Anecdotal History.* Ithaca: Cornell University Press, 1991.

Lyotard, Jean-François. *The Inhuman: Reflections on Time.* Trans. Geoffrey Bennington and Rachel Bowlby. Stanford: Stanford University Press, 1991.

Maeterlinck, Maurice. "In an Automobile." Trans. Alfred Sutro. *The Double Garden.* New York: Dodd, Mead, 1904.

Marinetti, Fillipo Tommaso. *Futurist Manifestos.* Ed. and intro. Umbro Apollonio. Trans. Robert Brain, R. W. Flint, J. C. Higgitt, and Caroline Tisdall. New York: Viking, 1970.

———. *Marinetti: Selected Writings*. Ed. and intro. R. W. Flint. Trans. R. W. Flint and Arthur A. Coppotelli. New York: Farrar, Straus and Giroux, 1971.

Marks, John. *Gilles Deleuze: Vitalism and Multiplicity*. London: Pluto Press, 1998.

Martin, Ronald B. *American Literature and the Universe of Force*. Durham: Duke University Press, 1981.

Marvin, Carolyn. *When Old Technologies Were New: Thinking about Electric Communication in the Late Nineteenth Century*. Oxford: Oxford University Press, 1988.

Marx, Karl. *Economic and Philosophical Manuscripts of 1844*. Trans. Martin Milligan. New York: International, 1968.

Matejka, Ladislav, and Krystyna Pomorska, eds. *Readings in Russian Poetics: Formalist and Structuralist Views*. Cambridge, MA: MIT Press, 1971.

Maugham, Somerset W. "On Writing for the Films." In *Authors on Film*, 181–87.

Max, D. T. "Day of the Dead: Malcolm Lowry's Mysterious Demons." *The New Yorker*, 17 December 2007.

McCarthy, Patrick A. *Forests of Symbols: World, Text, and Self in Malcolm Lowry's Fiction*. Athens: University of Georgia Press, 1994.

McCarthy, Patrick A., and Paul Tiessen, eds. *Joyce/Lowry: Critical Perspectives*. Lexington: University of Kentucky Press, 1997.

McElrath, Joseph R. Jr. "Frank Norris: A Biographical Essay." *American Literary Realism* 11 (1978): 219–34.

McElrath, Joseph R. Jr., and Douglass K. Burgess. "Textual Afterword." In *The Apprenticeship Writings of Frank Norris*, 2:261–76.

McElrath, Joseph R. Jr., and Jesse S. Crisler. *Frank Norris: A Life*. Urbana: University of Illinois Press, 2006.

McGann, Jerome. *Black Riders: The Visible Language of Modernism*. Princeton: Princeton University Press, 1993.

McGlynn, David. "*McTeague*'s Guilded Prison." *Rocky Mountain Review* 62, no. 1 (2008): 25–44.

McLuhan, Marshall. *The Gutenberg Galaxy: The Making of Typographic Man*. Toronto: University of Toronto Press, 1965.

———. *Understanding Media: The Extensions of Man*. Intro. Lewis H. Lapham. 1964. Reprint, Cambridge, MA: MIT Press, 1994.

Meadowsong, Zena. "Natural Monsters: The Genesis and Deformation of the 'Experimental Novel.'" *Studies in American Naturalism* 2, no. 1 (2007): 3–17.

Meijer, Marie. *Art Arche*, Program 3, *Life Is Short*. Videocassette. Meijer Films, 1991.

Merchant, Carolyn. *The Death of Nature: Women, Ecology, and the Scientific Revolution*. New York: HarperCollins, 1983.

Michaels, Walter Benn. *The Gold Standard and the Logic of Naturalism: American Literature at the Turn of the Century*. Berkeley: University of California Press, 1987.

Miller, D. A. *The Novel and the Police*. Berkeley: University of California Press, 1988.

Mink, Louis O. "Everyman His or Her Own Annalist." In *On Narrative*, ed. W.J.T. Mitchell. Chicago: University of Chicago Press, 1981. 233–39.

———. "Narrative Form as a Cognitive Instrument." In *The Writing of History: Literary Form and Historical Understanding*, ed. Robert H. Canary and Henry Kozicki. Madison: University of Wisconsin Press, 1978. 129–49.

Mitchell, William J. *City of Bits: Space, Place, and the Infobahn*. Cambridge, MA: MIT Press, 1995.

———. "Homer to Home-Page: Designing Digital Books." In *Rethinking Media Change*, 203–16.

Moore, Steven. *William Gaddis*. Boston: G. K. Hall, 1989.

Moraru, Christian. *Rewriting: Postmodern Narrative and Cultural Critique in the Age of Cloning*. Albany: State University of New York Press, 2001.

Moravec, Hans. *Mind Children: The Future of Robot and Human Intelligence*. Cambridge, MA: Harvard University Press, 1988.

Morris, Christopher D. *Models of Misrepresentation: On the Fiction of E. L. Doctorow*. Jackson: University Press of Mississippi, 1991.

Morse, Minna. "Facing a Bumpy History." *Smithsonian* 28, no. 7 (1997): 24–28.

Mota, Miguel, and Paul Tiessen. Introduction to *The Cinema of Malcolm Lowry*. 3–41.

———. "Re-Writing Fitzgerald: Malcolm Lowry's '*Tender Is the Night*.'" In *Transformations: From Literature to Film*, ed. Douglas Radcliff-Umstead. Kent: Kent State University International Film Conference Proceedings, 1987. 30–35.

Mottram, Ron. "Impulse toward the Visible: Frank Norris and Photographic Representation." *Texas Studies in Language and Literature* 25 (1983): 574–96.

Muller, John P., and William J. Richardson, eds. *The Purloined Poe: Lacan, Derrida, and Psychoanalytic Reading*. Baltimore: Johns Hopkins University Press, 1987.

Mumford, Lewis. *Sticks and Stones: A Study of American Architecture and Civilization*. New York: Dover, 1955.

Münsterberg, Hugo. *The Photoplay: A Psychological Study*. Reprinted as *The Film: A Psychological Study*. Intro. Richard Griffith. New York: Dover, 1970.

Murphy, Priscilla Coit. "Books Are Dead, Long Live Books." In *Rethinking Media Change*, 81–93.

Musser, Charles. *Before the Nickelodeon: Edwin S. Porter and the Edison Manufacturing Company*. Berkeley: University of California Press, 1991.

———. *Thomas A. Edison and His Kinetographic Motion Picture*. New Brunswick: Rutgers University Press, 1995.

Musser, Charles, with Carol Nelson. *High-Class Moving Pictures: Lyman H. Howe and the Forgotten Era of Traveling Exhibition, 1880–1920*. Princeton: Princeton University Press, 1991.

Muybridge, Eadweard. *Bodies in Motion*. Ed. Lewis S. Brown. New York: Dover, 1957.

Neilson, Jim. "Interview with Richard Powers." http://www.dalkeyarchive.com/catalog/show_comments/652 (18 April 2004). Originally published in *Review of Contemporary Fiction* 18, no. 3 (Fall 1998): 13–23.

New, William H. "Lowry's Reading: An Introductory Essay." *Canadian Literature* 44 (1970): 8–15.
Newton, Isaac. *Principia Mathematica.* Trans. Andrew Motte. Berkeley: University of California Press, 1934.
Nicholls, Peter. *Modernisms: A Literary Guide.* Berkeley: University of California Press, 1995.
Norris, Frank. *The Apprenticeship Writings of Frank Norris, 1896–1898.* 2 vols. Ed. Joseph R. McElrath and Douglass K. Burgess. Philadelphia: American Philosophical Society, 1996.
———. *Blix: The Complete Works of Frank Norris.* Vol. 4. New York: P. F. Collier, 1903.
———. *Collected Letters.* Ed. Jesse S. Crisler. San Francisco: Book Club of California, 1986.
———. Frank Norris Collection. Bancroft Library, University of California, Berkeley.
———. "Life in the Mining Region: A Study in Striking-Time of the Conditions of Living in Representative Mining Towns." *Everybody's Magazine* (September 1902): 241–48.
———. *The Literary Criticism of Frank Norris.* Ed. Donald Pizer. Austin: University of Texas Press, 1964.
———. *A Man's Woman: The Complete Works of Frank Norris.* Vol. 3. New York: Collier, 1903.
———. *McTeague.* 2nd ed. Ed. Donald Pizer. New York: Norton, 1997.
———. *The Octopus: A Story of California.* Ed. and intro. Kevin Starr. London: Penguin, 1986.
———. *The Pit: A Story of Chicago.* Ed. and intro. Joseph R. McElrath Jr. and Gwendolyn Jones. London: Penguin, 1994.
———. "She and the Other Fellow." *Overland Monthly* 23 (March 1894): 240–46.
———. "Student Life in Paris." *Colliers Weekly* 25 (12 May 1900): 33.
———. *Vandover and the Brute.* Ed. and intro. Warren French. Lincoln: University of Nebraska Press, 1978.
Olster, Stacey. *Reminiscence and Re-Creation in Contemporary American Fiction.* Cambridge: Cambridge University Press, 1989.
Ong, Father Walter J. *Orality and Literacy: The Technologizing of the Word.* London: Methuen, 1982.
Ortega y Gasset, José. *Toward a Philosophy of History.* Trans. Helene Weyl. New York: Norton, 1941.
Orvell, Miles. *The Real Thing: Imitation and Authenticity in American Culture, 1880–1940.* Chapel Hill: University of North Carolina Press, 1989.
Parks, John G. *E. L. Doctorow.* New York: Continuum, 1991.
Pasolini, Pier Paolo. "Aspects of a Semiology of Cinema." In *Writing in a Film Age,* 191–226.
Passaro, Vince. "Another Country." Review of E. L. Doctorow's *The March.* *The Nation,* 31 October 2005, 32–36.

Paterniti, Michael. "Driving Mr. Albert: A Trip across America with Einstein's Brain." *Harper's Magazine* (October 1997): 35–58.
Paulson, William R. "The Literary Canon in the Age of Its Technological Obsolescence." In *Reading Matters*, 227–49.
———. *The Noise of Culture: Literary Texts in a World of Information.* Ithaca: Cornell University Press, 1988.
Perloff, Marjorie. *The Futurist Moment: Avant-garde, Avant Guerre, and the Language of Rupture.* Chicago: University of Chicago Press, 1986.
Peterson, Nancy J. *Against Amnesia: Contemporary Women Writers and the Crises of Historical Memory.* Philadelphia: University of Pennsylvania Press, 2001.
Pinker, Steven. *How the Mind Works.* New York: Norton, 1997.
Poirier, Richard. "Venerable Complications: Literature, Technology, and People." In *The Renewal of Literature: Emersonian Reflections.* New Haven: Yale University Press, 1987. 114–34.
Popplestone, John A., and Marion White McPherson. *An Illustrated History of American Psychology.* Akron: University of Akron Press, 1994.
Postman, Neil. *Amusing Ourselves to Death: Public Discourse in the Age of Show Business.* New York: Penguin, 1986.
Pound, Ezra. *Machine Art & Other Writings: The Lost Thought of the Italian Years.* Ed. and intro. Maria Luisa Ardizzone. Durham: Duke University Press, 1996.
Pound, Reginald. *Mirror of the Century: The Strand Magazine 1891–1950.* New York: A. S. Barnes, 1966.
Powers, Richard. "The Art of Fiction" (interview with Kevin Berger). *Paris Review* 164 (Winter 2003): 106–38.
———. "Being and Seeming: The Technology of Representation." *Context: A Forum for Literary Arts and Culture*, no. 3 (2000). http://www.dalkeyarchive.com/article/show/120 (14 April 2005).
———. "A Dialogue: Richard Powers and Bradford Morrow." *Conjunctions* 34 (Spring 2000). http://www.conjunctions.com/archives/c34-rp.htm (18 April 2004).
———. *The Echo Maker.* New York: Farrar, Straus and Giroux, 2006.
———. *Galatea 2.2.* 1995. Reprint, New York: Picador 2004.
———. "How to Speak a Book." *New York Times*, 7 January 2007. http://www.nytimes.com/2007/01/07/books/review/Powers2.t.html (7 January 2008).
———. Interview with Sven Birkerts. *Bomb* (Summer 1998): 58–63.
———. *Three Farmers on Their Way to a Dance.* 1985. Reprint, New York: Harper-Perennial, 1992.
Puig, Manuel. "How the Provincial Argentine Left Literature for the Movies, Thereby Discovering the Immense Potentials of the Novel." In *Writing in a Film Age*, 271–76.
Rabb, Jane M., ed. *Literature & Photography: Interactions, 1840–1990.* Albuquerque: University of New Mexico Press, 1995.
Rabinbach, Anson. *The Human Motor: Energy, Fatigue, and the Origins of Modernity.* Berkeley: University of California Press, 1992.

Rank, Otto. *The Double: A Psychoanalytic Study.* Ed., trans., and intro. Harry Tucker Jr. Chapel Hill: University of North Carolina Press, 1971.

Reed, Walter L. *An Exemplary History of the Novel: The Quixotic versus the Picaresque.* Chicago: University of Chicago Press, 1981.

Reiser, Stanley. *Medicine and the Reign of Technology.* Cambridge: Cambridge University Press, 1978.

Rewald, John. *The History of Impressionism.* 4th ed. New York: Museum of Modern Art, 1973.

Rilke, Rainer Maria. *The Notebook of Malte Laurids Brigge.* Trans. M. D. Herter Norton. New York: 1949.

———. *Selected Works.* Vol. 1. Ed. G. Craig Houston. Norfolk, CT: New Directions, 1960.

Rindisbacher, Hans J. *The Smell of Books: A Cultural-Historical Study of Olfactory Perception in Literature.* Ann Arbor: University of Michigan Press, 1992.

Robbe-Grillet, Alain. "For a New Cinema." In *Writing in a Film Age,* 112–20.

Rourke, Brian. "Malcolm Lowry's Memory Machine: An Eclectic Systemë." *Journal of Modern Literature* 29, no. 3 (2006): 19–38.

Rowe, Katherine. *Dead Hands: Fictions of Agency, Renaissance to Modern.* Stanford: Stanford University Press, 1999.

Royle, Nicholas. *Telepathy and Literature: Essays on the Reading Mind.* Oxford: Basil Blackwell, 1991.

Rutsky, R. L. *High Technē: Art and Technology from the Machine Aesthetic to the Posthuman.* Minneapolis: University of Minnesota Press, 1999.

Ryan, Marie-Laure. "Postmodernism and the Doctrine of Panfictionality." *Narrative* 5, no. 2 (1997): 165–87.

Saltzman, Arthur M. *Designs of Darkness in Contemporary American Fiction.* Philadelphia: University of Pennsylvania Press, 1990.

Sanderson, Richard A. *The Development of American Motion Picture Content and Techniques Prior to 1904.* New York: Arno Press, 1977.

Schama, Simon. "New York, Gaslight Metropolis." Review of *The Waterworks. New York Times Book Review,* 19 June 1994, 1+.

Scharf, Aaron. *Art and Photography.* London: Penguin, 1974.

Schivelbusch, Wolfgang. *The Railway Journey: The Industrialization of Time and Space in the 19th Century.* Trans. Anselm Hollo. Berkeley: University of California Press, 1986.

Scott, A. O. "A Thinking Man's Miracle." Review of *City of God. New York Times Book Review,* 5 March 2000, 7.

Sekula, Allan. "The Body and the Archive." *October* 39 (1987): 3–64.

———. "The Traffic in Photographs." *Art Journal* 41 (Spring 1981): 15–25.

Seltzer, Mark. *Bodies and Machines.* New York: Routledge, 1992.

Shaw, George Bernard. *Complete Plays and Prefaces.* New York: Dodd, Mead, 1962.

Shi, David. *Facing Facts: Realism in American Thought and Culture, 1850–1920.* New York: Oxford University Press, 1995.

Siemion, Piotr. "No More Heroes: The Routinization of the Epic in Techno-Thrillers." In *Reading Matters*, 193–223.

Simmel, Georg. *Simmel on Culture*. Ed. David Frisby and Mike Featherstone. London: Sage, 1997.

Soustelle, Jacques. *The Daily Life of the Aztecs*. Trans. Patrick O'Brian. London: Weidenfeld, 1961.

Spariosu, Mihai. "Allegory, Hermeneutics, and Postmodernism." In *Exploring Postmodernism*, ed. Matei Calinescu and Douwe Fokkema. Amsterdam: Benjamins, 1988. 59–78.

Spender, Stephen. Introduction to *Under the Volcano*, by Malcolm Lowry. Philadelphia: Lippincott, 1965. xi–xxx.

Spolsky, Ellen. *Gaps in Nature: Literary Interpretation and the Modular Mind*. Albany: State University of New York Press, 1993.

Stallybrass, Peter, and Allon White. *The Politics and Poetics of Transgression*. Ithaca: Cornell University Press, 1986.

Steegmuller, Francis. *Apollinaire: Poet among the Painters*. New York: Farrar, Straus, 1963.

Sternberg, Meir. *The Poetics of Biblical Narrative: Ideological Literature and the Drama of Reading*. Bloomington: Indiana University Press, 1985.

Sterne, Jonathan. *The Audible Past: Cultural Origins of Sound Reproduction*. Durham: Duke University Press, 2003.

Stingelin, Martin. "Gehirntelegraphie: Die Rede der Paranoia von der Macht der Medien 1900. Falldarstellungen." In *Arsenale der Seele*, 51–69.

Stix, Gary. "The Elusive Goal of Machine Translation." *Scientific American* (March 2006): 92–95.

Sukenick, Ronald. "Film Digression." In *Writing in a Film Age*, 155–66.

Swanberg, Walter A. *Theodore Dreiser*. New York: Scribners, 1965.

Tabbi, Joseph. *Cognitive Fictions*. Minneapolis: University of Minnesota Press, 2002.

———. *Postmodern Sublime: Technology and American Writing from Mailer to Cyberpunk*. Ithaca: Cornell University Press, 1995.

Tabbi, Joseph, and Rone Shavers. *Paper Empire: William Gaddis and the World System*. Tuscaloosa: The University of Alabama Press, 2007.

Tabbi, Joseph, and Michael Wutz, eds. *Reading Matters: Narrative in the New Media Ecology*. Ithaca: Cornell University Press, 1997.

Tarkovsky, Andrei Arsenevich, dir. *Solaris*. Videorecording. New York: Fox Lorber, 1991 (1972).

Thagard, Paul. *Mind: Introduction to Cognitive Science*. 2nd ed. Cambridge, MA: MIT Press, 2005.

Thompson, Michael. *Rubbish Theory: The Creation and Destruction of Value*. Oxford: Oxford University Press, 1979.

Thorburn, Davis, and Henry Jenkins, eds. *Rethinking Media Change: The Aesthetics of Transition*. Cambridge, MA: MIT Press, 2003.

Tichi, Cecelia. *Shifting Gears: Technology, Literature, Culture in Modernist America*. Chapel Hill: University of North Carolina Press, 1987.

Tiessen, Paul, ed. *Apparently Incongruous Parts: The Worlds of Malcolm Lowry.* Metuchen, NJ: Scarecrow Press, 1990.

———. "Malcolm Lowry: Statements on Literature and Film." In *The Practical Vision: Essays in English Literature in Honour of Flora Roy,* ed. Jane Campbell and James Doyle. Waterloo: Wilfrid Laurier University Press, 1978. 119–32.

Tokarczyk, Michelle M. "Postmodernism Reconsidered on an Urban Landscape: *The Waterworks.*" In *E. L. Doctorow: Modern Critical Views,* ed. Harold Bloom. Philadelphia: Chelsea House, 2001. 179–94.

Tomashevsky, Boris. "Literature and Biography." In *Readings in Russian Poetics,* 47–55.

Tompkins, Jane. *Sensational Designs: The Cultural Work of American Fiction, 1790–1860.* New York: Oxford University Press, 1986.

Tortello, Michael. "Richard Powers: Industrial Evolution." *Raintaxi Online Edition.* Summer 1988. http://www.raintaxi.com/online/1998summer/powers.shtml (18 April 2004).

Trachtenberg, Alan. *The Incorporation of America: Culture and Society in the Gilded Age.* New York: Hill and Wang, 1982.

Tsimpouki, Theodora. "Millennial Maladies in E. L. Doctorow's *The Waterworks.*" *East European Monographs* 543 (1999): 177–89.

Tuman, Myron. *Word Perfect: Literacy in the Computer Age.* Pittsburgh: University of Pittsburgh Press, 1992.

Turbayne, Colin Murray. *The Myth of Metaphor.* Columbia: University of South Carolina Press, 1970.

Turkle, Sherry. *Life on the Screen: Identity in the Age of the Internet.* New York: Simon and Schuster, 1995.

———. *The Second Self: Computers and the Human Spirit.* New York: Simon and Schuster, 1984.

Turner, Mark. *Reading Minds: The Study of English in the Age of Cognitive Science.* Princeton: Princeton University Press, 1991.

Tynjanov, Jurij. "On Literary Evolution." In *Readings in Russian Poetics: Formalist and Structuralist Views,* ed. Ladislaw Matejka and Krystyna Pomorska. Cambridge, MA: MIT Press, 1971. 66–77.

Van de Grift Sanchez, Nellie. *The Life of Mrs. Robert Louis Stevenson.* New York: Scribners, 1920.

Varda, Agnès. *Gleaners and I.* DVD recording. New York: Zeitgeist Films, 2002.

Varela, J. Francisco, Evan Thompson, and Eleanor Rosch. *The Embodied Mind: Cognitive Science and Human Experience.* Cambridge, MA: MIT Press, 1991.

Veblen, Thorstein. *The Theory of the Leisure Class.* Intro. Robert Lekachman. New York: Penguin, 1979.

Virilio, Paul. *The Art of the Motor.* Trans. Julie Rose. Minneapolis: University of Minnesota Press, 1995.

———. *War and Cinema: The Logistics of Perception.* Trans. Patrick Camiller. London: Verso, 1989.

Walker, Franklin. *Frank Norris: A Biography.* New York: Russell and Russell, 1963.

———. Franklin Walker Collection. Bancroft Library, University of California, Berkeley.
Weinberg, Herman. *Saint Cinema: Selected Writings, 1929–1970.* Rev. ed. New York: Ungar, 1980.
Weinberger, Eliot. "Symposium: Twelve Visions." Comp. by Charles Barber. *Media Studies Journal* 6 (Summer 1992): 41–43.
Weisberg, Gabriel P. *Beyond Impressionism: The Naturalist Impulse.* New York: Abrams, 1992.
Werkbund Bayern, ed. *Der Mensch ohne Hand, oder die Zerstörung der menschlichen Ganzheit.* München: Deutscher Taschenbuchverlag, 1979.
White, Hayden. "The Fictions of Factual Representations." In *Tropics of Discourse: Essays in Cultural Criticism.* Baltimore: Johns Hopkins University Press, 1978. 121–34.
———. "The Narrativization of Real Events." In *On Narrative,* ed. W.J.T. Mitchell. Chicago: University of Chicago Press, 1981. 249–54.
———. "The Value of Narrativity in the Representation of Reality." *Critical Inquiry* 7, no. 1 (1980): 5–27.
Wieland, Schulz-Keil. "The Sixty-Seventh Reading: Malcolm Lowry's Novel *Under the Volcano* and Its Screenplays." In *Proceedings from the London Conference on Malcolm Lowry, 1984,* ed. Gordon Bowker and Paul Tiessen. London: University of London and Wilfrid Laurier University Press, 1985. 45–61.
"William Bouguereau." http://www.cahiers.naturalistes.com/pages/Bouguereaua.html (29 March 2006).
Williams, Jeffrey. "The Last Generalist: An Interview with Richard Powers." http://www.eserver.org/clogic/2-2/williams.html (18 April 2004).
Williams, Raymond. "Culture and Technology." In *The Politics of Modernism: Against the New Conformists,* ed. Tony Pinkney. London: Verso, 1989. 119–40.
———. *Television: Technology and Cultural Form.* New York: Schocken, 1975.
Williams, William Carlos. *Imaginations.* Ed. and intro. Webster Schott. New York: New Directions, 1970.
Wilson, Christopher P. *The Labor of Words: Literary Professionalism in the Progressive Era.* Athens: University of Georgia Press, 1985.
Winkler, Hartmut. "Discourses, Schemata, Technology, Monuments: Outline for a Theory of Cultural Continuity." *Configurations* 10 (2002): 91–109.
———. *Docuverse: Zur Medientheorie der Computer.* München: Boer, 1997.
Winthrop-Young, Geoffrey. "Drill and Distraction in the Yellow Submarine: On the Dominance of War in Friedrich Kittler's Media Theory." *Critical Inquiry* 28 (Summer 2002): 825–54.
———. *Friedrich Kittler zur Einführung.* Hamburg: Junius, 2005.
———. "The Informatics of Revenge: Telegraphy, Speed and Storage in *The Count of Monte Cristo.*" *Weber Studies* 14, no. 1 (1997): 5–17.
———. "Magic Media Mountain: Technology and the *Umbildungsroman.*" In *Reading Matters,* 29–52.

———. "Silicon Sociology, or, Two Kings on Hegel's Throne? Kittler, Luhmann, and the Postmodern Merger of German Media Theory." *Yale Journal of Criticism* 13, no. 2 (2000): 391–420.

———. "Undead Networks: Information Processing and Media Boundary Conflicts in *Dracula*." In *Literature and Science*, ed. Donald Bruce and Anthony Purdy. Amsterdam: Rodopi, 1994. 107–29.

Wittgenstein, Ludwig. *On Certainty*. Ed. G.E.M Anscombe and G. H. Von Wright. Trans. Denis Paul and G.E.M. Anscombe. Oxford: Basil Blackwell, 1969.

Wutz, Michael. "*The Reality of the Imagination*—A Conversation with Carlos Fuentes at 70." *Weber Studies* 17, no. 2 (2000): 2–18.

———. "The Waterworks." Review in *Review of Contemporary Fiction* 15, no. 1 (1995): 177–78.

———. "The Word and the Self in *The Ambassadors*." *Style* 25, no. 1 (1991): 89–103.

———. "Writing from between the Gaps: *Agapē Agape* and Twentieth-Century Media Culture." In *Paper Empire: Essays on the Art of William Gaddis*, ed. Joseph Tabbi and Rone Shavers. Tuscaloosa: The University of Alabama Press, 2007. 185–210.

Yeats, William Butler. *Selected Poems and Two Plays of William Butler Yeats*. Ed. and intro. M. L. Rosenthal. New York: Collier, 1966.

Young, Paul. "Telling Descriptions: Frank Norris' Kinetoscopic Naturalism and the Future of the Novel." *Modernism/modernity* 14, no. 4 (2007): 645–68.

Ziff, Larzer. *The American 1890s: Life and Times of a Lost Generation*. New York: Viking, 1966.

Index

Ackerley, Chris, 224n19, 228n29
Acocella, Joan, 207n17
Adams, Henry, 230n8
Aiken, Conrad, 221n5
Albérès, R. M., 224n20
Alter, Jonathan, 229n5
Anderson, Gregory, 51
Anderson, Paul Thomas: *There Will Be Blood*, 213n37
Anderson, Sherwood, 218n17
Anesko, Michael W., 208n3
Antheil, George, 115, 226n12
Antliff, Mark, 217n10
Armory Show, 56, 218n17
Armstrong, Tom, 236n9
Apollinaire, Guillaume, 23
Asals, Frederick, 104, 225n5
Ashbury, Herbert, 234n3, 239n30
Atlan, Henri, 102
Auden, W. H., 221n5
Auerbach, Erich, 14
Austen, Jane, 193
Auster, Paul, 9
Auschwitz, 157
authorship: anxieties of, 4; authorial agency, 21–22. *See also* Doctorow, E. L.; Lowry, Malcolm; Norris, Frank; Powers, Richard
autopoiesis, 9, 19, 185, 189
avant-garde, 1
Azetcs, 99, 100

Baldwin, Neil, 169, 172, 173
Barthelme, Donald, 228n1
Barthes, Roland, 104, 152, 158
Bateson, Gregory, 185, 241n9
Baudelaire, 23, 31, 58, 59, 60, 61, 63, 64, 145, 193, 217n13
Baudrillard, Jean, 232n20–21
Bawer, Bruce, 229n5
Beard, George M., 82, 167. *See also* neurasthenia
Beniger, James R., 18, 81, 157–58, 164
Benjamin, Walter: on art, 4–5, 210n17; on the collector, 79; on dandyism, 64–65; on filmic unconscious, 14, 117; on information, 74–75, 153; on modern shock, 41, 212n28; on photography, 40, 209n9; on the ragpicker, 141; on the storyteller, 152–53, 206n14, 233n30
Berger, Hans, 171
Berger, Kevin, 202
Bergson, Henri, 9, 109, 129–31, 205n2, 211n24, 228n29–30, 238n28
Berliner, Emile 4
Bertillon, Alphonse, 236n8
Birkerts, Sven, 202–03, 245n27
Blakeslee, Sandra, 239n31
Blériot, Louis, 107
Bloom, Harold, 230n10
Blumenthal, David R., 99
Bogart, Humphrey, 126

Bolter, J. David, 5, 26, 207n23, 244n23
Bowker, Gordon, 92, 93, 114, 122, 221n5, 222n9, 224n21, 226n17
Bouguereau, Guillaume-Adolphe, 66–68, 72, 218n17–19
Bower, Stephanie, 210n15
Bradbrook, Muriel, 108
Broca, Paul, 166, 172, 181, 237n17–18
Brooks, Peter, 100
Broude, Norma, 70, 219n23
Buck-Morss, Susan, 212n28
Buñuel, Luis, 225n4
Burroughs, William S., 182, 208n30, 226n11
Burton, Richard D. E., 60, 145, 207n18, 231n15, 231n17
Butler, Samuel, 238n28
Butor, Michael, 224n20

The Cabinet of Dr. Caligari. See Wiene, Robert
Cadigan, Pat, 8
Calvino, Italo, 15
Caponegro, Mary, 26
Caprettini, Gian Paolo, 236n12
Carlyle, Thomas, 137, 141, 148, 230n8, 232n21
Cartesian body-mind split, 164, 182, 203
Cendrars, Blaise, 55
Charcot, Jean Martin, 212n27, 213n32
Chevreul, Michel-Eugène, 69
Chinese Exclusion Act, 57
Chomsky, Noam, 187
Chopin, Frédéric, 220n27
cinema, 1–2, 4, 7, 14–16, 23
Chaplin, Charlie, 112
Citizen Cane. See Wells, Orson
Clancy, Tom, 150, 160, 233n27
Clark, Andy, 187, 241n8
Clifford, James, 134–35
Clipper, Lawrence J., 99
cognition and cognitive science, 7, 10, 18–20, 22, 157, 160–64, 169–72, 173–77
Cohen, Keith, 228n33
Coleridge, Samuel Taylor, 86, 114
Conrad, Joseph, 113, 142, 225n8
Cooter, Roger, 174, 235n7
Coover, Robert, 7
Coppola, Francis Ford, 210n19

Cragg, Tony, 134
Crane, Stephen, 36, 52, 94, 100, 214n44, 215n46
Crary, Jonathan, 212n31
Crisler, Jesse, 38, 47, 218n18
cyberpunk, 9, 173

Damasio, Antonio, 193
Danius, Sara, 7, 10, 100, 211n24, 212n31, 227n20
Dargis, Manohla, 213n37
Darwin, Charles, 22, 35, 175, 217n9
Darwinism, 45, 69, 175
Daumier, Honoré, 66, 210n17
Davis, J. Lennard, 23
Day, Douglas, 93, 221n6
D'Emilio, John, 218n17
de Certeau, Michel, 11, 127
de Chardin, Teilhard, 241n9
de Girardin, Emile, 179
de Gourmont, Remy, 217n9
de la Motte, Dean, 179
DeKoven, Marianne, 239n33
de Kerckhove, Derrick, 21, 25, 208n27
Degas, Edgar, 36, 69
Deleuze, Gilles, 6, 85, 103, 105, 145–47, 153, 163, 231n16, 231n18. *See also* Félix Guattari
DeLillo, Don, 8–9, 87, 207n19, 228n1
Den Tandt, Christophe, 61, 214n43, 216n51, 216n4, 216n6, 220n32
Denis, Maurice, 217n11
Dennett, Daniel, 19, 175, 196, 239n34, 242n13, 244n21
Deresiewicz, William, 242n14
Detaille, Édouard, 31, 69
Derrida, Jacques, 52, 106, 205n5, 221n5
Dick, Philip K., 9
Dickens, Charles, 40, 100, 112, 131, 156
Dickson, William, 39
Didion, Joan, 207n19
Dillingham, William, 34
distributed cognition, 9, 19, 184–86
Divisionism, 32, 69–71. *See also* Georges Seurat
Doctorow, E. L., 10; cognition in 18–19, 157, 160–62; and digital technologies, 16–17; *Big as Life*, 147; *Billy Bathgate*,

16, 17, 138, 139, 147, 149, 151; *The Book of Daniel*, 16, 136–37, 139, 143, 144, 149–50, 151; *City of God*, 16–17, 19, 139, 140, 141, 142, 148, 150–51, 155, 181–88, 192, 229n4-5, 230n9, 240n5; "Einstein: Seeing the Unseen," 240n4; "False Documents," 148, 232n20, 238n27; and film 16, 144, 150–51, 155, 187; intertextual recycling in, 135, 141–43; *Lamentation 9/11*, 231n12; *Lives of the Poets*, 142; *Loon Lake*, 16, 137, 141; *The March*, 141, 236n15; novel as "noisy channel," 18, 134; novel as "war machine," 145–47; "Quick Cuts," 151, 232n24, 233n26; *Ragtime*, 16, 138–39, 140, 141, 143, 173, 182, 231n11; *Reporting the Universe*, 232n25; technology of narrative, 135–36; *Three Screenplays*, 233n31; *The Waterworks*, 18, 141, 142, 143, 148, 151, 157–79, 186, 235n4, 235n6, 237n18, 238n23, 240n5; *Welcome to Hard Times*, 16, 142, 147; *World's Fair*, 138, 139, 140; writing practices, 17
Doolittle, Hilda, 244n23
Dos Passos, John, 222n8
Dostoyevsky, Fyodor, 125, 155, 227n27
Doyen, Victor, 124–25, 224n15, 227n23
Doyle, Sir Arthur Conan, 142, 156, 160, 162
Dracula, 156, 160, 201, 210n19, 237n18, 238n22
Dracobly, Alex, 236n14
Dreiser, Theodore, 53, 75, 206n14, 216n6, 223n13
Dreyfus, Hubert, 188
Drucker, Peter, 164
Duchamp, Marcel, 134
Dujardin, Éduard, 219n26
Dunne, J. W., 99
dynamical systems theory, 63, 217n14

Eakin, Emily, 200, 203, 242n13
Edelman, Gerald, 175
Edison, Thomas, 4, 6, 39, 46, 107, 169–73, 223n13, 238n23–24. *See also* phonograph; kinetoscope
Einstein, Albert, 19, 141, 142, 181–83, 186, 240n2-3

Eisenstein, Sergei, 40, 108, 115, 131, 212n27, 224n2
electroencephalography, 160, 166–67
Eliot, George, 193
Eliot, T. S., 60
Ellison, Ralph, 155, 192
embodiment, 9–10, 19–22, 37, 43–45, 47–48, 56, 72–74, 163–64, 172, 182–202. *See also* Hayles, N. Katherine
Emerson, Ralph Waldo, 186
The End of St. Petersburg. *See* Pudovkin, Svevolod
epigenesis, 175
Epstein, Jean, 228n33; *The Fall of the House of Usher*, 131
Everdell, William R., 69, 70, 92
Exner, Sigmund, 170
Ezekiel, 99, 100

Falk, David, 228n32
The Fall of the House of Usher. *See* Epstein, Jean
Faulkner, William, 111, 146
Fénéon, Félix, 70, 219n23
Fitzgerald, F. Scott, 14–15, 51, 75, 91, 108, 111–12, 115, 142, 213n34, 227n18
Flaubert, Gustave, 59, 60, 217n8
Flusser, Vilém, 2, 4, 16, 205n4
Ford, Ford Madox, 122
Foucault, Michel, 10, 206n11
Fowler, Orson and Lorenzo, 174, 235n7
Fox Talbot, William, 28
Frankenstein, 148, 156, 164, 193
Fraser, J. T., 224n18
Freedman, Estelle B., 218n17
Freud, Sigmund: on condensation (*Verdichtung*), 178–79; on phonographic memory, 170; psychoanalytical models and naturalism, 21; the scene of writing, 3, 207n24
Fried, Michael, 52, 94, 205n5, 214n44, 215n46
Fuentes, Carlos, 5, 225n4, 234n32

Gadamer, Hans-Georg, 240n7
Gaddis, William, 7–8, 10, 205n6, 207n18, 219n25, 228n1
Galton, Sir Francis, 35–36

Garelick, Rhonda, 65
Garland, Hamlin, 53
Gattaca. See Niccol, Andrew
Gaugain, Paul, 69
Gauld, Alan, 212n26, 213n32
Gebauer, Gunter, 184
Gentry, Bruce Marshall, 235n6
German Expressionism, 108, 118, 129, 224n2
George, Stefan, 94
Gibson, William, 8, 238n29. *See also* cyberpunk
Gilbert and Sullivan, 57
Ginzburg, Carlo, 235n8
Gitelman, Lisa, 6, 169, 206n9, 237n18, 238n24
Glaser, Otto, 210n11
The Gleaners and I. See Varda, Agnes
Gleick, James, 217n14
Godard, Jean-Luc, 116
Goldberg, Jonathan, 94, 215n47, 215n50
Goncourt brothers, 56
Grace, Sherrill, 88, 223n14, 224n17, 224n2, 225n4, 227n20, 227n25
Graham, Don, 211n22
Green-Lewis, Jennifer, 34, 210n13
Griffith, D. W., 46, 112, 113, 212n27
Grusin, Richard, 5, 244n23
Grüne, Karl: *The Street*, 108
Guattari, Félix, 145–47, 153, 163, 231n18. *See also* Deleuze, Gilles
Gunning, Tom, 117, 122
Gutenberg Galaxy, 4
Guyau, Jean-Marie, 170
Guys, Constantin, 66, 210n17

H.D. See Doolittle, Hilda
Habegger, Alfred, 215n48
handwriting, 4, 10, 46, 48, 214n39, 214n44, 216n5, 216n7. *See also* authorship; Doctorow, E. L.; Lowry, Malcolm; Norris, Frank; Powers, Richard
Haraway, Donna, 2, 54
Hardy, Thomas, 103, 114
Harnish, Robert M., 237n17
Harpham, Geoffrey Galt, 135–36
Harris, Zellig, 189
Hartman, Geoffrey, 147

Hartman Strom, Sharon, 214n42
Harvey, Thomas, 181–82
Hauser, Kaspar, 193
Hawkins, Harriett, 134
Hawthorne, Nathaniel, 57, 142, 152, 156, 234n1
Hayles, N. Katherine, 3, 9–10, 22, 172, 198, 201, 238n26, 238n29, 244n22. *See also* embodiment
Hearst, William Randolph, 169
Heidegger, Martin, 13, 85, 93, 171, 184, 223n10, 240n7
Heim, Michael, 26
Heise, Ursula, 208n25
Helmling, Steven, 231n14
Hemingway, Ernest, 57, 216n6
Henri, Robert, 217n11, 218n16
Herbert, Robert, 66
Herff, Geoffrey, 60, 217n10
Hirth, Georg, 156
Hitchcock, Alfred: *The 39 Steps*, 240n1
Hochman, Barbara, 83, 209n5, 216n2
Howells, William Dean, 59, 209n8
Huffman, Laton Alton, 211n20
Hugo, Victor, 155
Hulme, T. E., 60
Hume, David, 101
Husserl, Edmund, 30
Huston, John, 225n4
Hutcheon, Linda, 144
Huysmans, Joris-Karl, 56
Huyssen, Andreas, 60

Impressionism, 31, 32, 66, 67, 68, 69, 70
information processing: and the novel, 7–8, 15–17, 24–27, 152–54; in *McTeague*, 30–31; in *The Pit*, 74–83; in *The Waterworks*, 157–72
Invasion of the Body Snatchers, 156
Italian Futurism, 122
Iser, Wolfgang, 104, 143, 196, 239n33
Isherwood, Christopher, 94, 114, 227n18

James, Henry, 29, 174, 200, 208n3
James, William, 30
Jameson, Fredric, 2, 39–40, 87, 100, 143–45, 205n4, 206n14, 231n11, 231n13–14

Jenkins, Henry, 206n8
Johnson, Barbara, 236n10
Johnston, John, 8, 10, 233n30, 234n33
Joyce, James, 7, 15, 123, 142, 192, 193, 224n20, 239n34
Joyce, Michael, 27, 208n27, 208n30, 208n31
Jussim, Estelle, 211n20

Kafka, Franz, 48, 92
Kaplan, Amy, 213n35
Katz, Joseph, 30
Keller, Julia, 198, 200, 201
Kern, Stephen, 238n28
Kernan, Alvin, 26
Kilgallin, Toni, 110
kinetoscope, 4, 12, 39–40, 43, 46, 211n23–24. *See also* Edison, Thomas
King, Richard, 235n5
King, Rodney, 157
Kirby, Lynn, 11, 118
Kipling, Rudyard, 57, 122
Kiteley, Brian, 196
Kittler, Friedrich, 205n2, 206n11, 222n7; on chronophotography, 38; on handwriting, 53; on knowledge, 155; on Lacan/the real, 237n18, 238n22; on literature as information processing, 24; on the mother's mouth, 244n25; on Hugo Münsterberg/film, 228n30; on the phonograph, 170; on print and modern media, 2, 4; on thinking, 171; on typewriter 12, 91, 94
Kleist, Heinrich, 142, 147, 231n18
Kluge, Alexander, 117
Kolodny, Annette, 215n45
Koszarski, Richard, 37

Lacan, Jacques, 11, 237n18. *See also* Kittler, Friedrich
Landow, George, 177
Lang, Fritz, 121; *Metropolis,* 118, 243n18
Lanham, Richard, 206n8, 207n22
Latour, Bruno, 6, 206n9
Las Manos de Orlac, 93, 172
Lawrence, D. H., 216n6, 222n8, 236n14
Lears, Jackson, 58, 62
Le Corbusier, 88

LeClair, Tom, 7–8, 10, 153–54, 206n10, 208n26, 234n32–33
Le Guin, Ursula, 7
Léger, Fernand, 116, 226n12
Lehrer, Jonah, 45, 243n20
Lem, Stanislaw: *Solaris,* 156, 164, 168, 171, 181, 235n4
Lennard, Davis J., 233n29
Lenin, Vladimir, 181, 240n2
Leroi-Gourhan, André, 184
Leverenz, David, 214n41
Levy, Stephen, 240n2
Lewis, Wyndham, 58, 60, 80, 217n10
Leyda, Jay, 224n1
Liszt, Franz, 72, 219n25–26
Lombroso, Cesare, 34, 35
London, Jack, 75, 215n46, 216n6
Lowry, Malcolm: aesthetic of film, 14–15, 104; "Bulls of Resurrection," 227n20; car, bus, and railroad travel, 120–23, 226n15, 227n21; discourse of incarceration, 125–27; *Dark as the Grave Wherein My Friend Is Laid,* 15, 125–26, 131, 223n10; "Elephant and Colosseum," 88; "The Forest Path to the Spring," 86; "Ghostkeeper," 101, 103; handwriting and fear of manual incapacitation, 13, 91–98, 221n6; *Hear Us O Lord from Heaven Thy Dwelling Place,* 86–87, 88, 106, 221n2; "Hollywood and the War," 119; "June the 30th, 1934," 88, 226n15; *La Mordida,* 15, 226n12, 228n29; *Lunar Caustic,* 113; media schizophrenia, 15, 108–22, 123–32; narrative engineering, 13, 85; 88–89, 106, 221n3; narrative engines, 13, 85, 98, 101; "Noblesse Oblige," 88; *October Ferry to Gabriola,* 15, 86, 87, 88, 102, 109, 123–32, 227n28, 228n32; *Psalms and Songs,* 88, 93, 101, 103; "A Rainy Night," 226n15; *Tender Is the Night* (film script), 14–15, 91, 108, 115–22, 123–25, 128, 130, 223n11, 226n13, 228n34, 233n31; "Through the Panama," 88, 223n14; *Ultramarine,* 122, 125, 221n6, 226n13, 226n17; *Under the Volcano,* 15–16, 85, 88, 92, 93, 98–106, 109, 110, 118, 119, 188, 192, 223n13, 226n13;

on William Gaddis, 207n18; writer's block, 15, 90–91, 123, 203, 207n17, 227n22; writing practices, 13–14, 89–98; 223n11
Ludwig, Karl, 181, 237n20; kymographion, 168
Lumière brothers, 36, 107
Lumpenproletariat, 137, 145
Luhmann, Niklas, 22–23, 24
Lutz, Tom, 54, 82
Lyotard, Jean-François, 84, 186, 202, 207n20
Lythgoe, Mark, 240n3

Mach, Ernst, 101
Madame Blavatsky, 172
Maeterlinck, Maurice, 122, 227n20
Mailer, Norman, 57
Mann, Thomas, 7
Marey, Jules-Étienne, 12, 38, 168, 181, 237n20, 238n21
Marinetti, Fillipo Tommaso, 1–2, 11, 225n9. *See also* Italian Futurism
Marks, John, 231n16
Markson, David, 94, 224n15
Màrquez, Gabriel Garcia, 225n4
Martin, Ronald E., 208n1
Marx, Karl, 7
Marxism, 103, 136, 221n5, 223n10
Maudsley, Henry, 238n28
Maugham, William Somerset, 225n9
The May Irwin Kiss, 212n26
McCarthy, Patrick A., 90, 131, 207n17, 224n20, 227n26, 228n33
McCarthyism, 136, 226n17
McElrath, Joseph, Jr., 38, 214n40, 216n2, 218n18
McElroy, Joseph, 38, 47
McLuhan, Marshal, 20, 26, 81, 90, 114, 187, 206n9, 213n36, 241n9
McGann, Jerome, 3
Melville, Herman, 142, 193
Meissonier, Anton, 38
media ecology 4
Meijer, Marie, 134
Mengele, Joseph, 148
Merleau-Ponty, Maurice, 240n6

Metropolis. *See* Lang, Fritz
Michaels, Walter Benn, 61
Miller, D. A., 34
Mink, Louis O., 242n11
Minsky, Marvin, 238n29
Mitchell, J. William, 241n9
mobilized vision (car, bus, and train travel) 7, 11, 41–42, 118, 120, 121, 122, 123, 127. *See also* Kirby, Lynn; Lowry, Malcolm; Materlinck, Maurice; Norris, Frank; Schivelbusch, Wolfgang
Moraru, Christian, 135, 231n13, 232n22, 234n2
Moravec, Hans, 205n2, 238n29
Morris, Christopher D., 135, 233n31, 235n5
Morris, William, 49, 62, 80
Morrison, Toni, 239n33
Mota, Miguel, 108, 113, 125, 224n2, 228n32
Mottram, Ron, 39, 212n30
Mumford, Lewis, 88, 89
Munch, Edvard, 68, 70
Murnau, Friedrich Wilhelm, 227n25; *Sunrise* (*Sonnenaufgang*), 108, 118
Murphy, Priscilla Coit, 27, 208n29
Musil, Robert, 15
Musser, Charles, 39, 210n11, 211n22–23, 212n26
Muybridge, Eadweard, 12, 38, 211n20, 211n24
Münsterberg, Hugo, 129, 228n30

naturalism, 11–12, 21, 28–36, 39–45, 53–54, 56–60, 66
narrative engines, 11, 39, 85, 98
Neurasthenia, 82. *See also* Beard, George M.
Neilson, Jim, 188, 190, 192, 199
New, William H., 99
Newton, Isaac, 99, 100, 183
Niccol, Andrew: *Gattaca,* 240n7
Nicholls, Peter, 216n5, 217n8, 219n26
Nietzsche, Friedrich, 135, 157, 235n5
Night of the Living Dead, 156
Nordau, Max, 34
Norris, Frank: at Académie Julian, 31, 36, 66, 218n19, 219n21; "The Animal of a Buldy Jones," 218n16; animal painter, 38–39; authorial agency and fixation on

hands, 12–13, 46–51, 73–74, 214n39; *Blix*, 31, 41, 51, 52, 215n49, 220n30; "Charles Peter Rollo," 218n19; "The Coverfield Sweepstakes," 38; early film adaptations, 45–46; embodiment, 42–45, 47–48, 72–74; filmic sensibility, 35–46; "The Hopkins Institute," 218n19; idea of fiction, 31–33, 209n10; "Inside an Organ," 220n27; as journalist 29–34, 209n7; literary naturalism, 31–36, 37; *A Man's Woman*, 41, 42, 47, 52–54, 57, 75, 209n4, 215n49; *McTeague,* 11–12, 31, 33–34, 37, 39, 42, 45–46, 47, 52, 56, 57, 75, 78, 210n15, 212n26–27, 213n33–34, 214n44, 215n46; "Metropolitan Noises," 41; mobilized vision, 11–12; *Moran of the Lady Letty*, 49, 57; narrative engines, 11; *The Octopus*, 11, 45, 57, 61, 62, 75, 83, 212n27, 213n37; "An Opening for Novelists," 218n19; *The Pit*, 12, 31, 36, 46, 49, 50, 55–59, 70–74, 75–84, 216n1, 217n14, 220n29, 220n31; photography, 29–36; (proto)modernist sensibility, 12, 56, 216n2; "She and the Other Fellow," 212n29; "The Sketch Club Exhibit," 218n19; "Student Life in Paris," 218n16, 218n19; thermodynamic models, 11, 21; typewriter as engine of effeminacy and re-production, 13–14; *Vandover and the Brute*, 56, 215n46; *Yvernelle*, 49; "Western Types," 218n19; "The Winter Exhibition," 218n19. *See also* naturalism

Novel/print narrative: as carrier of information and knowledge, 24, 176–80; death of, 2; effect of realism, 4; fullness of literary experience, 11; materiality of, 3, 151; as "noisy channel," 134, 180; position in a postprint world, 2–6, 20–27, 133–34, 136–37, 149–50, 157, 172; ontological function, 22, 152, 164, 186; as encyclopedia, 133–34, 187

Noxon, Gerald, 112

Ong, Walter, 95–96
organicism, 189–90
Ortega y Gasset, Jose, 88, 89, 101, 124, 131, 221n2

Orvell, Miles, 29, 31, 34, 35, 206n15
Orwell, George, 146, 221n5

Parks, John, G., 142
Passaro, Vince, 207n19
Pasolini, Pier Paolo, 110
Pater, Walter, 57, 65
Paterniti, Michael, 181–82, 240n2
Paulson, William R., 84, 142, 154, 163–64, 193
Pearson, Karl, 101
Perloff, Marjorie, 205n1
Peterson, Nancy, 239n36
Pierce, Charles Sanders, 30
Pinker, Stephen, 173, 187, 239n31
Pissarro, Camille, 70
Pizer, Donald, 209n10, 216n3
phonograph, 1, 4, 6, 11, 23, 169–73, 201. *See also* Edison, Thomas
phrenology, 159, 166, 173–74, 235n7, 239n32
player piano, 4, 71, 205n6, 219n25
Poe, Edgar Allen, 164, 234n1, 236n10, 236n14
Poincaré, Henri, 101
Poirier, Richard, 21
Porter, Bruce, 218n15
(post)Impressionism, 68, 69, 70
Postman, Neil, 18, 26, 207n22
Pound, Ezra, 58, 60, 80, 216n5, 217n10
Pound, Reginald, 220n28
Powell, Bud, 222n9
Pudovkin, Svevolod: *The End of St. Petersburg*, 112
Pre-Raphaelites, 31
Proust, Marcel, 7, 15, 41, 100, 193, 211n24
Przyblyski, Jeannene M., 179
Powers, Richard, 9, 10; "Being and Seeming: The Technology of Representation," 202; cognitive science in, 19–20, 188–96; *The Echo Maker*, 242n14, 243n19; *Galatea 2.2*, 20–21, 188, 191–96, 197, 199, 202, 242n15, 244n25; *The Gold Bug Variations*, 190, 191, 198–99, 243n20; "How to Speak a Book," 201, 244n26; posthuman notion of authorship, 22, 196, 199; *Prisoner's Dilemma*, 191; on reading, 25, 202;

Three Farmers, 195, 196–97, 198, 199; writing practices, 199–202
Pulitzer, Joseph, 158
Pygmalion. *See* Shaw, George Bernard
Pygmalion myth, 20, 194, 242n16, 243n18
Pynchon, Thomas, 7–8, 230n9

Rabinbach, Anson, 38, 167, 168–69, 211n21, 237n19, 238n21
Rank, Otto, 128, 129
Reed, Walter L., 147
Reinhardt, Django, 222n9
Remington, Fredric, 38, 211n20
Reiser, Stanley Joel, 33, 159, 168, 169, 171, 237n20
Rexroth, Kenneth, 232n20
Ricord, Philippe, 166, 236n16
Rilke, Rainer Maria, 169
Rindisbacher, Hans, 45
Robbe-Grillet, Alain, 226n14
Roengten, Wilhelm Conrad, 169, 210n11. *See also* X-ray
Root, Ogden, 69
Rosenberg case, 136–37
Roth, Philip, 207n19
Rowe, Katherine, 223n10
Russell, Ken, 225n4
Ryan, Marie-Laure, 232n20

Saltzman, Arthur M., 135
Schama, Simon, 232n21
Scharf, Aaron, 36, 209n9
Schivelbusch, Wolfgang, 41–42, 120, 121, 122, 128, 212n29
Schoenberg, Arnold, 92
Scott, A. O., 229n5
Sekula, Allan, 34, 210n14, 210n16
Seltzer, Mark, 28, 100, 171, 206n12, 208n2, 213n35, 215n46, 216n51
Serres, Michel, 9, 18, 163
Sérusier, Paul, 217n11
Seurat, Georges, 69–71, 219n23. *See also* Divisionism
Shakespeare, William, 114
Shi, David, 216n6
Shaw, George Bernard: *Pygmalion*, 242n16
Siemion, Piotr, 233n27

Simmel, Georg, 12, 41, 167, 206n14
Snow, C. P., 224n18
Soderbergh, Steven: *Solaris* (film), 235n4
Solaris. *See* Lem, Stanislaw; Soderbergh, Steven
Sunrise (*Sonnenaufgang*). *See* Murnau, Friedrich Wilhelm
Spariosu, Mihai, 105
Spatial novel, 176–77, 239n35
Spender, Steven, 108, 121, 221n5, 224n2
sphygmograph. *See* Vierodt, Karl
Spolsky, Ellen, 174, 175, 176, 189, 239n34
Stallybrass, Peter, 155
Stein, Gertrude, 210n18
Steinbeck, John, 142
Stephenson, Neale, 9
Stevenson, Robert Louis, 59, 83, 206n13
Sternberg, Meir, 232n20
Sterne, Jonathan, 6
Stingelin, Martin, 210n15
Stix, Gary, 242n17
Stoker, Bram, 142, 238n28. *See also Dracula*
Stoppard, Tom, 16
The Street. *See* Grüne, Karl
Strickland, Stefanie, 9
The Student of Prague. *See* Wegener, Paul.
Soustelle, Jacques, 99
Sukenick, Ronald, 116
surrealist film, 115–16, 126, 129
Swift, Jonathan, 192
Symbolists, 45, 58, 60, 61, 68

Tabbi, John, 8–9, 10, 144, 188, 197, 206n7, 239n35, 242n12, 244n25
Tarkovsky, Andrei, 235n4
Tarzan, 193
Taylor, Frank, 110, 114
technological determinism, 6
Thagard, Paul, 182
There Will Be Blood. *See* Anderson, Paul Thomas
Theweleit, Klaus, 57
The 39 Steps. *See* Hitchcock, Alfred
Thompson, Michael, 229n2
Thorburn, David, 206n8
Tichi, Cecelia, 208n2, 221n4
Tit-Bits, 75, 220n28

Tiessen, Paul, 108, 113, 125, 224n2, 224n20, 225n7, 226n10, 228n32
Tokarczyk, Michelle M., 239n33
Tomashevsky, Boris, 227n22
Tompkins, Jane, 215n48
Tolstoy, Leo, 107
Tortello, Michael, 242n11
Tsimpouki, Theodora, 232n22
Tuman, Myron, 26
Turbayne, Colin Murray, 101
Turkle, Sherry, 207n24
Tynjanov, Jurij, 231n19

Updike, John, 207n19

Van de Grift, Sanchez, 206n13
Van der Rohe, Mies, 89
Varda, Agnès: *The Gleaners and I*, 229n3
Varela, J. Francisco, et. al., 19, 185, 240n6
Veblen, Thorstein, 59, 208n2, 219n20
Vidal, Gore, 25
Vierodt, Karl: sphygmograph, 168, 237n20
Villemessant, 74
Virilio, Paul, 2, 25, 43, 119, 208n27
Vitascope, 4, 39, 211n22–23
Vogt, Karl, 181
von Helmholtz, Herman, 168
von Stroheim, Erich, 12, 37, 40, 213n37

Wagner, Richard, 219n25
Walker, Franklin, 38, 47, 80, 210n12
Wegener, Paul: *The Student of Prague*, 128
Weinberg, Herman, 37
Weinberger, Eliot, 26
Weisberg, Gabriel P., 67, 218n16

Weller, Michael, 16
Welles, Orson: *Citizen Kane,* 113
Wells, H. G., 122, 146
West, Nathanael, 111
Whitman, Walt, 158, 174, 235n7
White, Allon, 155
White, Hayden, 152, 233n28, 242n11
Wieland, Schulz-Keil, 225n4
Wiene, Robert: *The Cabinet of Dr. Caligari*, 109, 118, 164
Wilde, Oscar, 56, 57, 65
Williams, Jeffrey, 189, 190
Williams, Raymond, 206n9
Williams, William Carlos, 122
Wilson, Christopher, 53, 216n7
Winkler, Hartmut, 24, 26, 178
Winthrop-Young, Geoffrey, 23, 206n11, 208n25, 210n19, 236n13, 238n25
Wittgenstein, Ludwig, 19, 139, 141, 183–84, 186
Wittgenstein, Paul, 240n7
Woodburn, John, 224n21
Woolf, Virginia, 206n16, 239n34
Wordsworth, William, 86, 200
Wright, Frank Lloyd, 88
Wutz, Michael, 144, 206n7, 234n32, 239n35

X-ray, 7, 11, 32–33, 169, 210n11, 238n23–24. *See also* Roentgen, Wilhelm Conrad

Yeats, William Butler, 60, 133
Young, Paul, 211n25

Ziff, Larzer, 83
Zola, Emile, 32, 61, 75, 100, 220n32